THE BIG PICTURE

McGILL-QUEEN'S STUDIES IN THE HISTORY OF RELIGION
VOLUMES IN THIS SERIES HAVE BEEN SUPPORTED BY THE JACKMAN FOUNDATION OF TORONTO.

SERIES ONE   G.A. RAWLYK, EDITOR

1 Small Differences
Irish Catholics and Irish Protestants, 1815–1922
An International Perspective
Donald Harman Akenson

2 Two Worlds
The Protestant Culture of Nineteenth-Century Ontario
William Westfall

3 An Evangelical Mind
Nathanael Burwash and the Methodist Tradition in Canada, 1839–1918
Marguerite Van Die

4 The Dévotes
Women and Church in Seventeenth-Century France
Elizabeth Rapley

5 The Evangelical Century
College and Creed in English Canada from the Great Revival to the Great Depression
Michael Gauvreau

6 The German Peasants' War and Anabaptist Community of Goods
James M. Stayer

7 A World Mission
Canadian Protestantism and the Quest for a New International Order, 1918–1939
Robert Wright

8 Serving the Present Age
Revivalism, Progressivism, and the Methodist Tradition in Canada
Phyllis D. Airhart

9 A Sensitive Independence
Canadian Methodist Women Missionaries in Canada and the Orient, 1881–1925
Rosemary R. Gagan

10 God's Peoples
Covenant and Land in South Africa, Israel, and Ulster
Donald Harman Akenson

11 Creed and Culture
The Place of English-Speaking Catholics in Canadian Society, 1750–1930
Edited by Terrence Murphy and Gerald Stortz

12 Piety and Nationalism
Lay Voluntary Associations and the Creation of an Irish-Catholic Community in Toronto, 1850–1895
Brian P. Clarke

13 Amazing Grace
Studies in Evangelicalism in Australia, Britain, Canada, and the United States
Edited by George Rawlyk and Mark A. Noll

14 Children of Peace
W. John McIntyre

15 A Solitary Pillar
Montreal's Anglican Church and the Quiet Revolution
Joan Marshall

16 Padres in No Man's Land
Canadian Chaplains and the Great War
Duff Crerar

17 Christian Ethics and Political Economy in North America
A Critical Analysis
P. Travis Kroeker

18 Pilgrims in Lotus Land
Conservative Protestantism in British Columbia, 1917–1981
Robert K. Burkinshaw

19 Through Sunshine and Shadow
The Woman's Christian Temperance Union, Evangelicalism, and Reform in Ontario, 1874–1930
Sharon Cook

20 Church, College, and Clergy
A History of Theological Education at Knox College, Toronto, 1844–1994
Brian J. Fraser

21 The Lord's Dominion
The History of Canadian Methodism
Neil Semple

22 A Full-Orbed Christianity
The Protestant Churches and Social Welfare in Canada, 1900–1940
Nancy Christie and Michael Gauvreau

23 Evangelism and Apostasy
The Evolution and Impact of Evangelicals in Modern Mexico
Kurt Bowen

24 The Chignecto Covenanters
A Regional History of Reformed Presbyterianism in New Brunswick and Nova Scotia, 1827– 1905
Eldon Hay

25 Methodists and Women's Education in Ontario, 1836–1925
Johanne Selles

26 Puritanism and Historical Controversy
William Lamont

SERIES TWO IN MEMORY OF GEORGE RAWLYK
DONALD HARMAN AKENSON, EDITOR

1 Marguerite Bourgeoys and Montreal, 1640–1665
Patricia Simpson

2 Aspects of the Canadian Evangelical Experience
Edited by G.A. Rawlyk

3 Infinity, Faith, and Time
Christian Humanism and Renaissance Literature
John Spencer Hill

4 The Contribution of Presbyterianism to the Maritime Provinces of Canada
Edited by Charles H.H. Scobie and G.A. Rawlyk

5 Labour, Love, and Prayer
Female Piety in Ulster Religious Literature, 1850–1914
Andrea Ebel Brozyna

6 The Waning of the Green
Catholics, the Irish, and Identity in Toronto, 1887–1922
Mark G. McGowan

7 Religion and Nationality in Western Ukraine
The Greek Catholic Church and the Ruthenian National Movement in Galicia, 1867–1900
John-Paul Himka

8 Good Citizens
British Missionaries and Imperial States, 1870–1918
James G. Greenlee and Charles M. Johnston

9 The Theology of the Oral Torah
Revealing the Justice of God
Jacob Neusner

10 Gentle Eminence
A Life of Cardinal Flahiff
P. Wallace Platt

11 Culture, Religion, and Demographic Behaviour
Catholics and Lutherans in Alsace, 1750–1870
Kevin McQuillan

12 Between Damnation and Starvation
Priests and Merchants in Newfoundland Politics, 1745–1855
John P. Greene

13 Martin Luther, German Saviour
German Evangelical Theological Factions and the Interpretation of Luther, 1917–1933
James M. Stayer

14 Modernity and the Dilemma of North American Anglican Identities, 1880–1950
William H. Katerberg

15 The Methodist Church on the Prairies, 1896–1914
George Emery

16 Christian Attitudes towards the State of Israel
Paul Charles Merkley

17 A Social History of the Cloister
Daily Life in the Teaching Monasteries of the Old Regime
Elizabeth Rapley

18 Households of Faith
Family, Gender, and Community in Canada, 1760–1969
Edited by Nancy Christie

19 Blood Ground
Colonialism, Missions, and the Contest for Christianity in the Cape Colony and Britain, 1799–1853
Elizabeth Elbourne

20 A History of Canadian Catholics
Gallicanism, Romanism, and Canadianism
Terence J. Fay

21 The View from Rome
Archbishop Stagni's 1915 Reports on the Ontario Bilingual Schools Question
Edited and translated by John Zucchi

22 The Founding Moment
Church, Society, and the Construction of Trinity College
William Westfall

23 The Holocaust, Israel, and Canadian Protestant Churches
Haim Genizi

24 Governing Charities
Church and State in Toronto's Catholic Archdiocese, 1850–1950
Paula Maurutto

25 Anglicans and the Atlantic World
High Churchmen, Evangelicals, and the Quebec Connection
Richard W. Vaudry

26 Evangelicals and the Continental Divide
The Conservative Protestant Subculture in Canada and the United States
Sam Reimer

27 Christians in a Secular World
The Canadian Experience
Kurt Bowen

28 Anatomy of a Seance
A History of Spirit Communication in Central Canada
Stan McMullin

29 With Skilful Hand
The Story of King David
David T. Barnard

30 Faithful Intellect
Samuel S. Nelles and Victoria University
Neil Semple

31 W. Stanford Reid
An Evangelical Calvinist in the Academy
Donald MacLeod

32 A Long Eclipse
The Liberal Protestant Establishment and the Canadian University, 1920–1970
Catherine Gidney

33 Forkhill Protestants and Forkhill Catholics, 1787–1858
Kyla Madden

34 For Canada's Sake
Public Religion, Centennial Celebrations, and the Re-making of Canada in the 1960s
Gary R. Miedema

35 Revival in the City
The Impact of American Evangelists in Canada, 1884–1914
Eric R. Crouse

36 The Lord for the Body
Religion, Medicine, and Protestant Faith Healing in Canada, 1880–1930
James Opp

37 Six Hundred Years of Reform
Bishops and the French Church, 1190–1789
J. Michael Hayden and Malcolm R. Greenshields

38 The Missionary Oblate Sisters
Vision and Mission
Rosa Bruno-Jofré

39 Religion, Family, and Community in Victorian Canada
The Colbys of Carrollcroft
Marguerite Van Die

40 Michael Power
The Struggle to Build the Catholic Church on the Canadian Frontier
Mark G. McGowan

41 The Catholic Origins of Quebec's Quiet Revolution, 1931–1970
Michael Gauvreau

42 Marguerite Bourgeoys and the Congregation of Notre Dame, 1665–1700
Patricia Simpson

43 To Heal a Fractured World
The Ethics of Responsibility
Jonathan Sacks

44 Revivalists
Marketing the Gospel in English Canada, 1884–1957
Kevin Kee

45 The Churches and Social Order in Nineteenth- and Twentieth-Century Canada
Edited by Michael Gauvreau and Ollivier Hubert

46 Political Ecumenism
Catholics, Jews, and Protestants in De Gaulle's Free France, 1940–1945
Geoffrey Adams

47 From Quaker to Upper Canadian Faith and Community among Yonge Street Friends, 1801–1850
Robynne Rogers Healey

48 The Congrégation de Notre-Dame, Superiors, and the Paradox of Power, 1693–1796
Colleen Gray

49 Canadian Pentecostalism Transition and Transformation
Edited by Michael Wilkinson

50 A War with a Silver Lining Canadian Protestant Churches and the South African War, 1899–1902
Gordon L. Heath

51 In the Aftermath of Catastrophe Founding Judaism, 70 to 640
Jacob Neusner

52 Imagining Holiness Classic Hasidic Tales in Modern Times
Justin Jaron Lewis

53 Shouting, Embracing, and Dancing with Ecstasy The Growth of Methodism in Newfoundland, 1774–1874
Calvin Hollett

54 Into Deep Waters Evangelical Spirituality and Maritime Calvinist Baptist Ministers, 1790–1855
Daniel C. Goodwin

55 Vanguard of the New Age The Toronto Theosophical Society, 1891–1945
Gillian McCann

56 A Commerce of Taste Church Architecture in Canada, 1867–1914
Barry Magrill

57 The Big Picture The Antigonish Movement of Eastern Nova Scotia
Santo Dodaro and Leonard Pluta

The Big Picture

The Antigonish Movement of Eastern Nova Scotia

SANTO DODARO AND LEONARD PLUTA

McGill-Queen's University Press
Montreal & Kingston • London • Ithaca

ISBN 978-0-7735-4014-9 (cloth)
ISBN 978-0-7735-4015-6 (paper)

Legal deposit third quarter 2012
Bibliothèque nationale du Québec

Printed in Canada on acid-free paper that is 100% ancient forest free (100% post-consumer recycled), processed chlorine free.

McGill-Queen's University Press acknowledges the support of the Canada Council for the Arts for our publishing program. We also acknowledge the financial support of the Government of Canada through the Canada Book Fund for our publishing activities.

Library and Archives Canada Cataloguing in Publication

Dodaro, Santo, 1950–
The big picture : the Antigonish movement of eastern Nova Scotia / Santo Dodaro and Leonard Pluta.

(McGill-Queen's studies in the history of religion.
Series two ; no. 57)
Includes bibliographical references and index.
ISBN 978-0-7735-4014-9 (bound).—ISBN 978-0-7735-4015-6 (pbk.)

1. Antigonish movement—Nova Scotia—History.
2. Cooperation—Nova Scotia—History. 3. Nova Scotia—Economic conditions—20th century. 4. Nova Scotia—Social conditions—20th century. I. Pluta, Leonard
II. Title. III. Series : McGill-Queen's studies in the history of Religion. Series two ; no. 57.

HD3450.A3N63 2012 334.09716'0904 C2012-901237-8

This book was typeset by True to Type in 10.5/13 Sabon

To Marion, Lucia, and Stefano
to Barbara
and to all the pioneers
of the Antigonish Movement

Contents

Acknowledgments

First of all, we are beholden to our respective families for their patience and their support in this endeavour.

We are grateful to the many members of McGill-Queen's University Press who have helped and supported us in the process. In particular, we thank Aurele Parisien, who first showed interest in the proposed work, and we are indebted to Donald Harman Akenson, who reviewed our first much longer and broader manuscript. In working with the revised copy, we were also greatly, and with much appreciated patience, assisted first by Kyla Madden and then by Mary-Lynne Ascough; their expertise, advice, and guidance were indispensable. We also thank Robert Lewis, who did such a phenomenal job of making the manuscript readable, and Ryan Van Huijstee, whose help got us through the final stage, including his sound advice on how to tackle the index. Further, we owe a special word of thanks to the two anonymous referees, who did a thorough review of the manuscript and offered a wealth of useful feedback that has greatly improved the quality of the work.

We would like to express our appreciation for the encouragement of Tom Webb, former director of the Extension Department of St Francis Xavier University, as well as many others who are associated with the department or with the cooperative sectors or who are interested in the Antigonish Movement and/or in other alternate approaches to economic organization and policymaking. We must also acknowledge two grants received from the former Centre for Research on the Future of Work, which got us involved in this area of inquiry. Of course, we are solely responsible for all errors and omissions.

Santo Dodaro
Leonard Pluta

Tables and Figures

TABLES

FIGURES

THE BIG PICTURE

1

Introduction

INTRODUCTION

The Antigonish Movement, born out of the socio-economic conditions existing in eastern Nova Scotia during the 1920s and set in motion by the creation of the Extension Department of St Francis Xavier University in 1928 with the Roman Catholic priest and professor Moses Michael Coady as its director, is one of a number of economic movements that have emerged in Western countries over the past two centuries. The first such economic movement of lasting significance originated in Rochdale, England, where a group of unemployed weavers started the first modern cooperative store in 1843. The Rochdale Movement, as it became known, has inspired, in addition to the Antigonish Movement, other economic movements such as the Raiffeisen-Schultze Credit Cooperative Movement of Germany, the Swedish Cooperative Union (KF), the Mondragon Movement of Spain, and the Caisse Populaire Movement of Quebec, Canada.[1] These economic movements represent a special category, although they are often included as part of the broader label of social movements.

ECONOMIC VERSUS SOCIAL MOVEMENTS

Although economic and social movements share some similarities, they are also characterized by significant differences. A social movement is generally defined as "a set of actions of a group of people directed toward changing the social structure and/or ideology of a society"[2] that arises largely in response to the perceived failure of the existing institutions to meet the needs and aspirations of a significant portion of the population. As such, a social movement tends to focus on bringing those who are perceived to be somehow marginalized or disenfranchised into the mainstream of society. The extent to which such a movement can succeed depends on the strength and consistency of its social vision and institutional structure, as well as on the action taken to implement its program of social change.

Social movements are heavily dependent on a vision, shared by their members, of the desired social order. Such a vision is generally couched in highly idealistic and even utopian terms and performs the essential function of sustaining the movement and promoting its growth. The desired social order also serves as the standard against which the existing order is compared. Thus a social movement entails a mix of idealism and criticism of the existing order – a criticism that can generate contempt for the existing order. Although the social vision must be perceived as essential, it needs to be complemented and reinforced by action if it is to give rise to a lasting movement.

Social movements have tended to address a wide range of issues and to employ many different tactics and actions that are often symbolic and appeal to the emotions, such as hunger strikes, sit-ins, demonstrations, rallies, letter writing, blockades, and the like. These sorts of actions are relatively easy to organize and limited both in duration and in the amount of resources required. Thus they can be successfully organized by a small number of dedicated individuals relying on the power of the mass media and other channels of communication to spread the message to the general public as well as to the political authorities. It is not surprising, therefore, that such strategies have been employed by the agrarian, suffragette, civil rights, labour, and other movements of the past and more recently by those involving women's rights, the environment, visible minorities, and gay rights, among other issues.[3] Generally, these movements entail promoting change through political action.

Economic movements strive to bring about change by means other than political action.[4] In effect, these aim at the promotion of economic development through the mobilization, development, and allocation of resources. They originate in response to the failure of existing economic conditions and institutions to meet perceived needs and aspirations and attempt to bring about socio-economic reform through the fundamental restructuring of economic institutions and the redistribution of economic power. Moreover, they also possess a clearly defined vision and program of action and the capability to initiate and sustain consistent economic activities involving a great many people over the long term. This economic action is real and direct and involves the utilization and mobilization of significant resources, both human and material. Symbolic action, which is often the mainstay of social movements, is of little significance here.[5]

Reliance on concrete economic action, even if largely limited to a particular sector or type of activity, requires a highly integrated, systemic approach, which helps to explain the tendency, at least in the past, of grassroots economic movements to be more regional in nature, seldom encompassing the whole national economy or crossing national frontiers.[6] An additional factor, which also points to the regional characteristic of grassroots economic movements, is economic homogeneity. For a movement to emerge and flourish, a sizable proportion of the population must share common economic interests and face common or similar economic problems and difficulties that in turn lead to agreement on a program of common action. Such a coincidence of interests and problems is more likely to be realized at the regional level than at the national or international levels, which would normally be associated with a more diversified economy and population. In the past, communication problems and limited linkages also favoured action at the regional level.

Common economic interests and problems constitute a necessary but not sufficient condition for the emergence of a successful grassroots economic movement. Normally, other bonds are also needed to supplement the economic ties, both during its initial stages and over time. Ethnic, linguistic, cultural, or religious affinity can often serve such a purpose by reinforcing the notion of common action for the common good. So too can the experience and memory of historic injustices such as economic exploitation, political oppression, social marginalization, and religious persecution. Thus the Mondragon Movement of Spain, in addition to the common economic interests of the population, was also promoted by the common ethnic and linguistic bonds between citizens as well as by the common bond of being subject to political repression in the past. Similarly, the Caisse Populaire Movement of Quebec, Canada, also relied on common cultural, linguistic, and religious ties as well as on the French citizenry's collective memory of political subjugation, social inferiority, and economic exploitation by a dominant English minority. The Antigonish Movement of eastern Nova Scotia, which initially involved the collective efforts of people of Scottish, Acadian, and Irish descent, was able to overcome linguistic and cultural barriers through the strength of its Roman Catholic affiliation, the people's memory of religious and political persecution, and their relegation to an inferior social and political status.

The need to be able to implement concrete economic activities also explains, at least in part, the relative rarity of economic movements vis-à-vis social movements. Indeed, aside from Mondragon, there has not been a new grassroots economic movement in Western countries since the end of the Second World War.[7] In part, the greater involvement of government in the economy and the general perception of prosperity have made grassroots approaches to resolving economic problems unappealing.[8]

THE CHARACTERISTICS OF GRASSROOTS ECONOMIC MOVEMENTS

Although economic movements can vary greatly, including in terms of their focus and coverage, they all tend to share a number of characteristics. Foremost, they entail shifting control over decision making and resources in the economic sphere to the individuals and members of the community as a whole so that basic needs, and other objectives as well, can be met.[9] Thus the people themselves are directly involved in the process as decision makers, as contributors of resources, and as beneficiaries, in contrast to the more passive stance inherent in the more conventional approaches to development.[10]

Fundamental to the grassroots approach is the notion that every community, no matter how poor or destitute, possesses resources, even if mainly human resources, which if properly harnessed can support economic activity and promote economic development. In effect, these resources, particularly in the case of labour, are either inefficiently utilized or underutilized, as in the case of both unemployment and underemployment. If no such resources or opportunities exist or if they are beyond the reach of the people, it will not be possible for economic activity to take place. Rather than simply an absolute lack of resources, the problem is a lack of complementary inputs, including adequate information and decision-making ability, which precludes the efficient utilization of resources. This lack of complementary inputs may also limit the possibility of developing new resources and hence expanding the resource base. Despite the low levels of income and widespread poverty, there still exists some amount of economic rent, which monopolistic elements manage to appropriate and remove from the community. Thus the immediate concern of a grassroots movement is not only to expand the resource base of the community but also to recover the existing rent. This scenario, which in many ways provides an effective way to mobilize existing resources and decision-making abilities, is also at the heart of the framework suggested more recently by Hernando De Soto.[11]

Economic rent is the payment made to a productive resource in excess of what is required to maintain the resource in a particular employment.[12] Generally, such payments are reflected in what we normally call "economic surplus," "profit," or "windfall." They are normally distributed, by market forces, among buyers and sellers, with their actual distribution dictated by relative economic power. The side that has most or all of the economic power also tends to appropriate most or all of the economic rent. Economic movements empower those who undertake collective action by granting them control over economic institutions and hence over economic rent.

The appropriation and/or distribution of rent payments can be carried out through market forces but can also result from government action and policy. In the case of the former, the process can be influenced by the implementation and expansion of grassroots activity and hence by "economic empowerment." In the case of the latter, the allocation is undertaken through legislation and hence through "political empowerment," which involves influencing the political establishment. Left on their own, those who posses monopoly power can usually capture most, if not all, of the rent by appropriate increases and decreases in prices depending on whether they are sellers or buyers respectively.[13] The local population, in turn, can appropriate this rent by forming its own organizations. Moreover, since all individuals participate, to a greater or lesser extent, in various markets (e.g., as consumers of final goods, purchasers of intermediate and capital goods, borrowers of funds, and suppliers of goods and services), the combined rent payments that can be appropriated can be substantial.

Generally, the emergence of a grassroots economic movement requires a large group of people located in a given region or undertaking a particular activity who constitute what may be labelled a regionally significant group. Such groups would likely be more homogeneous, at least in terms of their economic circumstances, than the national population as a whole. Examples of such groups would include the various primary producers in the Canadian maritime provinces, especially during the 1920s and 1930s, French Canadians in Quebec, and the Basques in Spain. In some cases, these groups are made up of people either bypassed by the development and progress experienced by the rest of the economy and mired in periods of prolonged stagnation or targeted by repressive policies on the part of the national government. In these instances, grassroots economic movements will also serve as vehicles for bringing people into the economic mainstream but on their own terms.

At the outset, such regional or local groups must be significant in terms of numbers, economic potential, and access to resources in order to be able to initiate economic activity and sustain it over time. Grassroots economic action requires people to pool their resources and share in both the risks and the rewards. As well, the various economic activities or projects must be integrated, requiring that all members of the group, to some extent, adopt common goals or a common vision in order to support the establishment of the necessary institutional framework. Such a framework is necessary for grassroots economic activity not only to flourish but also to achieve some degree of longevity. Indeed, without institutions there cannot be a movement.

Although not synonymous with the cooperative sector, grassroots economic movements necessarily imply cooperation, including between groups.[14] On a more general level, all economic activity, regardless of the social and institutional arrangements, must be based upon cooperation. Even the most basic transactions, such as exchanging one item for another, involve some degree of cooperation. In most economic activities, the necessary cooperation is fostered by some form of compulsion, whereby penalties are attached to the refusal to cooperate and/or rewards are associated with cooperation. Thus a worker must accept employment and carry out the associated tasks or suffer a loss in livelihood. A seller must sell goods or forgo revenue and hence production, and a buyer must purchase a commodity or forgo the benefit associated with its consumption.[15]

The pooling of otherwise inadequate resources allows participants to increase their market power both as producers and as consumers, increase their efficiency as a consequence of economies of scale, and generate new activities by mobilizing existing resources and developing new ones. These are, by and large, the same elements identified by the Economic Council of Canada as components of its community-based supply-side initiatives.[16]

Economies of scale generally refer to the reduction of per-unit costs, and hence the greater efficiency, arising from increasing the size of economic entities.[17] Moreover, expansion in the number of efficient economic institutions is associated with linkages, feedbacks, and agglomeration economies. Agglomeration economies entail cost reductions and gains in efficiency arising from the ability to share information, expertise, specialized skills, factors of production, and the like. These outcomes, in turn, promote additional expansion of a movement by lowering the risks and costs associated with new economic activity. Cooperation not only promotes empowerment, leading to the redistribution of economic rent, but also enhances both efficiency and the level of economic activity, thus expanding these rent payments as well.

Cooperation rests on group formation. As pointed out in the seminal work of Mancur Olson, the dynamics of group formation are complex, being dependent, in addition to economic incentives, on factors such as compulsion of various sorts, moral obligation, and philosophical belief.[18] The introduction of a socio-economic dimension to group formation and cooperation is particularly relevant to efforts at the grass-roots level, where activities, at least initially, are meant to be carried out in relatively small groups. Indeed, as Olson points out, by and large "social pressure and social incentives operate only in groups of smaller size, in the groups so small that the members can have face-to-face contact with one another."[19] The degree of homogeneity among group members and the degree of commonality of interests also play a key role by allowing agreement with respect to any course of action to be more readily achieved. For large groups to act together, and this must necessarily be the case if a movement is to thrive and expand, some sort of additional motivation is necessary, which requires some institutional arrangement or framework. As we shall see, the institutional framework constituted an important aspect of the Antigonish Movement in terms of both its early success and its later decline.

The free rider problem poses a serious impediment to effective cooperative action. As Olson points out, it is not rational for individuals to make sacrifices when they know that they can avail themselves of the benefits anyway.[20] Although the problem is more likely to arise in large group settings, where individuals cannot be identified and are most likely to believe that their actions will not make any difference, it can also arise in small groups unless precluded through some form of voluntary or involuntary compulsion. Social obligation and concern for the welfare of the group constitute voluntary compulsion, whereas consequences such as loss of social standing and ostracization constitute involuntary types of compulsion.[21]

Since grassroots economic activities are fundamentally voluntary in nature, the compulsion to cooperate must come largely from within; individuals must make a concerted effort to cooperate and not to cheat. This fundamental characteristic is a source both of strength and of weakness for the grassroots approach, and the Antigonish Movement was no exception.

Generally, cooperation is made necessary not primarily on philosophical or ideological grounds but by the fact that each member's resources, including human resources, are not sufficient to undertake significant economic activity. Although it may be possible for a few enterprising and energetic individuals to significantly improve their lot in life on their own, this outcome is unlikely for the vast majority of people in the absence of cooperation.[22] Although cooperation is an absolute necessity, economic movements are not inimical to competition.[23] Such competition occurs between various economic groups but within a clearly defined institutional framework and due to a coincidence of objectives and goals. Moreover, cooperative organizations, to be successful, must also ensure efficient utilization of resources.

An additional feature of economic movements is their generally holistic nature. The economic dimension, albeit important, is only one of many that impact the emergence, development, and ultimate success or failure of a movement. Economic factors are closely intertwined with social, cultural, moral, and spiritual dimensions and cannot be isolated from them. Separating the economic factors from their noneconomic moorings would distort reality and be both misleading and dangerous.

Historically, all grassroots economic movements that have flourished have rested on strong social, moral, and spiritual foundations. These movements have addressed not only the material needs and wants of the people but also their social, cultural, moral, and spiritual aspirations. In effect, a movement's economic goals, such as economic development, control over economic institutions, and higher incomes, are generally perceived as only an important first step in the attainment of loftier goals. Indeed, it is these loftier goals that are called upon to sustain the movement once some of its economic objectives have been realized.

The existence of a causal relationship between moral, intellectual, and economic development has long been implicitly recognized. Thus Adam Smith, the founder of the discipline of economics and a moral philosopher, traced the origin of the most important sources of individual and national wealth to moral foundations.[24] In a somewhat different vein, scholars from various disciplines, including economists, sociologists, anthropologists, and historians, have produced a body of literature around the notion of the moral economy.[25] Although we do not necessarily subscribe to all of the tenets of the moral economy, it nevertheless focuses attention on a notion that is often missing from much of modern economic analysis. Arguably, the causal relation that exists between virtue and wealth appears to be stronger and more complex than generally acknowledged and forms the implicit basis for much of the concern, for example, with corruption as a constraint to economic development. Moreover, in the holistic context of economic movements, moral and spiritual forces may be harnessed to promote economic activities, creating an improvement in wellbeing that can, in turn, lead to moral improvement and spiritual fulfilment.[26] This was clearly the case in the context of the Antigonish Movement, where the final goal was perceived as the attainment of the "good and abundant life for everyone."[27]

By way of summary, we can characterize grassroots economic movements as involving self-initiated and self-directed socio-economic activities of regionally significant and culturally or otherwise cohesive groups that share common objectives and are willing to cooperate to achieve them. Alternatively, they can be envisaged as the collective effort of groups of people to pull themselves up by their own collective economic bootstraps in order to reverse their state of poverty and stagnation and to continue doing so. Equally important is the fact that economic activity is driven by the needs and aspirations of the people (i.e., the people have direct control over economic activity), as opposed to the people reacting to external economic stimuli.

THE SOCIO-ECONOMIC ENVIRONMENT AND ECONOMIC MOVEMENTS

Both the emergence and the success of grassroots economic movements are predicated on the existence of particular socio-economic environments. As all such movements arise in response to a perceived failure on the part of the existing economy and its institutional apparatus, it is not surprising that their emergence has tended to coincide with periods characterized by upheaval and economic difficulties, such as the Great Depression, and periods of rapid structural transformation, such as the shift from subsistence to commercial agriculture or the advent of industrialization, when lagging regions are unable to adjust. In contrast, periods of prolonged prosperity and/or economic stability have tended to be inimical to economic movements, both discouraging the emergence of new ones by reducing the incentive to look for alternatives and weakening existing ones by presenting people with seemingly easier and more standardized options.

Economic Conditions

In Western countries, grassroots economic movements have tended to emerge in regions experiencing conditions of economic decline vis-à-vis the country as a whole.[28] This was certainly the case for the German Rhine district in the mid-1800s, the maritime provinces of Canada in the 1920s, and the Basque area of Spain in the 1940s.[29]

Normally, economic decline in comparison to the rest of the country gives rise to a number of serious problems for the region in question. Predominant among these problems is the out-migration of both human and material resources. In particular, the out-migration of the young, most highly educated, and most energetic people has a negative impact on the region by removing some of its most vital resources, leading to the underutilization of other resources and further weakening its economic base. Perhaps more important, out-migration threatens the very survival of communities and the viability of whole regions as the demoralized population that is left behind becomes increasingly engulfed in apathy, hopelessness, inertia, and resignation.[30]

Normally, a weak regional economy also translates into a situation of political marginalization, with inadequate political representation for the region as a whole as well as for the various constituent communities. A possible consequence of such marginalization may be that fewer than required resources, both public and private, are transferred to the declining region.[31] Private investment is particularly sensitive to the ways that limited markets, possible deficiencies in infrastructure, less productive labour (in part due to out-migration), and the like negatively affect profits. Under such circumstances, grassroots economic development predicated on self-reliance and cooperation emerges as perhaps the only available option. The alternative would most likely involve increased out-migration and outflows of resources and continued economic decline.

Interestingly, grassroots economic action can also be facilitated by more prosperous or more advanced contiguous regions. These regions can serve as markets as well as sources of capital goods and intermediate inputs once the appropriate network of economic institutions and economic activities has been established in the lagging regions. Markets, whether local, regional, national, or even international, play a key role in the grassroots approach. Generally, in a relatively isolated region, as was the case in eastern Nova Scotia in the 1920s and 1930s, local markets tend to be small and inefficient and, moreover, to be monopolized by a few individuals, who use their position to exploit the local population. Through their monopoly power, these individuals are able to exclude the local population from full participation in the local market and, by extension, in the wider regional and national markets. The primary source of local monopoly is the isolation of the area due to inadequate transportation and communication links with the rest of the region or country as a whole. Thus the grassroots approach, like any other, can make use of interregional linkages to reinforce its growth and development impulses.

Social Conditions

Since grassroots movements are predominantly community-based or at least regional in nature, it is the conditions at the level of the community and/or the region that are of particular importance, as these conditions must foster agreement on objectives and strategies and some degree of cohesion. As already suggested, such cohesion may arise from cultural, social, linguistic, religious, and/or other factors and can be further strengthened by the existence of hostile outside forces, such as social and/or economic exploitation and religious discrimination.

In addition to cohesion, there is also a need for a sufficient number of people with leadership abilities predicated on characteristics such as intelligence, education, charisma, social standing in the community, sheer willpower and discipline, and interpersonal skills. Such leaders are not only required to persuade the rest of the community to accept the vision of a movement but are also charged with ensuring the necessary organization and economic action. Despite the claim of democracy, whereby all members had a voice, dynamic, committed, and abundant leadership was a critical feature of the Antigonish Movement during its heyday and of other successful movements as well. At the same time, overdependence on one or a small number of leaders may thwart a movement's ability to survive over the longer term since new leaders may not be forthcoming and since the movement may not be allowed to evolve in the face of changing opportunities and circumstances, as the initial vision and motivation can be lost. One of the most pernicious effects of the out-migration that often accompanies economic stagnation is the fact that it robs the region of its leaders – the very resource that is required for stagnation to be overcome – thus making matters worse.

Political Conditions

For movements to emerge and thrive, the political environment must allow them to do so. In effect, the very nature of economic movements, and other types of movements as well, requires the voluntary association of independent individuals. As a result, the political apparatus must provide certain freedoms and guarantees, including things such as freedom of association, enforcement of contracts, protection of persons and property, and freedom of enterprise. It is not surprising therefore that whereas representative democracies are favourable to the grassroots approach, repressive, dictatorial, or totalitarian regimes are not. Thus there has been a dearth of grassroots movements in countries controlled by either fascist or communist governments.[32] A noteworthy exception involves the Mondragon Movement of Spain, which flourished under the rule of General Francisco Franco.[33]

Moral and Spiritual Conditions

Arguably, the strength and cohesion of a community and its leadership tend to reflect its moral and spiritual foundations. These foundations rest on the efforts of past generations and are in turn influenced by a wide array of historical factors and struggles against adversity. Consequently, they are an important element, particularly in mobilizing trust and working for the common good.

The Christian Church and religious leaders of its different denominations have been of particular significance in the emergence of grassroots movements in many Western countries. The church, due to its social inclusiveness, has tended to be the only institution open to the population that could provide it with a strong sense of identity. Nevertheless, economic stagnation and out-migration not only adversely affect the welfare of the population of a region but may also threaten the church's institutional viability. In the case of the Antigonish Movement, such pervasive mutual dependence between the population of the region and the Roman Catholic Church induced some enlightened clergy to examine the possibility of initiating a movement to improve not only the economic but also the social, moral, and spiritual conditions of the people. Indeed, both the Antigonish and Mondragon Movements flourished under the leadership of two formidable Roman Catholic priests: Rev. Moses Michael Coady and Rev. Jose Maria Arrizmendiarrieta respectively.

THE ROLE OF EDUCATION

Education is also a critical component of economic movements and looms particularly large in both the Antigonish and Mondragon Movements. The Antigonish Movement heavily relied on an education strategy that was predominantly nonformal in organization and that was aimed at problem solving and hence immediate in its impact, which was referred to as adult education. Education supplements existing knowledge and provides additional skills, especially those pertaining to decision making, and information required for economic action.[34] In effect, the knowledge and information emanating from the education process constitute human capital formation or the building-up of the requisite "intellectual infrastructure."[35]

Fundamentally, knowledge and information, and hence education, entail empowerment and control and also expand a movement's non-human resource base, particularly through the stimulus that is provided to entrepreneurial decision making. Within the context of the Antigonish Movement, this resource expansion involved measures such as going into the woods to cut lumber, which was then used to build a lobster-processing plant. In the process, existing resources were mobilized and others were developed. As well, education plays a role in forming the attitudes, habits, values, and social norms that are required to sustain cooperative undertakings. It is also of vital importance in fostering an understanding of existing conditions and creating awareness of what must be done to alter them.[36]

THE WINDOW OF OPPORTUNITY

A critical question is when, in situations of economic decline, a grassroots movement is most likely to be successfully implemented. Arguably, the best time may not be during an economic boom, when both the motivation may be low and the opportunity cost may be high, making grassroots activities unlikely to arise. There seems to be a relatively brief "window of opportunity," perhaps no longer than the span of a generation or two, when a grassroots movement can succeed in reversing the stagnation, out-migration, demoralization, and community decay that characterize economic decline. It is difficult to effect renewal once resignation, demoralization, and apathy are firmly entrenched in the very culture of the people. Thus it is during the relatively brief period between the start of economic decline and its effects becoming deeply engrained in the mindset of the people that a grassroots movement can be most effective in reversing the cumulative effects of economic stagnation and its accompanying social decay.

Once a grassroots movement is in place, a second "window of opportunity" arises as a consequence of improved links with and access to other outlying areas and markets (i.e., regional, national, and even international markets) and enlarged and more efficient local markets as more goods and services become available and monopolistic control is destroyed. As a result, there is a widening of options and possibilities, which fosters additional activities and injects optimism into the movement.

Historically, movements that have been successful have to a lesser or greater degree been able to exploit these "windows of opportunity." The Caisse Populaire Movement took advantage of widening financial markets in Quebec at the turn of the century, the Antigonish Movement expanded into the newly emerging financial, consumer, and producer markets in Atlantic Canada during the 1930s and 1940s, and the Mondragon Movement took advantage of the rapidly expanding markets for industrial goods in Europe during the 1950s and 1960s.

CONCLUSION

Grassroots economic movements involve self-directed and self-initiated socio-economic activities of a regionally significant and culturally or otherwise cohesive group whose members share a common vision and goals and are willing to voluntarily cooperate to achieve them. Whether such a movement is initiated and continues its expansion depends on a vast array of factors inherent in the social and cultural environment of the region as well as on existing political and economic conditions. The most favourable environment for the emergence of a grassroots movement appears to be a region experiencing economic stagnation in comparison to adjacent regions or countries but enjoying political and economic freedoms associated with representative democracy and the free enterprise system. It is also essential that the population of the region be relatively homogeneous, face the same economic problems, and retain a strong social, moral, and spiritual base. Also important is the existence of an institution or institutional apparatus that the people trust and whose survival is also threatened by the state of economic decline. Such a favourable constellation of factors may open up a "window of opportunity" for a grassroots movement to emerge.

Such movements, designed primarily to counter poverty and stagnation and their impacts on the human condition, are premised on a number of fundamental assumptions. First, solutions cannot come about through action initiated from outside but must come through self-reliant, community-based initiatives involving the establishment of an appropriate institutional framework. Second, solutions rest on economic action, which in turn requires the mobilization and development of resources. Third, the people themselves are able to exercise ownership and control of economic institutions by following a cooperative approach.

The Antigonish Movement emerged in eastern Nova Scotia in the midst of the Great Depression, which paradoxically constituted its window of opportunity. Unlike most other economic movements, which tend to be narrow both in focus and in terms of coverage, the Antigonish Movement set out to put in place an integrated alternate economic system based on cooperative economic institutions controlled and owned by the people themselves and with universal appeal and applicability. As a result, although it possessed some of the same characteristics as other economic movements, the Antigonish Movement was unique. The rest of this book is devoted to an analysis of this remarkable experiment.

2

The Birth of the Antigonish Movement

INTRODUCTION

The Antigonish Movement, which found formal expression in the creation of the Extension Department of St Francis Xavier University in 1928, was born out of the longstanding conditions of socio-economic decline that prevailed in eastern Nova Scotia during the late 1800s and early 1900s. It attracted local, national, and international attention and acclaim largely for two reasons. First, it introduced a unique approach to socio-economic reform based on the principles of mass education and self-reliance, an approach sustained and supported by ordinary people with little outside assistance. It promoted social and economic reform and change through the establishment of a unique alternate economic system based on cooperation and education that enabled people both to develop and to control economic institutions and resources, allowing them to meet their needs and aspirations. Second, it took place at the time of the Great Depression, when the Western countries were experiencing severe economic and political crises and when the options available to people were few.

The movement achieved an extraordinary degree of success, particularly during the 1930s, in mobilizing people and resources and in creating an appropriate network of new institutions owned and controlled by the people of eastern Nova Scotia and other parts of the Maritimes.[1] Its influence also spread to other parts of the world, particularly the developing world. The movement's history, evolution, and eventual decline can be traced through the work of the Extension Department of St Francis Xavier University – its institutional core. It also provided the basis for the establishment of the Coady International Institute in 1959, originally designed to promote the methods and techniques of the Antigonish Movement throughout the Third World.

The social, economic, political, and cultural conditions of eastern Nova Scotia determined the specific characteristics and institutional network of the Antigonish Movement as well as the geographical area over which it spread. However, although certain aspects were specific to the region and its particular environment, the Antigonish Movement also possessed features that were universal in terms of both their scope and their applicability. Thus, from the very outset, it was relevant, with some adaptation to more specific local conditions, for other areas and countries experiencing similar sorts of problems and pursuing similar objectives.

In this chapter, we present an analysis of the main socio-economic conditions existing at the time of the emergence of the Antigonish Movement and outline the process of establishment of the movement through the following phases: (1) the gradual clarification and development of the vision of the movement, particularly in the context of the problems faced by eastern Nova Scotia; (2) the implementation of this vision through the establishment of an institutional network, starting with the Extension Department of St Francis Xavier University; and (3) the mobilization and development of resources by these institutions.

Although our analysis focuses primarily on the socio-economic dimensions of the issues, particularly within the context of development and social and institutional reform, we also pay attention to other relevant factors and forces, including important historical ones. In the main, our objective is to derive a stylized version of the Antigonish model so that it can be more easily analyzed.

HISTORICAL BACKGROUND

Eastern Nova Scotia, popularly known as "the seven counties" (Pictou, Antigonish, Guysborough, Inverness, Victoria, Richmond, and Cape Breton), constituted the principal geographical area of operation as well as birth of the Antigonish Movement. The area also comprises the Diocese of Antigonish. The Catholic Church, both directly and indirectly, through its diocesan university, St Francis

Xavier, took the leading role not only in initiating the movement but also in establishing its direction and in providing the support required for its survival.

The population of the seven counties taken as a whole consisted predominantly of Catholics and of three distinct ethnic groups: Scots, Acadians, and Irish. In addition to Catholics, there was also a strong Scottish Presbyterian presence. The dominant group was of Highland Scottish origin, and the Acadians, living mostly in the coastal communities, came next. These two groups generally formed tightly knit communities. The third group, made up of those who were of Irish background, was widely dispersed and scattered among the farming, fishing, and industrial communities but, nevertheless, also played an important role in the movement.[2] In fact, the two main founders of the Antigonish Movement, Rev. Moses Michael Coady and Rev. James John (Jimmy) Tompkins, were of Irish origin and had been brought up in the Scottish communities of the Margaree Valley in Inverness County.[3]

These three ethnic groups were united not only by their common religious affiliation but also by a history of religious persecution, social and political discrimination, economic exploitation, and inferior social and political status. Among the Scots and the Irish, religious persecution and economic deprivation and poverty had common roots, as the Catholics of the British Empire were not allowed to purchase or inherit property prior to the Relief Bill of 1793. Furthermore, they could not hold public office prior to 1829. Religious persecution and the poverty associated with it led to lower levels of education and also to social and political marginalization, and the process perpetuated itself from one generation to the next. The only escape from this vicious cycle was through emigration. The Scottish and Irish groups that settled eastern Nova Scotia were largely parts of this process.

Generally, the Scottish and Irish immigrants found the conditions of eastern Nova Scotia to be harsh but, nevertheless, better than those they had left behind. Despite the early hardships associated with the settlement and clearing of land and with the lack of amenities or infrastructure, the settlers found large sections of land that, although not always very fertile, could provide a better existence and standard of living. In addition to land, they also had access to relatively abundant natural resources, particularly in the fisheries and forestry sectors.[4] Furthermore, the communities that they established were based on more egalitarian principles, and they were relatively free, due to their isolation, of the religious persecution and social discrimination from which they had largely escaped. As a consequence, they were able to enjoy better living conditions in terms of housing, diet, and the like, in addition to having relative social and political freedom. Moreover, under the leadership and financial support provided by the church, the Catholic communities established their own social, cultural, and educational institutions over time, and the same was true of other denominations as well.

Although the history of the Acadians differs from that of the Scots and the Irish, their migration was in response to somewhat similar forces. In any event, their treatment by the British, who forced them out of their original settlements, was just as severe as, if not worse than, that suffered by the Scots and the Irish.[5] After having been expelled from more fertile lands in the Annapolis Valley, the Acadians who settled along the seashores of eastern Nova Scotia began to harvest the abundant fish that was available there.[6] Although their historical experience may have been different, the Acadians shared with the Scots and the Irish the strong bond of the Catholic faith.

In 1853 the Diocese of Antigonish established its own university, St Francis Xavier, in the fishing community of Arichat, soon after in 1855 transferred to Antigonish, for the education of Catholic leaders, both religious and secular. Although the University was established for the purposes of supporting and strengthening the Catholic faith and training the Catholic youth for the religious and secular professions, it was hoped that it would also contribute to the social, cultural, economic, and political uplifting of the whole population of eastern Nova Scotia.[7]

Economic Conditions Prior to the 1920s

During the 1850s and 1860s, eastern Nova Scotia shared, to some extent, in the overall prosperity of the Maritimes based on the so-called "wood-wind-water" economy. Favourable demand conditions in Europe, the West Indies, and the United States – in the case of the latter, particularly as a consequence of the signing of the Reciprocity Treaty in 1854 – encouraged agriculture, fishing, trade, and shipbuilding.[8] As well, there was growth in the coal and steel industries, and there was an assortment of industrial and processing activity, especially in main urban areas such as Halifax.[9] There was also an expanding network of financial institutions, which included the Bank of New Brunswick, chartered in 1821, and the Bank of Nova Scotia, established in Halifax in 1832.[10] These were joined by the Merchant's Bank, established in Halifax in 1869.[11] As a consequence, the population of the Maritimes, including eastern Nova Scotia, increased and the general standard of living rose. Nevertheless, "poverty and destitution were common," and the "truck system," whereby primary producers, especially those in the fisheries, were dependent on the local merchants, was well established.[12]

The lucrative trade with the United States had been placed in jeopardy by the end of Reciprocity in 1866, one year after the end of the Civil War. Although Confederation offered the possibility of expanding trade with the rest of the Dominion, it required building additional railway links. Prime Minister John A. MacDonald's authorization of the construction of the intercolonial railway in 1869 (with a line to central Canada completed by 1876) was thus seen as a very important step.[13] In many ways, this undertaking provided the assurance that despite the detrimental political and economic imbalances of Confederation, the maritime provinces could still gain by being a part of the process.[14] The 1871 Treaty of Washington, which "provided free entry of Canadian fish into the American market,"[15] had a similar intent. Although Confederation linked the Maritimes more strongly with the rest of the Dominion, it still left open the option of maintaining the trade links of the Maritimes with Europe and elsewhere while also working to expand economic links with the United States. Thus, rather than simply looking west, Confederation also seemed to leave open the option of looking east and south.[16] However, the precipitous decline in shipbuilding, most notably during the 1870s, was a heavy blow, particularly given the importance of this industry.[17] According to Margaret Conrad and James Hiller, "without government encouragement and protection there was little incentive to build iron or steel vessels or to maintain a sizable merchant marine."[18] In effect, given the new circumstances, including that the decision-making apparatus was based on the existence of a federal government somewhat removed from the concerns of the region, the maritime provinces lost their comparative advantage in shipbuilding as iron and steel replaced wood. Combined with changes in demand in various overseas markets, the result was a much greater dependence on the western option, which also implied fundamental and difficult changes in the structure of the maritime economies. Confederation also reoriented trade away from the low-cost water transportation involved in the east and south options and toward the higher-cost transportation by rail involved in looking west. That the freight rates established by the intercolonial railway were low served as a mitigating factor, allowing the maritime provinces, particularly Nova Scotia, to export coal and other products, especially to central Canada.[19]

Within the context of the changes that were taking place, the federal government's National Policy of 1879, which put in place generally high protective tariffs, seemed to be beneficial to the Maritimes, although it would further disrupt the maritime provinces North-South links and provide additional incentive for them to move away from their traditional emphasis on trade and shipping. Initially, however, it contributed to an expansion in manufacturing activity, particularly in the coal and steel industries, which had become well established in eastern Nova Scotia.

The intercolonial railway played an important role, as much of the industrial activity was located along its corridor. As a consequence, new business activities sprang up in various parts of the Maritimes. In the case of northern Nova Scotia, assorted industrial activity flourished in towns served by railway lines, such as Amherst, Truro, New Glasgow, and Sydney.[20] In particular, the "growth of the coal-steel industry was spectacular"[21] and "seemed to confirm Nova Scotia's industrial pre-eminence."[22] Not only did Nova Scotia produce the bulk of Canadian coal, but two of the four corporations dominating the Canadian steel industry at the turn of the century were also located in eastern Nova Scotia: Nova Scotia Steel and Coal, which was established in Pictou County in 1882 and integrated at Sydney Mines in 1900; and Dominion Iron and Steel Company, which was incorporated in 1900 but began with the creation of the Dominion Coal Company in 1893.[23] Coal not only supported the iron and steel industry but also constituted an item exportable to central Canada – although only as a minor portion of that market's needs.[24]

A wide array of other industrial activities also emerged, particularly in the main urban areas, ranging from the building of railway cars (in Amherst) to the manufacture of textiles and the processing of foods. However, these industries "tended to be smaller and less efficient than those of central Canada."[25] Moreover, they were increasingly under the control of outside financial and corporate interests, particularly from central Canada. This trend was especially in evidence in the cotton industry, which by the early 1890s had been almost completely taken over by Montreal interests.[26] Thus, despite their seemingly impressive growth, the industrial development that took place in the maritime provinces was dwarfed by what was taking place in central Canada – the preferred location for new and even already existing firms and the recipient of large population inflows.[27] The situation in the Maritimes continued to deteriorate with the turn of the century.

The primary sectors also faced difficulties. Agriculture experienced slow growth and decreased prices in the face of increased competition, and there was also a decline in the forestry sector. However, the prospects of the fisheries, although negatively impacted by the expiry of the Treaty of Washington in 1885, were also enhanced by diversification, including the marketing of canned lobster, and by the fact that there was a generally expanding demand for fish in the rest of Canada and the United States, although there was a decline in overseas markets.[28] Nevertheless, the sector was plagued by structural problems that became increasingly evident over time.

By the turn of the century, the maritime provinces – once the more highly developed of the North American colonies due to efficient shipbuilding, trade, and finance – were experiencing steady decline compared to the rest of Canada. Financial institutions not only continued the trend of looking toward central Canada for their loans but also shifted their main operations out of the region. The Bank of Nova Scotia moved its headquarters to Toronto in 1901 (and later, in 1910, also absorbed the Bank of New Brunswick), and the Merchants' Bank, which had become the Royal Bank in 1901, similarly shifted its headquarters to Montreal in 1906.[29] In effect, the financial sector of the Maritimes had virtually disappeared.[30] The trend toward the greater dominance of central Canadian interests also prevailed in other sectors. Thus Dominion Coal and Dominion Iron and Steel, initially controlled by outside, largely American, interests, were taken over by Montreal interests in 1901 and became amalgamated as the Dominion Steel Corporation (DOSCO) in 1909, with control over most of Nova Scotia's coal.[31] The same applied to many other key maritime industries, leading in some instances to the shutdown of maritime production. These takeovers shifted decision-making power to powerful agents in central Canada and away from the region. This shift, along with the decline in the realm of political representation, further eroded the region's ability to participate in national policy-making, increasing its vulnerability and giving rise to serious repercussions for the local economy. Arguably, the outside control also fuelled labour unrest, as maritime workers "faced employers who had no particular attachment or loyalty to the region, and who were prepared to fight workers with any weapons at their disposal."[32] An important exception to the wave of foreign takeovers was the Nova Scotia Steel and Coal Company, which remained under local control until it was finally amalgamated, along with the Dominion Steel Corporation, into the foreign-controlled British Empire Steel Corporation (BESCO) in 1921.[33]

Overall, although the coal and iron and steel industries continued to flourish, the years prior to the First World War were also fraught with difficulties. These booming industries brought benefits to industrial centres such as those in Cape Breton County, but the sector was not without its weaknesses. The local coal production was largely absorbed by the local iron and steel industry, which in turn depended on markets being available, particularly outside the region, which made the region highly vulnerable to outside forces beyond its control. That the maritime provinces were not able to adequately diversify their industrial production, which was overly reliant on intermediate goods, and that foreign interests had significant control over what existed added to the problem.[34]

The primary sectors faced difficulties during the early years of the twentieth century. Although certain segments of the agricultural sector flourished, particularly apples and potatoes, others did not. The fisheries were generally in a state of decline, with the inshore fishermen faring particularly poorly.

The coming of the First World War provided a boost, especially to industrial activity, as coalmines, steel plants, metal works, and other operations worked at full capacity mainly in support of the war effort. However, the impact was short-lived and felt mainly in the industrial towns, which in the case of eastern Nova Scotia were confined largely to Pictou and Cape Breton Counties. The primary sectors also did well. The end of the war, however, dealt a heavy blow to the maritime economy, as many of the maritime industries, particularly those linked to mining and to steel and metal works, experienced great difficulty adjusting to the new peacetime circumstances. Perhaps most damaging of all was the increase in freight rates for the Maritimes in 1918 as a consequence of the reorganization of railway services, which saw the intercolonial railway and others amalgamated through the establishment of the Canadian National Railway over the 1919–23 period. Although there is some disagreement as to the importance of freight rates and whether the intercolonial railway in fact followed a policy of lower rates to foster regional development, the sharp increase in freight rates, which started around 1912, did not help maritime prospects.[35] Moreover, that they were now determined outside the region precluded any possibility that they could be used to foster maritime development.

The establishment of high, uniform freight rates, determined largely outside the maritime region, added to the economic decline that was already in progress and, some argue, already in evidence during the 1880s and 1890s. As rates skyrocketed, all sectors and occupational groups in the economy of the region, particularly those of eastern Nova Scotia, were affected.[36] The much higher freight rates, and hence higher transportation costs, reduced the competitiveness of maritime products in the rest of Canada while also increasing the price of imports to the region, such as agricultural inputs, making an already precarious situation even worse. To some extent, the higher freight rates and the economic plight of the region as a whole were also a reflection of the increasingly diminished ability of the maritime region to protect its interests through the political process.

The forces at work reshaping the maritime economy greatly impacted eastern Nova Scotia. The decline of the wood-wind-water economy caused shipbuilding to virtually disappear from many coastal communities and in the process severely curtailed the region's seafaring and trading tradition. However, new coalmines were opened up in the counties of Pictou, Inverness, and Cape Breton in conjunction with the steel and metal works complexes that were established in Trenton, New Glasgow, and Sydney.[37] Although the total population of the Diocese of Antigonish had continued to grow until the turn of the century, the growth was confined to two counties, Cape Breton and Pictou, where industrialization, driven by coal and steel, was predominant. The coalmines and steel mills also attracted immigrants from eastern and southern Europe, adding to the population mix but without fundamentally altering its region-wide composition.[38] The remaining five counties, which were predominantly rural, experienced a continuous stream of out-migration. The situation worsened after the turn of the century, leading to an overall decline in population.[39]

As was the case for the maritime provinces as a whole, the First World War gave rise to a period of short-lived prosperity in eastern Nova Scotia, particularly in the two industrial counties. However, the end of the war ushered in a period of economic stagnation and decline affecting all sectors, including within the industrial centres. Out-migration again increased, resulting in a drain of human resources that not only contributed to further stagnation but also placed the viability of the local economy and way of life at risk.[40] At the same time, the economy was undergoing fundamental structural changes.

The prolonged period of stagnation and decline that continued during the 1920s had a profound effect on a local population that was far removed from the early settler days. Attitudes of hopelessness, powerlessness, and resignation began to creep into the region as the still largely traditional subsistence economy that characterized many of the rural areas was challenged, to a greater extent than ever before, by an emerging market economy based upon money and credit. Primary producers were facing ever-increasing difficulties, and the industrial sector was being undermined by both internal and external forces.

THE ECONOMIC CONDITIONS OF THE 1920S The economic malaise that existed during the 1920s was tied not only to the long-standing decline of the wood-wind-water economy but also to the fundamental economic transformation that was taking place at the time.[41] To get a clearer picture of the conditions in the economic sphere, it is perhaps best to distinguish between the three basic occupational subgroups that comprised the bulk of the population of eastern Nova Scotia and that were certainly the most severely hit by the prevailing economic circumstances: (1) industrial workers concentrated primarily in Cape Breton County's industrial-urban area of Sydney and Glace Bay as well as in Pictou County, (2) farmers engaged mostly in subsistence agriculture, and (3) fishermen located in the numerous fishing villages dotting the eastern Nova Scotia coastline.[42]

By the 1920s conditions in the industrial-urban areas of eastern Nova Scotia, highly dependent on coal and steel, were rapidly deteriorating. The exploitation of workers, along with declining demand for the region's industrial output, created a situation of poor working conditions, labour unrest, strikes, and unemployment, with mines drastically cutting their output and steel furnaces shutting down. In turn, these circumstances promoted an increase in urban poverty, evident in poor housing, poor nutrition, and the like.[43] The results were anger and dissatisfaction with industrial capitalism, which elicited, at least in some quarters, a degree of sympathy toward the emerging alternate socio-economic system, embodied in communism and the emergence of the Soviet Union, as "Crowds flocked to hear of the Russian Revolution, broadcast at meeting after meeting."[44] However, this option did not attain widespread support as a viable alternative in the Maritimes.

As a consequence of changes that took place in the previous decades, industrial enterprise in eastern Nova Scotia during the 1920s was generally characterized by absentee ownership and monopsonistic-monopolistic conditions perhaps best typified by the "company towns."[45] At the same time, the inadequate investment and neglect that permeated the Maritimes, particularly as more profitable ventures emerged in central Canada and elsewhere, also affected the industrial-urban areas of eastern Nova Scotia.[46] Thus both the structure of industrial enterprise and demand conditions conspired to the detriment of the wellbeing of the urban workers. Desperate workers, especially the miners backed by District 26 of the United Mineworkers, the largest union in the Maritimes, fought bitterly against drastic wage cuts and layoffs imposed by management. Strikes were called, with some of them, such as the 1925 strike by miners in Sydney, turning violent and involving the loss of life.[47]

In the rural areas, conditions were also precarious. Much of the rural activity was primarily of a subsistence sort, with some cash crops, although the agricultural sector was becoming increasingly commercialized as a consequence of its greater incorporation into the monetized market economy, resulting from improvements in transportation, refrigeration, and the like, as well as from the growth of market transactions. This commercialization had a detrimental effect on the rural sector. The increased dependence on the market generated an increase in the demand for money, yet poor market conditions and monopsonistic buyers of produce limited the amount of money that could be earned.[48] Poor soil conditions and short growing seasons did not help matters, nor did inefficient production methods, which put local producers at a disadvantage vis-à-vis produce coming from outside the area.[49] At the same time, monopolistic sellers of consumer goods and agricultural inputs and implements ensured that the prices paid by the farmers remained relatively high.[50]

The same sort of problems plagued the fishermen. In particular, they were at the mercy of the monopsonistic fish buyers, who established very low prices for the fish, and of monopolistic sellers of fishing gear and equipment that the fishermen required to catch the fish.[51] These conditions were particularly damaging to the fishermen due to their greater degree of dependence on the market for the sale of their fish and purchase of inputs. Moreover, the situation became increasingly worse as the fish buyers lowered their prices even further as a way of insulating their position in response to adverse market conditions, particularly in the rest of Canada and south of the border.[52]

Often, the same individuals were involved in buying fish and produce, in selling fishing gear and equipment, agricultural implements, and consumer goods, and in providing loans and advances at high interest rates. These merchants could, and often did, exploit the primary producers, who depended on them to purchase their fish and produce and to supply them with goods as well as loans and advances. In turn, these merchants were controlled by outside interests and hence unable to make changes to the existing arrangements.[53] Such a situation resulted in the economic exploitation of farmers and fishermen, leading to their impoverishment while contributing to the affluence of a dependent "capitalist" merchant class.

In the economic sphere, therefore, the problems characterizing the bulk of the population of eastern Nova Scotia emanated from three basic sources: (1) the imbalance in market power between the capitalist and merchant class, on the one hand, and the worker and primary producer class, on the other; (2) the prevailing poor and deteriorating market conditions (i.e., demand conditions, particularly in the coal- and steel-dominated industrial sector and in the fisheries); and (3) the fact that the region was caught in a period of fundamental transition between traditional and modern economic organization, with the latter able to exploit the former. Added to these were elements of Canadian national policy that did relatively little for outlying regions such as eastern Nova Scotia.

Political, Social, and Cultural Conditions

In the political realm, the predominantly two-party free enterprise system did not perform well for eastern Nova Scotia in the 1920s.[54] At the time, there was little by way of a social-welfare safety net that could cushion some of the effects of economic decline, as the role of government in the economy was still limited. This state of events, particularly in the face of the dire conditions in which people found themselves, gave rise to discontentment reflected in the radicalization of the population, particularly in the industrial-urban areas, as manifested in strikes and riots as well as in communist agitation (reflected in the "Red Scare"), especially among immigrant workers who had already been exposed to communist ideology in Europe. However, such radicalization had a limited impact on the political system in eastern Nova Scotia and even less on that of the Maritimes as a whole. In other parts of Canada, particularly during the 1930s as the Great Depression caused discontentment to spread and intensify, there was perhaps a greater proclivity toward political experimentation and new approaches. Thus there was the birth of the Co-operative Commonwealth Federation, Social Credit, and Union Nationale political parties, arising from the search for new political ideologies and approaches that could address the emerging conditions. No such political movement loomed large in eastern Nova Scotia and the maritime provinces in general. The one possible exception was the Reconstruction Party in 1935, which we discuss later.

The social and cultural conditions of the various target groups were also important to the emergence and success of the Antigonish Movement. The whole of eastern Nova Scotia was characterized by a high degree of regional cohesion and by stable community structures that provided the basic social infrastructure that was vital to the spread and the acceptance of the movement.[55] In the rural areas, this cohesiveness stemmed from the nature of the traditional economy, particularly the absence of any significant degree of social and economic mobility and the absence of social stratification. The relative absence of mobility and social stratification tends to be characteristic of pre-market or rural-based traditional and subsistent societies. More traditional societies are also more inherently cooperative and community-based. In the industrial areas, mobility was also limited due to the relative geographical isolation. As well, to the extent that much of the urbanization was a rather recent phenomenon, social stratification among target groups both within the urban areas and between the urban and rural areas was also limited. Such a situation was a function largely of common rural roots and of a relatively small rural-urban gap in real income.

The relative isolation of eastern Nova Scotia, particularly in the case of its various rural and fishing communities, had likely worsened with the decline of the wood-wind-water economy, which had weakened some of its transportation and communication networks. Although the expansion of roads and railways mitigated these effects for the larger urban areas and towns, and in some instances constituted notable improvements, this was not the case in general. Many roads were often impassable during the winter, and the railway was not accessible to many rural and coastal communities.[56] As a result, the physical mobility of people was hampered, and more important, so was their access to information regarding matters such as market conditions, which enabled middlemen like livestock drovers and fish buyers to continue to flourish. In effect, filling in this information gap constituted a key component of the Extension Department's adult education programs over time.

At the regional and, even more so, community levels, the basic integrating elements were the Catholic Church and the cultural heritage of the people – particularly the dominant Scottish and Acadian heritages. The Catholic Church exerted a powerful integrating influence as a consequence of the variety of functions that it performed. Not only did it provide spiritual and moral guidance and carry out charitable work, but it was also at the forefront of education at all levels – including through the establishment of St Francis Xavier University – and of healthcare provision, with various religious orders operating hospitals and the like. Foremost in the health field was the pioneering work of the Sisters of St Martha, who established a regional hospital, schools of nursing, and outreach missions in the area and later across the nation and internationally as well.[57]

TOWARD SOCIO-ECONOMIC REFORMS

Economic stagnation, out-migration, and the social and moral decay associated with them became major concerns of the general public, particularly its socially minded educated leaders, both religious and secular. The steady decline in the economic and social base of the region undermined the economic position of teachers, lawyers, doctors, and other members of the liberal professions, even though the individual members of these professions had some occupational mobility. The Catholic Church and its clergy were affected to an even greater extent, for a number of reasons and in a number of ways. First, the depopulation of the rural areas reduced the number of church members, which was of concern to the Catholic Church since it affected both the church's influence and its fundamental mission to minister to the faithful. In addition, members of the clergy were much less occupationally mobile than those in the myriad secular professions. By and large, the members of the local clergy were tied to the Diocese of Antigonish, which in turn was territorially bound by eastern Nova Scotia. The Catholic Church and the clergy empathized with the plight of the local population, particularly in light of the church's social teachings.[58] It is not surprising that the clergy and, particularly, the Catholic priest-professors at the diocesan university became alarmed at the deteriorating conditions of the communities of their region and took a leading role in the various attempts at social and economic change. Furthermore, the priest-professors, being educated at seminaries outside the region, especially those who went to Rome, were familiar not only with the various papal encyclicals on the social teachings of the Catholic Church but also with the various attempts to put these into action in England, France, Denmark, Ireland, and elsewhere.[59] It became clear to them that economic decline had dire spiritual consequences that resulted in moral decay and loss of faith. The moral and spiritual foundations of the entire Diocese of Antigonish were thus being undermined. At stake was the survival not only of the communities but also of the Catholic Church itself as an integral part of the region.

The First Attempts

The first attempts at social and economic change in eastern Nova Scotia constituted, in the main, local responses to the several waves of social and political movements that swept the North American continent in the early 1900s. For example, various Protestant churches, alarmed by the emerging social problems, particularly in the urban areas, proclaimed a "Social Gospel" that entailed a mixture of social criticism and moral exhortation and eventually gave rise to the Temperance Movement.[60] The Catholic Church, led by Pope Leo XIII's encyclical *Rerum Novarum*, also joined the process, inspiring various priests and religious to work to improve the lives of the faithful. Farmers sought protection through the establishment of political parties. Similarly, industrial workers sought to improve their lot by joining labour organizations and by forming their own political parties. There were also some initiatives that were more local. These efforts were generally sporadic and disjointed and had little direct impact. In some instances, however, they contributed to the establishment of some of the foundations for the Antigonish Movement.

Although membership in organized labour increased dramatically, it did not improve the lot of industrial workers.[61] Some candidates of the United Farmers Party were elected to the Nova Scotia Legislature in 1920 and, allied with elected members of the independent labour parties, formed the official opposition.[62] This success was short-lived, as the party became discredited within two years. Labour, by comparison, achieved considerable success in municipal politics, especially in Cape Breton, and the radical wing of District 26 of the United Mine Workers even managed to get a resolution to join the Red International at its 1922 convention.[63] These efforts did not alleviate the plight of workers but caused alarm among the existing establishment, resulting in a hardening of the position of management while alienating the middle class and some workers.

These early efforts also comprised the so-called "progressive movements" of social and moral regeneration, which tended to be vaguely defined and unfocused. These movements inspired some priest-professors at St Francis Xavier University, led in particular by Rev. Tompkins, to establish the Forward Movement in Antigonish County in 1913, aimed at rural regeneration through the promotion and encouragement of immigration, improvement of agricultural practices, and creation of business and civic organizations.[64] Rev. Tompkins also raised relevant issues through the "For the People" column in the local diocesan newspaper, *The Casket*.[65] In these initiatives, heavy reliance was placed on fostering public awareness and the like. At the same time, there was also the important work done by Rev. Dr Hugh MacPherson, also a priest-professor at St Francis Xavier University, to promote agricultural cooperatives.[66]

Another major movement of the time, the Maritime Rights Movement, was primarily political in nature. It was loosely organized and employed political agitation and spontaneous protests as tools aimed at gaining economic concessions from the Dominion government. These concessions included lower freight rates for the movement of goods from the Maritimes as well as subsidies and port concessions.[67] In eastern Nova Scotia the movement had the support of local businessmen, the clergy, and assorted members of other professions. It also elicited interest from the two main political parties. Initially, it was championed by the Conservative Party, which failed to live up to its promises and faced retribution in the elections of 1921. The cause was then taken up by the Liberal Party but with similar results, causing the Liberals to lose most of their seats in the Maritimes in the elections of 1925.[68] This defeat prompted the government of Mackenzie King to establish the Duncan Commission to study the maritime provinces' grievances and establish a practical program to address them.[69] Although the Duncan Commission did recommend a reduction in freight rates for maritime products, resulting in the passing of the Maritime Freight Act of 1927, and an increase in subsidies to the maritime provincial governments, it did not resolve the deep-rooted structural problems that plagued the maritime economies.

Although short-lived, the Maritime Rights Movement did articulate the region's discontent with the status quo and was instrumental in prompting the establishment of a number of royal commissions to look into some of the more pressing problems.[70] In effect, the Maritime Rights Movement contributed to the precedent of setting up royal commissions to deal with maritime grievances. Moreover, the same clergy members who later came to play a critical role in the Antigonish Movement were also instrumental in articulating and popularizing the concerns of the Maritime Rights Movement.

Farmers, fishermen, and industrial workers also articulated and gave vent to their discontent and engaged in protest. Although the fishermen had been very active in searching for ways to improve their economic position even prior to the First World War, it was not until the 1920s that the farmers and workers joined the protests on an organized scale. As was the case elsewhere, their efforts to improve their economic conditions focused primarily on the existing institutional apparatus and thus revolved around the formation of political parties and labour unions.[71] An additional player that needs to be identified was the Scottish Catholic Society. Established in 1919, its primary concern was to save the agricultural sector by combating the rural decay that was becoming more apparent. As a result, it served as an ally of both the Catholic Church and the communities.[72]

These early attempts at social and political reform were generally not successful. They were not well organized, lacked focus and coherence, mobilized too few resources, and could not be sustained for long. They were nevertheless important, especially because they allowed the priest-professors and others to learn two important lessons. First, they learned that the causes of the economic and social stagnation of eastern Nova Scotia were deeply imbedded in the existing institutional framework, particularly in the economic structure of the region, and that overcoming these problems would thus require an organized and sustained effort, involving masses of the population, aimed at economic change and supported by an appropriate institutional apparatus. Second, they learned that the more traditional approaches did not address the specific social and economic problems of rural Nova Scotia, particularly the overriding problem of rural decay. These problems could be addressed only through the creation of an indigenous movement of social and economic reform.[73] Equally important, there had to be fundamental changes in human behaviour: people had to move away from traditional ways of doing things, which were often conditioned by fatalistic tendencies, and they had to adopt a willingness to take greater control of their resources and to exercise responsibility with respect to their uses. These changes did not occur on their own.

Putting these lessons into practice, of course, turned out to be the hard part. The obvious problems involved deciding where to begin and what steps to take. A particular dilemma revolved around the generally related problems of how to mobilize dispirited masses, where to find the resources required for the task, and how to use these resources most effectively. Although the problems facing the region were enormous, the actual resources initially at the people's disposal, and at the disposal of St Francis Xavier University, were minuscule. The leaders of the movement were aware, in light of past experience, that to deal with the existing circumstances they had to try something new and also something separate from the political process. Exactly what this new course of action entailed evolved slowly over the 1920s.[74]

Laying the Foundations

The Antigonish Movement adopted a strategy that, in retrospect, seems highly systematic, for it resulted from the leading role in the process played by the priest-professors, who were trained in logic, analysis, and the scientific method as well as in philosophy and the arts. The early leaders of the movement started with a theoretical approach based on in-depth analysis of the existing circumstances and a clear vision of what was to be accomplished, namely a fundamental reform of the existing socio-economic system. Their intuitive systematic process allowed them, through trial and error, to progressively narrow the range of appropriate action until they were able to formulate a relatively simple sequence of activities that proved to be extremely effective in promoting socio-economic change. Furthermore, this sequence of activity could be transferred elsewhere with similar results. In other words, they discovered an effective model of development that had wide applicability to other regions facing the same or similar problems. This model, which served as a guide and an instrument of motivation to action, became popularly known as the "Antigonish Way."[75]

During the 1920s, as a part of this systematic process, there was a flurry of activities that included the emergence of the People's School.[76] The first People's School was held in 1921 at St Francis Xavier University and constituted an effort to bring the people to the university.[77] It was repeated in 1922. Although well received, the outcome fell short of expectations, and the strategy was consequently reversed. Thus the People's Schools that were held in Glace Bay in 1923 and 1924 involved bringing the university to the people. The distinction is important for a number of reasons, as will become apparent later. At this stage, we need to note that it constituted a fundamental shift in terms of the role of the university vis-à-vis the community, consistent with the ideas expressed in Tompkins's influential 1921 pamphlet *Knowledge for the People*. In effect, the university went to the community rather than the other way around.[78] In 1924 there was also the first annual Rural Conference, renamed in 1934 the

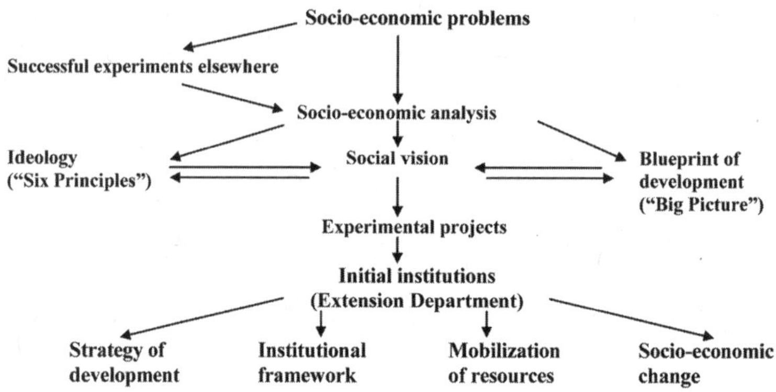

Figure 2.1 The process of the emergence of the Antigonish Movement

Rural and Industrial Conference.[79] These and other initiatives brought to the fore a wealth of ideas and strengthened the resolve to take action.

Although the Antigonish Movement's model of development turned out to be relatively simple, the process of discovering its unique sequence of activities to affect socio-economic change was in fact long and arduous. Rev. Coady and the other leaders of the movement had to ensure that the methods adopted fitted the socio-economic realities of the time, and these methods took them into uncharted territory. A highly stylized version of the process that was followed is delineated in figure 2.1.

The sequence, predicated on problem-analysis-vision-experiment, is similar to the scientific sequence of problem-hypothesis-experiment-theory. However, unlike scientists, who test their hypotheses through controlled experiments in laboratories, the priest-professors, especially Rev. Coady and Rev. Tompkins, did their testing and their analysis in the local communities and in the region on real people who had to be convinced of their importance and validity in order to be willing to participate. Failure in the case of these socio-economic experiments meant not only that resources would be wasted but also, and more important, that expectations would be crushed, reputations ruined, and people's lives seriously affected as the underlying problems of the region worsened. Undoubtedly, such a failure would compromise future efforts, as this approach did not entail a return to the laboratory, the reformulation of hypotheses, and the treatment of the failure itself as an addition to the stock of existing knowledge.

Of critical importance to getting the movement off the ground, as well as to formulating and then implementing its development model, was the ability to carry out an accurate and comprehensive analysis of the socio-economic conditions of the region. Such an analysis and the understanding that it generated served three basic functions. First, it identified the fundamental causes of the problems facing the region – a difficult but necessary task. It helped that the early leaders of the movement knew and understood the people, their environment, and the prevailing socio-economic structure and that they possessed a perspective that went well beyond the purely social and economic. As well, they had some understanding of and contact with the world outside of the region, which constituted an important additional dimension of their analysis. The identification of the underlying causes not only shaped the initial thrust of the movement but also determined the specific actions that were undertaken once the Extension Department was established.

Second, this analysis identified the forces within individual communities and the region at large that could, if unleashed, be powerful enough to overcome the existing inertia, hopelessness, stagnation, defeatism, and opposition to change. In effect, these would be the forces that could be harnessed to both initiate and foster socio-economic reform.

Third, this analysis identified an appropriate and practical course of action that people could accept as eventually leading to a solution to the existing problems – one that could satisfy their basic needs and aspirations.

The socio-economic analysis promoted a clearer understanding of the region's problems, provided crucial insights into causal relationships, allowed forces of change to be identified, and promoted the emergence of a vision that could later be transformed into action. These turned out to be vital components of the overall success of the Antigonish Movement in eastern Nova Scotia and other parts of the Maritimes but would have been relevant to other settings as well.

Socio-economic Analysis

The leaders of the Antigonish Movement started out with a good understanding of the people, their problems, and the forces at work in the region as a whole as well as in individual communities. They also understood that there were generally no easy solutions and, despite not being entirely clear about the specific type of actions that were required, knew what they wanted to achieve.[80]

Awareness of the local socio-economic environment, however, was not enough; by itself, it could not translate into a "grassroots" or "bottom-up" movement. For such a movement to be established, it was imperative that the population at large also be a part of the process. Thus the socio-economic analysis also had to be carried out at the grassroots level or, at least, had to ensure that the people were willing participants in the process and would play an ever-increasing role over time. It was understood that broad-based participation by the people – or by the masses – was critical. Indeed, the very notion of people being "Masters of Their Own Destiny," which emerged as the key component of the vision of the movement, clearly implied that this was the case. Moreover, the leaders of the movement understood, from the very beginning, that the involvement of the people in social and economic action would not come about automatically. Such involvement required that education and analysis be brought to the people – that is, to those at the grassroots. The pioneering work by Rev. Tompkins in establishing the People's Schools and his work in Canso, after having been transferred there to serve as a parish priest in 1922, were critical early components of this understanding. Also important was the work by Rev. Coady in mobilizing people to form study groups in Margaree.[81] The whole process of taking education and analysis to the people became more pronounced with the establishment of the Extension Department of St Francis Xavier University, which provided the institutional component that was necessary for the process to continue and become more effective.

The most obvious way of bringing socio-economic analysis to the people would have been simply to present the circumstances that prevailed in the region and then to suggest solutions based, in whole or in part, on how similar problems were successfully dealt with elsewhere. Such an approach, however, would have been of limited use in mobilizing the masses to form a movement since it would likely have appealed to intellectuals but not to the people at large. Logical and dispassionate analysis had to be repackaged so that it could appeal in a compelling way to both the intellectuals and the masses. That the Antigonish Movement was able to do this, at least during its early years, is a testament to the commitment and exceptional talent of its founders and early leaders.

Socio-economic Vision

By bringing the analysis of socio-economic conditions to the people, and also by allowing them to participate in the process, the leaders of the Antigonish Movement merged analytical rigour with an uplifting vision of future possibilities, expressed in language that the people could understand and that appealed to their emotion and to their reason. To the articulation of the existing circumstances, of which the people were well aware, was added the possibility that things could be better and that the way to make things better lay within their grasp. Although the people understood the problems that they faced, they generally lacked an understanding of their nature and causes, which could be provided by socio-economic analysis. In effect, by demystifying economic problems and their causes, the movement empowered people to push for change and to take control of their own affairs.

To appeal to the emotion and enthusiasm of the masses, the vision was usually couched in highly idealistic terms. The vision was appealing, but the benefits were by no means automatic; there was a lot of work to be done. Rev. Tompkins, Rev. Coady, and other early leaders of the movement insisted that the people should search out their own answers and that there was no easy or "lazy" way out of the existing circumstances. Thus the vision, even when expressed in somewhat abstract terms, was firmly rooted in relevant, accurate, and logical socio-economic analysis and predicated on the practical objective of social and economic improvement, with the consequence that what was being proposed was not merely a dream.

The vision of the Antigonish Movement appealed to the idealism and optimism of some as well as to the pragmatism and realism of others. Moreover, as some of the practical possibilities were in fact realized, particularly during the 1930s, the feasibility of the movement and the commitment to its vision increased.

In the main, the socio-economic analysis prompted by the movement helped to create and sustain a vision of a better social order and an alternate economic system more in tune with the people's needs and circumstances. Thus it went a long way toward addressing two of the crucial questions that often constrain attempts to implement reform and change: what must be done and how can one go about doing it? Although the appeal to emotion was important in getting the attention of the people, the actual content of the analysis was responsible for keeping this attention focused on the issues. The validity and relevance of the analysis and its accessibility to and acceptance by the people contributed not only to the emergence of the movement but also to the establishment of the institutional framework that was necessary for the success and survival of the movement, which had its own identity and fundamental uniqueness.

The importance of appropriate and accurate socio-economic analysis is, of course, not unique to the Antigonish Movement but is a part of every initiative aimed at social and economic reform. The implication is that grassroots economic movements, at least lasting ones, do not spring out of nowhere or come about on their own but emerge as a result of human actions based upon accurate knowledge and a compelling sense of purpose. Such was certainly true for the group of unemployed weavers in England who in 1844 formulated the Rochdale Principles and in the process founded the first modern cooperative, giving rise to the modern cooperative movement.[82] The same also holds true for the Caisse Populaire Movement in Quebec. Alphonse Desjardins, a county clerk, perceived that the major cause of stagnation and poverty among the working masses of Quebec could be traced to the financial sector, namely to the lack of community-based financial institutions able to meet the people's needs for financial services and to do so at a reasonable cost. Based on this analysis, the solution lay with the establishment of community-based people's banks, or credit unions. These would be controlled by the people themselves, granting them a hitherto unknown degree of financial independence. Desjardins's vision caught the imagination of a small number of followers, leading to the establishment of the first credit union at Lévis, Quebec, in 1900.[83] From this rather humble beginning, the Caisse Populaire Movement took hold and became a powerful force not only in Quebec but elsewhere as well. Similar stories can be told about the Raiffeisen-Schultze Credit Cooperative Movement of Germany and about other such movements. The Rochdale Principles and the Credit Union Movement were important components of the Antigonish Movement and were included in the items dealt with in the study clubs in the 1930s.[84]

The dynamic and evolutionary nature of grassroots economic movements requires analysis to be a continuous process carried out over time. In its absence, movements cannot adequately adapt to changing circumstances and thus lose their lasting power. The same holds true of the specifics of a movement's vision, which must remain open to clarification, modification, and adaptation to changes in the socio-economic environment.

THE EMERGENCE OF THE VISION OF THE ANTIGONISH MOVEMENT

The fundamental vision of the Antigonish Movement took shape primarily over the 1921-28 period.[85] The original spark that eventually became integrated into the core of the Antigonish Movement was the publication of Rev. Jimmy Tompkins's widely read and influential pamphlet *Knowledge for the People*. In this pamphlet, Rev. Tompkins repudiated, as he had in fact done many times before, the formal "elitist" education system of eastern Nova Scotia, of which he, as a vice president of St Francis Xavier University, was a prominent part, and called for the education of the masses as an instrument of social, economic, and spiritual betterment.[86] Outlining various experiments of adult education in other countries and in other regions of Canada, the pamphlet stressed the importance of better education as a remedy to the economic decay in evidence, particularly in the rural areas. Although its vision was broad and lacked a specific focus, it appealed to many. Indeed, it inspired Rev. Tompkins and his supporters to carry out what can be considered the first major experiment in adult education: the already noted People's Schools.[87] Another important development followed in 1924 when at the annual Rural Conference it was resolved that an Extension Department be established at St Francis Xavier University. Even though his transfer to Canso had radically altered Rev. Tompkins's position, transforming him from a priest-professor and administrator into a parish priest in a remote area, his influence remained both strong and vital.[88]

These various initiatives were consistent with Rev. Tompkins's notion of adult education as a tool of socio-economic change and transformation as well as of individual and spiritual betterment. The enthusiasm with which they were received must be interpreted as a perception among the people that the vision behind them was a valid one. Nevertheless, these initiatives also revealed major shortcomings and weaknesses that had to be rectified. These included the appropriateness of the education provided by the People's Schools, particularly for primary producers facing economic crisis, and the general failure to link education with action. In the context of the latter, the Rural Conferences were described by one participant as "all talk and no action."[89] The original emerging vision had to be modified to be more clearly focused so that it could be of more practical value as a guide to action. Calling for the establishment of an Extension Department at St Francis Xavier University constituted such a modification as it pertained to the institutional apparatus of the movement. To the focus on education and study were then added the notion of cooperation and the sharing of resources. Also important was the reinforcement of the vision by the strong message contained in the encyclicals *Rerum Novarum* and *Quadragesimo Anno*, which came out in 1891 and 1931 respectively and which guided the priest-professors and other early leaders of the movement.[90]

The experiments that took place in the first half of the 1920s pointed to the essential importance of socio-economic knowledge to the working masses, especially those involved in primary activities. However, the underlying vision of the movement still did not yield any sort of blueprint or offer clear practical guidance on how effectively to deliver such knowledge to the people in a way that could lead to action and positive change. In 1927 Rev. Moses Coady conducted what turned out to be an important and successful experiment when he organized a group of farmers into a study club. Of importance here was not only that people were able to get together in a study club but also that the process had the potential to translate into action.[91] As well, this small experiment led to the formalization of what can be described as the Antigonish method, which entailed organizing, participating in education, and acting cooperatively. Thus there was an additional modification to and clarification of the original vision: the conviction that education can be effectively and efficiently imparted to adults, resulting in economic action through informal organizations that involve small groups of friends, neighbours, and members of the community in general.

Even though a logical way of proceeding was now in place, the vision was still not complete. It still did not provide a clear rationale for the emergence of a movement and also lacked a clear focus, a clear sense of direction, and a clearly defined fundamental goal of economic action. There was a lot there, but something was missing as well, which limited the movement's power to persuade and motivate the people during its early stages. This shortcoming was overcome by Rev. Coady in 1931 when he articulated his theory of the "Great Default of the People." He argued that the people, particularly past generations, had to accept the blame for the social and economic plight of the region. Through their ignorance, lack of foresight, and inertia, they had lost control over economic resources and institutions.[92] The people were thus largely victims of their own failings. This was a critical issue because it directly implied that people actually had power and that it was their responsibility to exercise it. If they had lost control, they could also get it back. The "Great Default" was not a formal theory based on empirical analysis of the historical evolution of the local economy but an instrument of economic rhetoric meant to inspire and motivate people to take matters into their own hands.

Whatever criticism we may have of this notion, there is no question that it attracted adherents to the movement. Rather than viewing the people, however marginalized they may have been, as pathetic victims of forces beyond their control and as requiring others to intervene for the betterment of their condition, it viewed them as being fully capable of correcting the situation on their own. The people had the power to change their situation through education focused on delivering economic knowledge, particularly knowledge about economic institutions. The people themselves, working collectively, could regain their former control over the economic institutions of their communities and the region as a whole. In effect, they could become "Masters of Their Own Destiny."

The notion of the default of the people painted the past in broad strokes as a paradise lost or a missed opportunity so as to set a clear stage for the actions required during the present and in the future. The notion of the "Great Default of the People" assumed a mythical aura and became one of the most important complements to the vision of Antigonish Movement. Although the vision dealt primarily with the unlimited possibilities of a new and better socio-economic order, the notion of the great default provided a stylized explanation of the forces that had led to the existing one, predicated on poverty and exploitation arising from the loss of control over resources and economic institutions. Thus it provided a link between the distant and somewhat "golden" past of the pioneer age, the unjust present, and the possible ideal future. The notion of the great default became one part of a persuasive story endlessly repeated in various permutations not only by Rev. Coady but also by his associates to invoke a commitment on the part of the people to improving their socio-economic situation through their own efforts. The people had played a role in their own downfall, and they needed to play a role in their salvation.

The various components of its vision provided the Antigonish Movement with its unique identity and were responsible for its eventual success. In the main, this vision can be expressed in terms of four fundamental propositions that increased its clarity and narrowed its focus: (1) that the reform of eastern Nova Scotia begin with the mass education of adults, particularly among primary producers and industrial workers; (2) that the focus be on economic education, particularly in the initial stages, as this was most likely to result in economic action; (3) that education and economic action are most effective and efficient when undertaken by a group rather than individually; and (4) that the people should aim their economic action at regaining control over the economic institutions prevailing in their communities and in the region as a whole.

From Vision to a Program of Socio-economic Change

The four interrelated propositions cited above emerged slowly over the 1920s.[93] Collectively as well as individually, they served as guides to concrete, practical, and effective action. They were formulated and accepted as valid before the movement began to unfold on a large scale and reached its greatest momentum. Yet, during the crucial period of the 1930s, the movement did not have a clearly defined theoretical framework apart from the "Big Picture." The Big Picture reflected the movement's actual program for social change. In essence, it recognized that disparate economic actions had to be linked to a framework, or system, in order for them to contribute to social and economic progress over the longer term and throughout the region as a whole. We argue later that the failure to achieve integration into such a full-fledged economic system was a fundamental weakness of the movement, which contributed greatly to its eventual collapse.

The notion of the Big Picture was ingenious. Moreover, especially when expressed in a diagram (as represented in figure 2.2), it provided a comprehensive view of the future socio-economic order toward

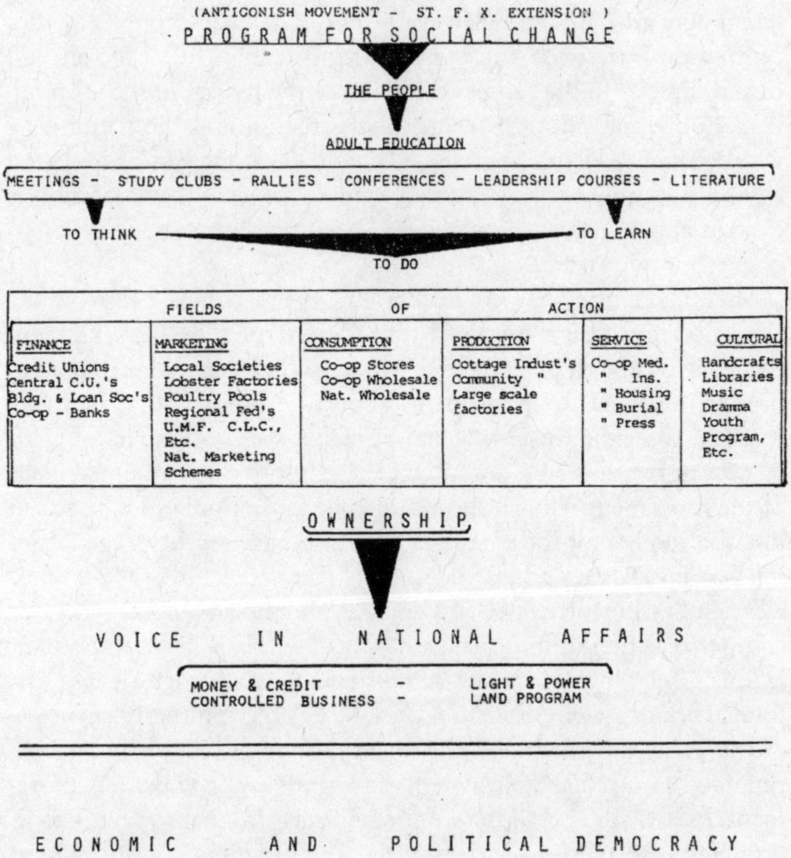

Figure 2.2 The "Big Picture"
Source: J.D. Nelson MacDonald, *Memoirs of an Unorthodox Clergyman* (Truro, NS: Cooperative Resources, 1986), 102.

which the movement was striving and enabled the participants to understand how their activities and actions fitted into the overall system. The movement's program for socio-economic change and its representation of the Big Picture identified the systematic link between education, economic action, and both the short-term and ultimate objectives. The ultimate objectives were specified in terms of economic and political democracy. In the notion of the Big Picture, all of the programs of the Antigonish Movement – all of its tools, techniques, economic projects, and education activities – were integrated into a comprehensive vision of a socio-economic order centred on ownership and control of institutions in all sectors and linked directly to the full participation of the masses in the economic, cultural, and political realms of the region and the nation as a whole. The Big Picture represented a cohesive framework stipulating an orderly sequence of progress en route to achieving socio-economic change and transformation through the establishment of an alternate economic system.

The "Big Picture" diagram inspired the enthusiasm and fostered the commitment of the participants in the movement by showing them that they were part of a larger, dynamic, and exciting whole. In addition, it informed the participants about the progress that they had made or were about to make and provided a sense of direction with respect to the next step toward achieving more clearly defined goals of the movement. Thus it moved the people not only to take action but also to plan for the next step. Its importance can be gauged from Ida Gallant Delaney's observation that "The big picture was a topic at all membership meetings, conferences, short courses and wherever co-operators met in informal gatherings."[94] Perhaps most important, it linked seemingly disparate actions and activities into a consistent framework or system of socio-economic change and transformation.

The great experiment of the 1930s, although seemingly ad hoc, unfolded in a remarkably systematic fashion. As a grassroots movement, its activities could not be programmed from above but had to originate with the people themselves. The prodding and inspiration provided by Rev. Coady, Rev. Tompkins, and others was of course critical, as was the support provided by the Extension Department of St Francis Xavier University. Nevertheless, it was the willingness of people to get together – that is, to organize, engage in study, and then move toward the implementation of economic activities – that was the central element. Because action stemmed from study and from the knowledge, information, and commitment that emerged from this process, it could not be programmed. The experiment was based on people solving their own problems cooperatively. The disparate actions by different groups were envisaged as parts of a larger whole and, more important, as fundamental building blocks to the attainment of the ultimate goals of the movement, predicated on the emergence of an alternate economic system. The systemic nature of the movement was captured in the notion of the Big Picture.

From Vision to Ideology

In the early years, the participants were busy working and creating a new socio-economic order consistent with the vision of the movement, and there was no need for an ideology to explain and justify what they were doing. The success of numerous economic, educational, and social activities and the enthusiasm of the thousands of people involved in the movement offered sufficient proof of its validity. Indeed, projects and ventures that had been considered impossible to achieve only a few years earlier became a reality in short order. Even after the Antigonish Movement had spread to other provinces and to other countries, there was no felt need for a formal theory and philosophy. The correct socio-economic analysis, the process outlined by Rev. Coady, and the implementation of projects based on what turned out to be sound economic principles were enough to push the movement forward, yielding tangible socio-economic benefits.

Eventually, as various programs were established, the most obvious types of economic projects were implemented, and the success of the movement began to garner national and international acclaim. Increasing numbers of people from outside the region wanted to know the secret of its undeniable success. In 1944 a young St Francis Xavier University professor of economics who later became internationally acclaimed, Harry Johnson, gave a talk to students at Acadia University. In his talk, and a subsequent article, Johnson, for the first time, summarized the essential elements of the Antigonish Movement in the form of "Six Principles": (1) the primacy of the individual, (2) social reform through education, (3) education beginning with the economic, (4) education through group action, (5) effective social reform through fundamental changes in social and economic institutions, and (6) full and abundant life for everyone.[95]

The principles were not very useful in establishing a sequence leading to the final outcome of a "full and abundant life for everyone." More important, they also left out some critical components of the movement. In particular, there was no mention of what must be seen as the essential element of the vision of the Antigonish Movement: the call for the people to become "Masters of Their Own Destiny" by exerting control over resources and economic activity. In effect, the Six Principles directed attention away from the fundamental task of putting in place an alternate economic system.

The Six Principles did, however, stress the critical importance attached to education and cooperation and explicitly recognized that these initiatives must be linked to the economic benefits that they were expected to generate. The principles also provided a clear distinction between the Antigonish Movement and socialism by stressing the individual even within the context of cooperation.

The form in which the Six Principles were presented was as important as their content. They were formulated as static, unchanging, and having universal applicability, in sharp contrast to the dynamic and flexible movement that they were intended to depict. The form of presentation seems consistent with Johnson's training in and allegiance to neoclassical economic theory, which is predicated on a series of fundamentally static, abstract, unchanging, and universally applicable principles. Johnson not only employed the neoclassical form but also incorporated two of the most basic principles of neoclassical theory into the "philosophy" of the Antigonish Movement. Thus the primacy of the individual corresponds to the individual as the centre of the economic system, which is also linked to the notion of consumer sovereignty. The notion of a "full and abundant life" also reflects the optimizing principle of neoclassical theory as embodied in the notion of utility maximization. Thus Johnson, who would not have been altogether comfortable with some of the anticapitalist rhetoric of the Antigonish Movement, framed the very principles that were to guide it within a fundamentally neoclassical context.

These Six Principles were endorsed by Rev. Coady and came to represent what can be regarded as the official philosophy and ideology of the Antigonish Movement.[96] In effect, however, they undermined the fundamental vitality of the movement by largely distorting its actual vision, especially by ignoring the importance of ownership and control of economic activity and hence the very notion of people being "Masters of Their Own Destiny."

Nevertheless, the Six Principles served a critical function by providing, however incomplete and misleading, an official philosophy and ideology that seemed to reflect the great array of activities that took place during the 1930s. The experiment had generated a phenomenal amount of economic activity and was deemed to be a success; it was now time to try to identify its components more formally. Such formalization, of course, would not change any of the things that had occurred in the 1930s but could be useful for the continuation of the movement. Arguably, the Six Principles affirmed faith in a movement that had already proven to be extremely successful in practice. Furthermore, they brought a measure of sophistication and formalism to a movement that was still highly experimental, activist, and pragmatic.

The Six Principles were articulated at a critical time near the end of the Second World War, which had itself ushered in a fundamental change in the socio-economic environment of eastern Nova Scotia and promised more changes to come. The war years had introduced a rupture in the movement, and the Six Principles constituted, in part, an attempt to keep its spirit alive.

Conflict between Ideology and Socio-economic Programs

For a time, the Six Principles and the Big Picture complemented each other by addressing different audiences. The former were primarily directed at the "outsiders" to the movement, whereas the latter was used to guide the activities of the participants. Yet the inherent conflict between these two fundamentally different representations of the philosophy of the movement could not be avoided for long. The Six Principles were static, inflexible, and universal and, moreover, did not suggest experimentation and innovation or constitute a plan of action. The Big Picture, in contrast, was flexible, adaptable to local conditions, and able to evolve in order to incorporate change over time. In effect, it constituted a plan that was intended to guide economic action as a part of a system. Over time, and with the passing of the older generation, the inherent conflict was eliminated by effectively discarding the Big Picture in favour of the Six Principles.

The triumph of the Six Principles was critical to the eventual demise of the Antigonish Movement. As Delaney puts it, "The devotion and hard work of the co-operative pioneers in the Maritimes was sustained by their belief that what they saw in the Big Picture could become a reality."[97] Thus the component that guided and focused the action of the movement as a means to an end was discarded, whereas the component that highlighted the movement's ideology and philosophy, in a superficial and not entirely accurate way, took over. Consequently, the whole process, which was a part of the great experiment, was undermined. The quarrel here is not with the Six Principles, even though they did distort to some extent the movement's fundamental nature, but with the fact that once they were articulated they became accepted as the blueprint of the movement rather than being regarded as simply the articulation of some of its main philosophical and ideological components.

Opting exclusively for the Six Principles also convinced the leaders of the movement that they had discovered a set of universally valid principles of socio-economic development that required little scrutiny, analysis, and adaptation to changing social, economic, and political circumstances. Indeed, as they stand, the principles do seem to have a universal appeal that requires little alteration. However, such universal appeal can be misleading since required changes and adaptations tend to come primarily at the practical level rather than at the philosophical or ideological one. The Six Principles, for example, do not spell out the process of organizing the people, the method employed in study, or the size, structure, and types of economic activities to be undertaken. All of these elements can and, indeed, must change over time and unless clearly defined can compromise the basic thrust of a movement. The adoption of the Six Principles, in effect, changed the Antigonish Movement from a dynamic enterprise to one that was predominantly static. The principles also ignored that there had to be something else to guide the actual progression and activities of the movement and in so doing introduced a fundamental break with its past.

In general terms, the 1930s yielded a fundamentally dynamic blueprint of the movement, manifested in the diagrammatic representation of the Big Picture. Thus, during much of the 1930s and up until the mid-1940s, the movement was guided by a practical plan of action. The eventual discarding of the Big Picture altered the experiment and over time caused the movement to lose sight of the importance of the economic and institutional framework that was being put in place. In particular, it lost sight of the fact that it was putting in place an economic system wherein education, economic action, and the building-up of an institutional apparatus were means to an end rather than ends in themselves.

EMERGENCE OF THE INSTITUTIONAL STRUCTURE

Rev. Coady and the other leaders understood that the Antigonish Movement could not thrive without its own institutions.[98] An institutional apparatus was required to plan, coordinate, direct, and provide support for sustainable economic activity and hence to transform into concrete action the movement's vision of mass education as the means for people to improve their socio-economic standing. Thus much attention was directed at setting up an appropriate institutional framework, starting with the Extension Department of St Francis Xavier University – the defining institution of the movement.

Establishment of the Extension Department

The background to the establishment of the Extension Department has been well documented in the literature.[99] Between 1924 and 1928 various groups, organizations, and individuals became actively engaged in efforts to establish such an institution. Since the vision called for the education of the masses, the focus of this institution had to be on education. Furthermore, as the most important educational institution in the region, pressure was put on St Francis Xavier University to create an Extension Department. Eventually, the combined efforts of the Roman Catholic clergy, influential priest-professors, the Scottish Catholic Society, and others convinced the university's Board of Governors to formally establish such an institution with Rev. Moses Coady as its director.

The Extension Department, as a part of an educational institution, was officially charged with the responsibility of implementing an adult education program and, through it, of promoting the spread of economic knowledge to the community rather than only to students on campus. The primary objective was to provide knowledge that would enable people to carry out socio-economic analysis of their prevailing conditions and then to engage in economic action that could lead to improvement. It constituted the official mechanism whereby the university could bring knowledge to the people, who would then use this knowledge to meet their basic needs and aspirations. Thus the establishment of the Extension Department put a concrete institutional face on the vision shared by Rev. Coady, Rev. Tompkins, and others that education aimed at the people at large could be a vehicle for socio-economic change and transformation.

Development Strategy of the Movement

The immediate problem facing the Extension Department was to find an effective means of discharging a mandate that was, despite the meagre resources at its disposal, of enormous scope and characterized by exaggerated expectations. With its initial staff of two, plus two secretaries, the department lacked the resources to directly implement programs of any significant scale.[100] Only a network of institutions, united by a common purpose, could perform the enormous task with which it was charged. Thus its first order of business was to design and create a supporting network of institutions that could carry out the various components of its perceived mandate and promote activities that would direct the Antigonish Movement toward the attainment of the goals and objectives inspired by its vision. For the movement to succeed and be able to satisfy its supporters, it had to promote economic action. It was perhaps fortunate that, due to Rev. Coady's involvement with the implementation of the recommendations of the MacLean Commission,[101] the work of the Extension Department was delayed until 1930, giving it some breathing space. Coady's commission undertakings also provided him with a track record in the establishment of cooperative ventures as a consequence of his work in organizing the United Maritime Fishermen as well as the opportunity to extol the benefits of cooperation and the importance of education in fishing communities throughout the Maritimes. In effect, the establishment of this union set the stage for the future longstanding involvement of the Extension Department in the fisheries.[102]

The structure of the institutional framework to be devised had to be internally coherent, mutually supporting, united by a common goal, and relatively free of internal conflicts, duplications, overlapping responsibilities, and waste of resources. A failure in any of these areas would be potentially fatal to the emerging movement, particularly in light of the severe shortage of resources in the initial stages. The movement's ability to avoid many of the pitfalls that stood in its way was due mostly to the ingenious and effective strategy of development that it pursued, which determined the overall institutional structure. Furthermore, the actual process of creating this institutional structure was both orderly and gradual, with the most simple and basic institutions being established first, followed by the more complex and larger ones. This process was assisted by a truly remarkable number of volunteers, particularly members of the Roman Catholic clergy and religious orders, as well as by the willingness of the people themselves to comply and cooperate with the Extension Department. The inspirational and charismatic leadership of Rev. Coady, complemented by

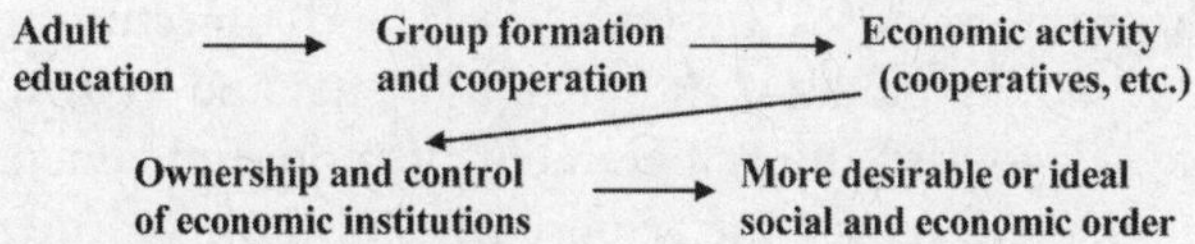

Figure 2.3 Strategy of the Antigonish Movement
Source: Adapted from Santo Dodaro and Leonard Pluta, "The Antigonish Movement as a Model of Regional Economic Development," in Masudul Alam Choudhury, ed., *Political Economy of Development in Atlantic Canada* (Sydney, NS: University College of Cape Breton Press, 1988), diagram 3, 56.

the organizational skills of Angus Bernard (A.B.) MacDonald, the associate director of the Extension Department, also played an important role.[103] The early leaders of the movement knew what they were doing and understood the people and their plight, which translated into the building of an appropriate institutional framework and enabled the movement to gain the support of the people in virtually all sectors of the economy.

The actual strategy of the movement, summarized in figure 2.3, was dictated by the fundamental notions of organizing, studying together, and engaging in cooperative action. It also reflected the basic vision of the movement with respect to the ownership and control question as embodied in the notion of people being "Masters of Their Own Destiny" and with respect to the final goal, which entailed the achievement of a more desirable social and economic order.

The first three items in the sequence presented in figure 2.3 were the key elements of the Antigonish Movement, particularly within the context of economic development and transformation. They highlighted its most fundamental aspects, including its community-based focus, while setting up the practical, broadly defined strategies for achieving its goals and objectives, as stated in the fourth and fifth components of the sequence. Those included in the fourth item constituted both an end result and a guiding principle of the economic development and institutional reform that the first three items of the sequence were set up to achieve. The final item in the sequence, representing the loftier ideals and promises of the movement, constituted the ultimate goal.

Although each economic activity contributed to improvements in the existing socio-economic conditions, it was their collective force as parts of the same framework, or system, that would prompt the attainment of a more desirable, even if not entirely ideal, socio-economic order. The movement's short-term goals and objectives generally addressed the more practical and pressing issues and in turn acted as steppingstones toward the achievement of more fundamental long-term outcomes. Moreover, the achievement of these short-term goals depended, particularly in the initial organizing and study stages, on the inspirational power of working toward a new order. This inspiration emanated, in the main, from the predominantly spiritual aspects of the human condition – that is, idealism and a yearning for the ultimate meaning of individual and collective existence – and from the powerful desire to escape the demoralizing and dehumanizing consequences of poverty and economic stagnation. Poverty, according to Rev. Tompkins, made the people "not only ignorant and despairing" but also "cringing and supplicant" since it stripped them of their sense of self-respect and dignity.[104] Thus the vision of a better spiritual and moral life founded on improved economic conditions emerged as an equally strong motivator in the call for action. The ultimate goal of the movement represents the fusion of the spiritual and the economic – that is, the spiritual ideal and the perceived basic material needs.

The strategy, summarized in figure 2.3, served as the bridge linking the vision to the institutional structure. Each institution, regardless of whether it was a unique creation of the movement or was brought in from outside, was chosen based on the task that it could perform for the movement under the existing circumstances, including the resources that were available. In turn, these institutions became parts of the framework, or system, of the movement, which implied that their conduct had to be consistent with the movement's vision; they had to be designed so that they could serve the purpose of transforming the vision into reality. Whereas the institutions acted as "the hands and feet" of the movement, the strategy, and by the same token the Extension Department, acted as "the head," which guided the work of the "hands and feet."

The vision of the movement determined the strategy that was to be adopted, and the strategy in turn dictated the institutional apparatus that was required. The institutional apparatus can be construed as the mirror image of the strategy inherent in the Antigonish model of development. The relationship between strategy and institutions is illustrated in figure 2.4.

Although the adult education program was predominantly the responsibility of the Extension Department, the institution that was

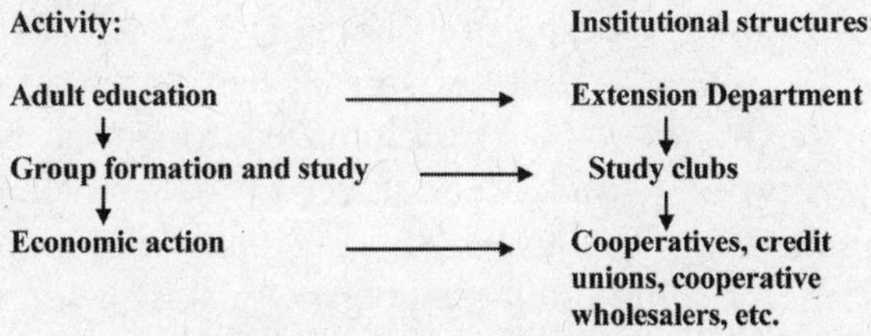

Figure 2.4 The relationship between strategy and institutional structures
Source: Adapted from Santo Dodaro and Leonard Pluta, "The Antigonish Movement as a Model of Regional Economic Development," in Masudul Alam Choudhury, ed., *Political Economy of Development in Atlantic Canada* (Sydney, NS: University College of Cape Breton Press, 1988), diagram 4, 65.

devised to carry it out was the study club. The study clubs not only provided the setting for people to engage in group study – and in the process to gain access to knowledge, information, and understanding – but also, through their weekly meetings and common programs of study, contributed to the formation of strong and committed groups of people capable of undertaking significant economic activities. The action arising from the process of study entailed the formation of economic institutions such as cooperatives and credit unions, as well as their federations and other secondary societies. The process enabled the people to collectively, gradually, and systematically acquire control over economic institutions in their communities and region, thus working toward the final goal of the movement. The initial successes strengthened the faith, confidence, and commitment of people in the practical implementation of the movement's vision, leading to new and more ambitious projects. In the process, the movement as a whole gained momentum and expanded.

Emergence of Supporting Institutions

The institutional structure of the Antigonish Movement could not be developed instantaneously, nor could the actual institutions that were required be predicted a priori. Thus the institutional apparatus evolved slowly and gradually, shaped by experience and practice as well as by the vision of the movement. One of the earliest of the new institutions was the study club, which proved to be an efficient and low-cost vehicle for the movement's adult education program. Modelled somewhat after the Danish Folk School concept and the

Swedish Discussion Circles approach, both of which had had an influence on Rev. Tompkins,[105] the study club concept became closely associated with the work of the Extension Department of St Francis Xavier University and played a central role in the Antigonish Movement during the 1930s. The study clubs consisted of groups of friends, neighbours, and/or community members with similar interests who were committed to meeting on a regular basis, at least once a week or so, to study the social-economic situation of their community and to participate in feasible economic projects, often in association with other study clubs pursuing a similar course of study.

The study clubs were thus truly grassroots, democratic, and participatory institutions that were able to elect their own leaders, choose where to meet, and the like. Nevertheless, the Extension Department played a critical role in their establishment and organization and in guiding and supporting their study process, especially by providing study materials and at times by bringing in experts when economic action was being contemplated.[106] Moreover, they did not stand alone but were the focal point of a larger educational and motivational framework. Once a month, a number of clubs in the community would get together in what was known as an "associated clubs rally" to compare notes, discuss the issues that had emerged from the study undertaken by the small groups, and so on. These were also supported by periodic regional conferences and by the larger annual Rural and Industrial Conferences. In addition, a host of other supporting activities, such as public speaking and debating contests, plays, and sporting contests, were put in place. The study clubs were normally established after rallies, or so-called "Mass Meetings," held by Rev. Coady and others, where the need was extolled for people to act in order to promote the betterment of their human condition.

The study club techniques proved to be very successful. In the main, this success can be attributed to five basic factors. First, people learn more effectively in groups and from each other. Second, people are generally most interested in finding out about issues that are of immediate concern to them. Thus the people were very interested in engaging in study that focused on their existing socio-economic situation, particularly on the causes of their poverty and the decay of their communities. Third, the knowledge generated concerning the nature and causes of the existing conditions was intended to form the basis for action aimed at finding a solution. Thus it became a powerful motivation for action, particularly when the action entailed doing something that the people could easily understand and with which they had some familiarity. Fourth, the more capable members of the group were generally eager to share their knowledge and their abilities with less capable members. Finally, there was the emergence of a wide array of capable leaders, which ensured that the study was properly conducted, that all participated, and that the focus remained on the ultimate purpose of implementing economic action.

The above overview begs the question of exactly what type of study and discussion took place in the clubs. Generally, the study revolved around not only understanding the basic causes of the existing conditions but also, and more important, searching for different alternatives. These alternatives were couched in terms of the implementation of community-based and -controlled economic activities. Thus the study required had to be practical in orientation as well as immediate in its impact. Nevertheless, the study clubs covered a wide array of topics, including philosophical issues, the Rochdale Principles, the technical and resource requirements for putting a project in place, and the legislation covering the activity being discussed. That those who participated in the study clubs generally dealt with economic action related to areas with which they had some familiarity contributed greatly to the study process.

Within a short time, some of the study clubs began to initiate economic projects, such as buying or marketing clubs, credit unions, and cooperatives. A limited number of cooperatives existed in the region prior to the establishment of the Extension Department. Indeed, a cooperative store was established in Stellarton as early as 1861.[107] By 1914 all of the maritime provinces had enacted co-op legislation, with governments playing an important role in the cooperative sector.[108] However, these cooperatives were not parts of a cohesive movement and were generally of limited consequence, as well as prone to failures.[109] Nevertheless, they did promote the acceptance of the cooperative approach fostered by the movement. The cooperative approach, being a part of the economic landscape, was something that the people understood and found easy to accept. Moreover, experience with one type of cooperative activity promoted the acceptance of other cooperative activities. Thus, for example, knowledge of the benefits arising from a cooperative store facilitated the acceptance of credit unions.[110]

Although many types of cooperative activities were already present in the region, others, such as credit unions, were brought in from outside. Credit unions, which were particularly prevalent in the early years of the Antigonish Movement, were brought in from the United States, which had imported them from the province of Quebec.[111] The American input has been recognized by the prominence given to names such as Bergengren.[112] Both newer and older types of cooperative institutions were incorporated into the framework of the Antigonish Movement and in the process were strengthened and made parts of a system. The same applies to organizations such as labour unions, which also predated the Antigonish Movement and had been very active in the region, especially in the steel and coal areas during the 1920s. The Antigonish Movement considerably strengthened the influence of the Labour Union Movement, particularly through its leader-training program, which produced a number of outstanding labour leaders both for the region and for the country as a whole. The Extension Department not only undertook the promotion of these institutions but in some cases was also instrumental in establishing their legislative basis, such as through its involvement in designing the credit union legislation in Nova Scotia.

The expansion in the number of study clubs and the ensuing emergence of economic organizations, such as credit unions and cooperatives, called for more specialized and technical training of individuals capable of assuming leadership positions in these new enterprises. It was one thing to mobilize the resources and decision making needed to establish economic activities, but their successful and efficient operation was another matter. The response of the Extension Department was to initiate its leadership courses and various other training programs of a specialized nature.

By being flexible, innovative, and responsive to the needs of the growing movement, the Extension Department contributed, both directly and indirectly, to the creation of a network of institutions that was, as outlined in figure 2.5, internally coherent, mutually supporting, and conditioned by the goal of allowing the people to gain control over resources and economic activity. In turn, this network acted as the conduit through which the vision of the movement was implemented and propagated. This network of institutions also reinforced the movement's practical bent and, in effect, gave rise to a de facto strategy.

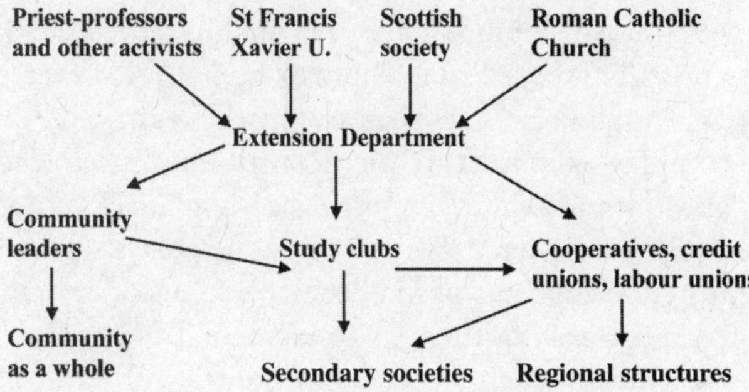

Figure 2.5 Internal relationship between institutions

The internal coherence of the institutional apparatus as a whole and the mutually supporting nature of its various individual components were also responsible for injecting dynamism into the process and for ensuring an expanding cumulative effect over time. Since education was the initial process upon which all others depended, the Extension Department necessarily had to precede all other institutions. The Extension Department, in turn, was instrumental in the creation and evolution of other institutions, including through the provision of some resources, both human and material.

MOBILIZATION OF RESOURCES

The general thrust of the institutional framework of the Antigonish Movement that emerged over the 1930s was economic.[113] More specifically, it served the purpose of mobilizing, developing, and creating resources to undertake economic activity aimed not only at meeting the basic needs of the local population and overcoming the existing state of economic stagnation but also at fundamentally changing the structure of the local economy and the role that people played in it. Thus the Antigonish Movement was revolutionary.[114]

The mobilization of resources entailed bringing into the production process factors that were idle, underutilized, or improperly utilized, such as in the production of less socially desirable goods and services. In addition to mobilization, some resources, both human and material, also needed to be developed. The development of human resources focused on the enhancement of attributes such as skills, decision-making ability, entrepreneurship, and knowledge – which are normally referred to as "human capital." However, there is much more to human resources than simply these attributes. Human beings are complex, as in turn are their contributions to the economic system. Thus attitudes, moral and social imperatives, and the like also needed to be considered. We can carry the analysis a bit further by highlighting the concepts of intellectual, social, and moral capital and infrastructure, viewing them as fundamental to the working of the economy. It was in such a broad and holistic context, of course, that adult education, particularly through the study clubs process, played a fundamental role in the Antigonish Movement. The development of nonhuman productive factors such as natural resources and physical capital was also essential, as in the case, during the early years of the movement, of the building of a lobster-processing plant by the people themselves utilizing local lumber and other resources.[115]

Since the movement was predicated on the notion of ownership and control of economic activity by the people, especially at the local or community level, and hence on the promotion of a great deal of self-reliance, the resources that needed to be mobilized and developed, at least initially, had to be largely local or from within the region.[116] Moreover, they had to be mobilized and developed by the people themselves. Since the movement was not aiming for a few isolated economic activities but for a whole network of activities that would effectively make people "Masters of Their Own Destiny," the amount of resources and decision making that needed to be mobilized was substantial. It could not be done all at once or without the establishment of an appropriate institutional apparatus.

A critical component in the mobilization of resources was the recognition of a hierarchy of resources, with the human element at the top. It was recognized from the outset that it is people who mobilize other resources. Indeed, this recognition was deeply ingrained not only in the sequence of institutions set up by the movement but also in the importance attached to education and the work of the study clubs. The role of the study clubs in this context is most relevant. In particular, they generated economic knowledge, and through the development of group entrepreneurship, they provided the basic decision-making capability to ensure action.

Economic Knowledge and Entrepreneurship

Economic knowledge is a valuable resource to the individuals and the community as a whole. Specialized knowledge of various sorts is normally considered to be a marketable commodity.[117] Just as knowledge is a source of economic power and income, lack of knowledge is associated with powerlessness and low income and poverty. The founders and early leaders of the Antigonish Movement, many of whom were educators, as in the case of the priest-professors, made the connection between knowledge and economic power very early on. Indeed, it was one of Rev. Tompkins's persistent themes.

The more technologically advanced the economy, the greater the importance of education and knowledge, particularly the knowledge that is obtained through formal channels. In less technologically advanced economies, less formal knowledge is generally required, which also translates into lower levels of economic activity and output. Nevertheless, even the relatively simple and traditional economy of eastern Nova Scotia of the 1930s, characterized by a large subsistence component, required a large stock of knowledge in order to function. The bulk of this knowledge pertained to the more traditional production techniques employed in farming, fishing, construction, mining, and other areas as well as to home production practices such as food preservation, weaving, and spinning. Most of this knowledge could be obtained informally through experience and practice and thus involved little formal training. Despite the rapid changes that had occurred in the local economy from the 1890s onward, knowledge about matters such as finance, marketing, distribution, processing, and quality control remained concentrated in the hands of a few people, mainly the monopolistic merchants and middlemen. Moreover, adding to the plight of the local population, even in the primary sectors, was the fact that new technologies and production methods were emerging that rendered much traditional knowledge obsolete or in need of adaptation.

During the 1920s, the eastern Nova Scotia region, as we suggested earlier, was in a state of fundamental transition. The primary producers and working masses found themselves at the mercy of the changes that were taking place around them, including the operation of the new market institutions, and in no position to acquire the required knowledge or resources needed to make the necessary adaptations.

The merchants, middlemen, and owners of enterprise, in contrast, understood the forces at work and were able to use them to exploit those who were powerless before them. That a key source of lack of power was a lack of knowledge and understanding of the forces at work is perhaps best illustrated by the words of Rev. Coady: "The coal miner comes out of the pit, cleans up at the wash-house, and calls it a day. The fisherman thinks he has done enough when he lands his catch on the wharf. The farmer puts in a day of drudgery and 'knocks off' until tomorrow. This is their great mistake."[118]

The failure to acquire the needed economic knowledge was one of the main underlying causes of the "Great Default of the People." The implication was not that people had no knowledge since they had necessarily acquired a substantial amount of it through their experience and participation in the economy. However, this knowledge was incomplete and in many instances also obsolete, inaccurate, or simply false. To make matters worse, merchants, fish buyers, cattle drovers, money lenders, and the like depended on their monopoly over specific economic knowledge and information, particularly about market conditions, to extract rent payments, or windfall profits, from the local population. Thus they normally guarded their monopoly jealously, often through the diffusion of misleading, inaccurate, or downright false information, which added to the general confusion and ignorance in the region.

There was no question that a great deal of relevant information and economic knowledge had to be acquired by the people before they could have a greater say in their economic lives and eventually become "Masters of Their Own Destiny." People needed to acquire knowledge concerning the functioning of the economy as a whole in order to be able to understand where they stood and why. They also needed to acquire specific knowledge concerning matters such as marketing, production techniques, management, finance, technology, accounting, and the working of the market in order to effectively undertake economic action.

Generally, education, particularly that taking place in a formal setting, requires advanced levels of literacy, mental discipline, concentration, and the comprehension of abstract concepts. In eastern Nova Scotia, the lack of these attributes rendered education on the part of adults, who lacked formal education to begin with, a difficult task. Opting for the study club mechanism served to place everyone on an equal footing. Although people may have lacked formal education and training, they possessed impressive analytical skills and logic acquired as a consequence of their work as well as during their everyday living; they possessed useful knowledge and understanding based on experience. Moreover, the clubs dealt largely with issues that all could understand and that made sense to everyone, which not only facilitated study and allowed the Extension Department to carry out its mandate with meagre resources but also fostered commitment on the part of the participants.

Study club participants had to possess courage, will, and determination and were often severely tested. They were not only asked to commit to undertaking the difficult task of mutual self-education but were also often subjected to scorn and ridicule by their neighbours, who, at least initially, often viewed the whole educational experiment, or program, as naive, wasteful, and even ridiculous. As well, the benefits expected from the study process, through the eventual implementation of economic projects, were highly uncertain and, in any event, generally not immediate. That so many persevered is a testament to the commitment to the movement that emerged fairly early on as well as to the participants' resilient character.

The focus on the economic circumstances of the people was particularly critical to the whole process. As they acquired knowledge, study club participants became increasingly aware of the economic conditions of their communities, of the extent to which they were being exploited by monopsonistic and monopolistic elements, and of the size of the economic rent payments, or windfall profits, that were being transferred out of their communities. Although one might expect the first reaction to such revelations to have been outrage and moral indignation, the study process also made people aware that there existed in their communities profitable economic opportunities of which they could take advantage and that they were not entirely powerless in the face of existing circumstances. Taking advantage of the existing economic opportunities required the mobilization and even the development of resources. Thus the knowledge gained through the study clubs led to the mobilization of resources, both human and material, and to the emergence of community-based, cooperative economic activities. Of particular importance in the whole process was the development of what we referred to earlier as "group entrepreneurship," denoting group decision-making ability.[119]

The role of entrepreneurship is critical in the process of initiating economic action. As in the case of entrepreneurship at the individual level, entrepreneurship at the group level entails three economic functions: (1) discovering economic opportunities by analyzing market conditions, production possibilities, and required resources; (2) undertaking the task of mobilizing, equipping, and organizing resources for production; and (3) accepting the risks associated with putting in place an economic venture.[120]

In essence, whether the study process actually led to economic action depended on the degree of success in developing entrepreneurship at the group level – the basic ingredient required to get economic activity started. The process of developing this group entrepreneurship was greatly aided by the fact that many of those participating in the study clubs were familiar with making entrepreneurial decisions in their capacities as farmers, fishermen, and the like. Even among urban industrial workers, there was some familiarity with cooperative activities. What was new to these people was not necessarily the entrepreneurial activity itself but the larger scale of operation as well as new production and marketing techniques.

The process of establishing such collective entrepreneurship required that study groups recognize their strengths and weaknesses and, more important, that the individuals in the groups trust and respect each other. Moreover, each group had to develop the confidence to face the risks involved in collective action. Given the limited resources available to individuals, which translated into standards of living that were quite low, the consequences of failure could be very great. People were called upon to undertake activities that under normal circumstances would have carried a relatively high risk factor. This risk factor was lowered by taking steps to ensure that projects not only got started but were also successful. The activities of the study clubs, and those of the Extension Department, were therefore also directed at ensuring that the knowledge and expertise required to run the projects were also developed. Moreover, in itself, that economic projects were intended to be parts of a system lowered the risks involved.

The dependence on group entrepreneurship was a natural outgrowth of the basic vision and philosophy of the Antigonish Movement. The call for people to overcome the powerful forces of disunity, jealousy, and distrust, as well as the overwhelming sense of apathy and helplessness, and to organize, engage in study, and undertake cooperative action was revolutionary in both intent and scope. It implied the mobilization of collective will and broad participation in the decision-making process, as well as a reversal of the implicit shortcomings or flaws of previous generations that had been presented as responsible for the "Great Default of the People." These were perceived as necessary if people were to become "Masters of their Own Destiny."

On a more practical level, it was understood that adequate resources to undertake new economic projects were often beyond the reach of any one study club's combined membership. A number of clubs in a particular locality would normally need to get together, and this was done through the Extension Department's institution of associated study clubs, which helped to translate education into action.[121] Once a month, study clubs in a given area would get together. In addition to discussing possible economic actions that could be undertaken jointly, study club members also engaged in social and cultural activities, which further cemented bonds within and between groups.[122]

In the process of undertaking economic activities, the movement relied on group entrepreneurship to serve as the catalyst for mobilizing and developing other resources. Thus, for example, credit unions mobilized local savings that could then be used as an input toward the expansion of the stock of capital. The setting up of cooperatives of various sorts mobilized additional labour as well as other resources. The mobilization of resources through the development of group entrepreneurship can be considered the practical process whereby the people's great default was reversed. The emergence of group entrepreneurship was the driving force leading to action, and at the same time it maintained ownership and control by the people who made up the group.

Mobilization of Capital and Financing

In addition to labour and decision making, or entrepreneurship, productive activity also requires capital. When we consider the notion of capital in the production process, we distinguish between physical capital (e.g., machinery, equipment, and buildings) and financial resources, which are essentially specified in monetary terms. Whereas physical capital is directly productive, financial resources are not, although they can become indirectly productive when used to purchase physical capital. Money, of course, is also required to pay workers, purchase intermediate goods, finance marketing operations, and so on. Thus, although not productive on its own, money facilitates production; without money, financial resources, or credit, production tends to be severely curtailed.

Unlike physical capital, especially in the short term, money or finance is generally very mobile and, moreover, can be used to acquire command or control of other resources such as labour, technology, and managerial and scientific expertise. Thus financial resources entail ownership and control, whereas physical capital entails production. This difference contributes to the separation of production from control and ownership. The power of money, or financial resources, is particularly great in a market-based economy, where political, social, religious, and cultural factors seldom act to curtail its power in any fundamental way – a state of affairs that is captured in the very notion of "capitalism." In the context of eastern Nova Scotia in the 1920s and 1930s, the separation of control from production was clearly evident in the absentee ownership of productive units and the concentration of finance in central Canada and abroad. The power yielded by the financial interests stood in stark contrast to the fundamental vision of the Antigonish Movement, which stressed not only greater egalitarianism but also a fundamental interrelationship between ownership and production.

The implementation of economic projects, as noted above, required both physical capital and access to financing. The latter was severely constrained by the nature of the economic activity the movement promoted as well as by its institutional structure, predicated on the cooperative model.[123] Rather than being based on the amounts of money injected into a project, the profit, or surplus, generated by an economic venture was attributed to the participation of members in the venture through their sales, purchases, or borrowings and, more important, was distributed accordingly. In addition, in the decision-making process, each member had a vote regardless of the amount of equity that was put into the operation. This cooperative structure was not conducive to the normal capitalist mode of financing. As a result, both the excessive power of finance and the danger of having the movement "hijacked" by financial interests were severely curtailed.

However, reliance on internal sources to finance investment posed some dangers as well. The internal reliance and the cooperative structure, in fact, conspired to give rise to severe undercapitalization and inefficiency in some of the ventures that were set up under the auspices of the Antigonish Movement.

Given the conditions of poverty and low incomes, which translated into very little saving, obtaining adequate resources to generate the physical capital required to implement desired economic projects constituted an important obstacle. One of the most common and most effective ways of mobilizing such resources was through "sweat equity." Thus, for example, study club members would pool their labour, particularly during the off season, in order to go into the woods to cut their own lumber for the erection of a building or structure. In the process, people would employ their abundant labour as well as lumber to directly generate a capital good, the building or structure, without having to go through the process of first generating savings that could then be used to get the structure built.[124] There were many such instances during the 1930s, especially in the fisheries.[125] Nevertheless, some money was still required to purchase machinery and other items that the people themselves could not produce. Moreover, it is difficult to envisage production efficiency without access to adequate credit.

A second method of mobilizing adequate resources was to come together to form savings groups, or credit unions. The members would pledge to deposit a certain amount on a regular basis, and eventually a sizable amount of money could be available that could be loaned out to members. Generally, the amounts that credit unions were able to mobilize were quite substantial, as will become clear later. Although these institutions were independent of others, they implied the presence of alternate sources of financing at the local level. A third alternative was community-based fundraising. These alternatives were not mutually exclusive and were often used simultaneously.[126]

Establishment of Formal Organizations

Once an economic activity was contemplated, the next stage involved the establishment of formal economic institutions separate from the study clubs and associated study clubs. These institutions were based on clearly defined rules and procedures pertaining to matters such as the ownership, control, use, and disposition of assets. These institutions constituted formal legal entities and were a far cry from the largely informal and voluntary setting of the study clubs. Moreover, the mechanisms that accompanied the setting-up of formal organizations such as cooperatives and credit unions were adopted later by the cooperative federations and centrals. These involved rules of behaviour to discourage cheating, shirking of work, and other abuses that would undermine any venture that was set up. These formal rules were also strengthened by the forces of compulsion emanating from the commitment of the people as well as from social penalties such as disapproval and ostracism that could be imposed informally at the community level to counter the free rider and other problems.[127] The participants needed some assurance that those who undertook the work also had access to a fair share of the benefits.

By establishing formal economic organizations or institutions, such as cooperatives and credit unions, over which they had control, the people of eastern Nova Scotia took the first step toward the concrete realization of their goal of becoming "Masters of Their Own Destiny." However, the new economic infrastructure, which initially consisted of several tiny credit unions, a handful of lobster-processing plants, isolated cooperative stores and supply depots, the occasional lumber mill, and the like, appeared very fragile and insignificant in comparison to the widespread poverty, unemployment, and human misery that characterized the local economy. Nevertheless, especially during the early stages of the development of the Antigonish Movement, these ventures had an impact that was far greater than their strict economic value, as measured in terms of sales, assets, and so on. These constituted what we identified earlier as the experimental projects of the movement. They offered visible proof of the power and relevance of the vision of the movement and, perhaps even more important, acted as a prelude of things to come in terms of what could be achieved by being part of the movement.

As a consequence of the movement, activities that were previously unimaginable were actually seeing the light of day. That these activities also turned out to be successful and profitable – in terms of increased incomes as well as improvements to people's lives – added legitimacy to the movement and enhanced people's commitment to it.[128] People were asked to work hard and to make substantial sacrifices, but they could also see that these things contributed to their wellbeing.

In addition to the establishment of formal rules and procedures, the new cooperatives and credit unions also adopted stringent and demanding business policies and practices, which were in keeping with the Rochdale Principles and which severely tested the moral commitment and willpower of their members. Thus, for example, many of the new consumers' cooperatives would not allow purchases on credit, despite the fact that the practice was widespread elsewhere in the private sector.[129] The practice of allowing customers to buy on credit was often fraught with abuses and exploitation, and many of the new organizations emerging from the Antigonish Movement refused to engage in it. These organizations were unwilling to implement practices that were associated with unethical and exploitative behaviour. Adopting a policy of cash trading in a situation of scarcity and irregularity of cash incomes was demanding and risky. In the systemic approach of the Antigonish Movement, however, the situation was to be mitigated by the emergence of credit unions as suppliers of credit.[130] At the same time, the credit unions required regular weekly deposits, no matter how small, to "teach" their members the importance of prudence and foresight – "economic virtues" that were deemed difficult but necessary if people were to again gain control over their economic lives.

The adoption of such strict business practices required high standards of business and personal ethics among the membership. People were required to develop habits such as saving regularly and planning for their purchases ahead of time. That most of these new organizations not only survived but also flourished must be seen as a testimony to the people's willingness to adhere to such standards in an environment that was previously characterized by widespread abuse, cheating, and mistrust. In effect, the high standards of business ethics adopted by the cooperatives and credit unions constituted a key factor in allowing them to compete with the often unethical and exploitative practices of the monopolies and monopsonies that were operating in the region but were normally controlled by outside interests.

The administration of these formal economic institutions required technical knowledge pertaining to matters such as accounting and management techniques, and such technical knowledge would most likely not have been available in the study clubs, even at the associated clubs level. The Extension Department addressed the issue by instituting new programs in areas such as leadership training, bookkeeping, and management training.

The Role of Women

During the 1920s, the vast majority of women worked in the home. According to the 1921 census, only 15 per cent of women were engaged in paid employment, mostly in the production of textiles and the provision of domestic services.[131] In eastern Nova Scotia, the proportion of women in paid employment was even lower, due to the structure of the local economy. Moreover, women had fewer educational opportunities and unequal access to property ownership. Thus there were also few women involved in business, the professions, and government.

Under such circumstances, it would not be surprising if women had been assigned a minor role in the emerging movement. However, the opposite was true, as women played an important role. The early leaders realized from the outset that without the dedication, energy, and commitment of women, particularly those in the rural areas, the movement would not be able to get off the ground and flourish. Women were responsible for many of the economic decisions within the households, which were vital to the future success of the movement. They generally managed household finances, made the decisions concerning which items to purchase, were responsible for the nutritional, health, and other needs of the family, and possessed many skills that could be used to supplement household incomes. Thus effective participation in cooperatives and credit unions could not take place without some degree of consent on the part of women. Consumers' cooperatives, in particular, "depended a great deal more upon the interest and support of women than of men."[132] In 1934 it was this recognition that led the Extension Department of St Francis Xavier University to establish the Women's Work program, which targeted women, particularly those in the rural sector, and sought to harness their energy, loyalty, and commitment in support of the new movement.

	INSTITUTIONAL STRUCTURES:	
Extension Department ↓	**Study clubs** **Rural and industrial conferences** **Associated study clubs**	**Cooperatives** **Credit unions** **Trade unions** **Etc.**
	MODES AND TECHNIQUES:	
Adult education techniques ↓	**Group dynamics** **Leadership development** **Specialized training**	**Cooperative education** **Labour education** **Etc.**
	RESOURCES:	
Economic resources	**Group entrepreneurship (decision making, etc.)** **Human capital (skills, knowledge, etc.)**	**Other resources (physical capital, natural resources, etc.)**

Figure 2.6 The relationship between the institutional structures and the mobilization and development of resources

Institutionalizing the Development Process

The process of institutional development and the mobilization and development of resources occurred simultaneously. As summarized in figure 2.6, the Extension Department was charged with the specific role of developing human resources through adult education, a task that was primarily achieved through the establishment of the study clubs. In turn, the study clubs focused not only on the generation and dissemination of appropriate economic knowledge but also on the promotion of change in the social, moral, and spiritual characteristics of the participants. These enhanced human resources, particularly in the case of group entrepreneurship, served to mobilize and develop other resources.

The whole process was not self-initiating but required a spark to get it going. During the 1930s, the needed spark was provided by the charismatic and forceful personality of Rev. Coady, who inspired the people to have faith in the movement and hence to get it started.[133] In addition, he was instrumental in getting the people to have faith in themselves and in the idea that they could effect the desired changes and transformation. His reference to the "Great Default of the People" suggested that just as people had contributed to their plight, they could now also contribute to its resolution. Thus the notion of a great default empowered the participants of the movement to take action.

During the 1930s, the process of organizing the people began with so-called "Mass Meetings" in which Rev. Coady or some of his associates would address the people in various communities. At such a meeting, the notion of the "Great Default of the People" would be invoked to clarify the community's plight and to challenge it to make changes, thus shaking the community out of its inertia. The mass meetings led to the formation of study clubs by groups of interested individuals. Study clubs in specific areas were encouraged to meet once a month to discuss common economic action and also encouraged to engage in social and cultural activities in larger forums, namely the associated clubs. Once a year, delegates from the study clubs and existing economic organizations attended the Rural and Industrial Conference held at St Francis Xavier University. This annual conference gave attendees the opportunity to hear of the achievements of the movement over the previous year, to listen to inspirational speakers, and to plan for the future. These conferences also attracted distinguished visitors from other parts of the country as well as from abroad.[134]

The various institutions – ranging from the Extension Department of St Francis Xavier University, the study clubs, cooperatives, and credit unions to the "secondary" societies that united all of the economic organizations of the movement into regional groupings – served the basic function of developing and mobilizing local resources in eastern Nova Scotia and elsewhere as the movement spread. The various economic organizations were charged with responsibilities such as the basic tasks of production, marketing, processing, saving and lending (i.e., financial intermediation), and improving wages and working conditions. The emergence of the various institutions was predicated on the prior development of human resources (through knowledge and information). This hierarchy, whereby the development of human resources was perceived as fundamental to the mobilization and development of other resources, necessitated setting up institutions in a certain sequence and also highlighted the critical importance of the Extension Department.

In 1939, partly as a response to the financial constraints faced by St Francis Xavier University, the task of organizing the study clubs was entrusted to the economic institutions that had been created by the movement. In effect, these economic institutions were charged with providing the spark to initiate the process of study and hence the expansion of economic activity. However, as some of these institutions broke away from the Extension Department in the early 1940s and devised their own, and much narrower, educational programs, the whole process and the movement as a whole began to be undermined.[135]

EMERGENCE OF THE NEW ORDER

The undeniable initial success of the movement imbued the participants with greater vigour and determination to undertake other ventures (i.e., to deepen their involvement and expand into other areas). It also attracted more members (i.e., widened the involvement) as people became convinced of the feasibility and validity of the message of the Antigonish Movement. In addition, its early successes served to silence the critics of the movement by demonstrating that there was, in fact, a viable and people-based alternative to the status quo. As a result, the mass meetings became more effective in spawning study clubs, and the associated study clubs were kept busy planning and organizing new ventures in the communities. The participants created a new order in which they were no longer victims of exploitation but active stakeholders in the economy who were in control of the emerging institutions.

Implementing the Big Picture

The notion of the Big Picture proved to be a very useful tool in the whole process. As we have already noted, it contained a broad but nevertheless comprehensive blueprint of economic action that could be applied at the community level, giving coherence and unity to the emerging economic institutions. Although at times some zealous local groups may have allowed their enthusiasm to get the better of them, leading to activities that could not be supported by the local economy and that were thus destined to fail, most community groups proceeded cautiously and methodically in establishing economic projects and activities. The cautious approach became known as the "go slow" approach and emerged as an important feature of the movement.[136] In effect, such an approach was consistent with the philosophy of the movement, which required careful and thorough study and then group action. The objective was to aim not at short-term, quick fixes but at setting up permanent institutions that would be capable of fostering permanent and fundamental changes.

Caution meant prudence but not timidity, as various groups set out to accomplish extraordinary deeds aimed at nothing short of transforming the whole economy. Even in communities where opportunities for new economic ventures seemed limited, local groups were quite ingenious in finding feasible ones. For example, a group of underemployed miners in Reserve Mines, who often worked only one day a week, organized a cooperative housing project. This project followed the establishment of a credit union in the community. Not only were these people able to build their own houses, but each home also had sufficient land to enable each family to keep some animals and to grow some of their own food. As a consequence, these miners and their families were no longer dependent on company houses and also less dependent on the infamous so-called "pluck me" company stores. The story of what came to be known as Tompkinsville is one of the more celebrated accomplishments of the Antigonish Movement during the 1930s.[137] The same desire for economic independence motivated the people in Acadian communities, such as Cheticamp and Pomquet, to link projects involving handicrafts and other manufactured products to existing cooperative ventures in their communities.[138]

The new organizations that emerged as a consequence of the Antigonish Movement promoted an increase in commercialization of economic activities in the various communities while redistributing economic power away from the traditional monopolistic and monopsonistic entities, leading to a democratization of economic power and control. In addition, the mobilization and development of resources and the expansion of economic activity generated increases in the amount of disposable income that was available for spending in the community. Greater spending could in turn support additional economic activities and projects, promoting the emergence of additional cooperative enterprises. Economic activities, therefore, prompted the establishment of additional ones primarily by exploiting the accompanying linkages.[139] The overriding objective was to acquire greater control over goods and services as well as over the resources available in the local community. In the process, the people took another step toward greater economic independence and becoming "Masters of Their Own Destiny."

Creating a New Socio-economic Reality

The economic success of the movement during the 1930s could not have occurred without the expansion of the people's ability to cooperate and reach collective decisions at the community level. The success of each new venture or project tended to bolster such cooperation and collective decision making, partly by promoting community pride and solidarity.[140] This interdependence between economic and social development was also recognized very early on by the leaders of the Antigonish Movement. Thus the study clubs were designed to be vehicles not only for acquiring economic knowledge but also for developing social skills, strengthening cooperation, and promoting solidarity. In the process, impulsive, unreliable, and antisocial elements tended to be weeded out. The same held true at the associated clubs level. The monthly meetings of the associated study clubs as well as the occasional conferences were structured in such a way as to integrate the economic activities, including the planning of new ventures and projects, into the social and cultural fabric of the people. This integration was accomplished by promoting social and cultural activities such as debating contests, dramatic presentations, and other festivities, as well as by stressing the participatory nature of the movement.

Perhaps the most important program designed to strengthen the link between the social and economic components of the movement involved the annual Rural and Industrial Conferences. As a rule, these conferences were also attended by distinguished foreign visitors and guests, who were generally impressed by what was being accomplished and usually lavished praise on the movement as a whole. To those who were parts of the movement, such praise served to bolster both their level of confidence in what they were doing or trying to do and their sense of civic pride.

Creating a New Moral and Spiritual Reality

The early leaders of the Antigonish Movement, especially the members of the Roman Catholic clergy, believed that, before anything else could be done, there had to be an improvement in the moral and spiritual attitudes of the people and that this improvement could best be accomplished through education and economic action. As noted earlier, the perceived harm done by the existence of poverty and economic stagnation went beyond mere waste and inefficiency. There was also the harm both to people as individuals and to the social fabric that binds communities. The struggle for scarce resources in order to survive generated widespread suspicion, jealousy, envy, and ill will among people, including neighbours. Poverty also affects the moral and spiritual fibre of individuals – a matter of particular concern to the early leaders of the Antigonish Movement, such as Rev. Tompkins.[141] Poverty, coupled with hopelessness, tends to destroy human dignity and undermine self-respect.

As people progressed through the study clubs, undertook group action, and implemented economic projects, their fundamental objective, apart from material gains, remained the achievement of continuous moral and spiritual improvement. The vision of the movement was based on strong moral and spiritual foundations designed to promote the achievement of a more humane and just society. Moreover, these moral and spiritual foundations held a powerful appeal and served as a strong motivator among those who participated in the movement. They also epitomized the more holistic approach to human existence, where both material and nonmaterial elements are important.[142]

The success of early economic projects initiated under the auspices of the Extension Department of St Francis Xavier University allowed the department to gain national and international recognition, in addition to its standing within the region. Initially, such recognition promoted greater discipline and commitment to the movement. It strengthened the participants' faith in the movement while also expanding its reach. Thus, although the economic and social development promoted by the movement depended on the moral and spiritual development of its participants, the latter also depended on the former. The issue here is a fundamental one, for ultimately it was the moral and spiritual uplift that was of primary concern to the early leaders of the Antigonish Movement. As Rev. Coady pointed out, it was not the objective of the movement "to create a nation of mere shopkeepers."[143]

THE MOVEMENT AND POLITICAL ACTION

The prolonged depression conditions of the 1920s and 1930s, as we have already noted, had a particularly severe impact on the primary producers and industrial workers of eastern Nova Scotia, strengthening their resolve to find a way to attain social and economic justice. Rather than giving rise to full-fledged political action, the pent-up energy and the desire for change were harnessed by the Antigonish Movement and redirected toward making primary producers and workers "Masters of Their Own Destiny." The movement jealously guarded its exclusive claim to social and economic justice and in the process distanced itself from political activity. Such an approach proved successful, particularly during the early 1930s, when the two traditional parties (the Conservatives and the Liberals) continued to propagate the discredited status quo and when the new protest parties, Social Credit and the Co-operative Commonwealth Federation, had not reached eastern Nova Scotia as organized political forces.[144] The situation seemed to change in 1935 with the founding of the Reconstruction Party.

The Reconstruction Party, which emerged in 1935 soon after its leader, H.H. Stevens, had split with the Conservative Party, seemed to replicate some of the concerns of the Antigonish Movement.[145] In particular, it was predicated on the concern for the "forgotten men," including "workers, agriculturalists, merchants, white collar class and small manufacturers," who were being exploited and undermined by the large financial and corporate interests comprising what it referred to as "big business."[146] The evidence of this exploitation rested on the spread between the prices paid to producers, including primary producers, and those paid by consumers, working conditions that resembled sweatshops, and the like.[147] Large entities, including enterprises and retail chains, were able to turn things in their favour through practices such as mass buying and the employment of loss leaders, to the detriment of small producers and retailers. In essence, these practices reflected the already noted monopsonistic and monopolistic nature of large businesses at the time. H.H. Stevens and the Reconstruction Party purported to provide a voice for the "little man," particularly against big business, through the political process and government regulation – an objective pursued largely by implementing the recommendations of the Royal Commission on Price Spreads and Mass Buying, which had been shelved by the Conservative Party – and to do so within the already existing capitalist framework.[148] Thus he presented a vision of change that was moderate and within the tradition of both the Liberal and the Conservative Parties and that was far removed from the approach that the Antigonish Movement was in the process of putting into place at the time.

Although many of the issues raised by the Reconstruction Party held some appeal to those who were involved in the Antigonish Movement, including fishermen, farmers, and industrial workers, in the case of Nova Scotia these issues found electoral support primarily among small retailers and businessmen as well as among some segments of the industrial labour force in high-unemployment areas such as Pictou and Cape Breton Counties. In the federal election of 1935, the Reconstruction Party captured 13.9 per cent of the popular vote (in excess of 38,000 votes), mostly in north-eastern Nova Scotia.[149] This percentage of the popular vote was the highest that the party received anywhere in Canada but did not translate into any seats.[150] After the election, the party disappeared nearly as quickly as it had emerged. Although it seemed to reflect the concerns of the Antigonish Movement, it could not offer a viable solution to the existing plight facing primary producers and workers in general through the political process.[151]

CONCLUSION

The Antigonish Movement, and its evolution, can be viewed as the result of a systemic chain of causation set in motion by the deteriorating socio-economic environment and nourished by a vision of economic democracy bent upon the promotion of active participation by all individuals in economic life, thus getting them "into the game and out of the bleachers." This vision determined not only the goals and objectives of the movement – particularly higher standards of living

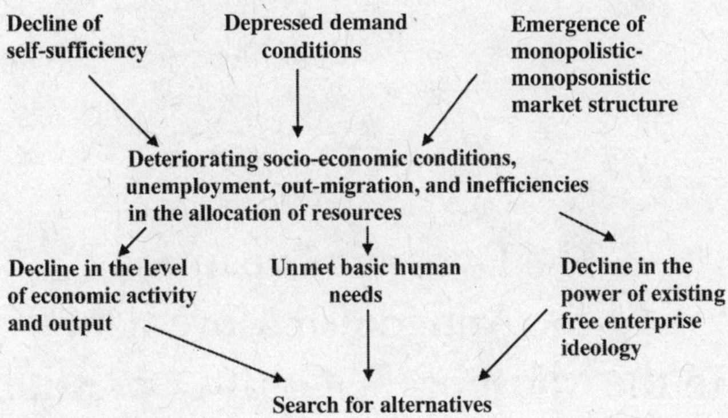

Figure 2.7 The systemic chain of causation
Source: Adapted from Santo Dodaro and Leonard Pluta, "The Antigonish Movement as a Model of Regional Economic Development," in Masudul Alam Choudhury, ed., *Political Economy of Development in Atlantic Canada* (Sydney, NS: University College of Cape Breton Press, 1988), diagram 1, 52.

and control over economic institutions – but also its strategy. This systemic chain of causation, which was dependent on the interaction between existing conditions and the movement's social vision – is summarized in figure 2.7.

The deteriorating socio-economic environment generated unemployment, out-migration, and widespread inefficiencies in the allocation of local resources. The decline in the level of production plus the concentration of power and wealth led to a failure to meet basic human needs and aspirations, as evidenced by outcomes such as poor housing and declining health standards. The sense of hopelessness and powerlessness in the face of the existing conditions led to a loss not only of motivation but also of human dignity and pride. These conditions also led to a state of fundamental moral and spiritual decay. The existing system, which was based upon the traditional tenets of the free enterprise system and promoted an ever-increasing gap between production and control, was clearly not working to the benefit of all. The Antigonish Movement provided an alternative that was both valid and consistent with the holistic and multidimensional nature of human experience.

3

The Dynamic Expansion of the Antigonish Movement in the Midst of the Great Depression

INTRODUCTION

The 1930s are generally perceived as the heyday of the young Antigonish Movement in action, characterized by a virtual explosion of wide-ranging activities. This period also witnessed the spread of the movement from its initial area of operation in eastern Nova Scotia to the other maritime provinces, Newfoundland, and the Magdalen Islands. At the same time, the movement also attracted national and international attention and support, creating enormous enthusiasm but also exaggerated confidence and expectations.[1] In retrospect, such dramatic expansion of the movement within less than a decade and the immediate international recognition that it received proved to be a mixed blessing. On the one hand, it contributed to the dynamism and increasing momentum of the movement, which created internal self-generating mechanisms that drew upon the initial successes and accomplishments as the base for a continuous and ever-expanding stream of activities. On the other hand, the early successes and recognition before the movement had fully taken root created a feeling of invincibility and exaggerated confidence on the part of the participants and, perhaps, impossible expectations among those viewing it from the outside.

The remarkable success of the movement appeared even more dramatic against the backdrop of the Great Depression and the widespread unemployment and hardship that afflicted the populace. However, amid the general enthusiasm, it was generally overlooked that the early successes were based primarily on the exploitation of the relatively easy economic opportunities, involving largely the redistribution of economic rent from the fish buyers, merchants, money lenders, and the like to the participants of the movement. The existence of opportunities that could be easily exploited and used to generate the early success stories was recognized by Rev. Moses Coady. He also recognized that these needed to form the basis for undertaking "more difficult ventures" and for tackling "problems in other more difficult spheres."[2]

The thrust of this chapter is empirical. Our primary intent is to provide a factual as well as analytical description of the Antigonish Movement during its most dynamic phase. Thus we record the remarkable process of transforming the movement's theory and vision into what may appear as the spontaneous emergence of a network of community-based institutions owned and controlled by the people themselves. Furthermore, these institutions mobilized an ever-growing stream of resources, leading to increased production and in some instances dramatically higher levels of income, which in turn resulted in a growth in civic pride, improved confidence, and a regained sense of dignity among the participants. The translation of the ideas, theory, and vision of the movement into concrete projects, institutions, and resources required guidance and institutional support as well as tools, techniques, and programs. It was in meeting these requirements, both directly and indirectly, that the Extension Department of St Francis Xavier University played the pivotal role in the whole process. Thus we begin this chapter by focusing on the empirical analysis of the programs and techniques used by the Extension Department to initiate and guide the movement, particularly its adult education programs and activities, including study clubs, mass meetings, leadership courses, and the provision of educational material (e.g., through travelling libraries).

Although these programs and activities formed the core of the Antigonish Movement, they were, in themselves, means rather than ends. In the main, especially in the context of the 1930s, they were the means whereby resources were mobilized, developed, and put to use in order to meet the basic needs and aspirations of the local population. The meeting of basic needs was in itself only a step toward the achievement of loftier goals as well as a part of a process of moral renewal. The mobilization of resources took place as a consequence of the establishment of cooperatives, credit unions, and other cooperative economic activities. At the same time, however, the process whereby these economic activities were put in place also promoted other and fundamentally more important human traits such as trust and honesty. The importance of these traits and their link to the socio-economic environment are perhaps best reflected in Rev. Jimmy Tompkins's concern with people stealing from each other in Little Dover – a fact, as already noted in the previous chapter, attributed to a moral breakdown resulting from poverty. Empowerment in the context of the Antigonish Movement also meant moral and ethical development.

THE EXTENSION DEPARTMENT AND THE INSTITUTIONAL STRUCTURE

The creation of the Extension Department at St Francis Xavier University in 1928 put in place the main institutional building block of the movement. Armed with a vision, the Extension Department went to work to translate it into practice with a minimum of resources, both human and material. The Extension Department had to discover how to best apply this vision to fulfil its mandate and resolve the problems that were plaguing the people of eastern Nova Scotia. In this process, it could rely on the lessons learned from the various educational experiments and initiatives, such as the People's Schools and the annual Rural Conferences, that were undertaken during the 1920s and that had also served to solidify the emerging vision. Furthermore, the experience of organizing the fishermen during the 1929-30 period provided Rev. Coady with additional insights into organizing and motivating the people. As well, it strengthened his legitimacy as a leader and that of the movement itself. As a result, the Extension Department was able to launch an educational program that was highly integrated and comprehensive in scope. Essentially, the educational program or strategy that emerged consisted of three parts: (1) the mass meetings, (2) the study clubs, and (3) the supporting programs, such as leadership courses, conferences, and the provision of educational materials, including those provided through circulating libraries.

The Mass Meetings

The initial, and also the most important, steps in the education program were the meetings attended by entire communities. These so-called "Mass Meetings" often introduced the communities to the Extension Department for the first time, and thus much importance was attached to them. Indeed, it was critical that these meetings go well and that the ideas that were presented be enthusiastically received, as the success or failure of the entire program greatly depended on them. Given their importance, much preparation went into the organization of these meetings. Usually, the local leaders – often comprised of parish priests, schoolteachers, and other influential community members – were approached first and asked for support. As well, information was gathered about the specific economic and social conditions prevailing in the various communities, and this information was forwarded to the main speaker. Every effort was made to ensure a good turnout and to heighten the expectation that a very important meeting was to take place. Finally, a dynamic speaker, usually Rev. Coady or his associate A.B. MacDonald, would undertake the "intellectual bombing operations" designed "to break mind sets" of those in attendance.[3] At these meetings, the theory of the "Great Default of the People" occupied a central position, followed by the outline of successful experiments of ordinary people organizing themselves and regaining control over their economic destiny. As well, Rev. Coady also stressed the important notion of scientific thinking, which he considered "The great secret of human progress."[4]

Prior to undertaking the mass meeting program, a crucial decision had to be made by the Extension Department. It had to decide whether to limit its educational activities to a selected number of local communities, and hence concentrate all of its resources in a relatively small area, or whether to spread the educational activities over the entire region of eastern Nova Scotia. The first option would have been less risky, as the very meager resources of the Extension Department could be used more effectively in a limited number of communities, thus assuring adequate support and the possibility of a few successful ventures. The success of these ventures could then be used as a demonstration of the practicality and validity of the program and as a basis for subsequent expansion over the wider area. On the nega-

Table 3.1
Number of mass meetings and number in attendance, 1931–36

Year	*Meetings*	*Attendance*	*Average attendance*
1931	192	14,856	77
1932	280	20,476	73
1933	380	23,000	60
1934	500	25,000	50
1935	450	27,000	60
1936	470	43,000	91

Source: St Francis Xavier Archives, RG 30.3/25/967, RG 30.3/25/972, RG 30.3/25/990, RG 30.3/25/999.

tive side, this option would commit the Extension Department to a slow process in the face of the dire and immediate needs of the people of the whole of eastern Nova Scotia. The second option of targeting the whole area posed the danger of spreading far too thinly the meager resources available to the department. However, if successful, this approach would ensure a much faster spread of the movement and greater momentum, while also putting into practice its concern for the population as a whole rather than for only a small number of target communities.

The second and more risky option was chosen. Within a short time, the Extension Department was able to cover the whole of eastern Nova Scotia with mass meetings.[5] The pace at which mass meetings were organized and took place was hectic, with three to six meetings per week. Given that the roads in eastern Nova Scotia in the 1930s were very poor and frequently impassable during the winter months, the pace must be considered nothing short of heroic. The average attendance at these meetings varied between fifty and ninety-one from 1931 to 1936, the period for which data are available. Although in absolute terms these numbers may not appear to be high, we must remember that the average rural community in eastern Nova Scotia consisted of seventy-five families, implying that virtually every family had at least one representative attending these mass meetings.

As shown in table 3.1, after the first two years, the average attendance at the mass meetings began to drop, going from between seventy-three and seventy-seven people over the 1931–32 period to as low as fifty in 1934. Attendance then rose again to a high of ninety-one in

1936. At the same time, the number of mass meetings went up from 192 in 1931 to a peak of 500 in 1934 and remained high over the 1935-36 period. Total attendance also increased throughout, going from almost 15,000 in 1931 to 43,000 in 1936.

These data offer a number of important insights into the movement and its spread. First, we can safely infer that attendance at the initial meetings was instigated by their novelty, coupled with the natural curiosity of the people. Normally, these are factors that disappear quickly and would not have been able to sustain the mass meetings for long. We must remember that the purpose of the mass meetings was to shake things up and then, far more important, to organize people into study clubs. Many of the initial study clubs failed in the first year of operation, which would normally be expected to have discouraged attendance at some meetings, especially when these were the second or even third mass meetings in a given community. Also, over time, mass meetings began to be held in some of the smaller and more remote communities that had initially been bypassed. Both of these factors would explain the lower attendance at individual mass meetings over the 1933–35 period. However, total attendance kept increasing, and the number of meetings mushroomed. Thus there was no loss of enthusiasm over the period as novelty and curiosity gave way to more concrete notions. Nevertheless, in terms of the number of people who were reached by the mass meetings, a sort of equilibrium was achieved that could easily have stalled and eventually undermined the movement. Arguably, by increasing the number of mass meetings, the Extension Department kept the vision alive during this most critical period.

The increase in attendance over the 1935-36 period represents a dramatic development. It suggests that the movement had overcome the initial difficulties and had demonstrated its validity. By 1936 numerous successful economic projects provided concrete evidence that the movement could in fact achieve what it promised. In other words, it had reached the mass movement stage, whereby it could expect to be pushed forward by its internal dynamics; it was no longer necessary to cajole people to come to the mass meetings, as the people themselves were flocking to them.

By 1937 the program of mass meetings had largely achieved its objective of introducing the Antigonish Movement to the people of eastern Nova Scotia. The movement was then spreading beyond the region and even to other countries. The technique of mass meetings was still being used but only to introduce the movement to the new regions and new provinces. The number of mass meetings declined rapidly, and their number was no longer recorded by the Extension Department. Their role in organizing the study clubs was passed on largely to the cooperative organizations that had been created by the movement.[6] As it turned out, these organizations were not up to the task over the longer term, which had serious implications for the movement in subsequent decades.

The Study Clubs

Study clubs were organized immediately following the mass meetings. Local leaders were identified and approached to undertake the responsibility of initiating and facilitating the educational activities within the clubs.[7] In many instances, the local leaders were identified prior to holding the community meetings and were even asked to help in organizing these meetings and in ensuring good attendance. In such cases, the mass meetings served to generate interest and enthusiasm that the local leaders could then channel into the formation of study clubs. Thus, although there was a great deal of spontaneity associated with the organization of study clubs, there was also a great deal of planning.

We have referred to the activities stemming from the Antigonish Movement during the 1930s as being remarkable. The data presented in table 3.2, concerning the number of study clubs functioning during each year, provide the most striking evidence of this fact. Interestingly, the level of participation in these study clubs climbed rapidly to a total membership of 10,000 in 1935 and then remained at about this level for the remainder of the 1930s – except for 1936, when there was a decline to about 8,000 members.

These data, however, do not convey the whole story. There was a great deal of turnover among the study clubs, particularly as a result of widespread failure in the initial wave during the first two years of the education program. In fact, few if any of the study clubs organized in 1931 survived the year.[8] Given that the fundamental purpose of the study clubs was to generate cooperative economic action over a relatively short time, a substantial turnover rate would seem normal. However, the high cessation rate during the first two years was fundamentally different from that of later years, when the turnover

Table 3.2
Study clubs and membership figures for eastern Nova Scotia, 1931–39

Year	*Clubs*	*Change from previous year*	*Membership*	*Average size*
1931	173	—	1,384	8.0
1932	179	+179	1,500	8.4
1933	350	+171	5,250	15.0
1934	650	+300	6,000	9.2
1935	940	+290	10,650	11.3
1936	860	-80	8,000	9.3
1937	1,013	+153	10,000	9.4
1938	1,100	+87	10,000	9.1
1939	1,300	+200	10,400	8.0

Source: St Francis Xavier University Archives, RG 30.3/25/966, RG 30.3/25/972, RG 30.3/25/975, RG 30.3/25/999, RG 30.3/25/1015.

among study clubs was motivated by their success in creating new economic organizations. Thus study clubs could be terminated not only as a result of failure but also as a result of success. Unfortunately, although available data provide a record of the net year-to-year changes in the number of study clubs, they do not include the rate at which study clubs were being terminated (or the reasons) and new ones established.

The widespread failure of the initial wave of the study clubs is not surprising and can be traced to several factors that can be linked to the process of learning by doing through which any new initiative must normally go. Rev. Coady suggested that these early efforts tended to lack focus and that "the education that was carried on through them was often superficial."[9] They were isolated and often hampered by inconsistent local club leaders. The initial support provided by the Extension Department was not always what was needed or timely. Notably, "In the early days of the movement it did not occur to the Extension workers to advocate the study of some specific economic ventures that ... would quickly demonstrate to them the value of adult education."[10] Furthermore, the gap between the study and discussion, on the one hand, and the concrete economic projects, on the other, appeared to the participants to be unbridgeable, which tended to dampen their educational efforts.

Although in theory the study club method appeared to be an appropriate tool of adult education, in practice a great deal of experimentation and fine-tuning had to be done to ensure the study clubs' eventual success and survival. Gradually, through trial and error, the Extension Department was able to narrow the focus of the clubs, improve the selection of the local leaders, and devise a more effective way of providing study materials. Also, it was able to organize complementary activities that broke down the study clubs' isolation, such as monthly rallies of all of the clubs in an area. Even the size of study clubs had to be adjusted to ensure their maximum effectiveness. Many of the early clubs were too large, consisting of fifteen to twenty individuals, which discouraged the participation of the members. At the same time, some study clubs were too small, comprising only four to five participants. Both instances contributed to their lackluster performance and frequent dissolution. After two years of experimentation, an optimum size of about ten members was identified, and this was generally the study club size that, for the most part, prevailed over the rest of the decade.

Another important factor, one that contributed to the improved effectiveness of the study clubs and that provided a strong impetus for the rapid spread of the movement, was the emergence of the early highly successful ventures created by the members themselves. These ventures, which would have been perceived as impossible only a few years earlier, provided indisputable evidence that the seemingly insurmountable obstacles facing impoverished fishermen, farmers, and industrial workers could be overcome. Ordinary people working together could collectively own their own fish-processing plants, marketing cooperatives, cooperative banks, and other cooperative enterprises and in the process, among other things, could increase their earnings, lower the cost of their purchases, increase their savings, and gain access to credit. These ventures became the early success stories that were repeated endlessly at mass meetings, study clubs, conferences, and other gatherings.

Among the most memorable of these early successes was the cooperative lobster plant established in Little Dover in 1932. The small, rocky, barren, isolated, and windswept village of Little Dover was an unlikely place for perhaps the most memorable of the early success stories. Prodded by the tireless Rev. Tompkins, a group of fishermen went into the woods and obtained the lumber that they used to construct their own lobster-canning factory. They took out a $1,000 loan that was guaranteed by Rev. Tompkins to purchase the canning machinery. By the end of their first year of operation, they had sold $8,000 worth of lobsters and were able to pay back the loan. During the next year, sales increased to $29,000, as many other fishermen joined the cooperative.[11]

Another success story emerged from a similar project undertaken in the village of Havre Boucher in north-eastern Nova Scotia. As had been the case in Little Dover, a group of fishermen contributed their own labour and "erected a canning factory in very short order."[12] The rewards for their labour and risk-taking were quick and substantial. During the first season, "they had received an average ... of twelve cents per pound for their lobsters, while the non-cooperators had got only about six cents per pound."[13] Three years later, the Havre Boucher cooperative had a surplus of $10,000, which was a large sum in those days, in addition to other benefits.[14] As well, each individual lobster fisherman earned on average an additional $200 for the year as a result of cooperation.[15]

Yet another improbable early success was the establishment of a cooperative bank in the depressed coalmining town of Glace Bay, in Cape Breton, by a group of poor, underemployed miners. When Rev. Coady made his usual rousing presentation at a mass meeting in 1931 in Glace Bay, the several hundred people in attendance were skeptical. Unlike the fishing and farming villages, those in the mining communities saw few possible ventures that they could organize and undertake, especially since the miners had been reduced to working one shift per week. Nevertheless, a few study clubs were organized, and although it took two years, in June 1933 thirty-four mostly young miners were confident enough to apply for a credit union charter, giving rise to the third credit union organized by the movement. The $1 fee for the charter had to be paid by the Extension Department, as the miners were unable to meet the expense, and the initial set-up cost of $15.36, to pay for pass books and deposit slips, had to be covered by fundraising activities for the same reason. Nevertheless, with each member depositing 25 cents per week on a regular basis, after six months the total deposits amounted to an impressive $1,062.95, with $590.25 loaned to members.[16] Two and a half years later, membership had increased to 900, total equity in the credit union amounted to a substantial $25,000, and $90,000 had been loaned to members.[17]

These loans were made for productive or providential purposes, such as "to repair homes ... to assist families in time of illness ... To buy artificial limbs."[18]

Although the success stories cited above were the result of the cooperation among a relatively large number of people, there were also examples of successful activities undertaken by very small groups. One such example involved four fishermen from Whitehead who broke with the accepted practice of selling their live lobsters to local buyers and collectively sent one crate to the Boston market, earning $24.00 instead of the $5.60 that they would have earned by selling locally.[19] Although their first reaction was to conclude that the $24.00 cheque was a mistake and that they would "have to send it back," they decided instead to send another crate, for which they received an even bigger cheque of $32.00.[20] This initial experience "marked the end of selling lobsters to local fish merchants ... along the Guysborough shore."[21]

Other examples emerged from other parts of eastern Nova Scotia. The small and impoverished community of Reserve Mines, which had the distinction of organizing the first study clubs in industrial Cape Breton, was also among the first to establish a successful credit union in English Canada in 1933.[22]

These and other early success stories inspired others to follow in their footsteps. They provided the models, techniques, and examples that others could rely upon in organizing their own cooperative ventures. Moreover, they emboldened their own communities to undertake more difficult and ambitious projects. Thus the early success in Reserve Mines was the precursor to even bigger ventures, as it spurred miners to envision the possibility of escaping from the dilapidated company houses, for which they had to pay very high rent, and owning their own homes, leading to the establishment of Tompkinsville in 1938. The people of Larry's River, following the successful establishment of a community-owned sawmill, went on to build a cooperative lobster-processing factory, a credit union, a consumers' cooperative store, and a blueberry-canning facility, among other undertakings.[23] Similarly, the Acadian community of Grand Etang followed an early success to establish five cooperative projects over eight years.[24]

A number of these ventures resulted from the study clubs, whereas others emerged outside of the study clubs network, some of which were organized by a few dedicated and persistent parish priests, among whom Rev. Tompkins occupied the leading role.[25] Nevertheless, even those early successes that emerged separately from the study clubs system acted as a boost to the movement, providing for the whole study clubs network an indispensable demonstration of the effectiveness of such initiatives. These activities were consistent with the vision and philosophy with which the study clubs were imbued.

Over the 1932–33 period, the movement established a foothold in the fisheries, agriculture, retail trade, and the financial sector. As a result, interest in the movement increased, causing the emergence of a second and bigger wave of study clubs. An additional 300 study clubs were operational in 1934, and another 290 were added in 1935, with the total number increasing from 350 in 1933 to 940 in 1935. In turn, these new study clubs led to additional successful economic ventures, which also instigated the emergence of additional study clubs. The mutual reinforcement between the new study clubs and the new economic organizations created an internal self-generating mechanism that drove the movement forward and effectively transformed it into a grassroots, people-based phenomenon as the 1930s progressed.

The data for 1936 point to a slight decline in the number of study clubs. However, this decline does not mean that the movement faltered. On the contrary, it was in 1936 that the movement began its most dynamic phase. The decline in the number of study clubs was, in part, the result of impatience on the part of new members, who rushed through the educational phase in order to establish their own economic organizations and benefit from their activities. Furthermore, the experience of the earlier study clubs reduced the study time and allowed for the accelerated conversion of study clubs into new cooperatives and credit unions. Given that, on average, it took five to seven study clubs to collectively form a credit union, and an even greater number to establish marketing or consumers' cooperatives, the decline in the number of study clubs in 1936 suggests that a large number of them were submerged in newly organized ventures. There were not enough new study clubs to offset those that terminated their existence as a consequence of the implementation of economic ventures, and thus the total number showed some decline. During the remaining years of the decade, the number of study clubs again increased, indicating that the newly organized study clubs exceeded the number of older clubs terminating their existence after having achieved their objective of implementing economic projects.

The study club as an institution was generally perceived as being transitional in nature, intended to operate until an economic project was put in place. To the extent that study clubs were instrumental in setting up many economic activities, they played a crucial role in the establishment and propagation of the Antigonish Movement. Furthermore, this role was carried out at little cost in terms of actual resource expended. Indeed, the study clubs did not overly tax the resources available to the Extension Department and to the participants, while also being easily accessible to everyone. Broad participation was further fostered by the combination of social and economic elements in the study clubs. Although the purpose of the study clubs was indeed serious, they provided an atmosphere where frank and friendly study and discussion could take place with all members as active participants, consistent with the social and cultural milieu of the people. The general flexibility and convenience of meeting places, which were often people's kitchens and living rooms, and the composition of the clubs enabled the social and economic dimensions to complement each other.

WOMEN STUDY CLUBS The resurgence of study clubs from 1934 onward was also helped by the establishment of the Women's Work program. This program, under the effective leadership of Sister Marie Michael (Mary Sarah MacKinnon) and Sister Mary Anselm (Irene Doyle), targeted the wives of farmers, fishermen, and industrial workers as agents of social reform.[26] An important function of the program was to identify women leaders for women study clubs. These study clubs addressed issues and activities of particular relevance to them, such as handicrafts and rug making, nutrition, canning, and food preservation, animal raising, financial management, and the marketing of products.[27] Study materials were provided from different sources, which initially included the "Women's Pages" of the *Extension Bulletin*. The astounding success of the program is demonstrated by the fact that in 1935, out of a total of 940 study clubs, 350 were composed solely of women – 290 of these in the rural areas.[28] The number of women study clubs remained high over the rest of the decade, with 350 active ones also reported for 1938. Indeed, over the period during which the program was in place, from 1934 to 1944, women study clubs made up about one-third of the total.[29] In many instances, women were engaged in the study of the same subjects as men, including credit unions and cooperatives of various sorts.

Supporting Educational Programs

The Extension Department's contribution to the education process was not limited to helping to organize study clubs and directly supporting their study endeavours with materials and the like. It also instituted programs that enabled not only the study clubs to be more effective but also the economic activities that emerged from them to be more efficiently managed.

THE LEADERSHIP COURSES In practical terms, the success of the study clubs was contingent on the ability of the leaders. In keeping with the general spirit of self-reliance and cooperation, the study club leaders were, in theory, envisaged largely as secretaries and facilitators. However, although their basic function was to ensure that meetings regularly took place, that study materials were made available to all members, that proper study methods were employed, and that all members actively participated in the process of study and discussion, they were also instrumental in establishing and organizing the clubs in the first place and acted as contact people for the Extension Department. The ability and dedication of these leaders, who were strictly volunteers, was thus very important not only in shaping and guiding the study clubs but also in promoting the spirit of self-reliance and cooperation. Their role is a classic example of Rev. Coady's notion that those who were more talented should put their talents at the disposal of the community.[30]

The role and importance of leaders became even more pronounced with the establishment of economic ventures. By 1933 the rapidly growing number of economic organizations created a need for technically capable and highly motivated personnel to manage them efficiently. Nothing would have been more detrimental to the young movement as the collapse or bankruptcy of the newly created credit unions and cooperatives. The Extension Department met this need by initiating a four-week leadership course, the so-called "short course."

This new educational program was to some extent a modified and improved version of the original People's School experiment of a

Table 3.3
Leadership course attendance, 1931–39

Year	*Attendance*
1931	—
1932	—
1933	86
1934	44
1935	30
1936	63
1937	78
1938	132
1939	130

Source: St Francis Xavier University Archives, RG 30.3/25/975.

decade earlier. However, there were significant differences between these two programs. In 1921 there was no mass movement in place, and there were no economic organizations created and owned by the people that required competent and efficient managers. The earlier People's School was unfocused in its curriculum, ranging from English literature to agriculture, and the selection of the candidates was haphazard. There was no clearly defined role for the new leaders, and there was no movement to lead, although there was hope that the new leaders would somehow assist in its emergence. By 1933 the situation had changed dramatically. A dynamic movement had emerged involving thousands of individuals engaged in study clubs, and new community-based economic organizations had been established. To ensure its stability and growth, the movement needed technically competent individuals who were also familiar with cooperative history and philosophy. The selection of candidates became highly competitive, with only the most capable and proven of the local study club leaders being chosen.

The leadership courses were designed primarily to train individuals who could effectively manage the cooperative enterprises that were emerging from the study clubs. However, they were also expected to improve the quality of leadership within the study clubs. Attendance at these courses, which over the decade ranged from a low of 30 candidates in 1935 to a high of 132 in 1938, is summarized in table 3.3.[31]

These courses were attended predominantly by the most promising young men of the region, although some women also participated. The curriculum was practical and oriented toward actual needs and requirements. A typical leadership course involved areas of study such as business arithmetic, business English, bookkeeping, elementary economics, cooperative business practices, history and principles of cooperation, legal aspects of cooperative operations, citizenship, community programs, debating, and public speaking.[32] Thus the leadership courses focused on specific and more technical areas with which the study clubs could not normally adequately deal. Moreover, their orientation offers evidence of the realization that although group entrepreneurship could set things in motion, individuals with some degree of specific knowledge and expertise were required for successful day-to-day operations in accordance with the exigencies of cooperative business activity.

OTHER SUPPORTING PROGRAMS The thousands of people engaged in the numerous study clubs required huge volumes of relevant study materials. Given the limited information-processing technology available at the time, essentially the manual typewriter and offset, the demands on the meager resources of the Extension Department were enormous. The problem was solved, at least in part, by adopting the use of "circulating libraries," which consisted of a number of boxes (each containing between twenty-five and thirty books) that were circulated among various study clubs and communities. Books were also mailed out upon request from an open-shelf library at the Extension Department. The number of volumes in this open-shelf library increased steadily from about 300 in the early 1930s to about 1,500 by 1939, with 700 volumes added in 1938–39 as the result of a Carnegie Library grant. During the 1930s, a library was also established in the Extension Department office at Glace Bay with help from a Carnegie grant and local tax levies. This library served ten branches in surrounding areas. Fundamental to the expansion of library facilities was legislation allowing towns and municipalities to levy taxes for the purpose of funding library development.[33]

The growth in the demand for books from the circulating libraries was accompanied by an even greater increase in demand for pamphlets and other mimeographed materials that even individuals with scant formal education could understand. Whereas books were gen-

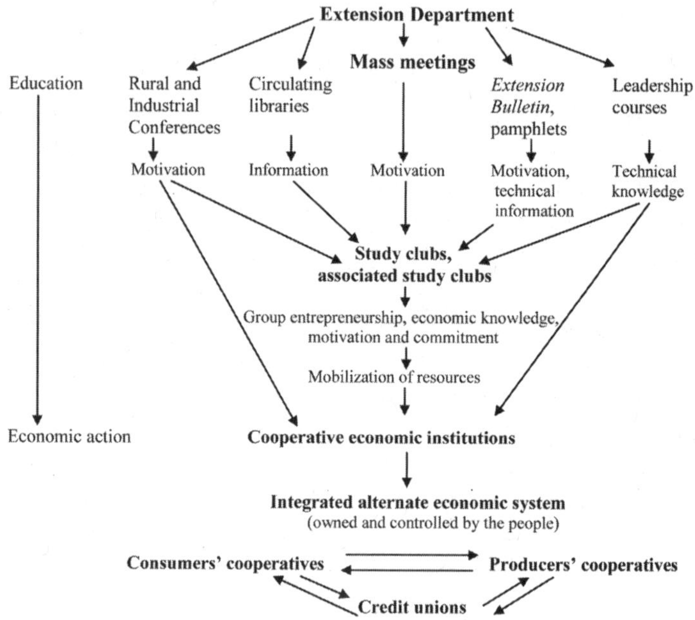

Figure 3.1 Integrated program in the 1930s

erally accessible only to the more educated study club members, a vast majority of them could understand the pamphlets. This demand for easily accessible study materials was met relatively early, in 1933, with the bimonthly publication of the *Extension Bulletin*, which continued its existence until 1939, when it was replaced by the monthly publication the *Maritime Co-operator*. The *Extension Bulletin* quickly became the main conduit of popular forms of study material, reaching a circulation of 7,000 in 1935. In addition to providing organized material on various topics of interest to study clubs, the *Extension Bulletin* also served as a forum for keeping up the level of enthusiasm in the Antigonish Movement.

The Integrated Education Program

The various components of the Extension Department's education program during the 1930s gave rise to a highly integrated system, as indicated in figure 3.1. The overall goal of the whole program was to encourage the undertaking of new cooperative economic projects as well as to ensure that once established these could be operated efficiently.

RESOURCES OF THE EXTENSION DEPARTMENT

The most remarkable aspect of the educational program of the Extension Department was that it was conducted with very few official resources – both human and financial. Indeed, both the staff and the budget of the Extension Department were pitifully small, particularly during the early years. Given the numerous mass meetings, the vast number of study clubs, and the large volume of study materials required to support them, the demands of the leadership courses, and the assistance required to manage the newly created economic ventures, what the small staff was able to do with few resources must be seen as astonishing.

During its first two years of operation, the Extension Department carried out its programs with only two people on staff: Rev. Coady and Kay Thompson Desjardin. They were joined by A.B. MacDonald in 1932 and by two sisters of St Martha – Marie Michael and Mary Anselm – over the next two years. This core group of two men and three women constituted the main driving force of the Antigonish Movement over much of the 1930s. Although the contribution by Coady and MacDonald has been widely recognized, the role of the women was also vital. They helped to organize study clubs, wrote and printed the *Extension Bulletin*, disseminated books and pamphlets, prepared speeches, assisted in the organization of the leadership courses and conferences, and carried out the many other tasks that gave shape to the Antigonish Movement. During the latter part of the decade, this initial core group was expanded with the addition of Alex S. MacIntyre, Ida Delaney, and Zita O'Hearn Cameron, among a number of others.

The Extension Department's ability to accomplish so much can be explained by its heavy reliance on outside resources and its policy of letting the participants do most of the work themselves – reflecting the Catholic doctrine of subsidiarity, which implies that people should be allowed to do for themselves the things of which they are capable.[34] Also, to conserve scarce resources, the Extension Department used and integrated existing community-based organizations into its own institutional network whenever possible, rather than creating all the necessary organizations itself. Among the outside resources, the parish priests provided invaluable services not only by assisting with the mass meetings and study clubs but also, as we have already noted, by initiating some of the first successful economic ventures. The clergy, particularly the Catholic parish priests and the priest-professors, constituted one of the few groups that could claim to be truly altruistic, with the welfare of the community being a primary objective. Moreover, the members of the clergy occupied a position of trust among a sizable segment of the largely homogenous population of eastern Nova Scotia, which made their espousal of the Antigonish Movement quite effective, particularly in the early years when evidence that it worked was not available.

In addition to the members of the clergy, many other local leaders, such as school teachers and agricultural representatives, were also called upon to help. The agricultural representatives, in particular, worked closely with the Extension Department in helping local farmers to improve their economic conditions. Their objectives coincided with those of the movement. The local and even regional structures already in place prior to the emergence of the movement also turned out to be particularly helpful. These structures included the shipping clubs organized under the Moncton-based Canadian Livestock Co-operative (CLC). In 1935, with the support of Rev. Tompkins, Rev. Coady, and A.B. MacDonald, the CLC was established as a cooperative wholesaler.[35] The association between the CLC and the Antigonish Movement was quite strong, although not necessarily smooth, in the latter part of the 1930s, and in 1938 a branch was established in Sydney called Cape Breton Co-operative Services, followed by another one in Antigonish in 1940 called Eastern Co-operative Services.[36] The CLC was renamed Maritime Co-operative Services in 1939.[37] F. Waldo Walsh identifies a number of other relevant initiatives by the Nova Scotia Department of Agriculture.[38] By incorporating these structures into its own institutional network, the movement not only economized on its scarce resources but also increased their effectiveness.

Nevertheless, the staff of the Extension Department would not have been able to do much if not for the fact that it motivated people who were willing to undertake the work themselves. Data on the staff of the Extension Department are presented in table 3.4.

Table 3.4
Human resources of the Extension Department, 1930–39

Year	*Full-time staff*	*Part-time staff*
1930	2	0
1931	2	0
1932	3	2
1933	4	2
1934	5	2
1935	5	3
1936	5	4
1937	7	9
1938	11	4
1939	11	7

Source: St Francis Xavier University Archives, RG 30.3/25/975, RG 30.3/25/1014.

Table 3.5
Budget of the Extension Department, 1929–39

Year	*Budget ($)*
1929–30	2,416.94
1930–31	8,187.15
1931–32	9,457.91
1932–33	14,990.23
1933–34	18,237.18
1934–35	17,244.33
1935–36	18,212.62
1936–37	21,154.47
1937–38	25,069.73
1938–39	47,660.58
TOTAL	182,631.14

Source: St Francis Xavier University Archives, RG 30.3/25/893.

Over the 1938-39 period, an additional thirty fieldworkers were hired as a result of the extra funds that the Extension Department received from the federal government to organize fishermen in the entire area of the Maritimes, Newfoundland, and the Magdalen Islands.[39]

Table 3.5 provides data on the budget of the Extension Department over the 1930s. Again, the figures are far from impressive, even in the

Table 3.6
Expenditures and sources of revenue of the Extension Department, 1929–39

1929–34		*Amounts ($)*
Expenditures		53,144.70
Revenue	Carnegie Corporation	29,500.00
	Other donations	5,311.03
	Sale of pamphlets, etc.	344.70
	Balance paid by university	17,998.97
		53,144.70
1934–39		
Expenditures		129,341.73
Revenue	Carnegie Corporation	27,382.20
	Other donations	9,373.93
	Sale of pamphlets, etc.	1,843.52
	Dominion Dept of Fisheries	25,094.49
	Balance paid by university	65,647.59
		129,341.73

Source: St Francis Xavier University Archives, RG 30.3/25/1439.

context of the time. However, for the reasons identified earlier, this limited budget went further than one would expect.

As can be seen in table 3.6, between 1929 and 1934 about 67 per cent of the Extension Department's funds came from private sources – particularly the Carnegie Corporation, which provided about 56 per cent of the total – with the university picking up about 33 per cent of the tab. The situation was much different for the 1934–39 period, when the university actually provided about 51 per cent of the total operating funds (and the Carnegie Corporation's contribution fell to about 21 per cent). This sort of situation created problems of financing, particularly after 1938–39 when the university started experiencing a serious financial squeeze.

Over the 1938–39 period, substantial funds – in terms of the Extension Department's overall budget – were obtained from the Dominion Department of Fisheries. This was an important development for a number of reasons. On the one hand, it introduced a new source of outside funds for the Extension Department, allowing its budget for

Table 3.7
Activity of the Extension Department in the fisheries of the maritime provinces and Magdalen Islands, November 1938–February 1939

	Nova Scotia	*New Brunswick*	*PEI*	*Magdalen Islands*	*Total*
Number of workers	13	13	6	2	34
Places visited	589	590	146	76	1,401
Meetings addressed	385	405	102	65	958
Attendance at meetings	13,923	24,670	3,331	4,184	46,108
Study clubs organized	437	661	103	57	1,258
Conferences with directors or committees	222	268	197	11	698
Personal interviews	1,595	1,549	770	246	4,160

Source: St Francis Xavier University Archives, RG 30.3/25/1009.

1939 to increase dramatically. On the other hand, these funds were earmarked for work among fishermen of the various maritime provinces, thus spreading the work of the Extension Department over a wider geographical area while also introducing an external governmental constraint on its activities. Although the partnership with the government was not entirely new to the Extension Department, or at least not to Rev. Coady, who had been previously involved in the implementation of the MacLean Commission recommendations,[40] such collaboration did not entirely fit in with the independent economic system that the Antigonish Movement was in the process of establishing.

The extent to which the activities of the Extension Department increased over the 1938–39 period is demonstrated in the data presented in table 3.7, covering the maritime provinces and the Magdalen Islands. The funds provided by the federal government mandated the Extension Department to establish an adult education program among the fishermen of maritime Canada that was designed to improve the lot of the fishermen and the health of the fishing industry as a whole, particularly through cooperative marketing and purchasing, more efficient production methods, and conservation. In the main, therefore, there was a fundamental congruence between the goals of the government and those of the Extension Department and the Antigonish Movement as a whole.

Such a drastic change in the scope and scale of operations of the Extension Department, especially its shift in responsibility from predominantly eastern Nova Scotia to virtually the whole of maritime Canada, proved to be a mixed blessing. On the one hand, it gave the Extension Department additional resources to expand the Antigonish Movement over a wider area and thereby to have positive impacts on the livelihood of a greater number of people. On the other hand, it stretched the department's resources and its leadership very thinly, magnifying the problems of coordination, direction, and guidance. Furthermore, the sudden expansion occurred at a time when the relatively easy economic opportunities had already been exploited and when the movement was faced with the challenges of tackling far more complex, although potentially more profitable, ventures, such as in processing and in production characterized by higher value added. In effect, the expansion widened the department's coverage at the very time when this coverage should also have been deepening. Moreover, it occurred on the eve of the Second World War, which ushered in radically different economic, political, and social conditions that required drastic adjustment and adaptation before the movement had a chance to become fully established.

In carrying out its new government-mandated fisheries program, the Extension Department adopted a two-pronged approach. The established program that earlier in the decade had proven so successful in eastern Nova Scotia, and in some parts of New Brunswick and Prince Edward Island, which consisted of measures such as mass meetings, study clubs, and the provision of study materials, was complemented by a more individualistic approach based on personal interviews with individual fishermen and on workshops.

The personal interviews and workshops, which were more specialized in content, were intended to complement and strengthen the effectiveness of the group-based traditional approach. In particular, they were intended largely to improve practices in the sector through what we later identify as a "Model Fisherman" approach. Newly hired Extension Department fieldworkers spent a great deal of time conducting interviews with individual fishermen, with each worker carrying out on average over 120 interviews during the period under consideration, as well as workshops for various committees and directors of new organizations. These new fieldworkers, lacking sufficient experience and knowledge of the movement, were expected to be more effective in these more individualistic endeavours than in the more group-based traditional approach. However, the new approach was not only more time-consuming but also not entirely consistent with the basic premise of the Antigonish Movement of organizing together, studying together, and acting together, although it could serve as a complement. The two-pronged approach was not entirely successful and set the stage for the shift away from the group approach that became increasingly evident over time.

THE MOBILIZATION AND DEVELOPMENT OF RESOURCES THROUGH COOPERATIVE ECONOMIC ACTION

The remarkable array of educational activities that took place under the auspices of the Extension Department during the 1930s was matched by an equally remarkable process of resource mobilization and development in various sectors of the economy of eastern Nova Scotia. These outcomes were achieved through the establishment and expansion of various cooperative economic institutions, owned and controlled by the people themselves, that were designed to enable them to regain control over their economic destiny. Rev. Coady and the other early leaders of the Antigonish Movement understood that without ownership and control of economic activity, there could be no real empowerment and socio-economic transformation.

Although they all shared the fundamental purpose of preparing the groundwork for collective economic action, the study clubs were not uniform, nor were their programs of study identical.[41] Both the type of economic action and the program of study differed among the distinct groups of fishermen, farmers, and industrial workers that made up the economy of eastern Nova Scotia. They also differed between producers and consumers as well as between men and women and between rural and urban dwellers. Distinguishing between the different groups highlights the diversity in the types of economic actions that the Antigonish Movement sought to promote. Nevertheless, they all shared the basic common purpose of bettering the lot of their participants and allowing them to become the "Masters of Their Own Destiny."

The Fisheries Sector

The fisheries provided the Antigonish Movement with its first significant successes, forming the base from which its activities spread to other economic sectors and geographical areas. A number of factors contributed to the fact that the fisheries, specifically the inshore fisheries, became the focal point in the emergence of the Antigonish Movement. The inshore fisheries were the most exploited sector, with fishermen receiving low prices for their fish while also having to pay high prices for their inputs and supplies. The plight of the inshore fisheries was described by the 1928 Royal Commission on the Fisheries (the MacLean Commission) as follows: "[The inshore fisherman] still sells, haphazardly, at a low level of prices and buys at a high level of retail cost. He has had heretofore no power whatsoever of bargaining; and having had little to say about the selling price of his product, unlike other producers he has been forced to take whatever price he could get – a price sometimes below the actual cost of production."[42]

The existing dire economic situation was a manifestation of deep-rooted causes. The inshore fishermen had neither effective organizations of their own nor any government support system.[43] Furthermore, the fisheries sector was largely dualistic, as it was characterized by modern and traditional practices existing side by side. The modern sector was made up of the more efficient capital-intensive offshore fisheries, whose trawlers processed fish at a low cost and thus flooded the market in the 1920s and 1930s. The traditional approach was predominant in the inshore fisheries and was characterized by the use of hook and line, small boats, and inefficient methods of fish preservation. The offshore sector was able not only to undersell its traditional rival but also to offer higher-quality products.

The fisheries also constituted the sector where a great deal of organizational work had been done by Rev. Coady, prior to the Extension Department becoming fully operational, as a result of his appointment by the federal government to implement the findings of the MacLean Commission. In fact, the work of Rev. Coady had resulted in the establishment in 1930 of both local and regional fisheries organizations: shipping clubs at the local level and the United Maritime Fishermen (UMF) cooperative at the regional level. There was also the work of Rev. Tompkins in Canso and Little Dover.[44] Thus the activities of the Extension Department were largely a continuation of this earlier work.

The early focus on the fisheries also involved facing and overcoming myriad obstacles and challenges, which in many ways were perhaps greater than those of other sectors. There was certainly serious opposition from the local fish buyers as well as from the owners of fish-processing plants. The fishermen themselves appeared to be more individualistic and stubbornly independent than any other primacy producers.[45] Furthermore, many of the fishermen were deeply indebted to the local fish merchant, which meant that they had forfeited their economic freedom and could not participate in cooperative marketing schemes. For example, in the fishing community of Port Sapin, New Brunswick, "Only a dozen or so were economically free men, and it was evident that the others could not take part in co-operative ventures."[46] Given their precarious economic conditions, it was also risky to participate in something that was largely untried and to sever existing links with middlemen and the like, even if these links tended to be disadvantageous. Thus, for example, fishermen, whose livelihoods were precarious to begin with, had reason to fear the wrath of the fish buyers if they undertook a cooperative venture to market their own fish and it failed.

Another difficulty involved in organizing fishermen was the complex nature of their industry. In addition to the inshore-offshore division, the industry was divided into separate and widely different market segments. Some inshore fishermen were involved in high-value, high-quality products such as lobster, salmon, and oysters, whereas others concentrated on lower-priced, lower-quality products such as cod, haddock, hake, and mackerel. Such a wide diversity in the fish markets, in turn, created a diversity of interests and often conflicts among different groups of fishermen. The lobster fishermen, for example, favoured low prices for mackerel, which they used as bait, a practice that conflicted with the economic interests of mackerel fishermen. Furthermore, the industry employed a wide variety of processing methods, such as slating, smoking, drying, freezing, and canning, which did not necessarily yield comparable qualities despite using the same labour inputs. All of these factors made it very difficult to organize the inshore fisheries and to induce them to try new ventures.

Despite these difficulties, the Extension Department chose the fisheries as a prime area of operation for the emerging movement, and there was no turning back. The collective activities took various forms, depending on the needs of the community and the economic opportunities that were available. However, these activities centred on collective marketing as offering the best chances of success in capturing the relatively large economic rent payments, or windfalls, that the local fish merchants and buyers had been extracting from the fishermen. The existence of rudimentary but not very effective organizations, namely the UMF and the local shipping clubs, also offered an institutional base on which a more effective marketing network could be established.

The fisheries also possessed characteristics that were conducive to the sort of economic actions and methods that the Extension Department was interested in fostering. Many inshore fishing communities were geographically isolated and, moreover, comprised of people who were engaged in a highly entrepreneurial type of economic activity. It was also in the fisheries that economic opportunities could most easily be identified and action taken. Rev. Coady's advice to "find your lobster" reflects this notion.[47]

COOPERATIVE LOBSTER FACTORIES Lobster fishermen were among the first to respond to the call for the formation of study clubs followed by economic action involving the collective processing and marketing of lobsters, which constituted some of the most striking early successes of the young movement. One of the reasons behind the early success in lobster processing and marketing was that the offshore fleet could not enter this segment of the market, meaning that only the private buyers were in competition with the cooperatives.

The marketing of lobster initially presented a seemingly impossible obstacle to the cooperative approach. The principal market for lobster was in the New England states, centred on the famous Boston fish market. Unfortunately, given the existing transportation system, this market was located too far away to be able to ship large volumes of live lobsters, which were more valuable and hence could fetch a higher price. The only way to reach this rich market was predominantly through processed or canned lobsters, which, although less immediately lucrative than shipping live lobsters, still offered significant economic opportunities. The problem was the lack of processing facilities. Although there were already a few cooperative lobster-processing plants in Prince Edward Island and western Nova Scotia, for the fishermen of eastern Nova Scotia the possibility of owning their own lobster-processing plants seemed to be well beyond their collective reach. Arguably, the very idea bordered on absurdity. Yet, as we have already noted, the desolate and impover-

Table 3.8
Cooperative activities in the fisheries of eastern Nova Scotia, 1931–39

Year	*Cooperative lobster factories*	*Communities affected by lobster factories*	*Cooperative fish plants*
1931	—	—	—
1932	3	9	n.a.
1933	8	27	3
1934	12	50	5
1935	14	60	5
1936	17	75	10
1937	17	n.a.	11
1938	17	75	11
1939	17	n.a.	11

Source: St Francis Xavier University Archives, RG 30.3/25/965, RG 30.3/25/975, RG 30.3/25/991, RG 30.3/25/1000.

ished fishing community of Little Dover, instigated by an indomitable Rev. Tompkins, succeeded in the construction of its own lobster-processing plant. So too had the lobster fishermen of Havre Boucher. Other communities soon followed the lead, and their ventures also turned out to be extremely successful.

By 1933 eight cooperative lobster factories were in operation, in Havre Boucher, Port Felix, Larry's River, Little Dover, Petit de Grat, Alder Point, Ingonish, and Grand Etang, affecting some twenty-seven communities.[48] These accomplishments were impressive, especially since they took place less than two years after the introduction of the first study club. In fact, it was among the lobster fishermen that some of the more heroic and influential demonstrations of the meaning of cooperative action emerged. As Rev. Coady noted, "The idea caught the imagination of other groups and the movement has been running like a prairie fire along the shore of Maritime Canada."[49]

As shown in table 3.8, the conversion of vision and ideas into concrete economic projects took place relatively quickly in the lobster fishery, although the process itself was arduous. Once the initial eight lobster-processing plants had been established, the movement spread with relative ease over the next few years, with the number of plants more than doubling by 1936 and remaining fixed at seventeen during the rest of the decade. Moreover, the number of communities served by these cooperatives in eastern Nova Scotia nearly tripled from twenty-seven in 1933 to seventy-five by 1938.[50]

In the mid-1930s the movement was able to develop the more lucrative market of shipping live lobsters to Boston. The problem of the high mortality rate of live lobsters shipped from eastern Nova Scotia, which plagued the efforts of cooperatives in the early 1930s, was resolved by 1936 through the combined effort of St Francis Xavier University scientists, the Nova Scotia Department of Marketing, and the local fishing cooperatives. In the process, the Antigonish Movement, through the agency of the Extension Department, demonstrated how available resources and agents could be mobilized to solve a very pressing problem and enhance the options available to its participants – in this instance, those in the lobster sector. The mortality rate of lobsters in transit was reduced to a negligible 2 per cent, making this avenue a preferred choice for marketing larger lobsters.[51] The smaller, less valuable lobsters were still being canned at the cooperative lobster canneries and shipped at lower cost, ensuring the maximum income to the local fishermen. The option of shipping live lobsters reduced the pressure to establish more cooperative lobster factories, which may help to explain the stable number of such operations from 1936 until the end of the decade.

The success of the cooperative marketing of live and processed lobsters encouraged the fishermen to tackle the more difficult problem of the financial indebtedness to local fish buyers that plagued many of them, as well as the equally difficult problem of marketing lower value species. The financial indebtedness, which was widespread among the poorer fishermen, not only prevented many of them from joining cooperative marketing initiatives but also undermined the loyalty of the existing members. Some of these members were forced to take loans from the fish buyers in exchange for the future sale of fish products, thus endangering the existence of the cooperative. The introduction of credit unions into fishing communities helped to greatly alleviate these problems. Now the members of a fish cooperative, when they needed to borrow, had an alternate and less costly source of credit. The emergence of credit unions served to strengthen cooperative fish marketing. At the same time, however, the local credit unions also benefited from the higher income of the members of these cooperatives, who found it convenient and profitable to deposit their savings with them. Thus, as the movement solved the pressing economic problems of its members, and in the process overcame myriad constraints, it also strengthened and integrated its own institutional structure and operations.

OTHER COOPERATIVE FISH PLANTS Other cooperative fish factories also emerged during the 1930s, involving primarily the sale of fresh and cured fish, especially herring, cod, mackerel, and haddock. Like the lobster factories, these plants emerged in 1933, with their number, as evident from the data in the last column of table 3.8, peaking in the mid-1930s – in this case, in 1937 at eleven – and then remaining constant for the rest of the decade. The number of fish plants almost quadrupled from 1933 to 1937, going from three to eleven.

The marketing of lower-value fish products was in many ways more difficult than the marketing of lobster. There was fierce competition from the more efficient offshore fleets as well as from other countries. Furthermore, the quality of fish varied considerably between different fishermen, and the small scale of the operations of cooperative enterprises made it difficult to maintain a high-quality product, affecting their ability to secure and maintain markets.[52] These difficulties explain, at least in part, why cooperative marketing and processing of lower-value species proceeded more slowly, as only three fish-marketing ventures were established by 1933, affecting a smaller number of communities than was the case with the lobster sector.

Some of these fish cooperatives also branched out into other and often unrelated activities. For example, on top of canning fish such as salmon and mackerel, there was also some involvement in canning foods such as blueberries and foxberries.[53] These items found ready markets and contributed to broadening the economic base of various communities. Thus some of the plants constructed for the processing of the fishermen's catch also promoted the processing of other primary products. Such a diversification was consistent with and facilitated by the fact that many of those involved in the fisheries were also involved in other activities, particularly small-scale and largely subsistent farming.

The significance of successful economic ventures in fisheries can hardly be overstated. They not only provided many fishermen with some degree of economic independence and higher income but also encouraged new forms of cooperative activity, such as credit unions and consumers' stores, in various fishing communities. In addition, they encouraged and stimulated other primary producers – farmers and woodlot owners – and industrial workers to engage in cooperative economic activities. The spread of the movement to other economic sectors was facilitated by the fact that many of the fishermen were also part-time farmers and woodlot owners and had family connections with industrial workers.[54]

The Agricultural Sector

Farmers were generally better organized, both economically and politically, than any other occupational group in eastern Nova Scotia. A wide range of services and assistance had been made available to farmers by the federal and provincial governments. In Nova Scotia the provincial government had encouraged the cooperative marketing of farm products more than a decade before the establishment of the Extension Department. In 1917 Rev. Dr Hugh MacPherson (a priest-professor popularly known as "Little Doc Hugh"), who had been appointed as the first agricultural representative east of Ontario, organized the first cooperative marketing of wool, lamb, and hogs.[55] In the 1920s the number of agricultural representatives had increased, as had the number of cooperative initiatives. At the same time, the Government of Nova Scotia established and operated several abattoirs to encourage greater agricultural production and cooperative marketing. Furthermore, various local marketing clubs were organized to market livestock in the Maritimes.[56] In 1927 there was the establishment of the Maritime Livestock Board, which gave rise to the Moncton-based Canadian Livestock Co-operative (CLC) – the precursor of Maritime Co-operative Services – in the early 1930s.[57] The various initiatives were not very successful and did not always receive the support of the farmers whom they were designed to help. In addition, they raised strong opposition from the private processors and packers as well as from the less politically strong livestock drovers. By the end of the decade, the main abattoir in Halifax was closed, and many of the shipping clubs were either inactive or on the verge of collapse, which in turn endangered the operation of the regional cooperative marketing organization.

The farmers turned out to be more difficult to organize than the inshore fishermen for a number of reasons. Production activities undertaken by farmers were more heterogeneous than those undertaken by fishermen. Moreover, compared to the fisheries, farming was neither as geographically concentrated nor as commercially oriented. Additional factors that conspired to increase the difficulty of cooperative economic action among farmers included the low value of produce, competition from other more efficient producing areas, and the general uncertainty surrounding agricultural output. More important, whereas in the fisheries cooperative economic action generally involved taking over processing and marketing activities, in the case of agricultural produce it involved, to a great degree, the actual development of products and markets. Consequently, fewer highly visible and specific cooperative actions were undertaken among farmers. However, farmers were not left out of the process, as they engaged in a wide array of cooperative activities ranging from cooperative purchasing to the cooperative marketing of produce. Nevertheless, even in the area of marketing of farm produce, there were serious problems. The generally small scale of production, which Coady recognized in his reference to "driblet producers,"[58] made it difficult to maintain standards of quality and, at the same time, raised the cost of both production and marketing. Equally serious was the lack of loyalty among farmers to their own cooperative organizations and their willingness to free ride.[59]

Despite these problems, the Extension Department was able to fully incorporate the agricultural sector into its grassroots movement, utilizing the existing organizations as a base for its own network of institutions and, in the process, saving a great deal of time and resources. Its educational programs and study clubs among farmers eventually led to the strengthening of the local shipping clubs, enabling them "to evolve into something more permanent"[60] as they became incorporated into farmers' marketing, supply, and consumers' cooperatives. The CLC was saved from possible failure by being transformed into a fully integrated cooperative wholesale organization and, together with Sydney and later Antigonish branches, "took on all co-operative activities of the farmers, both in the producers and consumers fields."[61]

In the mid-1930s the Government of Nova Scotia established a marketing division within the Department of Agriculture with the mandate to promote cooperative marketing of farm, fish, and forest products. Very close collaboration quickly developed between this new division and the Extension Department, resulting in a new wave of cooperative marketing activities not only in the agricultural sector but also in the fisheries and to a lesser extent in the forestry sector. By 1937 cooperative activities among the farmers had become so well established that the movement began to enter a more difficult phase of economic operations, namely the processing of farm products. The initial incursion into the area of processing took the form of a modern milk-pasteurizing plant in the Sydney area owned and operated by the farmers.[62] Far more ambitious ventures would be undertaken by the farmers in the following decades that would have a significant impact on the whole movement.

Cooperative Action in the Financial Sector: Credit Unions

The credit union concept had been brought to the attention of Nova Scotia farmers in the early 1920s. However, the idea of establishing and operating their own bank appeared to them to be so far-fetched that it elicited no serious interest. Although the credit union was in fact the most simple and most secure form of cooperative organization, it was difficult to "sell" this idea to a group of poor and often marginalized primary producers without a prior education program. Credit unions differ from the other economic activities described above in two fundamental ways. First, they entail the mobilization of saving and financial capital, and second, they are not directly productive in the conventional sense of the term. Essentially, the creation of credit unions allows local savings to be mobilized, which in turn can be used for local productive activity. This mobilization was, of course, an important consideration given that, for the most part, people would not have had access to any other sources of financing and credit, aside from largely informal and expensive sources, including the merchants and middlemen.

When the Extension Department began to organize its first study clubs in 1931, it quickly realized that most of these groups were in dire need of a simple and feasible economic organization that could serve as a basis for their study and discussion. In fact, many of the initial study clubs failed because they could not, on their own, find suitable and feasible projects to organize. In order to help solve the problem, in 1931 the leaders of the emerging movement invited Roy Bergengren, a noted expert of the US Credit Union Movement, to speak about credit unions at the annual Rural Conference in Antigonish. The concept

Table 3.9
Credit unions in the whole of Nova Scotia, 1931–39

Year	*Credit unions*	*Membership*
1931	—	—
1932	8	n.a.
1933	19	n.a.
1934	27	n.a.
1935	45	9,000
1936	65	12,000
1937	90	n.a.
1938	142	22,000
1939	170	30,000

Source: St Francis Xavier University Archives, RG 30.3/25/975.

immediately caught the attentions of the hundreds of study club delegates, and Bergengren was asked to assist in the drafting of the provincial credit union legislation, which was completed in 1932. That same year, a total of eight credit unions were organized through the study club mechanism. The study clubs and the credit unions seemed to form a perfect match. On the one hand, the study clubs needed the credit union idea to give them focus and motivation, and on the other hand, the credit unions depended on the study clubs not only for their establishment but also to motivate and train members so that they could serve on their boards of directors and various committees.

After the passing of the credit union legislation by the Government of Nova Scotia in 1932, a truly phenomenal expansion in credit unions took place. The extent of credit union activity over the decade is summarized in table 3.9.

According to Extension Department sources, by 1935 the total savings generated by credit unions were in the neighbourhood of $150,000 for the whole of Nova Scotia.[63] The data presented in table 3.10 paint a picture of very small operations able to mobilize rather limited amounts of resources. For example, none of them had total deposits in excess of $5,000 or total outstanding loans in excess of $5,000. Some of these operations, however, grew quite rapidly. By 1935, for example, the New Waterford Credit Union had a membership of 700 and total savings of $16,000, which were kept in constant circulation to satisfy its members' needs.[64]

Table 3.10
Sample of credit unions of eastern Nova Scotia as of May 1934

Credit union	*Membership*	*Savings ($)*	*Outstanding loans ($)*
Reserve Mines	309	4,875.46	3,530.00
Caledonia	265	2,670.25	1,100.00
Glace Bay	118	386.00	140.00
Glace Bay Fishermen	51	254.00	205.50
Coady (New Aberdeen)	287	3,079.92	1,550.00
McIntyre (Passchendaele)	176	3,300.00	1,500.00
New Waterford	220	1,008.00	245.00

Note: This sample includes credit union organizations that had been in operation for periods ranging from twelve months to two weeks as of May 1934.

Source: St Francis Xavier University Archives, RG 30.3/25/991.

The rapid expansion in the number of credit unions during the 1930s was the result of a number of factors. They were mostly community-based operations working out of parish halls and other such places, meaning that their fixed costs were minimal and that their break-even point was close to zero. Thus they could function even with a small number of members or very little savings and credit. Essentially, the cooperative activity was limited to two simple transactions: saving (usually once a week) and borrowing. Thus credit unions were easy to manage, and their operations were both inexpensive and easily understood by the membership.

Credit unions also faced only limited competition from other financial intermediaries, and there was very little institutional opposition to them. The lobster factories faced opposition from the private processors, the consumers' stores were opposed by the merchants, and the farmers' co-ops generated strong opposition from the private food processors and livestock dealers, whereas there were no institutions opposing the establishment of credit unions. The commercial banks were generally not involved in the business of providing credit to primary producers or industrial workers, who had limited earning power and lacked creditworthiness. The local merchants or fish buyers, who occasionally provided credit to farmers or fishermen, were concerned more with maintaining their primary business activity of selling consumer goods or buying fish than with acting as conduits for saving or with providing credit, which they normally considered a "business sideline."

The advantages associated with credit unions – simplicity, low risk, wide application, easy management, and the absence of institutional opposition – were precisely the reasons why these institutions were brought into the Antigonish Movement and the reasons they expanded so rapidly. Not only did the number of credit unions expand very rapidly, but this expansion also became more pronounced over time during the latter part of the 1930s. In the province of Nova Scotia as a whole, the number of credit unions increased from 8 in 1932 to 65 in 1936 and then to an impressive 170 in 1939.[65] Contributing to this expansion was that the already established cooperative organizations were branching out into new fields of cooperative activity. For many of these, expansion into the financial sector, through the establishment of credit unions, constituted perhaps the most obvious option. Thus many fishing or agricultural-marketing cooperatives organized credit unions among their members to help them deal with financial problems and to strengthen their own operations. The ease with which credit unions could be set up and their mass character – everybody at various times saves and/or borrows – contributed to this process. Thus, unlike the possibility for activities such as cooperatives in the fisheries, the potential for the establishment of credit unions was great and virtually open-ended. As time passed and people saw the effects and advantages of credit unions, the demand for them increased. Properly harnessed, the credit unions could become – and in some cases were – the foundation for an emerging dynamic and effective cooperative sector. As a result, they constituted an indispensable cog in the emerging integrated economic system that was being put in place by the Antigonish Movement. The movement had recognized early on that there were substantial financial resources that could be collectively mobilized to serve as an important source of credit and financing.[66]

These credit unions served to mobilize limited but nevertheless important financial resources by absorbing local savings, which could in turn be used to meet the pressing needs for credit among the membership as well as to finance other cooperative economic activities.[67] At the same time, they also lessened the power of noninstitutional moneylenders. In short, they provided a cooperative form of organized and highly effective financial intermediation.

In 1937 another factor came into play, which promoted another wave of newly organized credit unions. This new factor was the creation of the Nova Scotia Credit Union League, a central organization that was able to use the surplus funds from the established credit unions to assist with the organization of new entities. The credit union sector was thus able to establish the umbrella organization that was necessary for its propagation over the longer term.

The Consumer Sector

The consumer sector was believed to be of particular significance to the Antigonish Movement. Arguably, it was through consumers' cooperative stores and the like, rather than through marketing or the processing of primary products and production in general, that the people were ultimately able to regain control over their economic destiny.[68] According to Rev. Coady, the Industrial Revolution had deprived the workers of the ownership and control of production and, at the same time, had removed industrial activity from the rural communities, making them dependent on and subservient to the urban areas where much of the existing industry was relocated.[69] As a consequence, substantial numbers of people were being forced to move to the cities in search of work. The end result was the depopulation and the stagnation of the countryside and the rise in the power of the urban areas. The problem was compounded when the people in the rural communities lost control of their stores, banks, and other service organizations.

Following this line of argument, to regain lost control and economic independence, the people had to enter the consumer field on a cooperative basis and, in the process, begin to reverse the "Great Default" of their forebears. However, this entry into the consumer field would, at best, be a first step in the long process of the common people reclaiming their economic sovereignty. The cooperative stores would gradually lead to the creation of their own wholesale organizations, which in turn would lead to the establishment of the cooperative manufacturing base. In the words of Rev. Coady, "Consumer co-operation usually begins in the retail field and goes on through wholesales, to factories. This is a natural process."[70] Furthermore, the cooperative wholesalers and manufacturers would link with central cooperative marketing organizations selling primary goods such as fish, farm, and forestry products. In this way, the economic loop would be closed, and the cooperative sector, as envisioned in the "Big

Table 3.11
Cooperative stores and buying clubs in eastern Nova Scotia, 1931–39

Year	*Cooperative stores*	*New stores*	*Cooperative buying clubs*
1931	—	—	—
1932	2	2	n.a.
1933	4	2	n.a.
1934	6	2	3
1935	8	2	10
1936	18	10	5
1937	25	7	3
1938	39	14	4
1939	43	4	4

Source: St Francis Xavier University Archives, RG 30.3/25/975.

Picture," would become a fully integrated economic system, giving the primary producers and industrial workers, both as consumers and producers, control of their economic destiny.

The vision of using the cooperative stores as a stepping stone to economic sovereignty was lofty and inspiring but, unfortunately, far removed from the harsh reality of eastern Nova Scotia in the 1930s. Although cooperative stores were founded in some industrial areas, such as Sydney and Stellarton,[71] even before the turn of the century in the case of the latter, the movement found it very difficult to establish its own institutions. Two cooperative stores were established in 1932, but as table 3.11 indicates, their number increased at the slow pace of two new ones per year until 1935 and then more than quintupled by 1939.

There were a number of reasons for the consumer sector lagging behind all other sectors. At the retail level, there was strong competition not only from the local country stores but also from the more efficient and larger chain stores and the "mail-order houses ... that are using all the devices of the modern merchandising game to break up the cooperatives."[72] One of these "devices" was the widespread practice of selling on credit, which afforded them, given the conditions of poverty among the population, a definite advantage over the cooperative stores, especially those that, following the Rochdale Principles, insisted on cash trading.[73] Another factor discouraging the opening of new cooperative stores was the very large monetary expenditures on buildings, equipment, and inventories that were required, making their operations not only more difficult to fund but also more complex to manage efficiently and therefore more risky. In effect, their threshold size was greater than that of the other projects instituted during the early stages of the movement. The movement attempted to overcome these difficulties by organizing buying clubs, which would give the members and the new managers some experience and also the benefits of cooperation in the form of lower prices. However, this approach was not entirely successful, as the buying clubs were plagued by a number of problems of their own that emanated, in particular, from their unstable and informal nature. In short, they lacked the institutional integrity that was required for successful economic action, especially over time.

In 1936 the situation changed dramatically, with the number of consumers' stores more than doubling from the previous year. Moreover, the high rate of expansion lasted for the rest of the decade. An important contributing factor in the rapid expansion of consumers' cooperatives was the activities of the Women's Work program. Adopting the "Woman with the Basket" approach pioneered by the British Canadian Co-operative of Sydney Mines during the previous decades, the Extension Department sought to win the support of women through the "Women's Pages" of the *Extension Bulletin*, direct contact with women study clubs, and various other means. Indeed, it was only after women, particularly those in the rural areas, came on board that consumers' cooperatives began to flourish.

Moreover, as noted earlier, by 1936 the movement had successfully overcome many of its initial organizational difficulties and had created its own internal dynamics to rapidly become a truly mass movement, with each of its sectors – fisheries, agriculture, finance, and others – experiencing accelerated expansion. Another contributing factor in the rapid expansion of the cooperative stores was the incorporation into the movement of the local shipping clubs and their central organization, the CLC, which was converted into an integrated cooperative wholesaler serving the needs of both consumers and producers – in the case of the latter, by supplying inputs to farmers and fishermen. This was the first attempt to integrate the economic interests of primary producers, namely farmers and fishermen, with those of consumers. Moreover, there were also efforts to branch out into other

Table 3.12
Other cooperative enterprises in eastern Nova Scotia, 1931–39

Year	*Other cooperative enterprises*
1931	—
1932	n.a.
1933	n.a.
1934	2
1935	2
1936	2
1937	7
1938	7
1939	10

Source: St Francis Xavier University Archives, RG 30.3/25/975.

areas, such as the provision of cooperative health services.[74] By the end of the decade, it appeared that the movement's vision of the people regaining control over their economic destiny was beginning to converge with reality. In fact, the vision was beginning to shape the economic reality in its own image.

Other Cooperative Economic Activities

A wide range of other cooperative enterprises, often referred to as community industries, were also organized. These involved small-scale industries set up to increase the self-sufficiency of the community while also providing employment for local labour. Moreover, these industries depended largely on locally available resources. Sawmills, woodworking factories, and milk pasteurization facilities are examples of the activities that were undertaken. Some of these were intended not only to be commercial concerns but also to satisfy immediate local requirements. The extent to which such activities proliferated in eastern Nova Scotia is summarized in table 3.12.

These sorts of enterprises were forays into manufacturing activities. As such, they were intended not only to expand the economic base but also to generate powerful demonstration and spillover effects. However, these community industries began to take hold and expand only in the latter part of the 1930s as the movement, having emerged and experienced notable successes in its initial endeavours, was becoming poised to enter a new phase. These community industries were more difficult to establish in the initial rounds of the study clubs approach. Over time, however, the increase in technical sophistication, knowledge, and group entrepreneurship allowed for a widening of the movement's economic activities and enterprises, and additional components of the Big Picture were put in place.

Other Economic Initiatives

Other initiatives, which were fundamentally economic in nature, included the establishment of self-help clubs, cooperative housing, burial societies, and cooperative medical insurance. Through self-help clubs, individuals who were unemployed were able to barter their labour for goods and services, thus establishing an alternate non-monetized labour market. Moreover, through these clubs, people were able to engage in cooperative farming on land provided for this purpose with help from the provincial Department of Agriculture. These self-help clubs, which numbered about thirty-seven in 1933, were able to mobilize idle human and land resources for productive purposes.

Housing cooperatives, which are included in the tabulations in table 3.12, addressed one of the fundamental needs of people. The most prominent example of cooperative housing under the auspices of the Antigonish Movement was, as already noted, Tompkinsville in Reserve Mines, which formally opened on 13 August 1938. Tompkinsville was instigated by Rev. Tompkins after he was transferred to the Cape Breton community and subsequent to the work of Mary Arnold, a prominent cooperative housing expert from New York and one of the many notable volunteers who were invited to assist the movement. It also highlighted the importance of legislation in allowing cooperative activity.[75] Although, overall, cooperative housing was not particularly prominent in the 1930s, it became increasingly so later on, with the example of Tompkinsville looming particularly large.

CONCLUSION

The 1930s was the period when the Antigonish Movement emerged and achieved some of its most celebrated results. These outcomes appear even more surprising against the backdrop of the widespread unemployment and poverty of the Great Depression and given that they were achieved largely by the work of the people themselves: farmers, fishermen, and industrial workers. These outstanding achievements were not without setbacks, initial failures, difficulties, risks, and opposition. Indeed, at virtually every phase of their involvement, the Extension Department and the people who participated in the various activities had to overcome serious obstacles, accept various degrees of risk, and bounce back in the face of failure. The movement's first rudimentary organizations, the fledging study clubs, "were sickly things."[76] Even when the movement, against great odds, was able to organize its first economic organizations, such as lobster factories, small credit unions, and marketing cooperatives, it had to overcome widespread pessimism, disbelief, institutional opposition, inertia, and grinding poverty. That it was able to do so and in the process break out of these initial "beach heads" in order to reach the wider masses of people serves as a testament to the inherent power of the movement. In every sector it entered, the movement had to deal with specific problems and difficulties and had to develop relevant and often unique courses of action.

Despite these difficulties, the movement achieved what many believed to be the impossible feat of establishing a network of efficient economic organizations that were created, owned, and operated by the people themselves. By 1936 the movement had caught the imagination of thousands of people in eastern Nova Scotia and various other parts of maritime Canada, and it subsequently spread even further afield. Such success can be attributed to a number of factors. Foremost among these factors was the unshakable belief of the movement's leaders in the validity of the vision. Another contributing factor was its integrated and comprehensive approach to development. Each type of economic organization and educational tool used by the movement (e.g., credit unions, marketing cooperatives, regional marketing organizations, cooperative stores, study clubs, regional conferences, and leadership courses) had previously been introduced to the people of Nova Scotia, and each had failed to be accepted and adopted on any significant scale. However, when these tools and organizations were integrated into a comprehensive program of development and were combined with an inspiring vision, the results far exceeded the wildest expectations. Another factor contributing to the success of the movement was the emergence and development of local leaders

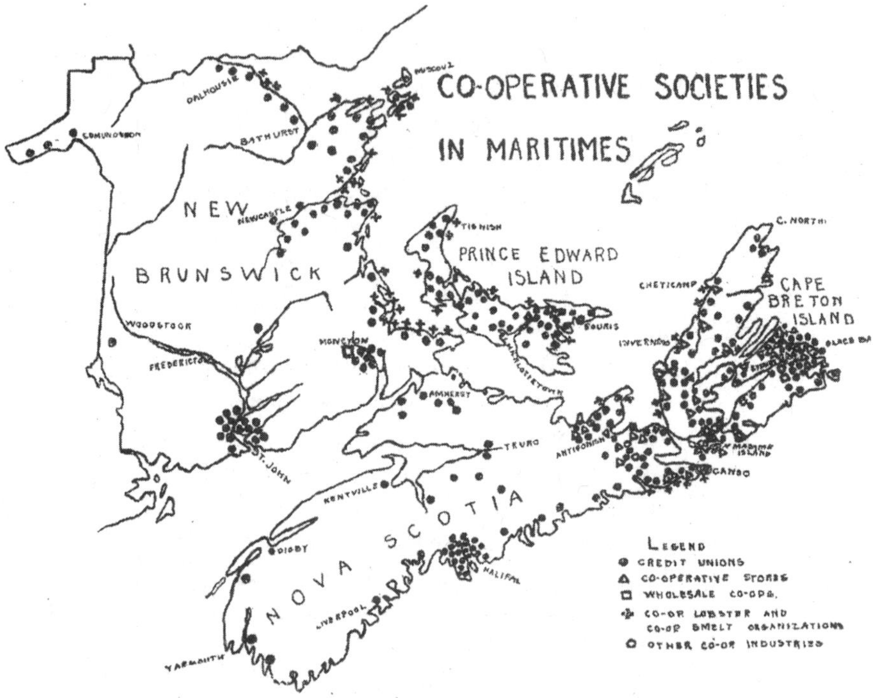

Figure 3.2 Cooperatives in the Maritimes as of 1939
Source: Extension Bulletin, 3 February 1939, 8.

through the study clubs, leadership courses, and the like. Finally, the discipline, courage, sacrifice, and hard work of the people themselves cannot be overlooked. Since the economic institutions that were put in place were legal entities, we must also recognize the important work that was done to establish the legislative framework.

Despite all of this, however, what was accomplished during the 1930s was the easy part, essentially involving the redistribution of rent payments. The hard part, involving the fundamental restructuring of the economy and the exploitation of new resources and opportunities, was still to come. Nevertheless, as shown in figure 3.2, by 1939 a highly heterogeneous network of cooperative enterprises and initiatives covering the broad economic spectrum of the maritime region was being put in place in the shape of the Big Picture.

4

The Years of Turbulence, 1940–49

INTRODUCTION

The 1940s began concurrently with the outbreak of the Second World War, catching the Antigonish Movement at its most critical time. The war effort depended on industrial capacity, technological sophistication, and the mobilization of the whole population and all available resources.[1]

The massive war effort, ironically, brought an end to the Great Depression, generated full employment, dramatically increased the country's industrial capacity, and raised the level of personal income and the stock of accumulated savings. Throughout the Maritimes, thousands of young men and women left the farms, fishing villages, and towns to join the armed forces. The miners went back to work, breaking production records, farmers and fishermen supplied vastly increased levels of output, and local factories and shipyards produced ammunition, planes, ships, and other items required by the war effort.

Just prior to the outbreak of the war, the federal Department of Fisheries had asked the Extension Department to take on the task of organizing the fishermen throughout the Maritimes, increasing the size of its grant to enable a large increase in its complement of fieldworkers. Within a year, however, the war conditions brought about a dramatic reversal in the operations of the Extension Department, from dynamic expansion to severe reduction in personnel and budget.[2] The shift from expansion to retrenchment, despite severely testing its flexibility and ingenuity, did not undermine the young movement. The Extension Department was able to fundamentally redesign its education program without losing its sense of direction.[3] Moreover, the existing cooperative sector, after some initial difficulties, adjusted to the war conditions and emerged from the conflict with a stronger financial base, increased membership, and a significantly greater volume of economic activity.[4]

The postwar conditions bought additional challenges to the Antigonish Movement. Its strong and experienced leadership group was broken up, creating a leadership vacuum that Rev. Moses Coady alone could not fill. The cooperative sector required additional training to adjust to changing circumstances. The accessibility of radio presented the Extension Department with new opportunities to expand its education programming but also posed significant dangers and pitfalls. Furthermore, ever-increasing demands for assistance, coming from other parts of Canada and abroad, imposed additional pressures on the limited available human and material resources of the Extension Department. Nevertheless, the movement was able to face these challenges and emerged from this turbulent decade remarkably strong, at least on the surface, and confident of its future progress. There was an unmistakable belief that something fundamental had been achieved.

THE ANTIGONISH MOVEMENT DURING THE WAR YEARS

The war years, 1939–45, came at a most inopportune time in the life of the young movement. The fisheries grant was reduced. Many fieldworkers and volunteers joined the armed forces. Moreover, St Francis Xavier University experienced financial difficulties of its own, adding additional pressure and uncertainty. The response of the Extension Department was to gradually reduce its staff and radically redesign its education program. The war affected the young movement in other ways as well. For example, changing international trade patterns and wartime restrictions, particularly the moratorium on capital expenditures, posed the danger of greatly reducing the activities of the various cooperative organizations and, in some cases, putting their very existence at risk.

The movement's future appeared particularly bleak during the early war years. Even Rev. Coady seemed to have been stripped of his normal optimism, as he noted: "At the present time, all the varied activities of the Department are being co-ordinated with the aim of assisting the war effort, and preparing for the *dubious aftermath*."[5] However, as the war progressed, the economic situation proved to be less bleak, and there was a fundamental shift toward greater optimism for the postconflict years.

During the later stages of the war, as its tide was shifting to the Allied side, the attention of the policymakers at the national and international levels turned to the question of planning for the postwar socio-economic order. The search for a new socio-economic order to replace the chaos of the Great Depression started as early as 1943 with the creation of the House of Commons Committee on Reconstruction and Rehabilitation, which invited Rev. Coady to present a brief on behalf of the Antigonish Movement.[6] Such planning was also carried out at the provincial level, with representatives of the movement fully participating in the deliberations. Thus the movement had become a force that was recognized by different levels of government.

The failure of the unfettered free enterprise system associated with the Great Depression prompted the planners of the new order to search for alternate solutions to the pressing economic problems of unemployment and poverty. Representatives of the successful movement, which had already caught international as well as national attention, were eagerly sought for their advice. The leaders of the Antigonish Movement, particularly Rev. Coady, were called upon to make numerous presentations before various committees, commissions, boards, and similar bodies at the provincial and national levels both during and after the war. Following the war, these invitations expanded to the international level, culminating with presentations to the US State Department and to United Nations agencies in 1949.

The Extension Department viewed such invitations as an opportunity both to gain greater exposure for the movement and its vision and to strengthen its relations with provincial and federal governments, as well as with the international community. Indeed, some tangible benefits did accrue from these activities. The fisheries grant was significantly increased during the postwar period, and the wartime campaign conducted by the Canadian Taxpayers Association to tax the profits of cooperatives was successfully blunted.[7] The Extension Department was very effective in carrying out the important function of keeping abreast of the legislative area to ensure that the interests of its institutions were promoted rather than undermined. Furthermore, additional publicity of the movement helped to spread its influence to other provinces in Canada as well as abroad.

Changes in the Socio-economic Conditions during the War Years

There were a number of important changes in the local environment as a result of the war. First, the enlisting of many young people generated a depopulation of some communities, with some detrimental effects on both the number and the effectiveness of study clubs. Prior to the war, the study clubs and cooperative enterprises were well represented, including in leadership positions, by young people who were normally expected to carry on well into the future while also adding dynamism to the movement.[8] Second, the national emergency created by the war diverted much of the attention and energy of the population away from other activities and concerns, including economic projects and social reform, and toward increasing war production. Winning the war and getting the young soldiers who had gone overseas home safely and as soon as possible became the primary concern. Third, the demand for war production brought about a situation of full employment. Indeed, during the war years, Canada's industrial capacity increased by 80 per cent, and personal incomes more than doubled.[9] At the same time, vast amounts of savings were mobilized for the war effort through the sale of "Victory Bonds."[10] Nova Scotia shared in the general prosperity and economic expansion, although not to the same extent as other parts of Canada. The demands of the war effort created a shortage of labour that was overcome by the entry of women into the labour force. As a result, women emerged from the war effort as more active participants in the production process.

The changes that took place in the socio-economic environment affected the activities of the Antigonish Movement in two fundamental ways. On the one hand, they reduced the amount of free time that people had available for study and implementing economic projects. On the other hand, since people were employed, the need for study and for the implementation of economic projects was less urgent.[11] These effects were counterbalanced by the fact that the institutions that the movement put in place in the 1930s also played a role in the war effort.

Adjustment to the Movement's Vision and Goals

The leaders of the Antigonish Movement recognized that the war years were extraordinary times. The original vision of the movement, formulated in the 1920s and propagated during the 1930s, could not be applied to wartime conditions. The call for the common people to become "Masters of Their Own Destiny" had been couched in terms of criticism of the existing socio-economic order based on the free enterprise system inherent in the "Great Default of the People." In conditions of endemic unemployment, poverty, and exploitation of both primary producers and industrial workers, such criticism was widespread and justified. The goal of the Antigonish Movement had been to correct the inherent weaknesses of capitalism through fundamental social reform and the creation of an alternative and superior economic system based on cooperation, equality, and efficiency. The criticism of the prevailing system had been confined primarily to the economic and social sphere but not to the political system of democracy and political freedom. In fact, the movement's goal was to defend and strengthen democracy, which was weakened by unemployment and poverty and under attack by the newly emergent totalitarian systems of communism and fascism, both of which were perceived as inefficient and wasteful.[12] Just as fascism had led to the militarization that had preceded war and destruction, communism had led to massive misallocations of resources and loss of freedom.[13]

In wartime conditions, criticism of the existing system would have been perceived both as unpatriotic and as unethical given that it could undermine the morale of the population, weaken the national resolve, and endanger the lives of the soldiers at the front. Although the goal of "fundamental social reforms" were enshrined in the "Six Principles" by Harry Johnson in 1944, and accepted by Rev. Coady a year later, the rhetoric used in speeches and writings often differed markedly from that of earlier times. The participants were urged to contribute to the wartime production. Miners were praised for achieving production records, credit union members were exhorted to invest their savings in "Victory Bonds," and farmers and fishermen were encouraged to increase production. At the same time, women's groups were organized to increase home and handicrafts production in order to alleviate the scarcity of consumer goods. These exhortations were very effective, as there was no inherent conflict between the objectives of the movement and the national goals. As the movement made contributions to the national war effort, which it proudly recorded and displayed, it also strengthened its own institutions and prestige.

Hidden beneath the rhetoric of patriotism and contributions to the war effort was the fundamental desire and objective of the survival of the Antigonish Movement. Thus the movement strove to consolidate its gains and to strengthen its membership and financial base for further expansion in the postwar era. Despite having to adapt to the requirements of an extraordinary event, the movement remained true to its vision. Its survival depended greatly on the effectiveness of the Extension Department's education program and on the survival of its economic institutions. Both of these were subjected to a great deal of uncertainty, especially in the early war years when the outcome was in doubt.

RESTRUCTURING THE EDUCATION PROGRAM The complex and highly effective education program of the 1930s, consisting of mass meetings, study clubs, monthly rallies, leadership courses, circulating libraries, the *Extension Bulletin*, the annual Rural and Industrial Conferences, and other instruments, could not be replicated under highly restrictive war conditions, with a significantly reduced budget, and with limited staff, including volunteers. Moreover, the traditional program was already in decline, even as early as the late 1930s when the movement was spreading across the maritime region, further stretching the Extension Department's resources, and the responsibility for organizing study clubs was passed onto the cooperative sector. As well, with the establishment of the Nova Scotia Co-operative Educational Council at the end of 1939, the Extension Department had brought the cooperative institutions into the educational fold. This process was further accentuated by the later formation of the Nova Scotia Co-operative Union as an affiliate of the Co-operative Union of Canada.[14] The Educational Council was financed primarily by the cooperative sector, and although it placed some emphasis on education at the local level, it had a narrower focus in tune more with the immediate needs of the cooperative enterprises than with those of the movement as a whole. This narrowing of focus became more pronounced as cooperatives also began to finance their own separate educational activities.[15]

In terms of the basic education program of the Extension Department, the war years called for innovative and effective adaptations if the movement was to survive and remain strong. The integrative nature of the different components that characterized the education strategy of the Extension Department in the 1930s, whereby each element played a unique role, and which constituted the source of the strength for the movement, had now become a major weakness. It would not permit piecemeal adjustments but required fundamental, even if only temporary, restructuring and redesigning of the entire program.

The need to make changes in order to ensure that the movement survived became evident early in the war period. The study clubs, which constituted part of the foundation for the entire movement and its education program, began to flounder, weakened by the enlisting of many young men and the long hours that those who stayed behind were required to work. As Ida Delaney points out, the "coal miners suddenly found themselves on full employment for the first time in many years. The young men rushed to join the armed forces. Very soon Canada's fuel requirements became so critical that the federal government 'froze' the miners in the pits and no more enlistment was permitted. But the loss of so many young miners was serious and the men who remained worked very hard. Their performance in the war effort was exemplary. They worked six days a week, often with overtime, and they 'hung up' records."[16]

Moreover, the role of the study clubs, at least in some instances, had changed. Whereas in the 1930s their purpose had been to establish cooperative economic enterprises, in the 1940s study clubs were being formed around already existing cooperative enterprises. As a result, as Delaney points out, study club numbers and attendance declined, as fewer people aside from "directors and committee members" felt the need to keep on studying.[17] They were no longer organized following mass meetings, which in the past had provided them with a direct link to the Extension Department and the vision of the movement. In the process, both their nature and purpose were compromised.

Along with the weak and ineffective study clubs, many of which existed only on paper,[18] the movement also found itself without the Rural and Industrial Conferences, which had been suspended in 1940, as well as without the leadership course.[19] Thus the individual components of the program were dramatically either suspended or downgraded, and the entire structure that had been systematically and meticulously put in place during the 1930s seems to have collapsed like a deck of cards.

The collapse of the entire education program greatly endangered the whole movement, as this program was its lifeline, circulating through and nourishing the entire system. There was a desperate need to replace the older education program, even if only on a temporary basis, with a simplified and less costly alternative in tune with the prevailing conditions and significantly reduced budget but also effective in sustaining the movement.

As a part of its response to the new set of circumstances, the Extension Department transferred additional education-related responsibilities to the cooperative sector. Thus, for example, the *Extension Bulletin* became the *Maritime Co-operator*, funded by the credit unions and cooperatives.[20] The Extension Department's new educational program eventually came to consist of two main components: (1) the so-called "short course," which replaced the four-week leadership course as well as the study clubs;[21] and (2) Regional and Vocational Conferences. These components were to be supported by the "University of the Air" radio program, which materialized in the postwar years. The desire to employ radio programs was given impetus by the establishment of Atlantic Broadcasters Limited to finance the radio station CJFX, which became operational in 1943.[22]

The short course, the key component of the new program, was largely a community-based course of three to five days conducted in the field by Extension Department workers with the support of agricultural representatives and the registrar of cooperatives. These courses dealt with the philosophical and historical dimensions of cooperatives and collective action in general as well as with the technical aspects of various projects. Both lectures and group discussions were employed – an approach that Delaney refers to as "The study club technique."[23]

Little information is provided concerning the content and fundamental purpose of these courses in the official documents of the Extension Department. However, much can be gleaned from the description provided by Delaney, who notes that each course "included instruction in group marketing for fishermen and farmers, agricultural topics, principles of co-operation, credit union practices, problems of consumer co-operatives."[24] Furthermore, according to

Table 4.1
Short courses during the war years of 1940–44

Year	*One-week courses*	*Average registration per course*
1940–41	11	30–80
1941–42	14	30–80
1942–43	20	n.a.
1943–44	22	50

Source: St Francis Xavier University Archives, RG 30.3/25/1018, RG 30.3/25/1023, RG 30.3/25/1028.

Delaney, "The short course was a valuable educational method because it provided sufficient time for a thorough discussion of local problems in co-operative enterprises and for the exposition of the whole program of adult education. Between classes and during free time the inspector of credit unions and co-operatives, and the agricultural representatives, were available to talk with individual students who had specific questions for which they sought answers."[25]

These short courses dominated the educational program of the Extension Department during the war years, as can be seen from table 4.1. They were complemented by mass meetings, held in the evenings at the same time that the short courses were taking place and open to all members of the community. In effect, the short course combined aspects of the three fundamental components of the Antigonish Movement's education program in the 1930s: mass meetings, study clubs, and leadership courses.

A prominent feature of these short courses was their emphasis on the "Big Picture."[26] This notion of the Big Picture, represented in a diagram similar to the one reproduced in chapter 2 as figure 2.2, was a product of the late 1930s, although it had been part of the rhetoric of the movement from the outset. In a manner that was both comprehensive and easy to understand, as we have already noted, it provided a representation of how all of the various components of the Antigonish Movement fitted together, as well as a sense of what was being achieved and what was to come next. The Big Picture had both a practical and an inspirational function: it provided people with a sense of accomplishment and a sense of direction as well as the perception of being part of a larger whole – a new economic system. This diagram was viewed as an important education tool, particularly given the nature of the short courses. According to Delaney, "That chart traveled to all the short courses in the Maritimes. It was a nuisance to carry, but we could not have run the short courses without it."[27]

The short courses were concentrated mainly in the fisheries sector due to their seasonality and the availability of funding specifically designated for the fisheries. Moreover, they were aimed predominantly at those who were already involved in a cooperative economic enterprise, meaning that their purpose was primarily to solidify and maintain what had already been achieved rather than to promote additional activities. In the process, they served to keep the vision of the movement alive. After the war, especially as new programs based on the mass media were introduced, these short courses became less important and were eventually discontinued.

Although the "short courses" constituted the mainstay of the Extension Department's education program during the war years, other courses were also held during the period. For example, a three-week course on business methods was offered during the period 1943–44, which was attended by fifty-six people (twenty-eight from Nova Scotia, twenty from New Brunswick, seven from Prince Edward Island, and one from the Magdalen Islands).[28]

The other major component of the new education program during the war years was the Regional and Vocational Conferences. These gatherings replaced the larger Rural and Industrial Conferences of the 1930s as well as monthly rallies and the meetings of associated study clubs. They were small in scale, covered a selected area or sector, were shorter in duration, could be arranged upon relatively short notice depending on the occasion, and were less costly to organize. Yet they performed important functions necessary to the survival of the movement under the war conditions. They provided a forum for both social and economic interaction and were indispensable in cementing belief in the vision of the movement and commitment to its activities. On the downside, however, because of their narrower scope and the fact that they were not fully under direct influence of the Extension Department, they also began to sow the seeds of fragmentation, undermining the fundamental unity of the movement as a system.

These conferences rapidly expanded, and Extension Department reports suggest that the people were enthusiastic about them. For example, in 1942 five Regional and Vocational Conferences were held

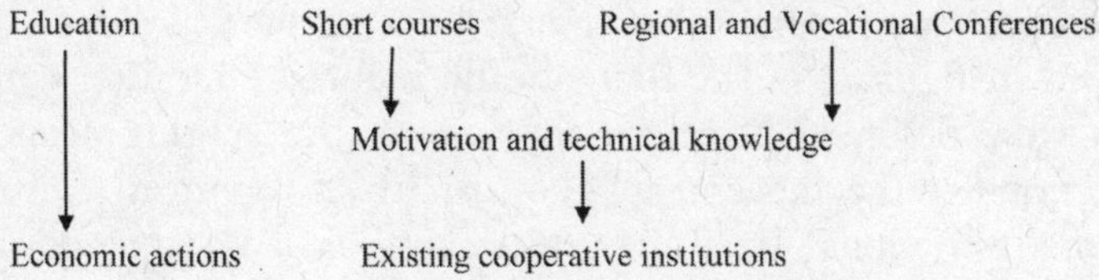

Figure 4.1 Education program during the war years, 1939-45

for fishermen, cooperative store managers, handicrafts, the Extension Department's staff, and women.[29]

The Extension Department still carried out its function of supplying study materials as well as books from its Antigonish and Sydney libraries. Although study clubs had declined in importance, they were nevertheless still supplied with pamphlets, books, and other study materials, including the biweekly *Maritime Co-operator*. The libraries, which were supported by grants from the Carnegie Corporation, were stressed during the period as important components of the Extension Department's program.[30] However, their function was increasingly separated from the notion of study for economic action.

The use of radio broadcasts was a particular war-years innovation that was to prove of great importance later on. The radio programs began with the establishment of the radio station CJFX in Antigonish in 1943. Although much of the initial programming was not highly focused, the short-lived weekly series "The Labor School of the Air," which started in 1943, was designed to mobilize and support study clubs in industrial Cape Breton.[31] This program was followed in 1945 by the "University of the Air" broadcasts.[32] These broadcasts marked a fundamental shift from the education approach of earlier times and served to further separate study from economic action in the postwar years.

The overall effectiveness of the wartime education program is evident in the fact that the Antigonish Movement not only survived the difficult war years but also retained some of its dynamism. The number of cooperative and credit union organizations as well as the volume of the resources controlled by the members increased over the period. Nevertheless, the war years caused changes to be implemented that had long-term negative consequences that became apparent only much later.

The education program that emerged during the war years is summarized in figure 4.1. The dramatically reduced education components were designed primarily to preserve the existing economic institutions of the movement. The scarcity of resources as well as wartime restrictions placed the undertaking of new cooperative economic ventures on hold.

THE ROLE OF WOMEN DURING THE WAR YEARS Although women were assigned an important role in the movement from the outset, during the 1930s it was largely within the context of the home and family environment. This role was not only consistent with Roman Catholic tradition and teaching but also reflected the temper of the times. Despite largely accepting this traditional role of women, the Extension Department, particularly through its highly influential female staff, strove to increase their effectiveness and productivity. In turn, they would directly contribute to their own and their families' wellbeing and would also contribute to the success of the various cooperative enterprises. Thus, despite the gender equality of cooperative principles, very few women occupied leadership positions, such as directors, managers, and members of important committees, in the various cooperative societies.[33]

The situation changed with the onset of the war and the exodus of a large number of men overseas, depleting the ranks of cooperative leadership and allowing many women to step "into more prominent roles as employees and managers of local co-operatives."[34] The Extension Department recognized that the survival and continuation of the movement now also depended on women's abilities in running some of the cooperative enterprises, and fieldworker Ida Delaney, along with her male counterparts, promoted the expansion of the scope and activities of the Women's Work program. Furthermore, the Extension Department organized a Maritime Women's Conference in November 1942, which was attended by 150 women from all over the region. It was followed by an additional four Regional Women's Conferences – two each in Nova Scotia and New Brunswick. These conferences provided opportunities for women to bring their ideas and concerns forward.[35]

The more active participation of women in the operation of cooperative enterprises brought to the fore the conflict between cooperative theory and practice. The women of the Extension Department took the initiative in remedying the situation, bringing forth proposals such as joint membership and a quota on women's representation but without any significant success.[36] Moreover, with the end of the war, most of the women working in the cooperatives "retreated to more traditional roles once the soldiers returned."[37] The Extension Department hastened the retreat by ending the Women's Work program in 1944, and women's increased rate of participation in the labour force, which put a constraint on their time, also contributed to the program's demise.[38] Nevertheless, a process was started that brought some changes during the postwar years. Undoubtedly, that the cooperatives and credit unions were not only able to survive but were also able to expand and strengthen their operations during the difficult war years owed a lot to the more active participation of women in their operations.

POSTWAR RECONSTRUCTION: 1945–49

The immediate postwar years were also extraordinary times. The war had destroyed or undermined many traditional institutions, and new institutions had not been firmly established to replace them. The new postwar order that gradually emerged, despite efforts to the contrary, was not entirely planned or anticipated. The peace attained at the end of the war was short-lived, as a new threat emerged. The Soviet Union, a wartime ally, assumed the role of the new enemy with the commencement of the Berlin Blockade in 1948 and the beginning of the Cold War. Furthermore, the threat of communism began to grow stronger with the communist victory in China in 1949. The independence of India in 1947 also marked the first sign of the dismantling of the existing colonial regimes. These and other events helped to shape the world in which the Antigonish Movement was to evolve and operate in the postwar years.

At the national level, a return to prewar economic depression conditions did not materialize. The gradual emergence of Keynesian economics marked the end of the presumed laissez-faire era, as the federal government assumed responsibility for economic stabilization, promoting full employment and stable incomes.[39] The injections of government spending into the economy prompted both by the war effort and by the gradual introduction of Keynesian economics contributed to generally rapid economic expansion and high levels of employment, although these effects were less pronounced in the Maritimes than in the country as a whole.[40]

In addition to greater prosperity, the postwar years were also characterized by a number of other changes, which had important effects on the working of the Antigonish Movement. These changes included new and more globally oriented, as opposed to community-centred, attitudes prompted by the war years. This process occurred particularly due to soldiers returning home from overseas[41] and to the vast improvements in communication, especially the increased popularity, expansion, and accessibility of radio programs. Indeed, the radio became very popular not only for entertainment purposes but also as a disseminator of information, reducing the dependence of the people in the area on the Extension Department. Other changes that became more pronounced during the next decade included the acceleration of the urbanization process, which also fostered migration out of the rural areas, to the detriment of the primary sectors.

POSTWAR ADAPTATION AND CHANGES IN THE MOVEMENT

The end of the Second World War brought new challenges to the Antigonish Movement, including changes in leadership, adaptating the movement's vision to new circumstances, designing a new education strategy, and streamlining its institutional framework. The continued progress of the movement required that all these challenges be met.

Changes in Leadership

During the 1930s, and also during the war years, a tightly knit leadership group, consisting predominantly of four individuals, each contributing unique talents and abilities, directed and guided the movement. The recognized leader of this group was Rev. Moses Coady, a founder of the movement whose influence was accepted by all and who, through his oratory skills and charismatic personality, forcefully articulated the vision and the ultimate goals of the movement. Rev. Coady was ably assisted by his long-time collaborator A.B. MacDonald, a superb organizer who kept abreast of all the operational details of the institutions of the movement and was respected and trusted as a man of the people. A.S. MacIntyre, a former labour leader, carried the movement into the industrial areas of eastern Nova Scotia and particularly into industrial Cape Breton, where he was able to organize and maintain the greatest concentration of cooperatives and credit unions in the Maritimes. These three were complemented by Rev. Jimmy Tompkins, a great visionary and innovator, who initiated and organized cooperative organizations in new and untried sectors and activities. In addition to their official position as members of the staff of the Extension Department, except for Tompkins, who laboured as a parish priest, the members of this group occupied key positions within the various cooperative organizations and, in the case of Tompkins and Coady, within the Roman Catholic Church. As a result, they were able to ensure the smooth operation and close cooperation between the Extension Department, key cooperative organizations, and the still influential Roman Catholic clergy of the Diocese of Antigonish. Thus A.B. MacDonald, in addition to his position as assistant director of the Extension Department, was, among other things, also the managing director of the Nova Scotia Credit Union League, a secondary society formed to support the community-based credit unions. Similarly, A.S. MacIntyre, a fieldworker of the Extension Department, occupied, among other things, the position of president of the Nova Scotia Credit Union League. Rev. Tompkins commanded a large following among the loyal and respectful rural clergy, who supported the movement with voluntary work and various forms of assistance. The same applied to Rev. Coady. These "interlocking directorships" and connections made such a small group very effective in exercising leadership within the movement and in carrying plans forward. At the same time, this arrangement also generated a great deal of cooperation among the various economic institutions of the movement.

This experienced and capable group was abruptly dissolved during the 1940s. A.B. MacDonald moved to Ottawa to join the Co-operative Union of Canada in 1943,[42] and A.S. MacIntyre was seconded to Newfoundland in 1948 and a year later to British Columbia in order to organize cooperatives there.[43] Rev. Tompkins, being terminally ill, retired that same year.[44] Of the original leadership group, only Rev. Coady remained active within the movement in its home base.

Thus, over a short period of time and under circumstances that were far from normal, the Antigonish Movement lost the organizational talents and dedication of A.B. MacDonald and the powerful presence of A.S. MacIntyre among the industrial workers. Arguably, an even greater loss was Rev. Tompkins, the beacon of the Antigonish Movement. He had provided the initial inspiration and direction to the adult education programs of the Extension Department and had demonstrated the powerful effects of cooperation, as in the cases of Little Dover and, later on, Reserve Mines with the advent of Tompkinsville. Tompkins, the frail priest and visionary, who was also Coady's cousin, had organized the first lobster-processing plant, the first credit union, the first housing cooperative, and the first circulating library and was truly a pioneer of the Antigonish Movement.

Prior to the demise of the leadership group in the 1940s, there was also a rift between Rev. Coady and Rev. Tompkins, arising from two fundamentally different philosophies of adult education, that had some implications for the movement, particularly in later years. Although both accepted the view that adult education was to play an important role in facilitating the work of the Antigonish Movement, they differed with respect to its nature. Rev. Tompkins, true to his earlier ideas in his pamphlet *Knowledge for the People* and in his People's School experiment, stressed intellectual and liberal arts education. Rev. Coady, based on his experience in mass meetings, study clubs, and leadership courses, believed that adult education must begin with practical, applied, and economic-oriented knowledge. Only after the pressing economic problems were resolved could adult education be directed at loftier goals. These longstanding differences did not prevent the two men from working together during the 1920s and 1930s. However, things began to change in the second part of the 1940s when Rev. Tompkins embarked on his last great life project, the establishment of regional libraries for Nova Scotia, equipping his pilot project, the People's Library in Reserve Mines, with books of general intellectual interest.[45] At the same time, Rev. Coady was in the process of setting up an Extension Library in Antigonish, amassing "pamphlets and print-outs ... as curriculum for immediate study use and as advertisement for co-operatives and credit unions."[46] At this junction, according to Rusty Neal, "the two men's missions firmly and finally separated."[47]

The Leadership Vacuum

The sudden departure of the experienced and dedicated leaders occurred at a most critical time, when the new postwar socio-economic order was emerging, and constituted a serious blow to the movement. Although A.B. MacDonald was replaced by Alexander Laidlaw, who became assistant director of the Extension Department in 1944, and although others were also brought into the fold,[48] there remained a leadership vacuum. Rev. Coady alone, despite his talents and dedication, could not fill the gap, especially as the demands on the Extension Department mounted during the immediate postwar years. Furthermore, demands on Rev. Coady's time and energy by outside commitments continued to mount, culminating in the 1949–50 period, during which he addressed meetings and conferences "in some forty centers in various parts of the United States and in all the provinces of Canada," with the high point being his address to the United Nations at Lake Success.[49] Moreover, in 1948, Rev. Coady also assumed the presidency of the Canadian Association of Adult Education, with its onerous responsibilities. In addition, Rev. Coady's health had begun to fail, forcing him to undergo serious operations involving prolonged hospital stays. Coady, who was born in 1882, was now well into his sixties and could not be expected to carry out all of these tasks while also single-handedly steering the movement during its most perilous period.

Given the circumstances, and especially the stature of the original leaders, it was not possible for new people to step in with the same effect, as they would need time before they could become established. Others, such as Ida Delaney, Sister Marie Michael, and Sister Mary Anselm (Irene Doyle), remained active but were involved in the actual fieldwork and programs, not in leading the movement.[50]

The leadership vacuum, dearth of resources, and increased demand on the Extension Department, all unfolding in a changing and uncertain environment, were not felt immediately by the economic institutions of the Antigonish Movement that were already in place. This delay was partly due to the overall buoyancy of the economy and to the persistent strength and relative independence of the cooperative organizations. However, evidence of the movement's problems can be easily detected. No annual reports from the Extension Department's director were submitted to St Francis Xavier University during much of this time. When such reports were resumed in 1949, they lacked substance and enthusiasm. A more serious implication was the failure of the Extension Department to revive its once successful education program. The study clubs, weakened during the wartime years, continued to decline in eastern Nova Scotia and other parts of the Maritimes, although they were being vigorously organized in places such as British Columbia and in parts of the United States, particularly in Ohio.[51] The leadership course, which had been suspended during the war years, was revived but now provided cooperative training mainly for bookkeepers and managers without any inspirational or motivational component to promote the expansion of the movement as a whole. The annual Rural and Industrial Conferences were not convened during this period. Although a great number of educational activities were undertaken, including new and bold educational experiments, these lacked unity and a coherent umbrella vision. In fact, what emerged was largely a collection of isolated and separate programs, each operating on its own. The movement seemed to have been put on automatic pilot at the very time that it entered fundamentally uncharted territory, requiring some fundamental changes and adaptations, especially in the realm of education and economic action. Coady was the indispensable visionary, but other leaders were required to guide the movement.

The Modified Vision

The original vision of the movement, calling for the common people to become "Masters of Their Own Destiny" and crystallized in the Big Picture, was the collective product of many individuals and evolved through the experiences of the 1930s. This vision was presented predominantly in economic terms and in a manner comprehensible to the people in general. With the spread of the movement to other parts of Canada and abroad, it became necessary to modify the original vision and present it in more abstract terms better suited to national and international audiences. The adaptation was undertaken by two men: Harry Johnson, a professor of economics at St Francis Xavier University, and Rev. Moses Coady. Johnson's contribution was to cast the vision in the form of abstract and general principles of universal applicability: the so-called "Six Principles." The deficiency of this adaptation has been discussed in chapter 2.

Rev. Coady's contribution was to couch the new vision in political language easily understood by international audiences – that is, as a "defense of democracy" against "monopoly capitalism" and, particularly, as an effective defence against communism.[52] According to Rev. Coady, the so-called "democratic formula," which the Antigonish Movement had apparently discovered and which was contained in the Six Principles, would enable the masses of humanity to enjoy the "full and abundant life." The anticommunist rhetoric of the movement, only occasionally used in the 1930s, became the dominant theme with the onset of the Cold War and was very attractive, particularly to audiences in the United States. This adaptation became the major "selling point" and was designed to overcome the opposition to the "collectivistic" and "socialistic" aspects of the movement. It enabled the movement to spread to other parts of Canada and abroad by staking a clear claim to a "Middle Way."[53] It also elicited a demand from abroad, especially from groups in the United States, to establish an international centre at St Francis Xavier University to train the leaders, especially from the developing countries, in the principles and techniques of the movement.

The impact of repackaging the original vision of the movement in the form of the Six Principles was largely negative at home in eastern Nova Scotia and other parts of maritime Canada. It detracted from the movement's ability to address immediate problems at home and contributed to the emergence of the unfounded conviction that a "scientific formula" had been discovered that could be applied to the problems of development in various regions, countries, and continents. The reality was that a great deal of work and adaptation still needed to be done before a viable alternate economic system could emerge. As a consequence, serious threats to the movement that were emerging at home were largely ignored. The conventional profit-driven private enterprises, based on the corporate form of ownership, were being revitalized using the financial techniques of mergers, acquisition, and amalgamation. The government was becoming more directly involved in the economy not as a partner but largely as a competitor, with unpredictable consequences for the movement. The government itself and its bureaucracy lacked the vision to fully understand and appreciate what was already in place.[54] In addition, improvements in transportation and communication facilities, coupled with the expansion in formal education, increased the spatial and social mobility of the people, particularly of the young, and in the process altered their attitudes and values. The "old nemesis" of out-migration from the rural communities reappeared again. The neglect of these threats, particularly by the leadership of the movement, the Extension Department, and the various cooperative economic institutions, was a serious error, as became evident in the decades to come.

Rev. Coady's conviction in the indestructibility of the movement, which rendered him somewhat oblivious to the "dark clouds gathering on the movement's horizon," was reinforced by the international recognition of the movement, the expansion of its cooperative sector during the postwar period, and the bold experiment in mass media education undertaken by the Extension Department through its radio programs. The future appeared to him to be "bright with progress."[55] However, Coady was not naive. He understood that lack of commitment, willingness to free ride, and general complacency could undermine all that had been accomplished. Moreover, although he had accepted the rhetoric of the Six Principles, he still adhered in practice to the Big Picture.

The Relationship with the State

From the outset, the movement relied on the support and cooperation of both the federal and provincial governments. The federal government, as already noted, financed a significant portion of the work of the Extension Department, with its fisheries grants starting during the latter part of the 1930s and continuing throughout the 1940s. The motivation on the part of the federal government, which had largely taken a stance of benign neglect toward the maritime provinces, despite its various royal commissions, was based largely on expediency. Nevertheless, it established a dependency that did not rest well with the movement's assertion of "self-reliance" and notion of making people "Masters of Their Own Destiny."

On the other hand, the relationship with the provincial government was more complex and also more strongly driven by political considerations. That farmers, fishermen, and industrial workers constituted an important voting block, along with their proclivity to seek political representation outside the two main parties, provided an incentive, on the part of both the provincial Liberal and Conservative Parties, to support programs designed to improve the welfare of these various groups, particularly in the case of the rural population.[56] This situation preceded the emergence of the Antigonish Movement. Thus the government provided assistance in the establishment of ventures such as cooperative creameries and abattoirs as well as the Maritime Livestock Board. There was a commonality of interests between the provincial government and the Antigonish Movement, particularly with respect to the rural population, that favoured cooperation between them, even if these interests were motivated by different factors.

During the 1930s, the collaboration between the Antigonish Movement and various provincial government departments and institutions proceeded on a largely ad hoc, piecemeal, and practical basis. Such collaboration was particularly close with the personnel from the Department of Agriculture, which promoted the establishment of cooperatives and credit unions among farmers.[57] With the establishment of the Department of Agriculture and Marketing in 1935, such collaboration extended to the marketing of fish products as well. Also important was the willingness of the provincial government to pass legislation that enabled cooperative institutions to be set up, as in the case of credit union legislation as well as amendments to the Housing Act, which extended low-interest loans, granted by the Housing Commission, to cooperative housing projects. Moreover, the library act was also amended to allow regional libraries to be established.

The collaborative relationship was facilitated by the presence of a number of individuals in the provincial government who were sympathetic toward the movement and its objectives. Among these was the long-serving premier of Nova Scotia, Angus L. MacDonald. MacDonald, who was born and raised in Cape Breton, was a graduate of St Francis Xavier University, where he also served a short stint as instructor, and a former student of Rev. Tompkins.[58] Angus L. MacDonald served as premier of Nova Scotia from 1933 until the start of the Second World War in 1939 and then again from 1945 until his death in 1954. Although MacDonald did not fully subscribe to the vision extolled by Rev. Tompkins and Rev. Coady, his ties to St Francis Xavier University, his Roman Catholic background, and his commitment to improve the lot of Nova Scotians ensured some sympathy toward the movement.[59] Moreover, MacDonald did not favour government involvement in the economy, which facilitated collaboration rather than competition with the movement.

The Extension Department's relationship with both the federal and the provincial governments, the latter in particular, benefited the movement during the 1930s and to some extent the 1940s as well. However, it also posed dangers for the Antigonish Movement that would become more evident later on as both levels of government became more interventionist with greater acceptance of Keynesianism.

The Postwar Education Strategy

During the postwar years, the financial situation of the Extension Department improved. Larger fisheries grants, combined with the willingness of the cooperative sector to devote part of its profit or surplus to educational activities, allowed the Extension Department to expand in size, increase the scope of its educational offerings, and launch a new innovative program using the radio as an education tool.[60] However, unlike the tightly integrated education programs of the 1930s, and even those of the war years, the new programs were largely isolated and fragmented. Although they were initiated in response to the needs of the movement, they lacked the guidance of its unified vision. In fact, the entire education program began to be pulled in different directions. On the one hand, the rapidly expanding cooperative sector demanded technical and practical training for its officers and especially its bookkeepers and managers. On the other hand, the adult educators within the movement and on the staff of the Extension Department, including Rev. Coady himself, began to deliver mass education programs independently of the existing cooperative structures and even independently of any concerted economic action. Additional pressure came from the increasing number of international visitors and students seeking knowledge of the movement's concepts, techniques, and principles, which could be applied in their own countries.

These divergent pressures and tendencies resulted in the creation of several independent streams in the educational program of the Extension Department. The first of these was technical cooperative training, comprising a variety of educational initiatives, such as the six-week Maritime Co-operative Training School, held at Amherst near the New Brunswick border and designed primarily for cooperative bookkeepers and managers, and the annual conferences of

Nova Scotia's cooperative store managers, designed to provide additional training in order to meet the needs of the expanding number of cooperative stores. In addition, numerous short courses were offered at various locations in Nova Scotia and New Brunswick in response to local needs.

The second stream, which was at the time hailed as an important innovation by the Extension Department, involved mass education through the medium of radio broadcasts. Initially envisioned during the latter part of the 1930s, the use of radio broadcasts started to take concrete form in the early 1940s with the conceptualization of the "University of the Air" radio program.[61] However, it was not until the postwar years that the new strategy began to take shape with the emergence of twin programs: the "Life in These Maritimes" broadcasts, aimed at the rural population and introduced in 1945-46 (i.e., the rural program); and the "People's School" broadcasts, intended for industrial workers, produced in collaboration with organized labour from Cape Breton, and introduced later in the decade (i.e., the urban program).[62] The "People's School" broadcasts emerged in 1948 out of two pre-existing programs: the Education for Urban Adults program, which was started in 1945 and was aimed primarily at providing economic knowledge to industrial workers and urban dwellers, and a newly instituted radio program modelled on the earlier "Labour School of the Air" broadcasts.[63] Aside from the first year of operations when it dealt with broad topics, many of which were directly linked to cooperation and the existing circumstances, the "Life in These Maritimes" broadcasts dealt mostly with specific rural issues, particularly matters linked to agricultural production and marketing. The "People's School" broadcasts dealt with issues of importance to the urban population, including organized labour.

Both of these mass education programs were initially conceived within the study club framework. Designed largely as replacements for the study club method, they attempted to retain the vital link between education and economic action. The broadcasts themselves replaced the mass meetings. They were perceived as a more efficient and less time-consuming way of getting people interested and willing to engage in study that would lead to the formation of study clubs. Although effective, the mass meetings of the 1930s had some serious drawbacks, including the need to travel to different communities – one community at a time – over roads that were difficult and unreli-

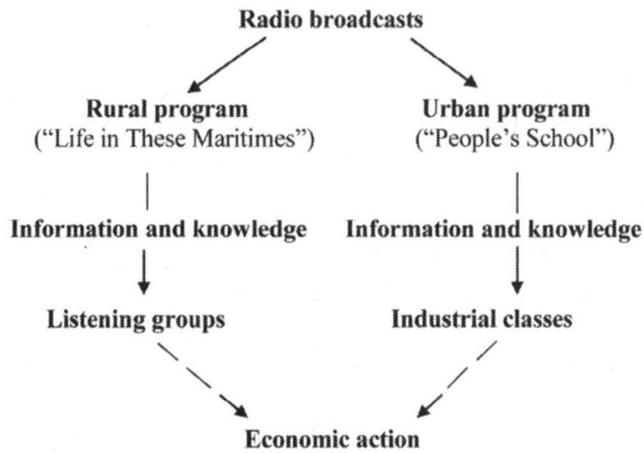

Figure 4.2 Postwar strategy for mass media education

able, especially in the winter. The radio broadcasts provided an enormous advantage by eliminating the need to travel and by being able to reach numerous communities at the same time and on a regular basis.[64] The broadcasts were supplemented by weekly lectures, bulletins, radio scripts, and small libraries. The crucial component of the original approach, the study clubs, was in effect replaced by industrial classes and listening groups. Thus the "People's School" broadcasts were followed by industrial classes in various urban centres, mostly in the industrial heartland of Cape Breton County, whereas the rural program was organized around listening groups, who were required to register with the Extension Department in order to receive weekly bulletins and radio scripts. Available data show that there were a total of 201 listening groups in 1946–47, 145 in 1947–48, and 115 in 1948–49.[65] The listening groups in a given area were to meet in "Monthly Forums" to discuss possible collective actions. The urban education program was often referred to as the "industrial study clubs." The new program that was being put in place is summarized in figure 4.2.

Although these mass education programs superficially resembled the educational strategy of the 1930s, giving an impression of continuity, there were important fundamental differences between the two. In the 1930s the study clubs and monthly rallies were directly linked to economic action. They constituted groups of interested individuals who came together to study and learn in order to put in place cooperative enterprises that would lead to an amelioration of their collective economic condition. This vital connection between study and economic action did not exist in the new programs. For example, the "People's School" broadcasts aimed to alter the attitudes of the industrial workers, to make them better citizens by making them more informed, and to promote the improvement of industrial relations in the area.[66] In this context, the "People's School" also tended to diminish militancy and radicalism in industrial Cape Breton by emphasizing the positive contribution that workers could make to the region's economy as they became equipped with better communication skills, greater knowledge, and the like. However, worker militancy would also have been reduced as a consequence of improvements in employment opportunities, higher wages, greater mobility, and participation in the local credit unions, consumers' cooperatives, and other cooperative undertakings.

Moreover, whereas the study club members had the decision-making power respecting the selection of topics, methods of study, and actions to be undertaken, such was not the case in the listening groups and industrial classes. Decision-making power in the new approach was transferred to the radio programmers and to the instructors of industrial classes. As well, the flexibility inherent in the mass meetings and the study clubs was lost because of the need to adhere to a specific timeframe and to target as wide an audience as possible, often implying general and superficial treatment of topics.

The new program could not replicate the conditions, particularly in terms of the development of trust, commitment, and conviction among the participants, that were necessary for economic action. Not surprisingly, most of the industrial groups never engaged in any collective economic activity. Similarly, the listening groups of the rural radio-education program were not involved in organizing any collective action, and the monthly forums, which had been poorly attended from the outset, were phased out. Nevertheless, both the urban and the rural mass-education programs enjoyed great popularity, assuming an institutional life of their own, and continued to expand well into the next decade.

Additional components of the postwar educational program included a two-year social and cooperative leadership program at St Francis Xavier University, primarily to deal with the demands of overseas students interested in the Antigonish Movement. Although the program had originally been introduced in 1941, it attracted few students until the postwar years.[67] The Extension Department also continued its involvement in organizing various conferences, including small-scale versions of the annual Rural and Industrial Conferences.[68]

On the surface, the postwar educational strategy of the movement appears to have been quite impressive. First, the total amounts of money spent on education were significantly higher than in the previous periods. For example, the total educational budget in 1946–47 for the movement as a whole was $50,000, of which more than half was contributed by the Extension Department.[69] This amount was more than the combined budget of the Extension Department over the entire 1931–35 period. Second, the new and experimental radio programs proved to be popular with both the urban and the rural population. Third, the education programs appear to have been responsive to the needs of the members in terms of the location and the content of the various courses and initiatives. However, behind the impressive appearance, there were some serious problems.

The major shortcoming of the new education approach was the lack of overall cohesion stemming from the replacement of the guiding vision contained in the Big Picture with the abstract Six Principles. Another, equally serious, problem was the growing divergence between what Rev. Coady called the "double-barrelled program of adult education and economic co-operation."[70] On the one hand, cooperative education was increasingly confined to technical training, ignoring the inspirational aspect of education. On the other hand, adult education became increasingly separated from any meaningful economic action. This increased divergence between education and action, unless reversed, could weaken and compromise the systemic unity of the movement over time.

The study clubs continued their war years' decline.[71] Those that were in operation, as had been the case during the war years, were a far cry from those of the previous decade, when they had constituted the mainstay of the Antigonish Movement. The absence of mass meetings and their greater links to already established cooperative enterprises changed their nature. Moreover, whereas the study clubs had been effective within the environment of the 1930s when the objective was to establish cooperative enterprises, they were much less effective and relevant once these initial enterprises were set up, especially in an environment where the other components of the education strategy were no longer present. The postwar years, however, did signal the emergence of kitchen meetings, largely an outgrowth of the

Table 4.2
Credit unions in Nova Scotia, 1940–49

Year	*Credit unions*	*Membership*	*Assets ($)*
1940	199	27,941	924,750.84
1941	201	28,144	1,055,730.85
1942	202	28,553	1,225,097.67
1943	204	28,850	1,469,280.53
1944	213	31,796	2,026,797.98
1945	218	33,645	2,567,054.68
1946	219	35,879	3,160,800.55
1947	219	36,216	3,441,580.37
1048	216	37,571	3,883,454.14
1949	219	38,883	4,255,823.35

Source: Nova Scotia Credit Union League, *Annual Reports* (1940–49).

original study clubs, which became increasingly important over time and were effective in revitalizing some of the already established cooperatives, such as the ailing credit union in St Andrews, a small community just outside of Antigonish.[72] We provide a fuller discussion of these institutions in the next chapter.

MOBILIZATION OF RESOURCES

At the outbreak of the war, the Antigonish Movement could lay claim to significant achievements in the Maritimes. It had a hand in the establishment of numerous cooperative enterprises, including credit unions, stores, lobster-processing plants, fish plants, smelt-marketing organizations (in New Brunswick), and other community ventures.[73] Despite the wartime restrictions, combined with the departure of many young men and women, the cooperative sector continued to expand during the early 1940s, although at a slower rate than during the very dynamic 1935–39 period. The pace picked up during the 1945–47 period and then slowed down again for the remainder of the decade.[74]

The end of the war and the removal of the wartime restrictions allowed the movement to resume its expansion, both in terms of organizing new cooperatives and credit unions and in terms of growing membership and the size of their operations. The credit union sector not only revived many of the troubled rural societies but also experi-

Table 4.3
Nova Scotia cooperatives, 1939–49

Year	*Cooperatives*	*Membership*
1939	61	10,695
1940	62	11,721
1941	65	11,604
1942	65	11,996
1943	64	12,369
1944	61	13,224
1945	70	15,200
1946	81	17,180
1947	103	21,917
1948	108	22,398
1949	116	24,267

Source: Nova Scotia Department of Agriculture and Marketing, *Annual Report of Co-operative Associations in Nova Scotia* (1950).

enced an expansion. There were 431 credit unions in 1948 in the Maritimes, and although this number remained virtually unchanged during the rest of the decade, reaching a total of 435 in 1950, the sector continued to grow in terms of membership and assets.[75] In the case of Nova Scotia, the credit union story is reflected in the data summarized in table 4.2.

The most rapid growth occurred in the cooperative sector. The growth was particularly pronounced for consumer stores, propelled by the relative postwar prosperity, accumulated savings, and the release of the pent-up consumer demand. Within the period of two years, from 1945 to 1947, the number of consumers' cooperative stores in the maritime provinces exploded from under 50 to 200, with combined sales of $10 million. This growth continued, reaching 245 stores with total sales of $20 million at the end of the decade.[76] In the case of Nova Scotia, this expansionary trend in the cooperative sector is represented in table 4.3. Although the data include all cooperatives, the cooperative stores constitute the dominant group.

Rapid expansion was also recorded by the cooperative housing sector, which grew from a dozen houses constructed before the war to 241 houses built or under construction in 1947 and 295 houses two years later.[77] However, the growth of cooperative housing was confined primarily to Nova Scotia because of the favourable financing

Table 4.4
Sales of fishermen's cooperatives, 1938, 1945, 1950

Cooperatives	*1938*	*1945*	*1950*
Amet Sound Packers	2,099.75	n.a.	n.a.
Bayview	3,749.27	n.a.	n.a.
Blue Ribbon Fisheries	22,600.94	71,318.65	59,592.35
Cape Breton Fishermen	16,968.52	76,410.03	7,555.67
Capeview	7,802.67	71,798.07	43,783.64
Cheticamp Fishermen	6,937.97	n.a.	163,878.17
Eastern Fishermen	36,970.32	7,761.78	129,332.08
Fundy	n.a.	26,463.16	10,387.26
Grand Etang Fishermen	n.a.	n.a.	123,992.29
Havre Boucher	9,461.65	24,161.16	n.a.
Lapoint	2,201.20	n.a.	n.a.
Little Harbour	n.a.	n.a.	14,152.43
Margaree Beach	n.a.	n.a.	35,755.04
Maryville	11,970.00	42,680.83	29,632.01
New Harbor	3,741.52	11,712.93	9,785.75
Northhumberland	n.a.	n.a.	96,367.58
Pleasant	n.a.	n.a.	15,085.82
Port Bickerton	n.a.	n.a.	142,824.51
Pubnico	n.a.	19,986.93	n.a.
Richmond	20,572.80	n.a.	n.a.
South Ingonish	5,646.89	13,970.43	n.a.
St George's	11,975.17	42,801.11	69,251.33
Tor Bay	11,237.16	98,661.29	189,916.88
Westport	n.a.	n.a.	63,877.04
TOTAL ($)	178,247.38	507,736.37	1,205,186.85

Source: Nova Scotia Department of Agriculture and Marketing, *Annual Reports of Co-operative Associations in Nova Scotia* (1938, 1945, 1950).

offered by the Nova Scotia Housing Commission, demonstrating the powerful positive impact of appropriate legislation.

Not all economic sectors, however, participated equally in this wave of expansion. The fisheries, in particular, showed little expansion. Arguably, since this sector had been among the first to be organized on a cooperative basis, it may have already approached the saturation point by this time. However, other and more important factors were also at work. The rapid expansion of the offshore sector limited the growth of the inshore fisheries within which the fishing cooperatives were operating. At the same time, more efficient profit-driven private-sector enterprises were emerging, limiting the potential for expansion by the cooperative sector. Nevertheless, the combined sales of the fisheries cooperatives continued to expand, reaching $3 million in 1947, and the United Maritime Fishermen cooperative, their central marketing organization, continued its steady growth. Table 4.4 provides some indication of the sales trends among fisheries cooperatives in the case of Nova Scotia.

The farm marketing cooperatives also experienced constraints to their further expansion arising from the difficulty of expanding agricultural production, a decline in the cultivated acreage, and increased competition from other, more productive areas. Nevertheless, the farm marketing cooperatives were able to sell in excess of $5 million worth of products by 1950 in the face of mounting difficulties.[78]

Interestingly, the growth and expansion that took place in the cooperative sector during the 1940s tended to be skewed in favour of the consumer and financial-service sectors as represented by the consumers' stores and the credit unions. Although not entirely surprising, this trend did signal an imbalance in the Big Picture, which goes back to the criticism that a fundamental weakness of the Antigonish Movement was inadequate emphasis on processing and manufacturing activities.[79] Nevertheless, the movement survived, and its economic institutions demonstrated remarkable resilience.

The large number of various cooperative organizations that had been spawned by the movement required support, coordination, and unified direction for their effective functioning and even their survival, especially over the long haul. It was necessary to create additional organizations in order to provide this required support and direction. The result was the creation of so-called "secondary societies," also organized on a cooperative basis. These were cooperative wholesalers, central marketing organizations, and the credit union centrals operating on a regional or provincial basis. The earliest of these organizations, of course, was the United Maritime Fishermen, which had been organized by Rev. Coady before the Extension Department had become fully operational. To some extent, the establishment of this cooperative had reversed the standard process. The credit unions were supported by their provincial centrals, of which the Nova Scotia Credit Union League, organized as early as 1935, was the most important.[80] The co-op stores acquired their own supporting organization with the establishment of the Canadian Livestock Co-operative as a wholesaler for the Maritimes in 1935, officially evolving into Maritime Co-operative Services (MCS) in 1944, which had two regional affiliates: Cape Breton Co-operative Services (CBCS), established in Sydney in 1938, and Eastern Co-operative Services (ECS), established in Antigonish in 1940.[81] These cooperative wholesalers, the latter two in particular, were closely aligned with the Antigonish Movement, acting as wholesalers and marketing agents for the local cooperatives as well as carrying out coordinating functions.[82] Thus they provided a link between producers and consumers. All three experienced growth throughout the 1940s, including during the war years. They also faced many challenges, including inadequate patronage by cooperators and cooperatives, whose members still bought from other sources, and financial difficulties.[83] Moreover, whereas MCS tended to be somewhat conservative in its operations, CBCS and ECS tended to be much more dynamic and willing to explore, promote, and become involved in different activities and hence to be more in tune with the notion of the Big Picture.[84]

The secondary societies themselves, in association with the Extension Department, formed another level of organizations: tertiary societies to coordinate some of the cooperatives' activities. Thus in Nova Scotia there was the emergence of the Co-operative Educational Council and later the Nova Scotia Co-operative Union.

The rather elaborate structure linking various components of the cooperative sector was necessary to direct the common activities of the local societies and institutions. Moreover, it enabled the Extension Department to work closely with the cooperative sector at different levels, particularly through its association with the secondary and tertiary organizations. The framework that was being put in place made it possible for the Extension Department to develop and implement a plan of action for the movement as a whole. The integrated institutional structure reflected the movement's attempt to put in place an alternate economic system that could sustain itself over time.

RESOURCES OF THE EXTENSION DEPARTMENT

Although financial resources were very scarce during the war years, the situation improved after the war. The fisheries grants were increased, and, moreover, the various secondary societies that had

Table 4.5
Revenue of the Extension Department, 1944–48

Year	*Revenue ($)*	*Fisheries grants ($)*
1944–45	53,653.71	38,247.51
1945–46	59,106.62	49,061.87
1946–47	56,709.14	39,840.34
1947–48	64,335.14	40,781.42

Source: St Francis Xavier University Archives, RG 30.3/25/1439.

Table 4.6
Human resources of the Extension Department, 1940–50

Year	*Full-time staff*	*Part-time staff*	*Fisheries part-time staff*
1940–41	11	7	15
1941–42	9	2	10
1942–43	10	—	9*
1943–44	10	—	15
1944–45	—	—	—
1945–46	13	—	12
1946–47	14	n.a.	n.a.
1947–48	16	n.a.	n.a.
1848–49	20	n.a.	n.a.
1949–50	23	n.a.	n.a.

* Engaged mostly, but not exclusively, in the fisheries.

Source: St Francis Xavier University, *Academic Calendars* (1940–50).

been created had at their disposal additional funds earmarked for educational purposes. That the Extension Department was able to finance various new initiatives, particularly those involving radio programs, also signalled the availability of additional financing during the latter part of the decade. Table 4.5 provides a summary of the direct revenue of the Extension Department, reflecting largely the fisheries grants and the contribution made by St Francis Xavier University, with the former making up the bulk of the total over the 1944–48 period.

The staff of the Extension Department also increased during the postwar years, as shown in table 4.6. However, the failure to fully revive the study clubs deprived the Extension Department of a vast pool of community volunteers, severely restricting its effective access to human resources. We must remember that in the 1930s the very small Extension Department staff was effectively complemented by a large cadre of capable and committed volunteers who did much of the organizing and other work.

Although the fisheries grants and the resources targeted by the cooperatives for specific purposes provided access to greater amounts of resources, they also created a dependence that could spell trouble for the movement in the future unless properly managed. More than ever before, the work of the Extension Department was being mandated by specific agents from both inside and outside the movement, limiting its independence.

CONCLUSION

The 1940s constituted a turbulent decade for the Antigonish Movement. During the first half of the decade, coinciding with the war years, severe limitations were imposed on the Extension Department and on the activities of its cooperative societies. Nevertheless, the movement was not only able to survive but also emerged from the wartime difficulties with a strong educational and economic base. With the postwar lifting of restrictions, the movement was able to take advantage of and benefit from the postwar prosperity. Indeed, it experienced accelerated expansion, particularly in the case of cooperative housing and consumers' stores, which increased substantially in number. The 1940s ended with a flurry of activities. Dominant among these were efforts to establish cooperative healthcare, especially in Cape Breton. Although the initiative failed, as doctors refused to get on board, it demonstrated the vitality of the movement.[85] There were also all sorts of plans to establish larger fish-processing plants, cold-storage facilities, produce-grading facilities, chick hatcheries, abbatoirs, and the like.[86] In the area of education, new and bold initiatives were launched through a mass media program predicated on the use of radio broadcasts. The continued success of the movement in the Maritimes, coupled with national and international acclaim, fostered its spread to other parts of Canada and abroad.

During the period, the movement also lost much of its experienced leadership, creating a leadership vacuum that Rev. Coady by himself could not overcome. Furthermore, the Extension Department failed to revive its successful educational strategy, particularly the study clubs. The various educational activities undertaken during the post-war period lacked overall unity and coherence. Yet, despite these limitations, the mood among the participants of the movement was one of confidence and high hopes for the future. The movement had survived difficult and extraordinary circumstances. At the end of the decade, its vision was surprisingly intact, and despite the articulation of the Six Principles, the notion of the Big Picture, although receding into the background, still had sufficient strength to keep the movement focused on the establishment of an integrated alternate economic system.

5

The Years of Transitions, 1950–59

INTRODUCTION

The 1950s, characterized by postwar economic expansion and prosperity, presented a series of additional challenges for the Antigonish Movement. Dramatic improvements in transportation and communications further reduced the relative isolation of the region, which had hitherto bestowed upon the Extension Department a virtual monopoly over information. At the same time, there was also an unprecedented expansion in public education, particularly at the postsecondary level, which increased the social and spatial mobility of the population, especially among the young. The expansion in education, along with increased urbanization and industrial development, prompted a new wave of out-migration from the rural areas, reaching unprecedented proportions during the decade.

The technological development that had been a part of the war effort was being successfully applied to the production of civilian goods and services. The adoption of the new technology as well as the expanded geographical market areas, resulting from the better communication and transportation, promoted larger-scale operations requiring greater amounts of capital. Thus there was an increase in the threshold size of economic enterprise. To finance the larger amounts of required investments, profit-driven private-sector corporations became more dependent on revitalized financial markets and on their various innovative structures and instruments. These markets posed a severe challenge to the cooperative sector and to the Antigonish Movement as a whole, which thus had to adapt and innovate.[1]

The government also became increasingly involved in the economy as it abandoned its traditional laissez-faire approach. During the 1950s, it became actively engaged in building up social infrastructure, developing an increasingly elaborate social-welfare system, and engaging in macroeconomic management and stabilization policies. As the government more fully embraced Keynesianism, with increased involvement in the economy, the principle of self-reliance and grassroots control over economic activity, which was pervasive in both the economic and intellectual spheres of the Antigonish Movement, began to weaken. Indeed, the new environment provided a formidable challenge to the belief that the people, through their own collective efforts, could become both the intellectual and economic "Masters of Their Own Destiny."

The seeming new prosperity also weakened the urgency of economic action. The difficult economic circumstances arising from the failure of the existing system during the 1920s and 1930s had initially provided a powerful and compelling incentive for the people to be receptive to new ideas that could improve their lot. As well, the reduction in widespread unemployment and underemployment among urban workers and the decline in the primary sectors reduced the time available for study.

Despite the substantially different circumstances and challenges, the Antigonish Movement was able to continue its expansion and mobilization of resources. Arguably, at the end of the decade, it stood at the height of its success, influence, and international recognition. By this time, it had been successfully transferred to other parts of Canada, most notably to British Columbia, the United States, particularly Ohio, and a host of other places, including Puerto Rico and Chile. Staff members of the Extension Department were regularly called upon to help organize people in other parts of the country as well as overseas.[2]

In the domestic sphere, the economic "pillars of the movement" – credit unions, fisheries organizations, consumers' stores, agricultural cooperatives, and cooperative housing organizations – continued to expand in terms of number of societies, membership, sales, assets, and membership capital. Although it had faded into the background, the "Big Picture" was still foremost in the minds of the leaders of the movement. However, the integrated network of economic institutions that was envisaged by the Big Picture was still to be completed; it still lacked some crucial components.

Farming and fisheries cooperatives were still selling primary products in unprocessed form and at very low prices to industrial processors located largely outside of the region. In turn, these processors sold the processed goods to local consumers' cooperatives at much higher prices. Moreover, the demand for consumer products grew rapidly, particularly in the urban areas, and consequently so did imports, including imports of food. To fully integrate its economic institutions, and forge direct links between the primary producers and consumers, the Antigonish Movement needed to establish its own processing and industrial facilities. The expanding demand for consumer goods as well as excess capacity in the primary sectors, particularly in the form of underutilized farmland and an abundance of fish, suggested that the time was ripe for such undertakings.[3] The Antigonish Movement responded with the Eastern Co-operative Services (ECS) mega project, which went into effect in the latter part of the decade. Based in Sydney, ECS was an integrated wholesale and processing complex. It was perceived as a crowning achievement of the Antigonish Movement.

An additional component of the institutional network that attracted a lot of attention, and one espoused by Rev. Moses Coady as early as 1939, was the establishment of an international arm of the movement to spread its principles, programs, and strategies abroad so that others could also benefit from it.[4] There was a strong belief that the Antigonish Movement was relevant to other countries and regions around the world, especially the developing countries and regions of Africa, Asia, and Latin America. The result was the establishment of the Coady International Institute in 1959.

CHANGES IN THE SOCIO-ECONOMIC ENVIRONMENT

The 1950s experienced profound changes in transportation. Prior to the war, the railway constituted the principal form of moving people and goods, with reliable road transport limited to the vicinity of larger urban areas. Federal and provincial involvement in postwar road construction led to fundamental improvements. Paved roads and highways facilitated year-round transportation, especially by truck and car, linking rural areas and urban areas and allowing people to travel far greater distances than ever before.[5]

In the realm of communication, the widespread use of radio and later television, the most powerful tool of the mass media, stands paramount.[6] The traditional forms of communication that the Extension Department relied on during the 1930s to provide information to the study clubs included books, magazines, pamphlets, and newspapers. Unlike printed material, which was accessible to one reader at a time, the new vehicles of the mass media – radio and television – could reach vast numbers of people at the same time. Thus they introduced a potentially more effective way of carrying out the movement's education program. Nonetheless, the new mass media were devoted primarily to entertainment and advertising rather than to the dissemination of information to foster study and economic action. Moreover, they were also instrumental in introducing and propagating new values and attitudes such as individualism, competition, and materialism.[7] The impact was strongest among the young, who had not experienced the hardships of earlier times. Thus the Extension Department had to compete for people's time and attention with rapidly expanding mass media, which offered different and well-packaged verbal and visual messages that often stressed values and attitudes that were in whole or in part contrary to those fostered by the Antigonish Movement.[8] The reports by fieldworkers of the Extension Department indicate that, indeed, television was the main culprit in the drop in attendance both in the study clubs and in weekly classes of the People's School.

The prosperity and high levels of employment that were experienced in the immediate postwar years and that continued into the 1950s were the result of high levels of capital accumulation, rapid technological progress, and the emergence of modern corporations characterized by larger-scale production, up-to-date technology, and highly trained managers.[9] These factors posed a formidable threat to the cooperative sector of the Antigonish Movement. Although existing cooperatives could effectively compete with small-scale and generally undercapitalized ventures such as family-run fishing plants, lobster-processing factories, and retail stores, they were no matches for the new enterprises. In order to survive, it was imperative for cooperative organizations to adapt to the changing conditions by increasing their scale of operation, modernizing their equipment and technology, and upgrading the skills of their workers, particularly their managers. To accomplish these things, existing cooperatives had to amalgamate and consolidate and, most of all, increase their capital accumulation (i.e., investment). Clearly, it was much more difficult for small groups to implement economic projects in this new environment through the traditional method of study clubs and associated study clubs; the resources and expertise required were generally in excess of what these clubs could muster on their own.[10] Both existing and new cooperatives needed the support of an integrated system.

During the 1950s, much of the social legislation that was already in place was broadened in scope, updated, and improved. As far as the effects on the movement are concerned, perhaps the most important factor was the increased transfers, particularly to the poorer provinces, by the federal government as a consequence of the Tax Rental Agreements and, after 1957, as a part of the Equalization Payments scheme.

The continued expansion of the welfare state and increased participation of the government in the management of the economy affected the Antigonish Movement in at least two ways. First, as mentioned earlier, it removed the urgency of self-reliant and grassroots-based economic action, as the people's basic needs were being met, at least in part, by the government. Second, it introduced an alternate way of solving economic problems. In addition to the self-reliant approach based on group study and cooperative economic action, there was now also an alternative based on "the lazy, easy way of political solution."[11]

The 1950s also witnessed an acceleration of the ongoing process of urbanization, aided by improvements in transportation and communication, with the agriculture sector continuing to decline in much of the Maritimes, including eastern Nova Scotia. The opportunities offered by urban areas, especially in other parts of Canada, prompted substantial rural-urban migration and out-migration from the maritime provinces.[12] For those in the Antigonish Movement who were dedicated to the growth and preservation of agricultural communities, this migration was a severe blow, particularly since it often resulted in the abandonment of the land as opposed to simply displacing surplus labour arising from greater efficiency and technological change. In Nova Scotia as a whole, the number of farm holdings declined from 33,000 in 1941 to 12,008 two decades later.[13] The situation in eastern Nova Scotia was equally dramatic.[14] Although mitigated by the Land Settlement program, put in place to try to reverse the land-abandonment trend with an influx of new farmers, including from abroad, the situation got worse. The out-migration that took place was reminiscent of the forces that had given rise to the founding of the Extension Department and the Antigonish Movement.

The agricultural sector had remained predominantly subsistent in nature, usually also involving part-time fishing and forestry. In 1951, in the six counties of eastern Nova Scotia (excluding Pictou), out of a total of 6,500 farms, only 108 were commercially viable, with yearly gross earnings in excess of $5,000, and another 400 or so had some commercial operations, with yearly gross earnings of $2,500. The remaining 6,000 were mostly subsistent, with very limited production, and their operators faced strong incentives to move to the urban areas and leave everything behind.[15]

The 1950s was the era of full commercialization, with agriculture in the country as a whole experiencing a great surge in productivity, which translated into lower prices.[16] The generally small-scale, mostly subsistent, and inefficient farming operations were caught in a bind. On the one hand, they could not compete, in the face of declining prices, with the more efficient producers from elsewhere, who faced lower per unit costs. On the other hand, the cost of their purchases went up along with the general increase in the cost of living. It was in this context that the importance attached to the establishment of Eastern Co-operative Services, discussed below, can be properly understood.

An additional factor that impacted the operations of the Extension Department and the Antigonish Movement as a whole was changes in provincial policies concerning formal education. During the 1950s, one-room country schools were closed and replaced by multiroom consolidated schools, with children transported, often over considerable distances, on newly improved country roads. This occurrence was a result of greater government involvement, at the provincial and federal levels, in education.[17] Although such a policy may have seemed justifiable, it was detrimental to the Antigonish Movement. The communities that lost their schools were often the same ones that were being negatively affected by the loss of farming families, country stores, and other economic institutions, meaning that the policy served to make a bad situation even worse. The rural village schools were often the only places where short courses and meetings could be held, and local teachers were often volunteers in the movement and leaders in the study clubs and other activities. At the same time, that children now spent so much time outside their communities also led to an eventual weakening of their attachment to them. Thus there was a deepening of the rural crisis, which had a pronounced impact on the Antigonish Movement given that concern with the preservation of the rural economy was one of the main motivating forces in its emergence.

The change in education increased social mobility, especially among the young, who were no longer bound to their local communities and the occupations of their parents and found it increasingly difficult to resist the lure of the opportunities offered by the expanding and prosperous urban centres, particularly those in central and western Canada. The greater spatial mobility increased the rewards of individual effort, initiative, and motivation but at the expense of community bonds, family ties, and local attachments. Such individualism, which was hitherto confined to the urban environment, invaded the rural areas, weakening the cooperative spirit of the younger generations. The pull from urban centres outside of the region implied that many of the more talented and dynamic members of the younger generation were no longer there to build and operate the new economic institutions that were required for the propagation of the movement.

Also of some importance was the change that occurred in the educational policy of St Francis Xavier University, the heart and brain of the Antigonish Movement. During the 1950s, the university became committed to academic excellence and to bolstering its faculty of science.[18] Although the university continued its commitment to the work of the Extension Department during the decade, this commitment weakened in subsequent years as a divergence occurred between the goals of the university and those of the Extension Department.[19] There was a lack of vision of how the Extension Department could be effectively integrated into the new academic environment. The university itself became a conduit for the exodus of the young from rural Nova Scotia, mostly to destinations outside of the Maritimes, in the process depriving the movement of their vital energy, initiative, and intellectual abilities. Such an exodus was an outcome that the initial leaders of the movement had railed against in their effort to bring education and empowerment to the people. To put the matter in perspective, we need to recall that, in the 1930s, the young and more educated men and women played a central role in the success of the study clubs and the economic activities that arose from them. Some of these were also recruited as fieldworkers for the Extension Department.

Overall, these negative effects were not recognized, and the attitude within the Antigonish Movement toward the emerging socio-economic realities was one of optimism; given that the movement had conquered difficult problems in the past, there was the belief that even greater things could now be achieved.[20] However, such confidence was predicated on the existence of a strong and expanding movement inspired by a compelling vision and equipped with an integrated network of economic institutions able to mobilize ever-growing amounts of resources. Such a tall order also required that the education programs of the Extension Department, which had become fragmented in the late 1940s, be reintegrated, revitalized, and reoriented toward their original nature and purpose, which was to foster and sustain economic action. However, over the decade, the gap between what was required and what was taking place continued to widen.

CHANGING LEADERSHIP

In addition to the different circumstances and various challenges with which the Antigonish Movement had to deal, there was also a further change in leadership. Rev. Coady officially retired at the beginning of 1952. Although his many commitments and failing health had required that he be frequently absent from his office during the preceding years, he had remained a critical constant in the evolution of both the Extension Department and the movement. The new director, Rev. Michael J. MacKinnon, a parish priest from industrial Cape Breton, had been active in the movement since the mid-1930s, initially as a volunteer and later as a member of the staff of the Extension Department in its Sydney office. In 1948 he had been appointed the director of labour education in Cape Breton and in 1950 head of the Sydney Extension Office.[21] Rev. Coady was given the title of director emeritus, and his influence still loomed large. Released from his irksome administrative duties, he was now able to devote his time and energy to the visionary and inspirational aspects of the movement –the tasks at which he excelled. Along with Rev. Coady's retirement, the deaths of A.B. MacDonald and A.S. MacIntyre in 1952 and of Rev. Jimmy Tompkins in 1953 also constituted important events for the Antigonish Movement.

Although the change in leadership itself was orderly and smooth, that Coady was no longer nominally at the helm was a psychological letdown.[22] Although Rev. MacKinnon experienced some initial difficulty in getting the cooperation of the Extension Department staff, fiercely loyal to the former director, a good working relation developed between the founder of the movement and the new director. Moreover, Rev. MacKinnon brought what seemed to be new vigour and enthusiasm to the Extension Department.

Rev. MacKinnon, who served as director of the Extension Department until 1958, when he was appointed vice president of the university and replaced by Rev. John A. Gillis, was a product of the Antigonish Movement and as such was committed to it and to its programs and vision. Thus it is not surprising that during the 1950s there was an attempt to resurrect many of the programs of the 1930s. However, unlike Rev. Coady, whose approach was inspirational and who relied on others such as A.B. MacDonald to do much of the actual management work, Rev. MacKinnon played more of a purely administrative role.[23] As well, Rev. MacKinnon's roots were in the industrial areas of Cape Breton, whereas Rev. Coady's were in the rural areas of Margaree but conditioned by a much broader worldview. Equally important was that Rev. MacKinnon inherited the Extension Department at a time when fundamentally different sets of challenges were arising for the movement.[24] In particular, Rev. MacKinnon and the Antigonish Movement faced two fundamental sets of challenges. First, the movement was now at a different stage in its evolution and hence had different requirements. Second, although economic difficulties still plagued the region, in the new socio-economic environment different and easier options now seemed to be available as alternatives to the movement.

Rev. MacKinnon's successor, Rev. Gillis, who also had some connection with the Antigonish Movement and strong links with the rural sector, was brought in to redirect the work of the Extension Department. His tenure was brief and tumultuous but also involved some attempts to preserve and promote essential features of the Antigonish Movement.[25]

Rev. Coady continued his involvement with the movement, remaining active in meetings and conventions, until his death in 1959. Although he attempted to do so, Rev. Coady was unable to provide an updated vision of the movement that could recapture its intrinsic nature and propel it into the future, and no other visionary emerged who could do so. Moreover, the movement was not subject to any rigorous economic analysis that could in itself maintain focus on the original vision, what had been accomplished, and why.

Yielding to pressures from the Extension Department staff, supporters, admirers, and even publishers, Coady spent a considerable amount of time in an attempt to write a new book on the Antigonish Movement. His first book, written in 1939, needed to be complemented by a new and more definitive work on the movement, which had now entered its third decade of existence. Unfortunately, his efforts came to naught. Coady was fundamentally a visionary and a doer who was at his best when a part of the action, having a unique ability to face intellectual challenges in the field. He found it very difficult to sit back and analyze, synthesize, and write. He was a man of action, not an abstract theorist. Nevertheless, the absence of a more formal articulation of the vision and the dearth of economic analysis constituted serious problems, especially as new participants less steeped in the tradition of the movement became more dominant.

Rev. Coady's Final Vision

In addition to speeches and articles, Rev. Coady left behind notes on and drafts of chapters of a never-completed book that provide some insight into the ideas and themes that he was preoccupied with during the last years of his life.[26] Looking back at the experience of the movement over the previous decades, Coady reiterated the crucial role of an inspiring vision in mobilizing people to action. He maintained that "if people study the possibilities of things in human society, the vision of these possibilities tend to become realities,"[27] and "the first step in progress is the vision of things."[28] Although he failed to produce a sequel to *Masters of Their Own Destiny* and hence to provide a statement of the vision for the future, he nevertheless publicly articulated a vision that harkened back to the original operation of the Antigonish Movement.

By the 1950s the Antigonish Movement had achieved recognition in many parts of the world, and this recognition is reflected in Rev. Coady's extension of his vision to cover the whole of humanity, to whom the movement offered "an adequate, positive, concrete and democratic formula by which the people can get for themselves the good and abundant life."[29] The people could gain economic independence through the type of adult education fostered by the movement and, even more so, through actual business experience gained in the management of economic activities. This economic independence could accrue both to the primary producers and, even more so, to the industrial workers, who by going "into business for themselves" could become bankers, managers, and so on.[30] The link between study and action was perceived as even more fundamental than in the original vision.

Underlying Rev. Coady's belief that the ordinary working people could become the "Masters of Their Own Destiny" was his unbounded faith not only in the people but also in the power of science and technology to work for the benefit of the masses.[31] Specifically, he believed that they could promote the development of natural resources to such an extent as to enable each individual to lead a rich and abundant life. Moreover, the technology embedded in modern industry could provide the means whereby "labor unions engaged in the consumer co-operative field" and at the wholesale level could meet farmers and fishermen as members of the various cooperative organizations, thus fostering cooperation among cooperators.[32] The economic integration between different economic groups through the secondary cooperative organization would assure social peace and remove the social strife and rivalry existing in modern capitalistic society. Thus, again, Rev. Coady couched his vision in terms of the establishment of an integrated economic system based on cooperation, in the process reaffirming the notion of the Big Picture but without identifying it as such.

He also reiterated that there was an order and a sequence within the process of equipping the people to build economic structures themselves, starting with the creation of community-based cooperative enterprises. These primary institutions, owned and controlled by the people, were to be followed by the wholesale and central organizations, which would integrate diverse economic groups into a cooperative strife-free regional society. Involvement in manufacturing and industry that integrated industrial workers would come next, followed by the establishment of cooperative housing and of services ranging from insurance and health to the provision of recreational and cultural opportunities.[33] As in the original vision, the process of building economic institutions, as one part of an alternate economic system, was not to be an end in itself but only a first step in the long progress toward the "full and abundant life."

The achievement of such a life was perceived not as an idle dream but as the culmination of a practical program. Rev. Coady suggested that, in fact, many communities in the Maritimes had practically completed the first stage of this process and in his view were actually solving the perennial economic problem of poverty or even of scarcity. He suggested that "Community X in the Maritime Prov. e.g. Port Bickerton, should after they have solved their economic problems, as they have in Port Bickerton ... study the recreational and cultural side of their life ... parks, little theatres, orchestra, music, recreation."[34] In these assertions, Coady was not only far too optimistic but also seemed to confuse a work in progress with the final product. The Antigonish Movement was a work in progress, and a lot more needed to be done. Nevertheless, it was important, during the 1950s, to stress its possibilities, as the people of Nova Scotia, and elsewhere, increasingly faced different options and opportunities. Rev. Coady had always been aware of the potential harm to the movement and to its economic institutions that could arise from a lack of commitment and a willingness to free ride. Thus he had often admonished people for being "half-cooperators."[35] He was also keenly aware of the importance of the education program to the success of the movement and of the importance of the Extension Department remaining fully engaged in the process.

Rev. Coady's vision favoured an agrarian, egalitarian, inclusive, and tightly knit society governed by Christian ethics that in practice could also be applied to other belief systems. From the outset, he sought to protect and defend this society against internal moral decay and the negative impacts from powerful outside forces, including those that were fuelling the rapid urbanization process.[36] He was steadfast in his belief that the serious problems plaguing the rural areas that had reemerged in the 1950s could be solved by the people themselves. Adaptation may have been required, but there was no need to throw away what was fundamental to the movement.

THE VISION OF THE MOVEMENT IN THE 1950S

In many ways, the 1950s were years of contradictions, being subject to substantial confusion concerning the vision, goals, and strategies of the Antigonish Movement. Although the rhetoric remained strong and largely consistent with the notion of ordinary people becoming "Masters of Their Own Destiny" through the ownership and control of their own economic institutions, there was an increased dichotomy between theory and action – between words and deeds.

The reports coming out of the Extension Department tended to be rather brief and vague, displaying a surprising sense of complacency. In the main, the attitude toward the new emerging socio-economic realities was one of optimism. The emerging serious problems, particularly those associated with the rural economy, were perceived to be of the sort that could be solved through the efforts of the Extension Department and the Antigonish Movement. Although this optimism was not entirely misplaced, it was not accompanied by the required adjustments in the institutional apparatus of the movement – adjustments that were necessary for the movement to remain effective and to take advantage of the emerging opportunities.

In principle, there was little reason for the Extension Department not to embrace the expansion of government involvement in the social and economic spheres. In many instances, it meant the deepening of government involvement in areas that are by their very nature best dealt with by the public sector. The greater involvement of the government in education was seen as a necessary step in the education of rural youth who would then become the future leaders of a rejuvenated rural sector and was consistent with the view advocated by Rev. Tompkins many years earlier.[37] Moreover, the Extension Department had a long history of cooperating with government departments, particularly with the provincial Department of Agriculture and the federal Department of Fisheries. The co-operation with personnel from the former had been particularly fruitful for the Antigonish Movement – a matter that loomed particularly large given the importance of the rural sector to the whole undertaking. By and large, the same held true for the latter, which had become an important financial contributor to the Extension Department since the late 1930s. Thus, arguably, the expansion of the government sector presented the Extension Department with greater possibilities for cooperation and for access to resources. Moreover, there seemed to be a fundamental congruence and complementarity between the objectives of the Extension Department and those of the federal and provincial governments.

In the same vein, the economic development and industrial expansion that had been precipitated by the war years were perceived as opening up new opportunities. People in rural communities were given access to newer technologies, expanded markets for their produce, and an expanded menu of goods and services that they could purchase. Technological progress in the form of mechanization could offer freedom from the yoke of drudgery and hard labour, which Rev. Coady associated with a dulling of the intellect and a limiting of aspirations.[38] Thus there was a greater possibility for people to have more time for education and for cultural, spiritual, and other activities, which were critical components of the ultimate goals envisaged by the Antigonish Movement. In concert with the seeming enthusiasm of the time, the architects of the movement were also putting in place what was perceived to be a key component needed to complete the economic structure that had been envisaged in the Big Picture – the Eastern Co-operative Services mega project.

Women continued to be critical to the success of the movement, but their role in the various cooperative organizations did not undergo any drastic change from what it was in the late 1940s. Although they were ready and eager to play a larger active role and had gained the right to attend meetings, cast votes, and hold office in the various cooperative institutions, they were still constrained in what they could do by their "home-based duties" and the norms of the times as well as by the adoption of family cooperative membership. Family membership implied that only the husband or the wife could cast votes or hold office, and it was often the former who did so.[39] As had been the cases in earlier periods, inadequate involvement of women in the decision-making process, beyond their role as consumers, served to dampen the success of some of the cooperative enterprises.

THE EDUCATION STRATEGY OF THE EXTENSION DEPARTMENT

The vision, despite the great deal of uncertainty and confusion, still focused on the critical role of education in fostering and sustaining economic action. Having survived the 1940s, the Antigonish Movement was ready to move forward, and the Extension Department was set to strengthen its leadership role through the revamping of its education program. In addition to attempts to revive elements of its original program, the Extension Department also became more deeply involved in the use of mass media education through radio and later television.

The Revival of Earlier Programs

Early in the decade, the decision was made to revive the entire education program that had proved so successful during the 1930s. The formerly annual Rural and Industrial Conferences, which had been suspended during the preceding decade, were the first component of the original strategy to be revived.[40] Starting in 1950, they were held on a biannual basis, except for special occasions, such as the twenty-fifth anniversary of the Extension Department in 1953. In 1951 the four-week leadership course – the School for Leaders – that had been discontinued during the war years was revived.[41] In addition to cooperative and credit union training, designed to improve the competence and effectiveness of cooperative officers and leaders, this course now also contained inspirational and motivational components in keeping with the objective of "re-adopting the general study programs used in the past."[42] However, the course now served a much more eclectic clientele, with increasingly more participants from outside of the region, especially from Third World countries and regions.[43] In this sense, it became a precursor of the Coady International Institute. Moreover, the course was no longer solely sponsored by the Extension Department but was also conducted in conjunction with the Nova Scotia Credit Union League and the Nova Scotia Co-operative Union, with each picking up one-third of the cost.[44] Thus the institutions that were created by the movement began to play a more active, albeit limited, role in its propagation. In addition to the leadership course, a wide array of additional courses dealing with specific issues or groups, including adaptations of the Cooperative Training School, proliferated during the 1950s, as they had during the 1940s.[45]

The Rural and Industrial Conferences and the leadership courses required the influx of a large number of enthusiastic and motivated community leaders, which in earlier times had emerged largely from the study clubs. The largely failed attempt to revive the study clubs was mitigated, to some extent, by the propagation of kitchen meetings. These kitchen meetings, which were first organized by the people themselves in the late 1940s in response to specific and pressing educational needs, became very popular during the 1950s, overshadowing and eventually displacing the study clubs. Like the study clubs, they involved groups of friends and neighbours meeting for the purpose of study related to collective economic action. Also, like the study clubs, they were supported by the Extension Department, which provided fieldworkers as well as the necessary study materials. In these meetings, groups "gathered in member homes ... with a local leader and an extension worker assigned to each group."[46] After a series of kitchen meetings, held over the course of about a month, all of the groups involved in the discussions would gather for a rally, after which they would be disbanded.

Although there were obvious similarities between the study clubs and the kitchen meetings, there were also significant differences. First, the study clubs were entrepreneurial, organized to exploit existing economic opportunities on a cooperative basis. The kitchen meetings, in contrast, were remedial, organized to improve the operation of existing community cooperatives or credit unions by focusing on specific problems and searching for solutions through common action, as in the case of the St Andrews Credit Union. Second, the study clubs were of longer-term duration, which could be a year or more, ending with the creation of permanent economic organizations. The kitchen meetings, in contrast, were of much shorter duration, usually, as already noted, of about one month and ending with the monthly rallies. If, after the initial month or so of study, the problem with a local organization persisted, another round of kitchen meetings would be organized. Some communities, such as Bras D'Or and New Waterford, organized kitchen meetings continuously for many years.[47] These meetings were usually organized in conjunction with the anniversary of the local cooperative organizations and were also used as a tool for maintaining the loyalty and motivation of the members and, thus, for enhancing their effectiveness. Third, the study clubs covered a wide range of concerns and could be organized in any community wherever the need arose. The kitchen meetings were generally confined to those communities where local cooperative organizations were already in place, and the issues that were dealt with were linked to the operation of those organizations. Where such organizations did not already exist, the kitchen meetings were of little consequence. Fourth, the study clubs were instrumental in expanding the number of cooperative organizations and spreading the movement to new communities. The kitchen meetings could only help to preserve and protect existing structures and institutions. Thus the kitchen meetings, rather than a smaller and more limited version of the study clubs, constituted a fundamentally different type of institution. In effect, they provided a better institutional tool for dealing with the preservation of economic institutions that were already in place. Given that the movement had moved beyond its initial stage of mobilizing group entrepreneurship and setting up the first cooperative enterprises and was now focused on the preservation of existing institutions, the kitchen meetings constituted an important innovation. However, there was still a need to establish new cooperative entities, meaning that although the kitchen meetings could effectively complement the study clubs, they could not replace them.

The attempts to revive the past education strategy seem, at least on the surface, to have met with some success during the first half of the decade. The new program aimed at adapting the best elements of the past program to the new socio-economic environment, thus retaining its traditional integrative nature, whereby each element contributed to the success of the entire program. As well, the new program included various social functions, such as public speaking contests and essay writing, that in addition to offering entertainment also provided motivation and cemented commitment.

Nevertheless, there were also substantial departures from the past. During the 1930s, the educational activities of the Extension Department had followed a well-established sequence of mass meetings, study clubs, meetings of associated study clubs, and the organization of new cooperatives and credit unions. As the 1950s progressed, this sequence underwent a reversal. The starting point and also the focus of the new education program was increasingly the existing local cooperative enterprises. Next came the organization of neigbourhood short courses (of one to seven days) and of local leadership courses to improve the operation of these enterprises and also to foster added enthusiasm for the cooperative approach. These courses usually coincided with the anniversary of the local cooperative organizations, which attracted the attention of the entire community.[48] The courses, which covered a broad range of topics, including issues related to the operations of the local cooperative organizations, were usually scheduled in the evening to ensure a good turnout. Members of the Extension Department and invited speakers would give talks followed by discussions.

The overall goal of the neigbourhood courses was to revive and strengthen the motivation of the members and their loyalty to the cooperative organizations and to enhance the community's civic pride. Following these courses, several kitchen meetings were usually organized among the more active members of the community. The program based on neigbourhood courses and kitchen meetings was integrated with the leadership courses.[49] A large number of candidates for the leadership courses would emerge from the neighbourhood courses and the kitchen meetings.

Perhaps the most dramatic difference between the program of the 1950s and that of the original Antigonish Movement, especially that of the 1930s, was that the 1950s program neither revived the study clubs, particularly outside of the fisheries sector, nor devised an adequate alternate institution that could establish new cooperative enterprises by carrying out the required entrepreneurial function. The exception was a brief and somewhat overly romanticized resurgence of study clubs around 1953, coinciding with both the twenty-fifth anniversary of the Extension Department and the centenary of St Francis Xavier University. Indeed, 1953–54 is referred to as the best year since the war for the Extension Department's "fundamental adult education" activities, which saw an increase in the number of kitchen meetings as well as a return to education through study clubs.[50] In fact, there does seem to have been a substantial amount of study club activity, especially in the fisheries, where 134 clubs were organized and active during the period. Reference is also made to 1,259 meetings attended by at least one staff member, for a total participation of 34,742 fishermen.[51] At the same time, 1,396 kitchen meetings and 128 study clubs were reported for the Diocese of Antigonish as a whole.[52] However, this resurgence was short-lived and of no lasting significance, and little mention is made of study clubs in the various reports of the Extension Department for the rest of the decade. By the end of the decade, they had become a spent force, both as tools of adult education and as propagators of economic activity, relegated largely to the history of the movement. In many respects, rather than a natural response to changing socio-economic circumstances, the decline of the study clubs reflected the progressive separation of education from economic action. It reflected that, given the integrated nature of the original education program, one component could not be revived without also reviving the other sustaining institutions – in this case, the mass meetings or something that could serve the same function of establishing and organizing the study clubs.

The decline of the study clubs also had an impact on the effectiveness of the now biannual Rural and Industrial Conferences over the 1950s. In the 1930s these conferences had provided a forum for both social and economic interaction and had played a critical role in supporting the work of the study clubs by cementing belief in the vision of the movement and fostering commitment to its activities. In the 1950s these conferences, deprived of support from active study clubs, began to revert back to their status of the 1920s, when, as noted in chapter 2, they were described as "all talk and no action."[53] Nevertheless, these conferences were still seen as successful and served some useful functions, including the exploration of new cooperative activities. Thus, for example, the conference of 16-18 August 1950 explored issues pertaining to health services and housing – two of the most important areas of concern for the Extension Department at the time. The 1953 conference was held in conjunction with the twenty-fifth anniversary of the Extension Department and, although primarily ceremonial and of a social nature, was also very inspirational.[54] Moreover, this particular conference also allowed for an articulation of some of the weaknesses that were emerging in how various cooperative enterprises operated and the degree of fragmentation that existed in the emerging alternate economic system.[55] As the 1950s progressed, however, the Rural and Industrial Conferences began to lose their significance and became less important.

Although the Extension Department and the Antigonish Movement strove to maintain key components of their traditional education strategy during the 1950s, by the end of the decade these components had to be largely abandoned. The study clubs, leadership courses, conferences, and so on were all parts of a system and could not operate effectively in isolation.

The Mass Media Programs

The decline in the study clubs was countered by an increase in the number of various types of courses, as well as by the adoption of radio and later television programs to spread information. In fact, as noted in the previous chapter, the new strategy based on radio broadcasts was envisioned as a replacement for the study club framework. The trend toward radio and later television programs, which had begun in the latter part of the 1940s, marked a radical departure from the Extension Department's earlier orientation and was enthusiastically envisioned as something akin to a great adventure in education. In the main, it intensified the shift in focus from the group to the individual, both in terms of study and in terms of action. Indeed, radio and television programs had to appeal to individuals in order to maintain their attention and could not address people as groups. More fundamentally, these programs marked a shift away from the active participatory approach of earlier years, premised on economic action and socio-economic transformation, and toward a more passive strategy, predicated on the dissemination of information. Community participation was undermined and rendered passive by transferring the initiative from the community groups to the course instructors and to those who were responsible for developing, scripting, and broadcasting the radio (and later the television) programs. In the traditional study club approach, the groups and the individuals within them were active participants in selecting topics, choosing study materials, deciding upon the study process, and taking effective action. In the new approach, people were involved primarily as passive absorbers of information.

The new mass media programs were also designed for the general public and thus tended to deal with matters of general interest rather than with fostering specific economic projects.[56] In the process, information became confused with knowledge, and group entrepreneurship and economic action were increasingly forgotten.

The use of radio (and later television) constituted a key innovation. The widespread accessibility of radio and television programs allowed information to be spread quickly and extensively throughout the region. These media also marked the Extension Department's immersion in modern mass communication techniques and, to some extent, were thus in keeping with the movement's pioneering spirit of being on the "cutting edge." The intention was to somehow integrate the old with the new and in the process devise an educational strategy for the future that would be able to reach a much greater population with limited resources.[57] The two major radio and later television programs that dominated the 1950s were the urban program and the rural program, instituted during the latter part of the 1940s. These were accompanied by a host of other broadcasts.[58]

THE URBAN PROGRAM The urban program, revolving around the "People's School" broadcasts, which dated back to 1948, was aimed specifically at the workers of industrial Cape Breton, although it was also extended to cover Inverness and Pictou Counties. The program, which reflected the Extension Department's continued preoccupation with the urban population of the region, particularly of industrial Cape Breton, sought to improve conditions among the urban workers and their families, predominantly through the development of responsible and socially conscious leaders.[59] The process involved influencing the attitudes, values, and ideals of urban dwellers while also providing them with needed information, especially concerning the economic and social conditions that prevailed in their communities. In addition to enhancing leadership skills, the People's School program also stressed the value of cooperation.

Following the pattern established since its inception in the late 1940s, the People's School consisted of radio broadcasts that were supplemented by classes conducted by volunteer instructors, mostly members of the Roman Catholic clergy, and by the distribution of copies of the radio scripts (or bulletins) and pamphlets.[60] In effect, although it incorporated the new technology of the mass media, the program also contained some basic elements of the study club method. These elements were reflected in the format that was adopted, which involved classes and the distribution of bulletins, as well as in the content to the extent that the focus was on basic economic knowledge, cooperation, and the like. Moreover, the combination of broadcasts, study classes, and the distribution of bulletins was perceived as a "significant pattern for urban adult education" that could also be used in other regions.[61]

The industrial classes, which were held in conjunction with the "People's School" radio broadcasts, were conceived as an integral part of the program and were initially well attended. For example, during 1950-51 industrial classes held in eleven communities reported a regular attendance of over 400 and a total registration of 700.[62] However, during the 1950s, attendance deteriorated and these classes became decreasingly important, although they were kept up. Thus, by 1953-54 average attendance in meetings held in fourteen communities was down to 240 and the total number of registrants down to 500.[63] Attendance at these classes was perceived as "disappointingly small."[64] From the mid-1950s onward, the People's School program switched from radio broadcasts to television shows aired by CJCETV of Sydney, and interestingly, the number of communities where People's School classes were being offered was drastically reduced.[65]

The topics covered by the "People's School" broadcasts were wide-ranging. For example, in 1950 they dealt with issues such as the problems of organized labour, government, public finance, education, and industrial development. Similarly, in 1953–54 "A breakdown of the twenty-one topics shows that two were related to education; three concerned housing; two were on co-operatives; nine concerned problems within the trade union field; and five were of general community interest."[66] The general focus of these programs was on information rather than on action, which became increasingly the case over the decade.

THE RURAL PROGRAM The rural program, revolving around the "Life in These Maritimes" broadcasts, dated back to the mid-1940s. As had been the case in the previous decade, these broadcasts provided information of various sorts perceived to be of relevance to rural dwellers. The topics covered in the broadcasts ranged from broader social issues involving health and education to more specific agricultural matters involving topics such as soils, livestock (e.g., sheep and cows), dairying, production methods, and marketing.[67] Many of the broadcasts provided technical information intended to promote improvements in agriculture, including through the adoption of new methods and technologies. Whereas in the 1940s these broadcasts had been accompanied by listening groups and monthly forums, these gatherings virtually disappeared in the 1950s, with only sixty-eight such groups reported for 1951–52 and no data available after that.[68] Thus the broadcasts' study club component, if not entirely eliminated, was severely curtailed, although the distribution of bulletins was continued. To a great extent, these broadcasts accentuated the predominantly rural roots of the movement.[69] This program was terminated in 1956 when the "People's School" moved to television and a new radio program, "Extension Speaks," primarily targeted at promoting the establishment of the new Eastern Co-operative Services, was instituted. Although the new program was aimed at the population of eastern Nova Scotia as a whole, it contained a strong rural-sector component.[70]

THE EXPANSION OF MASS MEDIA EDUCATION The rapid expansion of mass media programs peaked in the mid-1950s, when television was also adopted as a tool of adult education. The expansion of mass media programs during the first part of the 1950s resulted in the appointment of a full-time director of radio education, Rev. Dr Dan MacCormack, in 1951. Interestingly, whereas the broadcasts themselves were peaking, the actual study components were disappearing or, as in the case of the industrial classes, in decline. However, the number of bulletins distributed remained high until the mid-1950s.[71]

The proliferation of radio programs was facilitated by the fact that, although they originated with CJFX in Antigonish (or in Sydney), many other radio stations were able to run tape recordings of the broadcasts. Indeed, in 1953 in excess of 800 taped copies were requested by radio stations throughout the Maritimes. These copies could be cheaply and easily reproduced, allowing the broadcasts to reach a wide audience. Over time, increasing care went into the production of these broadcasts, improving their quality and expanding their scope. Thus, for example, with the use of tape recording, in 1953-54, "For the first time in the history of the People's School, men of nation-wide prominence in politics, business and trade unionism, were active participants."[72] Ironically, although these enhanced the technical quality of the programs, they also weakened their effectiveness as education tools.

The Extension Department's decision to replace radio with television in its People's School programming during the mid-1950s had a significant impact on both the scope and the nature of its adult education program. First, television programs were much more expensive to produce, so the Extension Department was forced to cut back on the scope of the coverage of its education program. The original rural and urban radio broadcasts were discontinued and replaced by half-hour "People's School" television programs – about twenty-five such programs each year. Second, the distribution of bulletins had to be terminated in order to save money, thus further constraining the coverage and intensity of the adult education program. The radio broadcasts, introduced as one part of the "Extension Speaks" series, could still reach a targeted wider audience, but they were intended to serve a more specific purpose.

By switching to television, the Extension Department also greatly reduced its audience. The reason for this is twofold. First, unlike the radio, not every family could afford a television set in the 1950s. Second, whereas radio broadcasts reached many remote communities throughout the Maritimes as a result of many local radio stations borrowing tapes from the Extension Department, such a possibility did not exist in the case of television programs. As a consequence, the target area was reduced to segments of the population of eastern Nova Scotia.

Television also proved less effective than radio as a tool of adult education. By and large, the radio programs used "ordinary" people as panelists – for example, people who were well known locally but could also be considered experts in the topic under consideration.[73] The format of the television programs, in contrast, was geared more toward the panel of "experts." Whereas the audience could identify with the speakers in the case of the former, such identification was less likely in the case of the latter. Thus the education program of the 1930s had evolved from one of intellectual independence into one of dependence on "experts." Moreover, the experts' sophisticated and often jargon-laden analysis tended to make the audience feel intellectually inferior and confused. The notion of people educating themselves so as to become "Masters of Their Own Destiny" was compromised, if not entirely laid to rest.

As already noted, the number of people who registered for the weekly classes kept declining after the switch to television. In 1957, in an attempt to revitalize the weekly classes, a formal four-year diploma program in social leadership was instituted, but it could not resolve the problem.[74] By the late 1950s, the era of the Extension Department's involvement in mass education was over. Although the "People's School" television broadcasts continued for more than another decade, their relevance to the Antigonish Movement steadily diminished, degenerating into public information programs of a subregional scope.

MASS MEDIA AND THE ANTIGONISH MOVEMENT On the surface, the decision to switch to radio programs starting in the latter part of the 1940s could be seen as both logical and reasonable. Even in the 1950s communication and transportation in eastern Nova Scotia were relatively slow, expensive, and unreliable, particularly during the winter months. Both Ida Delaney and J.D. Nelson MacDonald describe in vivid detail the waste of time and energy on the part of the staff of the Extension Department when travelling even over relatively short distances.[75] The radio and television programs not only eliminated this problem but also enabled the Extension Department to reach more people and to convey accurate and up-to-date information quickly and at a relatively low cost.

However, the radio and, even more so, the television programs had serious defects, which were not adequately recognized at first. Perhaps the most serious of these defects was that the programs did not provide any direct link between education and economic action. At best, they provided general information that could perhaps motivate some unspecified future action by influencing, for example, attitudes and values. There was clearly no direct call for economic action through the mobilization of entrepreneurship to identify and implement cooperative economic projects. Thus they were woefully inadequate as replacements for the study club method.

Since the direct link between education and action was broken, the reinforcing feedback between the two was also eliminated. The self-generating, self-sustaining educational process was replaced by an externally motivated and remotely controlled information program.

Another, and equally important, limitation of the radio and television programs was that they neglected group dynamics. Both the "Life in These Maritimes" and the "People's School" broadcasts were supplemented and complemented by study activities for small groups – the listening groups in the case of the former and the weekly classes, directed by volunteer instructors, in the case of the latter. However, they were not substitutes for the study clubs and not even for the type of short courses that had proliferated during the war years. The strength of the study clubs was that they not only generated knowledge and spread information but also influenced beliefs, commitment, and collective entrepreneurial decisions. The radio and television programs, even when complemented by the classes, were primarily aimed at the individual rather than the group, thus weakening the belief in and commitment to cooperative action and self-reliance. They effectively eliminated the social process of transformation of information into a commitment to act, thus contributing to the delinking of information and action.

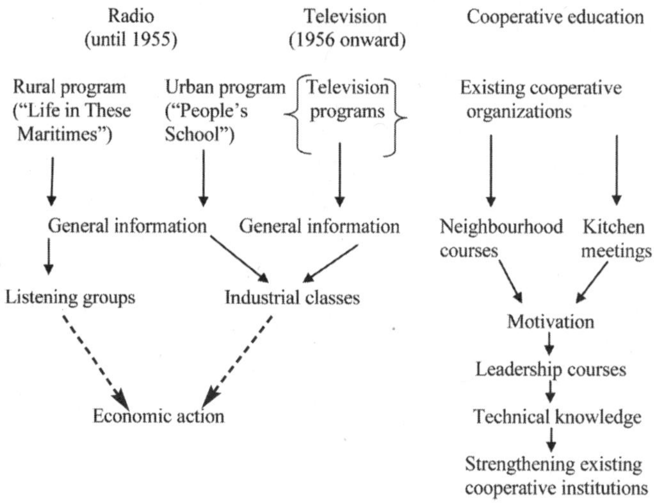

Figure 5.1 Educational Strategy in the 1950s

Given the above, it is not surprising that the use of the mass media was neither effective in terms of promoting economic activity nor useful in consolidating what had already been achieved. Rev. Tompkins's vision of adult education was turned on its head and divorced from the notion that "St. F.X. would teach people to learn, to think, and to do."[76] The education program that was envisaged during the 1950s, largely an extension of what was put in place in the latter part of the 1940s, is summarized in figure 5.1.

Although the link between education and economic activity was severed in the mass media programs, the combined short courses and kitchen meetings introduced a new component into the program. They attempted to put into effect a mechanism that could address the requirements of the cooperative economic institutions already in place while also preserving their link to the Extension Department. That there was no education program aimed at creating new cooperative ventures, however, imposed severe limitations on the movement's ability to expand and become sustainable.

The Education Program in the Fisheries

In its fisheries program, due to the inflow of government funding, the Extension Department was more successful both in maintaining the link between education and economic action and in actively promoting group dynamics. Even in the fisheries, however, it was much more difficult to begin new economic projects, particularly as a consequence of larger threshold size and of technological and managerial sophistication. Moreover, the preservation of what had already been put in place required consolidation, improved management, more effective quality-control mechanisms, and the like. These factors posed a challenge to the traditional study club approach, which, despite its decline during the war and postwar years, still remained of some importance in the sector well into the 1950s.

For most of the period under consideration, the Extension Department's fisheries program followed, as it had done since the late 1930s, a two-pronged strategy combining both group-based and more individualistic approaches, with the latter becoming increasingly dominant over the decade. The group-based approach involved the study clubs actively discussing and investigating the possibility of implementing schemes of various sorts, such as health programs and the provision of insurance. Thus their focus was on widening the cooperative approach to cover different sorts of activities, as suggested by the Big Picture. In terms of deepening the cooperative approach within the fisheries sector itself, the focus was on increasing the efficiency and competitiveness of what was already in place, which involved providing education and information concerning new technologies, upgrading managerial skills, exploring alternate means of raising necessary funds, and so on. Also critical was the need to expand markets by devising publicity programs aimed at providing information about the nutritional properties of fish as well as by stressing the importance of the fisheries to the Canadian economy. Of perhaps even greater importance was making sure that what was put on the market was "a high quality product, efficiently and scientifically produced, processed and distributed."[77] These priorities, together with a need to more properly manage the resource, required a different approach.

The newer and more individualistic approach, which became more predominant over the 1950s, was particularly evident in the strategy focusing on the "Model Fisherman." Typically, this model fisherman would be younger and more enterprising and, consequently, more receptive to new ideas and more capable of expanding operations by adopting newer and larger-scale technology. Once the individual fisherman had succeeded in increasing his production, lowering his average or per unit cost, and increasing his income or profits, it was expected that other, initially less enterprising, fishermen would follow suit. The increased production would be handled by fishing cooperatives, whose members would benefit from the greater volume and the lower cost. Thus the Model Fisherman program was intended to serve a threefold purpose: (1) it would provide information on new techniques, (2) it would reduce the perceived risk factor involved in adopting new techniques, equipment, and practices,[78] and (3) it would increase the scale of operations of the fishing cooperatives and improve their economic viability and performance.

The role of the Extension Department fieldworkers was to provide the information required by the model fisherman. Such information concerned not only new technologies – especially the use of longliners – and new techniques but also issues such as how to secure necessary funds from the local credit union or, most likely, from the Fishermen's Loan Board.[79] The main educational instrument employed by the Extension Department fieldworkers was the personal interview, which had been in use since as early as the late 1930s. As this model became more predominant over the 1950s, the number of personal interviews by fieldworkers also increased.

The group approach became increasingly unimportant and ineffective in the fisheries over the 1950s. As can be ascertained from the complaints of fieldworkers, radio and television programs helped to precipitate this shift through their adverse effect on attendance at study clubs and other group activities.[80] These radio and television programs were competitors not only in the information field but also with the entertainment and social functions that were an integral part of the study clubs, the various conferences, and other activities of the Antigonish Movement.

The traditional strategy based on the study clubs seemed less relevant as the problems facing the fisheries changed. Whereas the types of activities undertaken by fishermen in the 1930s involved primarily marketing, basic processing, and finance, those of the 1950s involved more complex production processes requiring greater expertise and resources than the traditional individual or associated study clubs could muster. Increasingly, specialized knowledge was required to deal with the growing complexity and threshold size of economic projects. The two-pronged approach adopted by the Extension Department in the fisheries is summarized in figure 5.2.

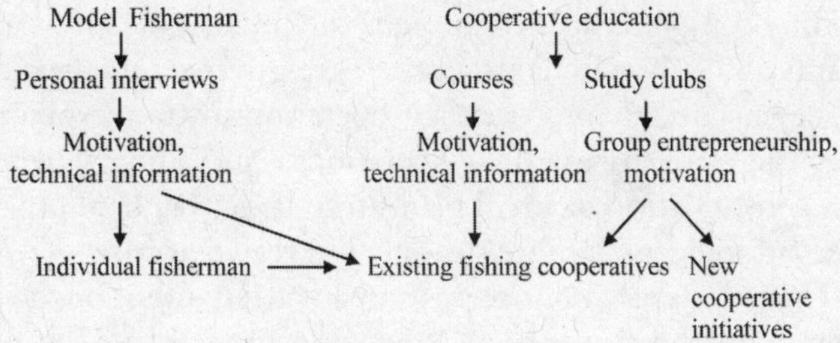

Figure 5.2 Educational Program in the Fisheries in the 1950s

The education program in the fisheries strove to preserve the link between education and economic activity. However, this link was largely with existing cooperatives. The two-pronged approach – based on the study clubs and the model fisherman – was aimed at improving the economic conditions of the individual fishermen as well as bolstering the fishing cooperatives.

The Education Program and the Cooperative Sector

The 1950s ushered in an era of rapid expansion in productive capacity, and nowhere was this more in evidence than in the Atlantic fisheries, particularly the offshore ones. In the fisheries and elsewhere, this new era was characterized by the emergence of a new form of enterprise based on the corporate form of ownership, large-scale production, modern technology, and highly trained management. Moreover, some of these were foreign-controlled. This corporate enterprise was responsible for much of the increased capacity in the fisheries through the introduction of offshore fleets of draggers, long-liners, seiners, and the like, leading to an expansion in onshore processing activities. Interestingly, this increase in capacity involved substantial financial input by the Canadian government both directly and indirectly through expenditures to support infrastructure such as wharves, windbreakers, roads, and channels.

The existing cooperative sector in the fisheries found itself at a competitive disadvantage vis-à-vis these new enterprises. The problem, therefore, was predominantly not one of establishing new cooperatives but one of making those that were already in place more efficient and competitive. Whereas in the 1930s the fisheries cooperatives had successfully competed against the generally small and family-oriented fish plants and fish merchants, in the 1950s, to meet the new competition, they needed to improve their operations by modernizing their facilities and reorganizing their operations – including, where necessary, the consolidation of small plants into larger regional units – and they needed to become more strongly integrated as parts of a system. The Extension Department seems to have been aware of the overall situation, with the thrust of its education program in the fisheries being increasingly focused on modernization and consolidation, aptly expressed in the slogan "Bigger and Better." However, the need for the cooperatives to become more integrated as parts of a system, although recognized, was largely ignored.

Bringing about the required changes in the fisheries, as in the cooperative sector as a whole, was fraught with obstacles, predominantly in the areas of capital accumulation and management – the two areas where the cooperative form of enterprise turned out to be particularly vulnerable. The negative connotation attached to the notion of profit or surplus among cooperators, who are generally more concerned with maximizing services or benefits to the membership, led to widespread undercapitalization. The problem was further aggravated by management, whose performance was measured largely on the basis of fish prices as well as the size of rebates and dividends paid to the membership. Higher prices, rebates, and dividends were associated with more successful management at the cost of capital accumulation, future growth, and even institutional survival.

The fisheries and other cooperatives also faced problems in the recruitment and retention of competent managers. The salaries paid to managers of cooperatives were relatively low in comparison to those of managers in the noncooperative private sector. Most of the managers of the early cooperatives were recruited from within – in the case of the fisheries cooperatives, from among the fishermen themselves. These were generally the brightest leaders of study clubs who received some business training from the Extension Department. As long as cooperatives remained small and had fairly simple objectives and tasks, these people could adequately and efficiently manage them. They were motivated by the spirit of cooperation, and their position in the organization gave them social prestige, which compensated for the modest monetary rewards that they received. Furthermore, their opportunity cost was very low, and some of them were even employed by the Extension Department or the United Maritime Fishermen cooperative on a part-time basis as fieldworkers. Thus monetary remuneration was not a serious obstacle to the recruitment and retention of efficient managers, and the study clubs provided a steady stream of such people.

As the complexity of the cooperative organizations increased, the skills and knowledge required for effective management also grew, contracting the pool of suitable candidates from within the movement and increasing the need to attract competent managers from outside sources. The relatively low remuneration levels precluded success in recruitment efforts, forcing at least some cooperatives to rely on people who lacked the experience and/or the ability for the task. The problem was further accentuated by the fact that the cooperative set-up made it very difficult to dismiss incompetent managers. Whereas managers could be easily fired in the more traditional private firm, the dismissal of a manager in a cooperative organization could cause a split in the membership, with potentially disastrous consequences. Indeed, reports by fisheries fieldworkers suggest that there was widespread tolerance of incompetent managers in order to avoid the risk of splitting the membership. Despite numerous short courses, leadership-type courses, and the like, this issue was not adequately addressed over the decade.

MOBILIZATION OF RESOURCES

Despite the forces at work and the changes that were taking place in the education program of the Extension Department, especially the weakening of the link between education and economic action and the failure to adequately address problems such as those related to management and capitalization, the cooperative sector remained remarkably resilient. That many of the economic institutions in place since the 1930s were able not only to survive but also to expand seemed to augur well for the soundness of the movement as a whole, regardless of what was happening on other fronts. In many ways, however, the relative buoyancy in the cooperative sector served to mask the fundamental problems that were quickly overtaking both the Extension Department and the movement as a whole.

The Fisheries

The number of fisheries cooperatives in eastern Nova Scotia remained relatively stable over the decade, hovering at around sixteen. However, as documented in table 5.1, their combined sales nearly tripled, with the value of fish products handled by local cooperatives being in excess of $3 million in 1960. The exceptional performance of fisheries cooperatives, however, was more apparent than real. In 1960 nearly 60 per cent of sales were generated by the four strongest cooperatives: Port Bickerton, Cheticamp, Grand Etang, and Isle Madame.[81] Moreover, there was a substantial turnover during the decade as some ceased operations and new ones were organized.

Fisheries cooperatives proved to be unstable, with even the strongest ones facing the possibility of decline and even bankruptcy in short order. In 1950, and 1945 as well, Tor Bay was the largest and most efficient fisheries cooperative in eastern Nova Scotia, responsible for over 15 per cent of total cooperative sales. Although it had lost its leadership position, by 1955 it had gotten even stronger, posting sales of nearly $300,000. By 1960 its sales were less than $10,000, leading to its dissolution a few years later. The case of the Northhumberland cooperative was equally dramatic, as it went from being the sixth largest in the region in 1950 to bankruptcy by the end of the decade. The small number of societies that seemed to prosper consisted of those that were able to acquire larger and more efficient boats and equipment, especially for offshore fishing, and to establish more modern and larger-scale fish-processing plants. These included the ones that the fisheries fieldworkers were able to organize between 1955 and 1960 to replace some of the older and weaker entities. The new cooperatives were able to tap into the funds provided by the Fishermen's Board of Nova Scotia to access larger boats and newer technologies. Most of the other existing cooperatives, unable to expand or otherwise adapt to the changing environment, even if they survived, remained vulnerable and susceptible to myriad dangers, including loss of members loyalty, undercapitalization, and obsolete technology, in addition to the factors that emanated from the nature of the fishing industry, with its short harvesting season, changing weather patterns, unpredictable movements of fish stocks, and so on.

The same factors were at work in New Brunswick and Prince Edward Island as well. In the case of New Brunswick, between 1945

Table 5.1
Sales of fishermen's cooperatives in eastern Nova Scotia, 1950, 1955, 1960

Cooperatives	*1950*	*1955*	*1960*
Antigonish	n.a.	175,594.99	150,639.51
Blue Ribbon Fisheries	59,592.35	55,910.37	60,673.71
Cape Breton Fishermen	7,555.67	n.a.	12,784.25
Capeview	43,783.64	n.a.	n.a
Cheticamp Fishermen	163,878.17	171,791.24	450,649.1
Eastern Fishermen	129,332.08	117,981.81	84,127.77
Fundy	10,387.26	n.a.	n.a.
Grand Etang Fishermen	123,992.29	357,263.72	346,947.61
Guysborough Fishermen	n.a.	n.a.	108,243.35
Isle Madame	n.a.	n.a.	366,175.69
Little Harbour	14,152.43	n.a.	n.a.
Margaree Beach	35,755.04	2,532.43	n.a.
Maryville	29,632.01	42,097.13	80,075.86
New Harbor	9,785.75	n.a.	n.a.
Northhumberland	96,367.58	76,135.95	n.a.
Pleasant	15,085.82	3,521.30	n.a.
Port Bickerton	142,824.51	326,663.83	602,158.04
Pubnico	n.a.	n.a.	140,205.79
St George's	69,251.33	90,072.88	112,219.41
St Michael's	n.a.	n.a.	139,862.65
St Paul's	n.a.	49,331.84	n.a.
Tor Bay	189,916.88	292,914.74	9,670.44
Victoria Fishermen	n.a.	n.a.	176,173.76
Westport	63,877.04	73,520.00	115,284.99
TOTAL ($)	1,205,186.85	1,835,332.65	3,070,950.96

Source: Nova Scotia Department of Agriculture and Marketing, *Annual Reports of Co-operative Associations in Nova Scotia* (1950, 1955, 1960).

and 1957 a total of twelve cooperative lobster canneries failed, leaving only six in operation. Moreover, three of the remaining canneries were barely surviving.[82]

Credit Unions and the Financial Sector

Credit unions prospered over the whole of Nova Scotia, as can be gleaned from the data presented in table 5.2. They also flourished in the rest of the country.[83] Although the number of credit unions in Nova Scotia decreased from 221 in 1950 to 219 in 1960, the member-

Table 5.2
Credit unions in Nova Scotia, 1950–60

Year	*Credit unions*	*Membership*	*Assets ($)*
1950	221	41,882	4,686,966.86
1951	217	44,600	5,439,573.48
1952	218	47,823	6,290,025.64
1953	221	49,831	7,255,455.11
1954	220	51,952	7,927,069.37
1955	218	51,985	8,654,479.64
1956	222	51,824	9,656,665.81
1957	212	53,545	10,817,101.57
1958	212	58,005	12,496,564.51
1959	221	59,553	14,111,896.77
1960	219	60,577	15,567,204.97

Source: Nova Scotia Credit Union League, *Annual Reports* (1950–60).

ship increased by about 50 per cent and the value of total assets in 1960 was over three times that of 1950 (and over fifteen times that of 1940, when the value of total assets was, as noted in the previous chapter, $924,750.84). Nonetheless, there were also many instances of failure, and some of the surviving credit unions were on relatively shaky ground.[84] Credit unions were particularly strong in eastern Nova Scotia, which contributed the bulk of the total assets. For example, in 1954 the seven eastern counties of Nova Scotia comprised about 65 per cent of the total membership and 67 per cent of the total assets of credit unions in Nova Scotia.[85] Overall, the credit union sector seems to have been quite dynamic during the period, which, at least on the surface, augured well for the movement in the future. The credit unions also benefited from the overall expansion of the local economy outside of the cooperative sector.

Consumers' and Other Cooperatives

As demonstrated in table 5.3, cooperative stores declined in number over the decade, going from seventy-nine in 1950 to fifty-nine in 1960. Moreover, although their total sales increased, the increase was relatively small, especially from 1955 to 1960, which suggests that the drop in numbers was due more to failure than to consolidation into

Table 5.3
Nova Scotia cooperatives by sector, 1950, 1955, 1960

Sector	*Year*	*Cooperatives*	*Sales ($)*
Consumers' stores	1950	79	10,334,694.09
	1955	74	12,199,888.91
	1960	59	12,897,169.70
Fishermen's cooperatives	1950	17	1,205,186.85
	1955	15	1,835,332.65
	1960	17	3,070,950.96
Other cooperatives	1950	17	2,627,065.42
	1955	25	3,799,284.98
	1960	36	5,176,999.71

Source: Nova Scotia Department of Agriculture and Marketing, *Annual Reports of Co-operative Associations in Nova Scotia* (1950, 1955, 1960).

Table 5.4
Nova Scotia cooperatives, 1950–60

Year	*Cooperatives*	*Membership*
1950	113	21,464
1951	110	21,649
1952	116	22,950
1953	109	20,456
1954	112	23,675
1955	115	24,152
1956	121	25,421
1957	118	26,514
1958	118	28,210
1959	114	28,631
1960	114	28,647

Source: Nova Scotia Department of Agriculture and Marketing, *Annual Report of Co-operative Associations in Nova Scotia* (1960).

other units. Fisheries cooperatives, as we have already seen, stayed fairly constant in number while increasing in total sales. Other cooperatives, mostly in the agricultural sector, including the cooperative dairies, experienced an increase in terms of both number – more than doubling from 17 to 36 – and sales. Overall, as indicated in table 5.4, the number of cooperative entities did not change very much over the decade, increasing from 113 in 1950 to 121 in 1956 and then dropping to 114 in 1959 and 1960. Interestingly, the low point of 109 was achieved in 1953, the year that marked the centenary of St Francis Xavier University and the twenty fifth anniversary of the Extension Department. In terms of membership, there was an overall increase during the period, from 21,464 in 1950 to in excess of 28,000 from 1958 onward. Again, the low point was achieved in 1953, with the membership dropping to 20,456. It is also important to note that it took until 1955 to bring the membership up to the 1949 level of in excess of 24,000.[86] Both the numbers of cooperative organizations and the fact that cooperative membership remained stagnant in the late 1950s can be taken as evidence of the creeping malaise that was taking over the movement at the end of the decade.

The Crowning Achievement: Eastern Co-operative Services

Although the two regional wholesalers, Eastern Co-operative Services (ECS) of Antigonish and Cape Breton Co-operative Services (CBCS) of Sydney, experienced growth and expansion during the 1940s, both began to face difficulties starting in 1949 and continuing into the 1950s, despite generally experiencing increases in total sales. These difficulties arose from a number of factors.[87] Local agricultural production was generally not only inadequate but also, and more important, could not be marketed by the wholesalers or purchased by cooperative stores since farmers were not able to "grade, process, package and store their produce and guarantee a continuity of supply."[88] The farmers lacked access to the facilities that would have allowed them to undertake these tasks. This state of affairs contributed to the serious crisis in the agricultural sector, which the Extension Department was prompted to address through the establishment of a division of rural education with its own full-time director in 1955. However, in addition to limited facilities, the two wholesalers were hampered by the fact that cooperative stores bypassed them in favour of private suppliers as well as by shortages of working capital worsened due to the withdrawals by members of cooperatives, conflicting interests between consumers and producers, increased competition from grocery chains, and a host of other problems.[89] These issues were particularly serious in the case of CBCS.[90] After a period of intense study and consultation, the proposed solution to the problems faced by ECS and CBCS as well as by the agricultural sector as a whole was to merge the two wholesalers and, in the process, expand the services provided (including those required to be able to market local produce), establish the possibility of expanding into other areas of economic activity, and integrate both consumers and producers into the same institutional apparatus.[91] The new ECS was not only a part of a rural rehabilitation program designed to boost efficiency as well as local production and diversification but also an important part of the completion of the Big Picture. Not surprisingly, it was strongly supported by Rev. Coady, who, as he was nearing the end of his life, saw it as a crowning achievement of the Antigonish Movement.[92] Writing in 1958, Rev. Coady referred to ECS as "the synthesis of all our education and all our activity for the whole twenty-nine years of our existence."[93]

The proposal elicited both enthusiasm and opposition. The enthusiasm came from various cooperators in eastern Nova Scotia, who saw it as a possible anchor for the movement and as the secondary society that was needed to revive the agricultural sector and reverse the serious problem of rural decline.[94] Among the detractors were the leaders of Moncton-based Maritime Co-operative Services, particularly W.H. McEwen, and the Nova Scotia Department of Agriculture.[95] Stefan Haley suggests that McEwen's opposition was premised on three fundamental concerns: (1) that increasing the capacity to handle agricultural output did not necessarily imply an increase in output, (2) that local produce would not be able to compete with imports, and (3) that there were limits to the expansion of local output given the limited potential of the region's agricultural sector.[96] Similar concerns were also echoed by the Nova Scotia Department of Agriculture.

On the face of it, however, the objections were no more compelling than the supposed advantages. Merging two somewhat struggling operations entailed a process of rationalization that could, under proper circumstances, have been beneficial to both of the existing operations. Expanding operations, including adding additional capabilities for further processing, was another matter. Its outcome would depend on a number of factors, including the ability of the agricultural sector to increase its commercial production, how the various operations were managed, and the degree to which it was supported by the people of eastern Nova Scotia, including the various cooperative institutions already in place.[97] A lot of emphasis was placed on the education program of the Extension Department, which involved short courses, group meetings, kitchen meetings, radio and television programs, news bulletins, and the like.[98]

The merger was adopted in 1956, and the new Sydney-based ECS Limited became fully operational, with new facilities, in September 1959. In keeping with the objective of boosting agricultural activity through expanded processing, the new ECS included cold-storage facilities, a poultry-processing plant, an egg-grading station, and grading and packing facilities for fruits and vegetables.[99] These facilities were complemented by the establishment of a cooperative abbattoir in Halifax, which also went into operation in 1959.[100] ECS also offered to provide, among other things, "education and field services, a group medical plan, farm mutual insurance, Co-op Life and Auto insurance, farm credit, land settlement, forest product marketing, and a livestock shipping agency."[101] In contrast to the cautious approach of Maritime Co-operative Services, the new ECS followed the more adventurous and expansive approach of the original ECS and CBCS. Moreover, although during 1957, its first year of operation, its performance was satisfactory and sales continued to increase, difficulties also arose, and these became more pronounced over the rest of the decade.[102]

The actual establishment of the new ECS proved to be more difficult than anticipated and severely taxed the resources of both the Extension Department and the Antigonish Movement as a whole. It also soured relations between the Extension Department and some of its supporters, particularly the provincial Department of Agriculture.[103] Moreover, both the nature and the scope of the project pushed the movement into a fundamentally different type of activity that required much greater financial resources, skill, and coordination among various cooperative entities than any previous undertaking had required.[104] The whole process of getting the project off the ground also exposed many of the weaknesses of the Antigonish Movement, including the fragmentation of the existing cooperative sector. Nevertheless, the project went ahead, and the importance of the fact that both the Extension Department and the movement had the ability to establish something of such a magnitude cannot be underestimated. The movement was still able to motivate the establishment of a complex and large-scale operation.

Table 5.5
Human resources of the Extension Department, 1950–60

Year	*Full-time and part-time staff**
1950–51	23
1951–52	25
1952–53	26
1953–54	21
1954–55	24
1955–56	23
1956–57	23
1957–58	28
1958–59	26
1959–60	26

* Includes Rev. Moses Michael Coady.

Source: St Francis Xavier University, *Academic Calendars* (1950–60).

Other Cooperative Activities

During the decade, some progress was made in cooperative housing, with numerous groups being formed. According to Ellie Mae Sowder, in 1958 there were "700 families in Nova Scotia, some 4,000 persons in all," living in cooperative houses.[105] Sowder also notes that 134 cooperative houses were built over the 1950–54 period and 449 over the 1955–59 period.[106] The movement also had made some incursions into other service areas, most notably into insurance and into health-related areas.

RESOURCES OF THE EXTENSION DEPARTMENT

The inadequacy of resources, both human and material, was a constant problem for the Extension Department from the outset. In the 1930s the constraint of meager resources had been effectively overcome by the degree to which volunteers carried out much of the organizing and other work of the Antigonish Movement. Volunteers also helped during the extraordinary circumstances of the war and postwar years, when many activities were largely put on hold, although the circumstances themselves had a dampening effect on volunteerism.

In the 1950s, as shown in table 5.5, the staff of the Extension Department – both full-time and part-time – ranged from a low of twenty-one in 1953–54 to a high of twenty-eight in 1957–58. There was also a resurgence in the number of volunteers. Given the challenges faced by both the Extension Department and the Antigonish Movement as a whole, the staffing was still inadequate, especially since the staff's work was no longer limited to the local area but even included forays overseas.

The financial resources were also limited, especially in view of the myriad demands that were being made on the Extension Department. That even after two decades of operation it had failed to secure a reliable and stable financial base acted as an important constraint to its work. The financial difficulties were perhaps the most obvious symptom of the inability of the movement to act as a system – and of the cooperative sector to appreciate the importance not only of education but also of being a part of an integrated and broad-based economic system.[107]

With the exception of the fisheries grant, the Extension Department had no secure long-term funding. Moreover, this grant increased in size and hence in importance to the Extension Department over time. For example, whereas the grant was only $5,000 in 1938, it had grown to about $47,000 by 1954 and to nearly $70,000 by 1960.[108] Indeed, during the 1950s, the fisheries grant accounted for anywhere from 50 to 75 per cent of the Extension Department's budget.[109] At the same time, the Extension Department itself did not pursue an active strategy of generating a more balanced and secure source of funding.

The Extension Department's situation is put in perspective by the fact that over the 1953–54 period, the Nova Scotia Credit Union League and the Nova Scotia Co-operative Union, both of which had departments of education, had a combined amount of $50,000 available for their own adult education programs, an amount that was in excess of the budget of the Extension Department, estimated to be less than $40,000.[110] Arguably, the department did not appreciate the importance of maintaining control over the adult education program in order to propagate the movement as a whole, as opposed to dealing with the concerns of individual institutions.

THE COADY INTERNATIONAL INSTITUTE

The idea of putting in place an international branch of the movement first appeared in Rev. Coady's book *Masters of Their Destiny*, where he proposed the creation of a people's research institute.[111] Over time, the idea of establishing an institution capable of training individuals from overseas in the principles, techniques, and practices of the Antigonish Movement became increasingly appealing. The trainees, upon returning to their countries of origin, would organize various cooperatives, credit unions, and other institutions suitable to the local conditions. The success of these enterprises would not only directly benefit the masses of the poor but would also encourage the creation of even more cooperatives and credit unions, as it had in the Maritimes, giving rise to the emergence of alternate economic systems, indigenous to the various countries, that could tackle the problems of development.[112] At the same time, the influence of the Antigonish Movement would be spread over wider areas. This optimistic global vision of the movement appeared not only enticing but also plausible and possible. After all, the movement was spreading overseas spontaneously and the establishment of an international institute would only accelerate and formalize the process.

The idea was accepted uncritically and with a great deal of enthusiasm, but financial considerations kept it from being realized. The severe resource limitations and challenges of the war years relegated it to the back burner as more pressing problems and concerns took centre stage. The postwar revival in the late 1940s, combined with the further spread of the movement overseas, brought the idea of an international institute to the fore again. The revival of the idea was influenced by a number of specific factors, foremost being the steady and growing stream of international visitors and admirers eager to learn the secrets of this successful movement in order to apply them in their own countries or regions. However, the movement had neither the resources nor the facilities to meet their expectations and needs. Although some of them were placed in the short courses designed to train the local leaders and others were able to enrol in the university programs, most of them were simply unloaded upon overworked fieldworkers, who often complained that, as a result, their effectiveness was being hampered by the constant interruptions, questions, and inquiries with which they had to deal. A specialized training institute would be a far more effective and systematic vehicle for transferring the experience of the Antigonish Movement to the overseas visitors and students.

Another factor contributing to the promotion of the establishment of an international institute revolved around the drastic changes taking place in the international political relations of the time, particularly the start of the Cold War in 1948 and the decolonization process set in motion by India's independence in 1947. These two momentous events had a bearing on the Antigonish Movement and the establishment of its international institute. The Antigonish Movement, with its focus on voluntary cooperative action, claimed the middle ground between unbridled individualism and collectivism. For many in the newly or soon to become independent developing countries, this "Middle Way" constituted a preferred alternative to both capitalism and communism. In particular, the perception that the movement represented an alternative capable of forestalling the spread of communism among the developing counties allowed it to gain a great number of new sympathizers and supporters, particularly in the United States. This support coincided with the formation of the Friends of Antigonish Movement in Boston and New York in the late 1940s, with the goal of fundraising for the purpose of establishing an international training institute in the Extension Department.

Two additional factors were also at work. The first was the widespread belief among both the leaders and the members of the movement that its undeniable benefits ought to be spread to all corners of the globe for the good of others. The second emanated from the desire on the part of many friends and followers of Rev. Moses Coady to create an institute bearing his name to honour the man and his accomplishments.

Financial constraints were finally overcome in 1959 by a generous donation from Cardinal Richard James Cushing of Boston, and the institute bearing Rev. Coady's name was established.[113] Its programs, modelled after the successful leadership course – the so-called "short course" – provided students with general knowledge comprising the principles of economics, sociology, and politics in addition to the theory and practices of the Antigonish Movement. Upon the successful completion of the eight-month course, candidates were awarded a diploma in social leadership.

It is beyond the scope of this volume to analyze the workings and merits of the Coady International Institute. Notably, it emerged at the very time that the Antigonish Movement was in a state of fundamental transition and confusion – a circumstance that eventually led the institute to define its own role in terms fundamentally different from those of the Extension Department and the Antigonish Movement. Since the movement was no longer able to promote the establishment of an alternate economic system at home, it remained to be seen whether it could do so abroad.

CONCLUSION

The 1950s were years of transitions for the Antigonish Movement. There was the transition from the fundamentally extraordinary circumstances of the war and postwar years to a new era characterized by seemingly greater options and the gradual adoption of Keynesianism. There was the transition associated with the appointment of a new director to replace Rev. Coady. By the end of the decade, the vision predicated on the establishment of an alternate economic system that would enable the common people to become "Masters of Their Own Destiny" was being severely challenged, even though it could still motivate the establishment of Eastern Co-operative Services – in effect, the last stand for the Big Picture. Finally, by the end of the decade, all four of the key early leaders, Rev. Coady, Rev. Tompkins, MacDonald, and MacIntyre, had died.

During the 1950s, the Extension Department instigated fundamental changes in its education program. Whereas some were attempts to return to the successful program of the 1930s, others, such as the mass media programs, were novel and intended to adapt to the changing circumstances and the new socio-economic environment.

Although the movement was predicated on education, study, and analysis, it failed to carry out any analysis of what had been done in the past. Specifically, it failed to establish its own "think-tank," or analytical centre, to serve as a guide for future action. Instead, it maintained its reliance on the imagination, intuition, trial and error methods, and pragmatism of its leaders, which had proven effective in the past but were no longer adequate. In the absence of analysis and a clear sense of direction, the disintegration of its numerous programs and activities, so tightly knit in the past, was allowed unchecked.

The cooperative sector managed to survive, with the number of institutions remaining stable and with generally increasing membership and/or sales. However, the weaknesses, which were apparent at the start of the decade and even earlier, ranging from fragmentation to inadequate capitalization and poor management, became increasingly pronounced. The changes in the socio-economic environment required that the cooperative organizations make fundamental adaptations, including increasing their size of operation, introducing new technologies, and improving management. The movement could not effectively deal with these factors. At the same time, the adopted education programs were fragmented and ineffective. The general failure to revive the study club method eliminated the movement's most powerful tool of widening the cooperative approach by establishing additional enterprises through the development of group entrepreneurship and decision making.

Nevertheless, a sense of unbound optimism permeated both the Extension Department and the movement as a whole. This optimism was evident in the establishment of ECS and of the Coady International Institute. It was perhaps this optimism that allowed many of the emerging problems either to go unnoticed or to be underestimated. Thus the Extension Department and the Antigonish Movement as a whole ignored the urgency of maintaining or reestablishing the link between education and economic action by reviving, revitalizing, and adapting traditional tools such as study clubs and mass meetings.

6

The Unravelling of the Movement, 1960–69

INTRODUCTION

Despite facing mounting difficulties, the Antigonish Movement was able to adapt to the changing conditions of the 1950s and thus not only survived the decade but also did so with a seemingly remarkable degree of vitality and vigour. That all was far from well came fully to the fore in the 1960s as the movement began to quickly unravel. Faced with deteriorating economic conditions in the region, the persistent difficulties and eventual collapse of its most ambitious undertaking in the form of Eastern Co-operative Services (ECS), and a fundamental change in the role of the Extension Department, the movement lost both its vitality and its fundamental vision as an economic force. The notion of people becoming "Masters of Their Own Destiny" ceased to be, in any meaningful way, its rallying cry.

An important contributor to the unravelling of the movement over the decade was the growing gap between the idealistic and pragmatic components of its vision. In earlier decades, these two components had been able to coexist more or less harmoniously since they were seen as fundamentally complementary. Idealism inspired and led the way, and pragmatism took care of the details required to build the economic system that would lead to the achievement of the lofty goals prescribed in the "Big Picture." Such coexistence, which had already been disturbed by the emergence and enthusiastic adoption of the "Six Principles" in the latter part of the 1940s, became further strained in the 1950s as the Big Picture was relegated to the background and then virtually disappeared in the 1960s.

The persistent difficulties and eventual collapse of ECS must be considered a critical turning point. Arguably, the establishment of such a large-scale enterprise in the 1950s was in itself a reflection of the widening gap between idealism and pragmatism, although it could also be interpreted as a last gasp to combine the two. The establishment of the Coady International Institute in 1959 was also a reflection of the same trend. The shift toward greater idealism could not fail to develop a universal appeal that would engulf many of the primarily newly independent and overwhelmingly poor developing countries. Whereas such an idealistic bent had generally benign effects on the work of the Coady International Institute, it had the opposite effect locally, where the more practical concerns of running existing enterprises to ensure their survival and expansion, as well as promoting the establishment of new ones, loomed much larger.

The establishment of the ill-fated ECS was construed by its supporters as a necessary cog in the structure of the Big Picture and hence as consistent with the original vision of the movement. It was designed as a grandiose project of rural transformation, whose size was far too large given the market area to be served, the agricultural resource base upon which it could draw, and the available financial and management resources. The circumstances called for a facility more modest in terms of both size and scope, with a better chance of surviving and in the process strengthening the agricultural base of the region and the Antigonish Movement as a whole. Arguably, its establishment can also be seen as an attempt to keep the dream of an economic system alive after nearly three decades of operation.

The persistent problems and eventual collapse of ECS by the middle of the decade brought into question the original vision of the movement. The weakening of this once inspiring vision created a vacuum, adversely affecting both the morale and the motivation of its participants. The staff of the Extension Department, a majority of whom were new, untried, and generally far removed from its early and pioneering work, was strongly affected by this vacuum. With Rev. Moses Coady no longer physically present to establish a link with the past, the inexperienced director and staff of the Extension Department felt compelled to find a new faith, a new vision, and a new identity for their organization.[1] The result was the rejection of the very essence of the Antigonish Movement, predicated on the establishment of an alternate economic system based on control and ownership by the people themselves. That the vision of the movement was so quickly undermined suggests that it had been deteriorating for some time and, moreover, that there had been a fundamental lack of understanding of what it was all about.

The search for a new vision and a new role led the Extension Department to rely on the emerging social sciences for guidance in the belief that the scientific knowledge of highly trained professionals and academics at St Francis Xavier University could determine the best course of action for the university's Extension Department and what was left of the entire movement. Thus, in the new vision that emerged out of the 1960s, the people were no longer deemed capable of solving their own socio-economic problems. These were to be solved primarily through the application of discoveries made by social scientists. In the process, the past accomplishments of the movement, although still often lauded, were made largely irrelevant.

In many ways, the faith in the social sciences, and in the social engineering imposed by experts, reflected the temper of the times. Indeed, the 1960s saw these ideas being adopted by an ever-increasing cadre of government officials who occupied administrative positions in the various agencies and departments created to solve the economic problems of the maritime provinces. Thus there developed a strong bond of common interests between the Extension Department and the heads of various government agencies and departments. There was a strong belief that, together and through the application of the new knowledge provided by the social sciences, the problems that afflicted Atlantic Canada could be solved.

The stronger ties that were forged with the various government agencies and departments proved to be a mixed blessing for the Extension Department and severely damaging for the Antigonish Movement. On the one hand, they enabled the Extension Department to tap into new and significant sources of public funds, allowing it to increase the size of its budget and staff and hence not only to maintain its existing education programs but also to initiate new ones, such as the "Indian," forestry, and civic education programs. On the other hand, the reliance on public funds, particularly those earmarked for specific purposes, caused the Extension Department to lose its intellectual independence, undermining even further its identity and, perhaps most important, its ties with the cooperative sector and other institutions of the Antigonish Movement. Ironically, even as they were expanded, the effectiveness of the Extension Department's education activities – the life line of the movement – was declining as a result of their increasing fragmentation and their separation from meaningful economic activities and from the institutional structure of the movement.

The weakening of the Extension Department's historical bonds with the cooperative sector – its own institutional child and key component of the alternate economic system – was particularly damaging. Although this weakening resulted from a complex series of factors, some of them dating as far back as the 1940s, the loss of vision by the Extension Department and its increasingly stronger links with government agencies and departments in the 1960s certainly played a key role. The cooperative sector suffered a setback as a result of the difficulties faced by ECS. It was further weakened by the declining effectiveness of the education programs of the Extension Department, forcing it to assume even greater responsibility for the education of its members and officers. The cooperative sector, made up of economic entities with much narrower and more immediate concerns, was ill equipped to carry out the sort of education that was required by the movement as a whole.[2]

The combination of factors proved disastrous for the Antigonish Movement. The cooperative structures were greatly weakened as they lost not only control over their resources but also, and more important, the commitment and loyalty of their members. No longer inspired and motivated, and with seemingly many more options, members of cooperatives were looking elsewhere and in the process were draining the cooperative enterprises of their capital. The loss of capital and loyalty of the members pushed weaker cooperative organizations into bankruptcy, which set in motion a snowball effect that undermined stronger ones as well. Bankruptcies, and the growing perception that these organizations were not efficient, also discouraged entry into the sector, further weakening the movement. The movement had failed to integrate its cooperative institutions into an economic system, leaving individual enterprises largely on their own in an increasingly competitive environment.

As a result, during the 1960s, the Antigonish Movement experienced a vicious cycle of decline and disintegration. This process of internal disintegration was augmented and accelerated by external threats and by the pressures emanating from the rapid changes in the socio-economic environment of the region.

THE SOCIO-ECONOMIC ENVIRONMENT

The socio-economic environment of eastern Nova Scotia and the rest of Atlantic Canada during the 1960s differed greatly from that of previous periods. Improvements in communication and transportation eliminated the isolation of the region. A network of highways and secondary roads made even the most remote communities accessible, and cheap gasoline and the spread of the automobile increased the mobility of people.

The 1960s, even more so than the 1950s, saw the emergence of television as the most powerful tool not only for entertainment but also for the dissemination of information. It became an effective avenue of adult education, able to reach millions of viewers in the comfort of their living rooms. This education, along with the entertainment, was seemingly provided free to the public, as it was financed by the large national companies that were using television programs to advertise their goods and services.[3] The programs themselves were rated by their popularity among the viewing public and were continuously modified, improved, and frequently replaced. The television commercials, inserted at the most exciting moments of the programs, were also improved in attractiveness and effectiveness, generating attachment and loyalty to particular brands, products, and services, notably among the younger generation. In the process, television also had a subtler but nevertheless important effect on the people's attitudes and values, promoting consumption, gratification, and even self-indulgence at the expense of self-denial, sacrifice, and cooperation with others.

The program of adult education that had been adopted by the Extension Department since the 1930s, with its combination of hands-on group study and social interaction, could not compete with the adult education provided through the mass media, particularly television. Thus, over time, as the mass media became more pervasive, the more traditional and time-consuming study clubs, kitchen meetings, and even weekly industrial study sessions were scaled down and eventually discontinued. Moreover, cooperative managers had to be increasingly ingenious in hiding profits or surpluses to prevent the members from draining capital from their organizations – in some cases, in order to buy new and heavily advertised consumer goods. The dream of becoming "Masters of Their Own Destiny" through self-reliance, hard work, and cooperation began to lose its appeal altogether, and the Antigonish Movement ceased to be seen, by many of its adherents, as a viable alternative.

The Social-Welfare Safety Net

The steady expansion of the welfare state and the general increase in the involvement of the government in the economy following the full-fledged adoption of Keynesianism turned out to be important factors in undermining the Antigonish Movement during the 1960s. The avalanche of legislation and programs that permeated the decade reduced the incentive to promote economic activity and change through the movement's seemingly harder route of study and cooperative economic action. Indeed, what Rev. Coady had earlier termed the "lazy way" out of difficulty through political action became more predominant. However, although the various public-sector programs and initiatives cushioned the effects of economic difficulties, they did not eradicate them.[4]

The building of the social safety net was only one aspect of the increased involvement of the government in the economy. The decade also witnessed a wide array of government programs and agencies instituted to promote regional economic development, as it became concerned with the persistence of regional disparity, especially in view of the general growth and prosperity that engulfed the nation as a whole. Instead of resisting the negative impacts of such interventions or at least attempting to modify them – or, indeed, to turn them to its advantage – the Extension Department and hence the Antigonish Movement as a whole were willingly co-opted into the process. This complicity was particularly evident in the case of the leadership of the Extension Department, which was willing to accept a much-reduced role as a junior partner in the development process.

At the international level, the 1960s also coincided with the "development decade," which was supposed to transform Third World countries, many of which achieved independence during the decade, into industrialized and prosperous entities. Indeed, the 1950s and 1960s witnessed the proliferation of numerous theories and approaches and their applications to the problems of economic development. Most of these perspectives stressed capital accumulation and industrialization either through the market mechanism or through heavy doses of economic planning.[5] Generally, there was great optimism that the social sciences, especially the new theories and approaches developed by economic theorists, would yield the correct policy instruments to deal with disparities at the local and regional levels and with the promotion of development in the developing countries at the international level.

The Canadian government's more formal involvement in regional economic development added new programs to the plethora already in place, such as tax write-offs and other incentives for firms locating in high-unemployment areas, with the seeming total exclusion of the cooperative sector. Thus the 1960s saw the emergence of agencies such as the Agricultural and Rural Development Agency in 1961, the Atlantic Development Board in 1962, the Area Development Agency in 1966, the Fund for Rural Economic Development in 1966, and most important, the Department of Regional Economic Expansion (DREE) in 1968. These agencies covered virtually all aspects of the regional economy, addressing issues such as rural development, the expansion of manufacturing, the promotion of research, and the build-up of infrastructure. DREE itself came on stream to coordinate the work of all of the other agencies and to foster broad-based regional development through various incentives.[6]

St Francis Xavier University

At the more immediate level, St Francis Xavier University experienced the most rapid period of expansion in its history. Enrolment increased, and so too did the size of the campus as new buildings were erected. Moreover, the university was no longer financed by contributions from the diocesan population but primarily by funding from the federal and provincial governments, which provided increasing amounts for both operating and capital expenditures. Education funds, transferred from the federal government through the provincial government, became the most important source of operating revenue, and the expansion of new buildings and facilities was financed almost entirely by government capital grants and loans. With increased enrolment, there also came a need to hire additional faculty. Traditionally, the faculty of the university was provided largely by the diocesan clergy, along with some of the brightest graduates, who received financial support in their graduate work under the condition that they return to teach at their alma mater. However, the demand for faculty in the 1960s greatly exceeded the numbers that could be obtained through these traditional channels, resulting in the recruitment of new faculty from outside of the region and even outside of the country. Moreover, there was also a trend toward faculty with higher academic credentials, with a doctorate being increasingly required for appointment to the university as well as for tenure eligibility.[7]

There was also a shift in the areas of study undertaken at the university, particularly toward the natural and social sciences and professional programs, with more emphasis on scientific and technical training, and away from the liberal arts. At the same time, faculty members were strongly encouraged to become increasingly involved in academic and scientific research and explorations, with tenure and promotions being increasingly linked to these activities.

In earlier times, the faculty of the university had played a critical role in the emergence and progress of the Antigonish Movement, particularly through their association with the Extension Department. It was from the faculty of the university that many of the innovators and pioneers of the movement, such as Rev. Coady, Rev. Jimmy Tompkins, and Rev. Dr Hugh MacPherson, had emerged. The faculty members, especially those who also belonged to the Roman Catholic clergy, provided the movement with a core of volunteers for study club meetings, kitchen meetings, weekly industrial classes, and the like. They assisted with the preparation of the scripts for and the broadcasting of the radio programs, participated in the annual Rural and Industrial Conferences, and played key roles in the activities of many cooperatives, credit unions, and other economic institutions. The new faculty was less able and at times less willing to assume such a role. First, many of the new faculty members were not familiar with the socioeconomic conditions prevailing in the region, nor were they aware of the activities of the Extension Department and of the Antigonish Movement. Second, their training and research, although more rigorous than that of earlier faculty members, were often limited by narrow disciplinary boundaries, whereas the problems in the region were complex and multidimensional. Third, the research of the new faculty was generally more theoretical and based on national or international perspectives of little direct relevance to the local problems. Fourth, even if appropriate, such research could not easily be applied to the problems of the region since the required institutional mechanism for doing so no longer existed. During the 1960s, the links between the Extension Department and the cooperative sector became progressively too tenuous and fragile, especially as the unifying vision of the movement was being undermined. The economic institutions and the Extension Department were no longer seen as parts of an effective and dynamic economic system but, at best, only as fragments of it.

While the university was rapidly expanding its range of expertise and its body of knowledge, the mechanisms for the transfer and the utilization of such expertise and knowledge in order to address the pressing socio-economic problems of the region were being eroded. The gap between the university and its surrounding communities began to widen, with the Extension Department being increasingly unable and unwilling to do anything about it. Thus, as the academic side of the university increased in size and importance, making it a more powerful source of new knowledge, the institutional apparatus that could translate this new knowledge into greater local economic activity and efficiency was being undermined. Moreover, the role of the Extension Department within the university also declined, eventually leading to its de facto marginalization.

The Role of the Roman Catholic Church

Equally important for both the Extension Department and the Antigonish Movement in the 1960s was the decline in the influence and involvement of the Roman Catholic Church and its institutions. During the 1930s, 1940s, and even 1950s, the influence of the Catholic Church in eastern Nova Scotia, and other parts of the Maritimes where the Antigonish Movement flourished, was pervasive.[8] Roman Catholic parish priests and members of various religious orders, such as the sisters of St Martha, played pivotal roles in organizing meetings, motivating people, and carrying out programs. Their volunteer work on behalf of the Antigonish Movement was part of their vocation. In the postwar period and especially in the 1960s, the situation began to change drastically due to a number of factors. First, there was the government incursion in areas that were hitherto subject to generally benign neglect, such as in the spheres of education and health.[9] Second, the change in moral outlook and aspirations, especially among the young, shifted attention away from the message of local community service and toward the search for economic gain and other options and hence, to some extent, also away from the church and toward the market.[10] These effects were perhaps most pronounced in the case of women, who found themselves with increased options both in terms of their access to education and in terms of their role in the workplace and community at large. The result was not only a reduction in the number of priests and sisters but also a decline in the extent to which religious and economic aspirations coincided. The Antigonish Movement and the Roman Catholic Church viewed economic wellbeing as a means to moral and spiritual growth and development, whereas the new social reality increasingly tended to view economic wellbeing as an ultimate end in itself.[11] For many, the system, whose perceived failure had occasioned the emergence of the Antigonish Movement to begin with, seemed to be working once again. That far greater options had opened up that allowed some people, both men and women, to become highly educated and to contribute to society at large through secular means also played an important part in weakening the role of the church.

In the process, the role of priests, sisters, and other religious – as well as social – leaders declined, leaving a void that came to be filled by an ever-expanding army of professionals and specialists, such as civil servants and consultants. Coming largely from outside the movement, these new social leaders had little or no appreciation for the economic system that it had been building up. In particular, their very professionalism made them reluctant to accept a bottom-up approach where the people, rather than the experts, would be the main decision makers.

The far-reaching reform program of the Catholic Church, encompassed in what is known as Vatican II, can also be identified as a contributing factor during the decade. Of particular relevance to the present discussion was the placing of laity on par with the religious.[12] The immediate post–Vatican II period ushered in an exodus of young priests and sisters at the same time that new religious vocations were in decline.

The declining role of the priests and other religious persons was also influenced by the Catholic Church's own view about its role in society, particularly in helping to foster economic activity. As religious vocations declined and Roman Catholic priests and sisters left, it also became harder for the ones who stayed to remain as involved in community matters as they had in the past. That the movement had not been able to lessen its dependence on such leaders presented an important and difficult problem that had not been addressed.

The Changing Role of Women

Women remained important to the movement during the 1960s, particularly in their traditional roles as spenders and savers. However, their readiness to take on a more direct role in running and holding office in the various cooperative economic institutions was even greater in the 1960s than it had been in the 1940s and 1950s. Technological and other changes were freeing increasingly educated women from some of their "home-based duties," and there was greater general acceptance of even married women working outside of the home. Many of them, particularly those who were younger, more educated, and less bound to the conditions of the past, found increasing options and opportunities outside of the movement and the cooperatives, especially as these were in decline and of less consequence to the well-being of both families and individuals. In turn, this impacted the movement as a whole, weakening women's traditional role as well as precluding their more active participation in the various cooperative economic institutions.

Mounting Economic Difficulties

In the 1950s eastern Nova Scotia had shared in the postwar economic expansion of the country, driven especially by industrial development, technological progress, capital accumulation, and urbanization. With the exception of agriculture, the region generally experienced greater volumes of production, higher sales, and increasing incomes. Even the fisheries seem to have benefited from the shift toward larger boats and from improvements in fishing gear. The industrial sector, particularly the coal and steel industries, experienced further expansion, driven by the ever-increasing demand for goods such as electricity, housing, automobiles, and assorted appliances, which more than offset the effect of the postwar decline in military procurement. Although there were problems, the 1950s were also optimistic times.

In the 1960s the economic fortunes of the region changed drastically and for the worse. The postwar expansion of the 1950s proved to be a short-term phenomenon and was replaced by significant economic decline. The most dramatic reversal of fortune occurred in manufacturing and the fisheries. Manufacturing, based on coal and steel, was never particularly strong, even at the best of times. By the 1960s the coalmines in Cape Breton and Pictou Counties, which were undercapitalized, employed obsolete technology, and were producing low-quality coal, could not compete with more efficient and centrally located producers in Canada and the United States. Coal was also falling behind in its competition with oil and natural gas. Thus the region's coalmining sector was in crisis. Initially, the least efficient mines were closed and hundreds of miners were laid off, but as the decline in the mining sector continued, every mine in the region was in danger of closure, creating a great deal of uncertainty.[13] The lack of diversification in the industrial economic base meant that there was little to cushion the impact of the crisis.

The worldwide steel industry experienced a dramatic increase in productive capacity in the 1960s, particularly in Asia and Europe, as the war-torn countries rebuilt their economies and their steel industries. This expansion, however, took place at the same time that the demand for steel products was being eroded by the effective competition from plastics, aluminum, alloys, and other related products. The North American steel producers found themselves in a difficult position and were losing market share to other producers, especially the Japanese and Europeans, while also facing declining prices. The situation was even bleaker for relatively high-cost steel producers of Atlantic Canada, leading to an imminent shutdown of steel operations in Cape Breton near the end of the decade. The near total collapse of the coal and steel industries was averted, at the last minute, when the federal and provincial governments stepped in and undertook to continue coal and steel operations, although at significantly reduced levels of production and employment.

The fisheries sector also experienced difficulties, especially in the second part of the decade. The enormous expansions of productive capacity, particularly in the offshore sector, undertaken during the preceding decade and enhanced further by the expansion in the Canadian corporate fleet in the late 1960s resulted in a glut of fish products on the market, leading to a precipitous decline in fish prices.[14]

The inshore fisheries, once again, were facing an economic crisis of a magnitude similar to that of the 1920s. The efforts that had been expended on this sector by the Extension Department and the Antigonish Movement over the previous three decades turned out to be insufficient to prevent the crisis. To a great extent, the problem stemmed not from the economic institutions promoted by the Antigonish Movement but from their failure to expand and operate efficiently and to become integrated as parts of a system, especially in the face of renewed and more formidable competition from both domestic and foreign harvesters and processors.[15]

The remaining sectors where the movement had managed to make significant inroads during the previous decades, especially the financial sector through the establishment of credit unions and the consumer sector though the establishment of consumers' stores, were in relatively better shape. The credit unions continued their expansion in terms of assets, loans, and membership, although at a much slower rate than in the preceding decade. Most of the credit union expansion occurred in the urban centres and the towns. Rural, community-based credit unions remained stagnant, with no expansion at all. Furthermore, the rate of expansion of credit unions in the region as a whole lagged behind that of credit unions in other parts of the country. Extension Department sources point out that "many Credit Unions are not aware of their potential. They are satisfied to remain small and have no real desire to grow and extend their services. At the same time finance institutions along side of them are thriving and budget plans are growing fat. Credit Unions are doing only a small part of the Credit business in every community whether rural or urban."[16]

The cooperative stores, although shaken by the collapse of Eastern Co-operative Services in the early years of the decade, remained relatively insulated from the deteriorating economic conditions of the region. Rising prices of consumer goods and rising incomes of members in the more urban areas, especially the main towns and cities, who were increasingly dependent on the public sector, provided some degree of insulation from the overall economic stagnation of the region. The increased government involvement in the region, along with the growth in the social-welfare safety net, served to boost or at least support local consumption. The collapse of ECS, however, had a negative impact on the agricultural sector.

The Impact of Economic Decline on the Movement

In the 1920s the economic crisis facing eastern Nova Scotia had given rise to the Antigonish Movement. Ironically, during the 1960s the mounting economic difficulties of the primary and industrial sectors of the region imposed severe strains on the cooperative organizations of the movement and undermined it. Hardest hit by the economic circumstances were the farming and the fisheries cooperatives, although some showed remarkable resilience. The decline in farm produce and fish prices negatively impacted the value of sales, the size of mark-ups, and eventually the profitability of these organizations. The exodus from the farms and, to a lesser extent, from the fishing communities, reduced the membership of the cooperative organizations and their scale of operations, increasing their average cost of production and further endangering their existence. Moreover, the cooperatives, as hybrid economic and social institutions, faced additional challenges unique to these types of organizations.

The "social" character of the cooperatives, summarized in the slogan "not for profit but for service," had given them an advantage over the more traditional profit-driven private firms. In the 1930s the unswerving loyalty of the members and the dedication of their leaders, both of which resulted partly from the education strategy of the Extension Department, had enabled the cooperatives to compete successfully against existing private organizations. In the 1960s, even more so than in the 1950s, the changing attitudes and values of the members, the emergence of seemingly attractive other options, and the lack of education placed the cooperatives at a competitive disadvantage vis-à-vis the larger, better capitalized conventional private firms and corporations. The continuing tendency of members to press for higher returns on their investment in the cooperatives, coupled with the tendency of cooperative managers to offer higher prices for their inputs, higher rebates, and higher dividends than justified by market conditions, practices that were even a requirement for some, resulted in cooperative organizations that were too small in scale, that were undercapitalized, and that employed obsolete technologies. Furthermore, faced with the risk of causing a split in the community, the cooperatives, as in previous times, had to tolerate incompetent mangers and staff members. Thus both confusion about their socioeconomic nature and their need to operate efficiently and in conjunction with market conditions severely handicapped the cooperative enterprises, especially at a time when the vision of the movement itself was being undermined and when the socio-economic environment was less forgiving.

During the 1960s, more than ever before, the movement required greater levels of management competence and expertise to enable its economic institutions to survive and flourish. However, the commitment both to the movement and to the cooperative institutions was weak. Given the general weakness of many of the surviving institutions, even the revival of education programs that would foster loyalty, commitment, and enhanced participation by members of cooperatives would not have been enough. Making the cooperative sector more efficient while maintaining its fundamentally broader objectives was the real challenge, and neither the Extension Department nor the fragmented and increasingly self-absorbed cooperative institutions, often struggling to survive, were up to the task. As a result, there was a tendency on the part of various cooperatives to become increasingly isolated and also divorced from their own members.[17] Moreover, the mechanism that could act as an effective generator of new cooperative ventures, the study club method, had been extinguished. The movement could no longer count on new economic projects to provide it with much needed dynamism.

THE CHANGING LEADERSHIP OF THE EXTENSION DEPARTMENT

In July 1961, after a short and tumultuous tenure, Rev. John A. Gillis was unceremoniously removed from his position as director of the Extension Department, assigned to a rural parish, and replaced with Rev. Dr Joseph N. MacNeil.[18] Unlike all of his predecessors, Rev. MacNeil, who remained the director until 1969, when he was succeeded by Rev. George Topshee, had little knowledge of or experience with the Antigonish Movement or the work of the Extension Department. He was a canon lawyer by training whose previous experience, including as chancellor of the Diocese of Antigonish and of St Francis Xavier University, was entirely in the area of clerical administration – a career that he successfully resumed after his tenure at the Extension Department, first as the bishop of Saint John in New Brunswick and then as the archbishop of Edmonton in Alberta. The new director, urbane, sophisticated, and possessing a great deal of personal charm, appeared to be a suitable appointment to deal with various government agencies and departments recently created to advance regional and community development. In terms of this objective, there is no doubt that the new director was eminently well qualified and, indeed, that he gained a great deal of respect and recognition in public circles, perhaps best exemplified by his appointment as an economic advisor to the premier of Nova Scotia.[19]

Lacking experience and knowledge of the movement, and given the existing state of flux, the new director quite prudently appointed consultants and co-directors to assist him with his leadership tasks.[20] By the middle of the decade, six consultants[21] were advising four co-directors to chart the course of the Extension Department and, indirectly, of the entire movement, or what was left of it. Numerous committees and task forces, creating a bureaucratic labyrinth of considerable proportions, augmented the ever-increasing collective leadership of the Extension Department. Moreover, although the number of co-directors and the office staff was increasing, the number of fieldworkers was not, making the Extension Department administratively top-heavy and reducing its presence in the field – a reversal of the situation in earlier times.

Along with the change in leadership, the Extension Department also experienced a large turnover in its staff. Many of its experienced and seasoned workers were replaced with younger, more educated, but inexperienced counterparts. These new staff members, although better versed in the new formal theories and approaches and sympathetic to the plight of the people, generally lacked any direct link to the past operations of the movement.[22] Thus, at the very time when the movement was undergoing internal fragmentation and the external challenges were mounting, the Extension Department was being led by an inexperienced director with a tendency to exercise leadership by committee and consensus and a supporting staff that was equally inexperienced and untried. Furthermore, as the marginalization of the Extension Department within the university proceeded during the decade, the staff members could no longer count on receiving support and encouragement from their academic colleagues. The situation only grew worse as both prestige and university resources were increasingly shifted to the academic endeavours, with decreasing importance attached to extension work. Thus there also emerged a morale problem among the field staff, in contrast to the situation experienced by the highly appreciated and praised field-workers of previous decades.

THE SEARCH FOR A NEW VISION AND A NEW ROLE FOR THE EXTENSION DEPARTMENT

At the start of the 1960s, the Antigonish Movement was in disarray – a condition further accentuated by the collapse of Eastern Co-operative Services. Adding to confusion were the combined effects of rapidly changing socio-economic conditions, mounting economic problems, and the entrusting of the Extension Department to less experienced leaders and staff, who also turned out to be fundamentally out of step with the movement.

A logical outcome of these various factors was the belief that a radically different vision for the movement and a new role for the Extension Department were in order. The enduring and inspiring vision of enabling the ordinary people to become masters of their economic destiny through the implementation of a new and dynamic economic system was replaced by a vision deemed more appropriate to the new emerging realities.

On the surface, the calls for a new vision and a new role for the Extension Department were motivated by factors that appeared to be compelling. First, the persistent and worsening socio-economic problems of the region were taken as an indication that the existing approach could no longer deal with them. Second, the field of socio-economic development had been invaded by numerous government departments and agencies with far greater financial and human resources than those at the disposal of the Extension Department, giving possible legitimacy to the view that "These days, huge amounts of money and large staffs are being used to assist every phase of economic life in the Atlantic area. Extension must find its proper role in relation to these agencies."[23] Third, there was the belief that a new scientifically driven community development approach constituted a more efficient and effective tool for dealing with the problems of the region. In fact, the Extension Department proclaimed the new approach to be "more scientific and adaptable for more complex and changing social and economic conditions."[24] Fourth, it was believed, mistakenly, that the cooperative and credit union sectors had acquired a cadre of competent leaders who could provide for their own educational and motivational requirements, thus freeing the Extension Department from carrying out some of its traditional functions. Fifth, the adoption of a new vision was consistent with the innovating and pioneering nature of the Extension Department and thus couched in terms of the continuation of a proud tradition. Finally, there was the belief that the most important decisions regarding the welfare of the people were no longer made within the institutional framework of the Antigonish Movement but by various government agencies, task forces, boards, and institutions. For the Extension Department to remain relevant, it had to become more closely aligned with them.

The New Vision

The formal search for a new vision and a new identity for the Extension Department was set in motion in 1961, when an associate director was appointed to evaluate the existing policies and programs of the Extension Department. In addition, the university appointed a committee to assist the new director in the formulation of new policies for the department. These initiatives were further augmented by the establishment of a number of committees, including committees of priests and committees of fieldworkers, put in place for largely the same purpose. The ever-increasing number of such committees, combined with a growing number of consultants and co-directors, illustrates how pressing the task was perceived to be. It also demonstrates the degree of confusion and uncertainty that existed about the very nature of the Antigonish Movement and about the vision that had propelled it over the previous three decades.

The Extension Department's search for a new vision placed heavy reliance on the theories and methods that were being brought to the fore by the emerging social sciences. These, which also influenced various public-sector initiatives, seemed to promise quick and easy fixes for some very deeply entrenched socio-economic problems.[25] More important, they posited an approach that was fundamentally top-down, suggesting that people's problems could be solved for them by experts, which removed all responsibility from the people themselves. The collective experience of the Antigonish Movement was largely ignored and effectively undermined, as its traditional vision was rejected and the Extension Department began to sever its remaining links with its various institutions and components. Rather than people becoming "Masters of Their Own Destiny" through the creation of a dynamic economic system in which they exercised ownership and control of economic activity, the new vision was predicated on working within the existing system and in step with the various initiatives taken by the government.[26]

To a great extent, the new vision of the Extension Department came to be embodied in the "community development" approach.[27] What is surprising and indeed ironic is that the Extension Department failed to realize that it had in fact been engaged in a process of community development for three decades and had achieved some remarkable results. Indeed, that the unique economic system that the Antigonish Movement had been putting in place was the embodiment of an effective community development strategy seems to have been completely ignored. The reason for this was that the nature and true accomplishments of the Antigonish Movement were simply not understood. Although it was clear that the Antigonish Movement had accomplished some remarkable things, what and why remained clouded in misleading rhetoric that was focused rather exclusively on adult education.

It is remarkable that much of the true nature of the movement escaped rigorous and broad-based economic analysis and that it was so easily ignored and dismissed in the 1960s. Hidden behind the rhetoric of adult education, a coherent economic system was being established that few seemed to notice, especially once the Big Picture was no longer in vogue. What was noticed was not the whole but some of its parts, and it was assumed that they were independent and should be fully freed to be on their own.[28]

The new, and by its very nature fundamentally fragmented, community development approach was believed to be superior, as "the new contributions of sociology, economics and adult education to the field make this approach more scientific."[29] To a great extent, the faith placed in the possibilities of scientific research and the social sciences must be understood in the context of the times. Postwar prosperity was largely credited to the application of science not only to industry and technology but also to society as a whole, with the successful application of Keynesian economics as the prime example. Nevertheless, the abandonment of traditional methods, techniques, and approaches, which had proved to be successful in the past, is difficult to justify. In the process, the most fundamental principles of the movement – self-reliance through economic cooperation, participants' control and ownership of economic activity, and moral commitment and even sacrifice for the common good – were abandoned. Indeed, the reports coming out of the Extension Department during the early 1960s openly stated that the economic problems of the region were too great for the people themselves to resolve and that government intervention was imperative. Rather than being "Masters of Their Own Destiny," the people were largely relegated to the role of recipients of public generosity.

Problems in Applying the New Vision

The task of distancing itself from its historical ties to the Antigonish Movement proved more difficult, prolonged, and controversial than the Extension Department had initially expected. There were numerous practical issues and problems that needed to be resolved before the process could be completed satisfactorily. First, since most of its established programs were either entirely or partially financed by outside or affiliated agencies, they could not be terminated or altered without a loss of revenue to the Extension Department. Of these, the longstanding fisheries program, which was based on the specific goal of promoting economic cooperation among the fishermen of the Maritimes, was by far the most important. Other programs, such as those linked to cooperative and credit union training, also constituted important sources of funds. The termination of these programs had to be accomplished gradually, skilfully, and through mutual agreement. Second, terminating its historical ties to the movement and abandoning its traditional leadership role was bound to create controversy and mobilize criticism among the loyal supporters of the movement, the still influential clergy, the older faculty of the university, and the Extension Department's own more experienced staff and fieldworkers. Such criticism had to be diffused, allayed, and overcome, and the task required diplomacy, patience, and time. However, the Extension Department, as already noted, no longer had to deal with Rev. Coady, who until his death at the end of the 1950s was able to muster a great deal of power in defence of the Antigonish Movement and its vision, even though he had failed to provide a final blueprint for it. Third, in addition to securing its support, the question of the competence and skill of its staff had to be addressed. Many of the remaining fieldworkers, who had risen from the ranks of community leadership, were either too close to retirement or lacked adequate educational background to be able to acquire new, research-based skills and techniques. These needed to be replaced by younger, more educated, and also more pliant ones. Fourth, as the Extension Department terminated its ties with its former allies and affiliates, such as cooperatives and credit unions, it had to find new partners and allies and to establish stronger links with public-sector development agencies and institutions in order to secure the necessary financial, research, and even political support.

The Extension Department also faced difficulty with the implementation of its new and supposedly more scientific approach. The new approach turned out to be much more expensive than the former one, which relied heavily on a large number of volunteers, poorly paid but dedicated fieldworkers, and an overworked but highly effective office staff. The new approach was predicated on the employment of economists, sociologists, consultants, and other highly trained experts. Ideally, it required the Extension Department to establish its own research capacity, which involved adding such professional and specialized personnel to its staff. Its fieldworkers, who would be carrying out much of the actual research in the field, would also require higher formal-education qualifications, which also involved higher costs for the Extension Department.[30]

The new approach was also largely experimental and untried, making it necessary to test its effectiveness in the field before committing more resources. Thus, to implement the new program, the Extension Department had to secure substantial and longer-term financial resources from outside sources, without being able to prove that the approach was one that could succeed. In effect, its only option was to adopt the programs of those outside agencies that were willing to provide the funding.

The Adoption of the New Community Development Model

The adoption of the new community development approach came at the cost of severing the Extension Department's traditional ties with the Antigonish Movement and its institutions. In the process, it undermined the rationale that lay behind the establishment and existence of the Extension Department itself.

This new approach not only required different types of fieldworkers and other staff members but also involved a great deal of experimentation through the establishment of numerous pilot projects.[31] The rural community of Inverness in Cape Breton emerged with the dubious distinction of having the largest number of such pilot projects. As can be expected when putting in place something that is new, some initial difficulties arose. The research projects undertaken were ill defined and not appropriate to the existing conditions, and the communities responded with less than the expected enthusiasm.[32] Moreover, even where responses where promising, the lack of immediate results made it difficult to sustain the interest of community groups.

The community development program was launched during the mid-1960s. It was an ambitious undertaking, and the Extension Department was optimistic and had "great hope for this approach."[33] The first step in the community development program was the establishment of a local Community Development Council. In turn, the council, assisted by experts from St Francis Xavier University and/or by fieldworkers from the Extension Department, sponsored a study or survey of the community, with financing provided by the Agricultural and Rural Development Agency (ARDA). St Francis Xavier University was given the responsibility of carrying out ARDA-sponsored research in the seven counties of eastern Nova Scotia.[34] The purpose of the study or survey was to identify the various economic opportunities existing in the community and, in so doing, to serve as the basis for local groups and entrepreneurs to start new economic projects. The production of these studies or reports, which were sent to ARDA, elicited a great deal of excitement within the Extension Department. A three-part resource study completed for ARDA in the mid-1960s was viewed as a success.[35] Shortly afterward, it was announced that "Extension likely produced more studies and surveys in 1966–67 than in any period of its existence."[36] Moreover, the approach was also introduced in some of the more urban areas, particularly Glace Bay and New Waterford, as well as in seven Aboriginal communities of eastern Nova Scotia. This involvement then paved the way for the partnership between the Extension Department and ARDA to also be extended to educational and organizational programs in the forestry sector among woodlot owners.[37] The approach was also adopted in the fisheries program, where the Extension Department believed that out of a number of potential alternatives, "the most promising is the community development approach where people are encouraged to study and solve their own problems."[38] However, the focus was on the studies and reports themselves rather than on the action that they elicited.

Very few local groups and/or entrepreneurs emerged to implement successful new economic projects. The whole exercise of community development generally ended with the publishing of the studies or surveys. At this stage, it was up to the local groups and/or entrepreneurs to carry the ball, as evident in the statement that "The research projects completed to date have identified a wide range of local development projects which will be followed up by Extension if local leadership maintains sufficient interest in them."[39] Usually, since local leadership did not maintain sufficient interest, the "scientific" community development approach turned into a paper exercise. We were unable to identify any successful economic project that emerged from the community-development program during the decade. The fundamental weakness of the whole program, and indeed of all Extension Department programs in the 1960s, was that there was no direct connection between education – as embodied in the surveys and studies – and economic action.

The New Role for the Extension Department

The new vision for the movement called for a new role and a new identity for the Extension Department. Rather than remaining the active and dynamic centre of an economic system in which it mobilized and inspired the common people to acquire control over their economic institutions, it adopted a largely passive and less directly involved bridging role between the experts and the community. However, in keeping with the rhetoric of the past, it also maintained that "the role of St. F.X. Extension [is] to ensure that the plans, funds, and personnel involved in these programs are used in a way that will really help our people to help themselves."[40]

As a first step in carrying out this new bridging role, the Extension Department attempted to develop its own independent research capabilities in order to initiate, carry out, and supervise community-based development research in the region. Thus it proposed to "assist in the establishment of a Research Commission staffed by full time qualified economists and sociologists."[41] The new research-based approach was seen as useful for tackling the economic problems of, for example, industrial Cape Breton, where the greatest concentration of cooperatives and credit unions existed. In fact, it was suggested that "The salvation of the industrial communities in Cape Breton may rest, in large measure, upon this kind of scientific approach to its economic and social problems."[42] In the three previous decades, the Extension Department had not sought to develop its own research capability – in the main, because it was always able to access the necessary expertise free of charge. Its reputation and attraction were so great that it was able to obtain the services of even international experts by simply inviting them to come and help out. Thus the Extension Department was able to gain the valuable services of Roy Bergengren, Mary Arnold, and many others, who were instrumental in setting up credit unions, cooperative housing projects, and the like. However, by the 1960s the era of the paid professional experts and consultants had begun, and free help was no longer as easy to obtain.

The Extension Department's requests to the Board of Governors of St Francis Xavier University for resources to boost its research capabilities fell on deaf ears. The university had committed an increasing share of its resources to the academic programs, and rather than providing more resources, its contribution to the Extension Department was frozen for most of the decade.

Although the Extension Department failed to establish its own independent research capabilities, the faith in the scientific approach was retained. In 1965 the Extension Department reached an agreement with the various social science departments of the university to continue its ARDA-financed research on community economic development in various parts of eastern Nova Scotia. This agreement, however, failed to turn the Extension Department into an "institutional bridge" between the academic side of the university and the community at large.

The Extension Department's failure to transform itself into an effective bridging institution, at the same time that it had also largely abandoned its more activist stance in terms of the mobilization of resources and the promotion of economic activity, constituted a double failure. Moreover, when it did try, it could no longer revert back to its former role of "rallying the local people" and "giving leadership."[43] By the end of the decade, the harsh economic realities and the Extension Department's reduced standing in the university had forced it to dramatically reduce its role to primarily that of, in the words of Rev. George Topshee, who took over as director of the department in 1969, "educational upgrading and retraining of adult workers."[44] Thus, within the span of one decade, the Extension Department had transformed itself from a remarkable agent of socio-economic reform as the centre of an independent and self-contained economic system into something akin to a vocational school. In the process, it had discarded three decades of pioneering action.

The Extension Department did achieve some success in upgrading the professional qualifications and research skills of its staff members. In 1963 three of its office staff members returned to the Extension Department after having successfully completed graduate studies at American universities, and more followed over the next two years.[45] By the middle of the decade, the retraining and turnover of the staff had been largely completed. A memorandum issued in 1964 claimed that "Today, those who staff the Antigonish and Sydney offices are by and large newcomers to Extension"[46] – and, as noted earlier, increasingly fewer of them had any links with the early pioneers of the movement.

Over the 1960s, the activities of the Extension Department became increasingly divorced from the requirements of the various cooperative institutions and, hence, of the Antigonish Movement. These cooperatives remained starved of the economic knowledge and managerial expertise that were absolutely necessary for them to flourish both individually and as parts of an economic system, especially at a time when efficiency improvements and greater market access were becoming increasingly important. At the same time, there was also no mechanism in place for the establishment of new cooperative enterprises.[47] The result was an increasingly fragmented and stagnant movement.

EDUCATION STRATEGY

The education program of the Extension Department was an essential component in the systemic approach of the Antigonish Movement, especially in the process of transforming its abstract ultimate goals and vision into the concrete and effective economic system envisaged in the Big Picture. Education and knowledge were critical ingredients in the establishment of economic projects and the mobilization of the wide array of resources that such projects required. In turn, these projects provided direct economic benefits to the participants as well as enhancing their social standing. Thus education and economic activity were closely entwined in the movement and could not be separated. As a fieldworker of the Extension Department noted in 1964, "it is practically impossible to draw a line between the economic and educational phases of our program ... there is a close relationship between the success of our economic cooperative ventures and the effectiveness of our educational program."[48]

The fundamental link between education and economic activity called for an education program that was coherent, practical, and unified in its various components. Moreover, given the dynamic nature of the socio-economic environment and the economic system itself, the education program had to be able to adapt to change without undermining its very nature or the nature of the economic system that was being put in place. In the previous three decades, although not without its problems, the education program of the Extension Department had managed to meet the various challenges facing both the region and the movement to a considerable extent. Innovative programs such as the wartime short courses, the Regional and Vocational Conferences, the women's programs, the kitchen meetings, and perhaps even the Model Fisherman program had served to push the movement forward. The various programs were generally consistent with the needs of the movement and those of the various economic activities.

The adoption of a new vision in the 1960s, however, led to fundamental changes in the education program of the Extension Department, despite the fact that, on the surface, some of the programs seemed quite similar to those of the previous decade. There seemed to be a similar emphasis on short courses of various sorts, mostly in response to requests and perceived need, and also on the classes and television programs of the People's School. The Rural and Industrial Conferences were also a part of the program at the start of the decade.[49] However, study clubs were largely a thing of the past, and even kitchen meetings were rare. The new strategy, in keeping with the new vision, focused on the provision of information and no longer linked study and action.

The education strategy of the Extension Department had undergone significant changes over the previous three decades, particularly the 1950s. Thus the changes that occurred in the 1960s were, to some extent, the culmination of these trends, perhaps taken to their logical conclusion. The Extension Department's progressive withdrawal from cooperative education stands out as perhaps the best example of this culmination. Nevertheless, the changes that took place during the 1960s compounded the problem and, to some extent, ensured that there would be no possible reversal of the process. To flourish, the movement required an institutional component or core that could serve the needs of the system as a whole as well as its individual economic entities. As the Extension Department moved away from this function, the crisis in the movement also deepened over time. Perhaps the most symbolic action in terms of signalling the nature of the changes that were taking place was the closing down of the Extension Library, which had been so closely linked with the Antigonish Movement from the outset, in 1964.[50]

During the first part of the 1960s, the Extension Department's main preoccupation was the establishment of the financial, personnel, and research base to launch its new community development initiative later in the decade. As a result, it generally not only kept its existing programs but also tried to revive some of the ones that had been deemed successful in the past. Nevertheless, the Extension Department also made it clear to its development partners and allies that its involvement in most of these programs would be terminated in the not too distant future.

The People's School

The People's School remained in place virtually unchanged from the latter part of the previous decade, relying exclusively on television programming. On average, twenty-three half-hour television programs were produced each year, although a lack of financing reduced the number to sixteen during the 1969–70 period. These programs, which were generally well done and highly praised, covered a wide array of topics that involved most areas of concern to the local population.[51] Near the end of the decade, to make them more attractive, the programs underwent a change in format: from the panel-type studio-produced programs to on-location programs with interviews in coalmines, in people's offices, and so on.[52] Nevertheless, by the end of the decade, increasing production costs and the formidable competition from private and public information programs, particularly those transmitted by the Canadian Broadcasting Corporation, had contrived to reduce their effectiveness even further. In effect, they were one of a number of alternate sources of packaged information.

In the early part of the 1960s, the "People's School" broadcasts were still complemented by classes held in various communities. Attendance at these classes was generally small, as had been the case during the latter part of the 1950s, and their effectiveness was also hampered by a lack of qualified instructors.[53] Pamphlets and bulletins also accompanied the broadcasts, at least for a time.

The television programs were not, as we noted in the context of the 1950s, very successful in mobilizing people to undertake economic action and create new cooperative enterprises. Moreover, the People's School was not designed to prompt economic action but to deal more effectively with existing circumstances, primarily in the main urban areas. Indeed, one of the stated objectives of the People's School was to "help Cape Breton's industrial workers to understand the legitimate role of the labor movement in the life of a healthy community."[54] To the extent that economic development remained an area of concern, the main thrust of the People's School became the promotion of the "new" notion of community economic development both through government and through private-sector agencies. Very little emphasis was placed on the workings of the Antigonish Movement.

Courses, Seminars, Schools, and Institutes

The 1960s saw a proliferation of courses given by the Extension Department. Generally of short duration and of a specific and often nonrecurring nature, these courses were the mainstay of the Extension Department's program. It was precisely the increased importance of these types of courses that transformed the Extension Department into a sort of vocational school as it adopted a more passive strategy.

The shift in focus – with a marked emphasis on adult education per se, designed to upgrade the education level of the population, rather than on education for economic action – may have been a reflection of the perception that greater expertise was required to enable cooperative economic institutions to function more efficiently. Such would have been the case for the summer school courses for credit union officers and short courses for directors and managers of local cooperative stores.[55] However, despite strong opposition from several quarters, by the end of the decade the courses in cooperative and credit union education had been terminated. Although the effectiveness and relevance of these courses had been on the wane for some time and although by the middle of the 1960s the Extension Department's involvement with the cooperative sector entailed largely "participating in training programs and giving guidance in policy decisions",[56] this termination was nevertheless important. It was symbolic of the fact that there was no concerted effort to serve the educational needs of the Antigonish Movement as a system.

The many courses, seminars, and meetings kept the Extension Department involved in the community, enabling it to respond to many concerns in need of attention. However, its ability to respond was compromised by the fact that its education agenda and programs were increasingly being dictated from outside.[57] Moreover, its education focus became increasingly segmented into labour education, urban education, and so on – a continuation of the trend in evidence in the 1950s – which added to the fragmentation that was taking place within the movement and within the Extension Department itself.

THE FISHERIES

The Extension Department remained active in the fisheries throughout the decade. However, its role tended to be much different than previously and its achievements of much less consequence, especially from the mid-1960s onward.[58] It was in the fisheries that the Extension Department most prominently saw itself as a bridge between the experts and the fishermen. The Extension Department increasingly saw its role as one of providing a liaison between the experts and researchers and the fishermen. In keeping with this new role, a main function of its fieldworkers in the fisheries was to make sure that the fishermen were kept up to date concerning new fishing techniques. They were also active participants in annual fisheries schools and conferences, including those involving managers of fisheries cooperatives. The Extension Department also sponsored a television program, "Sea Harvest," aimed at the fisheries.[59]

During the earlier years of the 1960s, the overall situation in the fisheries was not particularly discouraging, although there were certainly some problems. In the annual reports, references are made to gains by fishermen belonging to cooperatives in terms of higher prices received for their fish. There was also a sizable amount of new investment in larger boats, better fish-processing equipment, and the like by various fisheries cooperatives, which served to increase both the size of the catch and the quality of the product while also increasing efficiency, lowering costs, and promoting diversification.[60] Nevertheless, many cooperatives were also experiencing difficulties as a consequence of small boats, the small size of operations, and other inefficiencies.[61]

The Extension Department stressed the importance of new developments in a number of fishing communities. These included the Canso Development Company, set up by the Canso Community Development Council to provide inshore fishermen with credit that would allow them to modernize, and the special fisheries in L'Ardoise, again set up by the local Community Development Council. Indeed, the establishment of Community Development Councils in various fishing communities was hailed as being particularly noteworthy. These councils also placed a great deal of emphasis on carrying out studies, in keeping with the more analytical approach followed by the Extension Department and its fieldworkers.[62]

The overall situation in the fisheries masked, even in the early 1960s, the severe plight facing the inshore fishermen. The Extension Department stated in its 1965-66 annual report that "The large and heavily capitalized offshore sector of the industry reported its greatest expansion in history, while the inshore fisheries continue to struggle for survival."[63] The same report went on to say that "The economic condition of many inshore fishermen is almost as pathetic as during the depression years."[64] The small inshore fishing communities, even where the fishermen belonged to cooperatives, did not benefit from the expansion in the fisheries.[65] Indeed, it was no longer possible to earn an income above the poverty line in inshore fishing. To earn a higher wage, fishermen needed to engage in either offshore or intermediate-range fishing. In the second half of the 1960s, the situation became even worse for the inshore fishermen, as the fisheries were hit by a depression created by an overexpansion in productive capacity, primarily as a result of new technology and the expansion of the offshore fleet.

As far as the inshore fishermen were concerned, their circumstances had gone full circle, bringing them back largely to the conditions that they had experienced during the 1930s. However, there was one important difference. Whereas in the 1930s the fishermen had faith in their ability to better their condition and to change the existing economic order through group study and cooperative economic action, in the 1960s this was not the case. Cooperative institutions were already in place. They needed to evolve and expand as parts of a flexible and dynamic economic system.[66] Moreover, whereas in the 1930s the Extension Department saw itself as the instigator of changes that would turn people into "Masters of Their Own Destiny," in the 1960s it saw itself in a different light and was not up to the task of revitalizing the cooperative sector.

The matter was further complicated by the amendment, in 1956, of the unemployment insurance legislation to cover the self-employed inshore fishermen.[67] Although introduced as a temporary measure, this amendment, which made inshore fishermen eligible to receive benefits during the off season, was never repealed and became a permanent fixture in the inshore fishery, with its full effects being felt in the 1960s. The fishermen were now receiving a portion of their income from outside of their involvement in the operations of the cooperatives. Moreover, they were also tempted to sell their catches to private buyers in order to increase the value of their sales during the insurable weeks, thereby obtaining greater benefits. Consequently, the fishermen were further alienated from their cooperatives, and the Extension Department's role in the sector was weakened.

Indeed, aside from promoting the restructuring of the United Maritime Fishermen (UMF) cooperative by amalgamating local cooperatives into a central UMF, which provided some potential relief to inshore fisheries, and aside from initiatives involving Community Development Councils, the Extension Department's suggestions for resolving the existing plight of the fishermen followed very conventional lines. For example, the 1966–67 annual review of the Extension Department suggested the following:

1 a bailout in the form of "generous grants and low-interest loans to U.M.F. to enable it to do the job in many fishing communities that no other organizations or agency seem prepared to do";
2 a program to assist young people to leave the fisheries and find employment elsewhere, described as "A massive training and mobility program ... for many young people who can not find employment in either offshore or intermediate range fishing operations"; and

3 "for those who cannot participate in either of these programs, an alternate solution based on generous early retirement schemes or relocation."[68]

These proposals conflicted with the traditional core principles of the Antigonish Movement, which would have envisaged the solution to the emerging problems in terms of setting up new cooperative enterprises, strengthening existing ones, and promoting better management of the fisheries. The Extension Department adopted the stance that the only way it could directly assist the fisheries in solving the problems facing them was by obtaining information and data on socio-economic factors through studies, surveys, and the like. In part, this reflected the shift toward placing greater reliance on the top-down scientific process.

Despite the change in strategy, aimed at facilitating adjustment rather than promoting new economic action, the Extension Department's rhetoric remained remarkably consistent with its more traditional role. Thus, for example, the function of the fisheries field-workers was still "to aid in fisheries development especially through the promotion of cooperatives and credit unions."[69] Over the 1960s, the gap between rhetoric and reality became increasingly greater. During the second half of the 1960s, the Extension Department became involved in various training and education-upgrading programs, establishing schools for fishing communities to provide grade 10 equivalency in basic subjects such as mathematics, English, and science for some of the younger people and, in the process, enhancing their chances of finding employment outside of the fisheries. Nevertheless, it still also carried out some of its traditional tasks of providing basic training designed to support the cooperative sector, such as in bookkeeping and management.[70]

Increasingly, many of the activities of the Extension Department became linked to the "lazy man's" solutions, which involved political action. These more politically oriented activities, which included recommendations aimed at obtaining federal grants for the UMF and the proposal for relocation and retirement schemes for fishermen, were driven by the belief that government intervention was required to resolve the pressing problems facing the fisheries sector and others as well. Thus government interventions such as the establishment of the Fisheries Price Support Board in 1968, which helped to halt the fall in the prices of a number of varieties of fish that had begun in 1966, and the lobster licensing policy, which was viewed "as an important step towards rationalizing the overcrowded industry," were increasingly seen as the way of the future.[71]

The seeming failure to find a solution to the new plight facing the inshore fishermen of eastern Nova Scotia and other parts of Atlantic Canada, coupled with the belief that government intervention was required, severely compromised the relevance of the Extension Department and the Antigonish Movement in the sector. Thus the termination of the Extension Department's involvement in the fisheries in 1969, when the federal Department of Fisheries did not renew its funding for 1970, should not have come as a surprise. The termination of the fisheries program also had important symbolic implications since the fisheries comprised the initial successes of the Antigonish Movement.

The termination of the federal government's fisheries grants, after thirty-three years, marked the end of a remarkable era predicated on the dream of self-reliance and socio-economic transformation. The Extension Department's involvement in the fisheries, which predated the availability of government funding, was prompted by the plight of the inshore fishermen during the 1920s and 1930s. By the time the program was terminated at the end of the 1960s, the inshore fisheries seem to have gone full circle, returning to the conditions that had characterized them prior to the fisheries program, but now there was no help from the Antigonish Movement. Indeed, the 1969–70 annual review of the Extension Department perhaps said it best: "The plight of many of the inshore fishermen in Atlantic Canada is a sorry one. The numbers of inshore fishermen continue to decline, but there are still far too many trying to eke out a living from a small boat operation with inadequate equipment and facilities. Consolidation of these operations in larger, cooperative units, would seem to be the answer. The pursuit of this objective must be left to the UMF or some other body because the Extension Department no longer employs fieldworkers in fisheries."[72]

In the fisheries, the weaknesses in the cooperative sector that were already evident in the 1940s and 1950s became even more pronounced and devastating in the 1960s. The generally undercapitalized and small-scale cooperatives, having failed not only to evolve into more competitive units but also to become integrated parts of an economic system, quickly lost ground to increasingly formidable competitors. Some benefits could still be obtained through greater efficiency by amalgamating the smaller fisheries cooperatives, but this action in itself would not resolve the problem. The fisheries were simply too overcrowded and fragmented. Government policies regulating prices and catches were probably the most effective policies for the short term, and this began to occur in the 1960s as the government started to put in place its own resource-management system.[73] More important, the Extension Department itself lacked the resources and the imagination to adapt to the new circumstances and to come up with new pioneering solutions. Rather, it left the task up to the government and to the universities. The more fundamental issue here, however, is that the movement had failed as a system since it had not allowed the emergence of the institutional apparatus that was required for a successful grassroots movement. Evidence of what was occurring overall in the fisheries of eastern Nova Scotia during the 1960s is presented in table 6.1. In many ways, these data overstate the health of most of these enterprises and hide the plight of the inshore fishermen, which by the late 1960s was also affecting some cooperative stalwarts, such as the cooperative fish plant at Port Bickerton.[74]

CREDIT UNIONS

Despite the longstanding history of credit unions as critical components of the Antigonish Movement, during the 1960s the Extension Department's involvement with these institutions was generally limited to providing some training and personnel upgrading, through the short courses, and to attempts, particularly during the second half of the decade, at promoting the amalgamation of some of the smaller and weaker ones. Only about one-half of the credit unions on Cape Breton Island participated in the Extension Department's education program, and even among those who participated, the commitment to education was generally weak.[75] Innovations such as organizing credit unions into chapters also proved generally ineffective.[76] In the mid-1960s in a number of communities in Cape Breton, there was a resurgence of kitchen meetings associated with credit unions, and these meetings were generally perceived as effective tools of revitalization.[77] Generally, rather than being integrated as key components of an economic system, the credit unions stood on their

Table 6.1
Sales of fishermen's cooperatives, 1960, 1965, 1970

Cooperatives	*1960*	*1965*	*1970*
Antigonish	150,639.51	239,098.00	259,118.00
Blue Ribbon Fisheries	60,673.71	91,889.94	123,680.00
Cape Breton Fishermen	12,784.25	206,246.61	n.a.
Chedabucto	n.a.	93,171.43	n.a.
Cheticamp Fishermen	450,649.13	666,516.77	942,626.00
Eastern Fishermen	84,127.77	n.a.	n.a.
Grand Etang Fishermen	346,947.61	261,282.26	449,105.00
Guysborough Fishermen	108,243.35	107,882.02	n.a.
Isle Madame	366,175.69	252,701.28	382,883.00
Mabou Fishermen	n.a.	n.a.	26,413.00
Maryville	80,075.86	100,442.97	149,111.00
Port Bickerton	602,158.04	1,534,393.69	1,854,692.00
Port Maitland	n.a.	198,619.62	217,086.00
Pubnico	140,205.79	333,771.75	291,858.00
St Gerorge's	112,219.41	155,726.16	264,461.00
St Michael's	139,862.25	184,133.53	720,967.00
Tor Bay	9,670.44	n.a.	n.a.
Victoria Fishermen	176,173.76	246,517.23	371,537.00
Westport	115,284.99	187,366.05	n.a.
Woods Harbour Fishermen	n.a.	n.a.	496,655.00
TOTAL ($)	3,070,950.96	4,853,759.31	6,550,192.00

Source: Nova Scotia Department of Agriculture and Marketing, *Annual Reports of Co-operative Associations in Nova Scotia* (1960, 1965, 1970).

own, having relatively weak links with the Extension Department and, despite a few exceptions, with the other economic institutions of the movement.

The credit union sector as a whole continued to grow on its own in terms of assets and membership. However, this growth was concentrated mainly in the larger ones that had moved to permanent premises, that were staffed by trained, full-time personnel, and that served a relatively large number of people. These included the Dosco Credit Union of Sydney and the Bergengren Credit Union of Antigonish. The smaller and simpler operations, such as village and parish credit unions, were, at best, struggling to survive. Although a few additional charters were granted during the period, these were more than offset by the number of dissolutions. The number of credit unions in Nova

Scotia as a whole declined from 219 in 1960 to 186 in 1965 and 147 in 1970.[78] The only new initiative that was put in place was the School Credit Union program, which involved the creation of savings clubs operated by and for students in public schools. In effect, the credit unions fell far short of becoming a banking system for the Antigonish Movement and the cooperatives sector.[79]

The Extension Department's limited involvement with credit unions can be attributed to a number of factors. The abandonment of the original vision by the Extension Department meant that their importance was no longer recognized. With the Big Picture and economic action no longer seen as the critical components of the movement, especially once the government became involved in the development process, the fundamental role of finance in the mobilization and allocation of resources was less relevant. Rather than a building block for an economic system, credit unions came to be seen more as providers of financial services similar to those of chartered banks and other financial institutions. Moreover, the credit unions had become largely a separate entity able to cater to their own needs and were unlikely to feel that the Extension Department had much to offer them, especially given its increasingly passive role. They had been able to thrive and to establish their own institutional links at different levels as parts of essentially a separate system.

COOPERATIVE HOUSING

Cooperative housing, the last of the major programs put into effect by the Extension Department during previous decades, was continued during the 1960s. Although it was hampered by practical matters such as the availability and cost of land and financing, increases in the price of building materials, the effects of direct and indirect taxes levied by the various levels of government, and the proliferation of government regulation, as well as the effects of economic fluctuations, it remained remarkably dynamic during the decade, expanding its coverage to also include low-cost housing in some of the black communities.[80]

The program experienced a decline during the first part of the 1960s as the number of houses being built fell from over 120 per year in the late 1950s to 49 around 1961 and 59 in 1966.[81] In 1967, however, with its publication of the *Co-operative Housing Handbook*, the Extension Department in collaboration with the Nova Scotia Housing Commission (NSHC) introduced a new design for low-cost housing that provided a needed dramatic boost for the program. The magnitude of the impact of this new design can be easily gauged from the fact that between 1968 and 1970, on average, about 300 new cooperative houses were built per year on a self-help basis in eastern Nova Scotia (and 600 in the province as a whole over the period June 1969 to June 1970).[82] Moreover, the cooperative housing program also spread to the other provinces of Atlantic Canada.

The relative dynamism of the program, particularly during the late 1960s, can be ascertained not only from the number of houses constructed but also from the number of groups engaged in study and the number of fieldworkers, especially volunteers, involved in the sector. For example, the 1968-69 annual report of the Extension Department refers to twenty-five fieldworkers associated with the housing program. This cohort was made up mostly of either volunteers, especially Roman Catholic priests and clergymen of various denominations, or part-time workers. The emergence of a sizable number of volunteers is particularly interesting since it signalled grassroots involvement and was also consistent with the more traditional Antigonish Movement approach.

The program's relative dynamism also owed a great deal to the nature of the housing sector. Since shelter is among the most basic of human needs, the benefits arising from having a house were obvious to all. Moreover, the logistics involved in the construction of basic housing were generally well understood. Thus it was possible for people to plan and carry out projects with limited outside help once the required resources were mustered.

Even in this sector, however, there is evidence of a trend toward solutions of a more political nature, particularly near the end of the decade when the Extension Department's attention shifted more toward public and government-subsidized housing. Moreover, it also attempted to establish closer links with the public sector and to broaden its influence by, for example, having a member appointed to the NSHC, working more closely with the Central Mortgage and Housing Corporation, assisting the Atlantic Labour Co-operative Committee, and having a member on the board of directors of the Washington-based International Self-Help Housing Association.[83]

Unfortunately, the cooperative housing program came to a sudden halt in 1970 when the NSHC assumed total responsibility for cooperative housing, thus effectively pushing the Extension Department out of the sector. To carry out its functions, the NSHC increased the number of its staff members so that they could displace volunteers working for the Extension Department, which, left with no alternative, shifted its housing program toward the provision of public housing for low-income families, particularly among minority groups: the so-called "specialized housing projects."

THE COOPERATIVE SECTOR AND EASTERN CO-OPERATIVE SERVICES

As mentioned in the previous chapter, the Eastern Co-operative Services (ECS)) mega project began to experience difficulties virtually from the outset. The severity and implications of these difficulties were not adequately appreciated by the Extension Department, aside from Rev. Gillis, who had been wary of the enterprise from the outset of his brief tenure as director.[84] Even Rev. Gillis, in an optimistic vein, reported in May 1960 that "The position of Eastern Co-operative Services is improving day by day. Great efforts have been made during the past year to get efficiency into its business."[85] He noted, moreover, that it had done in excess of $5 million worth of business. A year later, he was quite pessimistic, noting that "The business of Eastern Co-operative Services, during the past year has been disappointing. The organization is having financial difficulties stemming from a lack of sufficient working capital."[86] This pessimistic stand was moderated by a suggestion that some steps were being taken to resolve the difficulties.[87] In a report written a few months later, the new director, Rev. MacNeil, states that "E.C.S. seems to have gotten on its feet again after a most unfortunate tottering on the brink of bankruptcy."[88] A similar view is expressed in the Extension Department's annual report for the period May 1961 to June 1962.[89] These statements, particularly those by Rev. MacNeil, tended to offer an overly optimistic view of things. W.H. McEwen has suggested that during 1960–61, ECS was in fact facing bankruptcy.[90] Its difficulties could not be successfully addressed, and after its collapse in 1964 it became amalgamated, starting in 1965, as a branch of Moncton-based Maritime Co-operative Services.

As noted in the previous chapter, proponents of the Antigonish Movement attached a great deal of importance to the setting-up of

ECS. It was seen, particularly by Rev. Coady, as a culmination of the Big Picture. It would certainly have established, if it had been successful, an unmistakable anchor for the Antigonish Movement in eastern Nova Scotia. At the same time, it could have provided a mechanism to foster the further development of the troubled rural sector in eastern Nova Scotia and to enable expansion into cooperative manufacturing activities. Although the failure of ECS cast a pall over the movement as a whole, it elicited no passionate debate and analysis but was met by a remarkable silence and by recrimination, leaving little opportunity for renewal.

The establishment of ECS as a separate entity amalgamating Cape Breton Co-operative Services of Sydney and Eastern Co-operative Services of Antigonish, as we noted in the previous chapter, was fraught with controversy emanating from a number of sources. It suffered from a wide array of inefficiencies at the management level, which was something that afflicted many of the cooperative enterprises of the movement. From the outset, the project was too large and tried to cover too many activities, as evident in its organization structure, which comprised seven divisions.[91] Its complex structure made ECS difficult to manage and was also hampered by skepticism, including among some of its management personnel.[92] The fundamental problems inherent in inadequate local agricultural output, severe shortages of working capital, lack of support by cooperatives and individual producers, and increased competition from supermarkets all conspired to make ECS's bankruptcy and reorganization in 1961 inevitable.[93] Despite the reorganization, which brought new management and new money, the problems persisted. Moreover, from 1961 until its demise in 1964, the operations of ECS were driven by the objective of survival rather than the loftier notion of social transformation, and thus it had lost much of its original purpose.[94]

To some extent the establishment of ECS was also premature, given that the groundwork upon which it stood was inadequately developed. Indeed, Rev. Gillis, taking an extreme position, characterized the setting-up of ECS as "a furtive, panicky attempt to build something to show for extension's twenty five year efforts in agriculture."[95] Yet the fact that individual operations had been in place in Sydney and Antigonish for some time suggests that such a project, perhaps one more appropriate in scale and scope and based on more solid cooperative foundations, could have succeeded. To succeed, however, it had to be part of an economic system, and perhaps more than anything else, this was the crux of the matter.

The establishment of ECS involved the application of a more top-down approach than had been employed in other economic institutions spawned by the Antigonish Movement. Despite the flurry of activity, there was, in the final analysis, inadequate consultation with cooperative leaders and other members of the affected communities and sectors.[96] Aside from violating the basic principle of people being fully involved in the decision-making process as well as in controlling the economic activities that were put in place, inadequate consultation also limited the extent to which an informed decision could be made and the extent to which commitment to it could be fostered. The movement, particularly in the establishment of economic institutions, had developed some well-established mechanisms that allowed the people to be a part of the decision-making process. In the case of the establishment of earlier economic projects and institutions, however, the requirements in terms of threshold size, levels of expertise, and the like were such that the people organized in groups could establish them on their own. The establishment of an enterprise the magnitude of ECS was an entirely different matter. Ideally, it required the input and resources of a dynamic Extension Department and a unified cooperative sector. The extent to which the cooperative sector had already been fragmented in the 1950s, with each entity narrowly concerned with its own survival, would have made economic cooperation among its various components very difficult. Without such mutual cooperation and support, however, the success of the project was compromised. The problems faced by ECS were due as much to the movement's disarray as to any of the other factors. Ironically, its failure further worsened the disarray. That Rev. Gillis, during his brief stint as director of the Extension Department, was openly critical of the establishment of ECS also did not augur well.

The nature of the project, the way that it was planned and implemented, and the conflicting views about it all conspired to make its failure particularly damaging to the Antigonish Movement. The establishment of ECS represented something of a new chapter in the evolution of the movement. As such, it had to succeed to benefit the movement – just as the first incursions into the fisheries had to be successful to ensure that the Antigonish Movement could take hold to begin with. That the movement was already in decline, of course, rendered the failure more catastrophic. The fragmentation that existed, however, shielded many of the cooperative organizations from the effects of this failure, at least in the short term.

One of the key weaknesses of the cooperative services sector and indeed of the cooperative sector as a whole, of which the Extension Department seemed well aware, was the lack of adequately trained personnel, especially competent managers. Although the department instituted, particularly in conjunction with the Maritime Co-operative Council, numerous courses and programs designed to address the problem, it did not have in place a formal and rigorous academic program that could train managers and other professionals to operate effectively and efficiently in the cooperative sector. Competent management would have been particularly important in the case of ECS.

THE NEW PROGRAMS

Over the 1960s, the Extension Department became increasingly reliant on new programs. However, these reflected a different vision of the Antigonish Movement that was not predicated on the establishment of an integrated economic system. Although some of these programs had originated earlier on, particularly during the late 1950s, it was not until the 1960s that they gained some degree of prominence, and consequently, they can be treated as new programs.

In many respects, these programs arose from the Extension Department's attempt to remain relevant, as many of its traditional programs were either facing difficulties or were being largely phased out. Moreover, these new programs were increasingly marginal and disjointed, generally dependent on government funding, and subject to government directives. As such, they reflected the abandonment of the movement's vision to transform the whole of society. The problem was not that the new areas of involvement were inappropriate but that they had no links with the existing institutions of the movement. On their own, they were not likely to succeed. That the Extension Department had failed to secure the resources to become an effective independent development agent had perhaps largely undermined its ability to follow a different course of action.

The Forestry Program

The forestry program was perhaps the most ambitious of the Extension Department's new undertakings.[97] During the late 1950s and early 1960s, forest products, which previously were of little commercial value to local producers, suddenly became valuable. Pulpwood, for example, became a valuable resource as a result of the establishment of a pulp and paper mill in the Strait of Canso area. At the same time, it was recognized that other forest products such as lumber and Christmas trees were not being adequately and effectively exploited. The Extension Department had anticipated these developments and, during the late 1950s, had employed a forestry specialist to devise a forestry program for the subsequent decade.

The main objectives of the Extension Department's forestry program involved resource management and the marketing of forest products. In many respects, therefore, the forestry program was somewhat similar to the fisheries program, where resource management and marketing were also cited as primary concerns. Nevertheless, it was marketing that received the most attention, as it was the component that promised to yield immediate results and that elicited the more enthusiastic response. Thus the Extension Department's main immediate goal in the forestry sector was to establish a provincial marketing agency, owned and controlled by the members, for its products. Such an agency would bargain with the pulp companies on behalf of individual woodlot owners and at the same time promote better forest management. In 1961 such an organization was in fact created, in the form of the Nova Scotia Woodlot Owners' Association. However, it was not very successful and quickly disappeared, in spite of changes in government legislation that allowed orderly marketing practices to be extended to forestry products.

By 1964 there was much uncertainty about the forestry program, but the Extension Department did not give up and in the ensuing years carried out an extensive educational campaign aimed at establishing local associations of woodlot owners who would, in turn, create a more effective organization at the provincial level – that is, a provincial organization of woodlot owners similar to but more effective than the original one. This endeavour was facilitated in the second half of the 1960s by cooperation between the Extension Department and the Agricultural and Rural Development Agency.

In 1966 ARDA provided the funding for an organizational and educational program for woodlot owners, which allowed the Extension Department to employ three full-time fieldworkers and a part-time director in the sector.[98]

The methods employed by the Extension Department in the forestry sector included radio and television programs, short courses, meetings, and conferences. Nevertheless, the task of effectively organizing the woodlot owners was not a simple one, and it took a number of years before anything of any consequence was accomplished. However, by 1968 thirteen local organizations of woodlot owners had been created, and a year later the Nova Scotia Woodlot Owners' Association (NSWOA) was established at a meeting held in Truro, attended by some forty-five representatives of twelve woodlot organizations.[99] In 1970 the NSWOA was certified as a bargaining agent for its members. It was also decided that on 31 March 1971 the NSWOA would take over promotional and educational functions from the Extension Department.[100] Thus, having achieved its goal of creating the NSWOA, the Extension Department terminated its involvement in the forestry program. By so quickly distancing itself from the organization once it was established, the Extension Department ensured that its influence over the sector would be kept at a minimum. In this respect, it acted in a manner consistent with its behaviour toward the cooperative sector from the 1950s onward, abandoning the role of providing education to the cooperatives.

The creation of the NSWOA came too late to have any impact on the forestry industry during the 1960s. Nevertheless, its establishment was an important achievement, as the local woodlot owners' associations that preceded it were not equal to the tasks of achieving better prices, promoting conservation, improving management, expanding the industry, and improving its efficiency.[101]

In implementing its forestry program, the Extension Department faced different and more serious problems than it did, for example, in the fisheries. First, the forestry program involved getting people to exploit a new resource rather than simply pursuing, albeit more efficiently, an activity that was already being undertaken and upon which people depended for their immediate survival, as was the case in the fisheries. Thus a greater amount of outside knowledge was required, and the sense of urgency was not great. Second, cooperation among woodlot owners was rendered more difficult by their geographical dispersion. Third, the market facing the woodlot owners was much different from that prevailing in the fisheries, particularly in the case of pulpwood, where multinational corporations with access to alternate sources of supply were in a very strong bargaining position. Thus the scenario that prevailed in the forestry sector was significantly different from that in the fisheries during the early years, where initial gains were obtained by simply gaining control of the marketing process and, consequently, of the distribution of rents and quasi rents. Equally important was that in the forestry sector, the focus was on strengthening the position of the woodlot owners within the existing framework rather than on promoting fundamental new activities and transforming the sector. Again, this marked a significant shift away from the original model of the Antigonish Movement.

The "Indian" Program

The second new major program undertaken by the Extension Department involved education for the Aboriginal population. The actual start of this program can also be traced to the late 1950s. However, in the 1960s it was greatly expanded in scope and in terms of the financial, human, and other resources devoted to it. The program, which involved an array of short courses, folk schools, training, and organizational activities and meetings of various sorts, was financed by the Indian Affairs Branch of the federal Department of Citizenship and Immigration. Its objective was to develop social leadership among the Aboriginals of Nova Scotia under the assumption that the lack of such leadership was a key element constraining their socio-economic development.[102]

The program was terminated in 1970 and must be classified largely as a failure.[103] Indeed, after more than a decade of operation, its tangible achievements were negligible, with the possible exception of the establishment of the Union of Nova Scotia Indians, small projects such as the organization of fourteen oyster fishermen on the Eskasoni reserve to look at the possibility of establishing an oyster hatchery there, and some improvements in terms of training provided, educational upgrading, and the like. In 1970 the Union of Nova Scotia Indians took over the functions previously discharged by the Extension Department, including the administration of the federal government grants and the implementation of projects and programs. The desire on the part of the Aboriginal communities to take control of their own affairs can be easily understood and in fact makes sense in the context of the promotion of grassroots development.

In many ways, the "Indian" program presented challenges that the weakened Extension Department simply could not meet. It required not only a clear vision but also the ability to make the necessary adaptation to different organizational and institutional circumstances. The Antigonish Movement was predicated on education for economic action, with the latter being the objective and the former serving as a tool. Moreover, the economic action had to be perceived as successful in order to establish the legitimacy of the approach and engender commitment to it. This economic action involved undertakings that the people themselves, in this case the Aboriginal communities, could devise and implement, driven by their own fundamental objectives and resources. That the Extension Department was acting as an intermediary for the government also contributed to the outcome since it would not have been free to pursue its own vision and independent courses of action.[104]

The Civics and Other Programs

A third new program involved a short-lived civics project centred in Cape Breton. The objective of this program was to educate and generally enlighten civic leaders in the virtues of larger and more efficient municipal units and, in so doing, to assist in the amalgamation of small municipalities in industrial Cape Breton. After the Extension Department hired a consulting firm to study the situation, classes on civic government were offered to local civic leaders. These classes enjoyed some short-lived popularity, but the ultimate goal of the project – amalgamation of small municipal units – was never realized. The civics program is perhaps the clearest indication of how far the Extension Department had strayed from its roots.

The Extension Department was also involved in numerous other small projects that tended to have in common a lack of focus, a very short life span, and a general uncertainty as to their rationale. Moreover, they did not yield much by way of concrete results and more than any others fitted the pattern of a haphazard search by the Extension Department for some niche in the economy of eastern Nova Scotia in order to remain relevant. This search was usually instigated by outside forces, often the government.

CONCLUSION

The 1960s witnessed the steady decline of both the Extension Department of St Francis Xavier University and the Antigonish Movement as a whole in its home base. The Extension Department lost faith in its original vision of self-help and socio-economic reform predicated on education and cooperative economic action as the underpinnings of a new economic system owned and controlled by the people themselves. Instead, to foster improvements within the existing system, it adopted a new vision that was founded on academically driven scientific research and was largely government funded.

The new vision gave rise to programs and activities that were largely ineffective. All of the Extension Department's major programs, with the possible exception of housing, experienced a decline in effectiveness over the decade, and virtually all of them were eventually terminated. Of its major new programs, only the one involving the forestry sector achieved any measure of success. These new programs had also been largely terminated by the start of the 1970s. As well, and perhaps of even greater importance, the Extension Department became isolated institutionally – a serious shortcoming for an organization involved primarily in fostering bottom-up development and highly dependent on its ability to motivate people. While its links with the cooperative sector were being cut, those with the academic world of St Francis Xavier University were never developed. By the end of the decade, its longstanding partnership with the federal Department of Fisheries had been terminated. The newer public-sector partners, which included the Department of Indian Affairs, the Agricultural and Rural Development Agency, and the Area Development Agency, were much less supportive, offering limited financial support for generally short-term projects.[105]

Much of the Extension Department's work during the decade was linked to the delivery of public programs for government departments and newly created agencies that lacked their own capabilities. However, these bodies did not hesitate to terminate their arrangements with the Extension Department once such program-delivery capabilities were developed.

During the 1960s, to a greater extent than ever before, the focus of the cooperative sector was on the consolidation and rationalization of existing enterprises to ensure adequate capitalization and modernization. The resource, decision-making, and other requirements of cooperative enterprises necessitated the existence of an integrated economic system that would be able to link the various entities and, in the process, enable them to exploit various linkages as well as agglomeration and scale economies. These linkages and economies, in turn, would have added to both the efficiency and the dynamism of the individual cooperatives.

In many ways, the 1960s started with a bang and ended with a whimper for the Antigonish Movement as a whole. The Big Picture quickly evaporated, leaving behind the Six Principles, which romanticized the movement as a relic of the past. During the 1960s, all pretense of creating an integrated economic system was dropped. What was left of the movement was neither strong enough to withstand adversity nor flexible enough to adjust to changing circumstances. Ironically, while the movement was being transferred abroad through the work of the Coady International Institute, it was collapsing at home.

By the end of the 1960s, the role of the Extension Department had been reduced to primarily the educational upgrading and retraining of adult workers. Thus, within the span of one decade, the Extension Department of St Francis Xavier University was transformed from an agent of socio-economic change into something akin to a vocational school – a rather remarkable journey. Although many cooperatives survived, the cooperative sector became markedly weaker during the decade, no longer maintaining even the pretence of working toward integration into a dynamic alternate economic system. Generally, the cooperatives that achieved success did so on their own. Those that were floundering were largely left to flounder, and there was no substantive help for them.

7

The Last Hurrah, 1970–2000

INTRODUCTION

At the beginning of the 1970s, the Extension Department of St Francis Xavier University found itself in an unenviable position. As a result of the radical transformation that had taken place during the 1960s, its programs were floundering in disarray, and it was dropped by practically every development partner, notably the federal Department of Fisheries, the Nova Scotia Housing Commission, and those in the cooperative sector. Many of its programs and functions were taken over by government and other agencies, and its finances were in tatters. The Antigonish Movement, predicated on the establishment of an alternate economic system, made up of its own independent institutions owned and controlled by the people, was largely relegated to the past. Adult education, rather than a tool, became largely the sole objective of the Extension Department.

The forces unleashed during the 1960s continued to dominate, and the Extension Department's effective involvement in the community, although still substantial, continued to wane while also becoming increasingly marginalized within the university. In the process, the links that had been fostered between the university and the community at large were also weakened as was any notion that the Extension Department could be an effective bridge between the campus and the community.

Over the next three decades, the Extension Department did make some efforts to recover its former vitality, dynamism, and support base in order to reestablish its relevance and that of the movement as a whole. Attempts were made to regain the power and attraction of the past vision, to revive and create a new educational strategy, to revitalize economic cooperation in the fisheries, finance, and other areas, to resurrect or to initiate innovative and promising programs, to enter new fields of social action, to establish new sources of permanent funding, to find new clienteles and new development partners, and so on. However, there were few efforts to resurrect the notion of the Antigonish Movement as an economic system and to reintroduce or adapt the notion of the "Big Picture."

The period under consideration coincided with the tenure of three directors of the Extension Department: Rev. George Topshee from 1969 to 1982, Dr Teresa MacNeil from 1982 to 1992, and Tom Webb from 1994 to 2000.[1] Although each faced the same challenge of restoring and revitalizing the Extension Department's leadership role in order to make the department more relevant and capable of dealing with the socio-economic difficulties facing the region, they brought different perspectives and visions to the position. Consequently, each adopted a different approach, defined the nature and identity of the Extension Department in fundamentally different terms, and sought different alliances, supporting structures, and partners.

For most of the period under consideration, the approaches adopted conspired with the accelerating rate of change in the socio-economic environment, the deteriorating economic base, and the continuing out-migration from the region to the detriment of both the Extension Department and the Antigonish Movement. Despite the department's various activities and efforts, the loss of vision, institutional fragmentation, and especially the failure to grasp that the effectiveness of the Antigonish Movement lay in its attempt to establish a dynamic and highly integrated economic system proved insurmountable. The legacy of the 1960s proved to be irreversible – it had become too deeply entrenched both intellectually and institutionally. Despite this failure to revive the movement, the various educational programs and activities of the Extension Department provided significant assistance to numerous organizations working in the region, and they were of great benefit to a large number of individuals in the local communities over the years. However, this assistance was a far cry from the stirring vision and the lofty aims of the Antigonish Movement.

THE EXTENSION DEPARTMENT AND THE UNIVERSITY

Over the period under consideration, St Francis Xavier University steadily reduced its financial contribution to the Extension Department. Moreover, the process of marginalization within the university community continued unabated, transforming the Extension Department from a powerful and vital component of the institution into a mere appendage.[2] Both the university, which was no longer dependent on the financial contribution of the local communities, and its highly qualified faculty and administration had decreasing or no attachment to the Antigonish Movement and the historical mission of the Extension Department. The university became increasingly preoccupied with academic standards and concerns and less so with the plight of the local communities. In the process, it became largely indistinguishable from other undergraduate universities in Canada, except in terms of its location and perhaps size and history. In effect, the university experienced a fundamental reversal of its impact on the surrounding region when compared to earlier decades, including to some extent the 1960s.

Whereas during earlier times St Francis Xavier University, through its Extension Department, had helped the local communities of the region to develop economically and socially, it now reverted to educating the region's brightest and most active youth, who in turn tended to leave and find employment and seek opportunities elsewhere. Thus the university was now contributing, albeit indirectly, to the process of economic and social stagnation in the region and reproducing exactly the circumstances that Rev. Jimmy Tompkins and the other early pioneers of the movement had initially railed against.

The academic faculty came increasingly from outside the region, with the hiring being done on the basis of academic training and research capabilities. As would be expected, these people were preoccupied with research and publications in areas that, generally, had little immediate relevance to the socio-economic conditions of the region. Although some faculty members continued to become involved in the work of the Extension Department and what remained of the institutional framework of the Antigonish Movement, such involvement was often restricted to the delivery of short courses, workshops, and the like. In any event, rather than becoming a source of the new technologies, innovation, and expertise that would be required for the Antigonish Movement to reemerge and flourish, especially in a new knowledge- and technology-driven economy, the university increasingly removed itself from the whole process, achieving a virtually complete retrenchment with the coming of the new millennium that created an almost complete separation of the campus from the community. Even among the students, interest in and concern with the Antigonish Movement seem to have largely disappeared along with the cooperative bookstore, cooperative barbershop, two credit unions, and the International Club.

The goals and the objectives of the university and those of the Extension Department and what remained of the Antigonish Movement became fundamentally at odds, and over time the gap widened. With continued expansion and the growth of its academic and professional programs, the university was bound to prevail, mitigating the Extension Department's efforts to revive its former vitality and relevance, regardless of the ability and commitment of its director and staff.

THE SOCIO-ECONOMIC ENVIRONMENT

From the 1970s onward, the socio-economic environment proved to be increasingly hostile to the operations of the Extension Department and to the fundamental vision of the Antigonish Movement as a whole. Having failed to establish a viable and dynamic economic system, and unable to depend on substantive support from the university, neither the Extension Department nor what was left of the movement could elicit broad-based support. Marginal and often disjointed local activities could not satisfy the imagination of the people, who now had greater options, nor could these activities meet the needs of communities and sectors in decline. In many ways, the labour unrest and strife in the fisheries that ushered in the 1970s constituted manifestations of such a state of events. In the fisheries, declining conditions were further exacerbated by the lack of intercooperative cooperation, which precluded the formation of stronger, more dynamic, and flexible economic institutions able to compete with the emerging large-scale, for-profit enterprises.[3] By the end of the 1960s, with the termination of the fisheries grant, the Extension Department had passed on to the United Maritime Fishermen cooperative the task of dealing with the fisheries sector. Thus it had been forced, to a great extent, to the sidelines in the very sector where many of its early successes where achieved.[4]

Among other things, the weakened Extension Department had to deal with the impact of the mass media, which became the most significant and influential tool of adult education in the region and a powerful opinion- and value-forming agent. The proliferation of the mass media took its toll on the traditional way of life as eastern Nova Scotia and the whole of Atlantic Canada became increasingly integrated into the North American economy.[5] Furthermore, the entry of the baby boomers, the first generation raised in conditions of relative security and affluence, into public life and leadership accelerated the transformation of the traditional culture, which stressed self-denial, cooperation, stability, and the permanence of social relations, into the modern culture, which placed greater emphasis on materialism, individualism, self-gratification, mobility, and adaptability to ceaseless and accelerating change. Educated, energetic, and adaptable individuals excelled in this new environment of mobility and opportunity, moving rapidly within the network of social and educational institutions and assuming positions of greater responsibility, prestige, and income. Such individuals were drawn into and constituted the leadership of cooperatives and credit unions in previous decades. In this period, the public and private institutions, mostly located in other regions, offered them much more attractive opportunities than the generally small, undercapitalized, and often marginal local cooperative enterprises. To some extent, there was no place in much of what remained of the movement for the new generation of leaders and skilled and highly educated entrants into the labour force.

On the other extreme, the less skilled and educated, who generally entered the social and economic institutions at their lower rungs, faced entirely different situations and prospects. Some of them left the region seeking a better life in the industrial and commercial centres of central and western Canada. Those who remained, especially as a result of additional changes that further eroded many of the more traditional jobs, generally faced reduced prospects. Many who remained engaged in primary activities were forced to supplement their income from farming, fishing, or forestry with part-time employment in low-paying jobs or, alternatively, with unemployment benefits, social assistance, and other benefits available from the expanding social-welfare safety net. The same situation afflicted many of those who worked in the service sectors. Although the social safety net mitigated some of the worst outcomes, it did not alter the underlying factors at work.[6] Moreover, for those who had few skills that could be transferred to other activities, migration to low-paying jobs in other parts of the country entailed a further drop in their living standards. During the earlier decades, the latter social group constituted the main body of the membership of the cooperatives and credit unions. From the 1970s onward, such participation was must less evident, largely as a result of the decline of the cooperative sector.

The emergence of new and improved social legislation in the 1970s and afterward weakened commitment to self-reliant economic action, especially given that it seemed to offer little in terms of additional benefit and that there was neither a grand vision nor an institutional framework to point the way. Thus, in circumstances where it was evident largely in increasingly marginal activities and where there was no longer a vision that allowed people to establish their own institutions, the strengthening of the social safety net had a negative impact on the Antigonish Movement. Many became alienated from the existing cooperatives and sought alternate mechanisms. In what is often referred to as the "Rochdale cul-de-sac," cooperatives began to be controlled by management teams who were concerned with running them more as businesses than as cooperative enterprises. As a result, the cooperative nature of the enterprises was undermined, which led to a loss of commitment among the membership. In some cases, members established other institutions to ensure that their interests were safeguarded by their own cooperative organizations.[7]

In between the two extremes of the population identified above, there were those who were able to take advantage of the opportunities created by the new socio-economic environment. These included some of those in the primary sectors, such as the fisheries and agriculture, who faced expanded prospects, higher incomes, and better standards of living as a result largely of unearned economic windfalls arising from the reappearance of rents and quasi rents due to government policies that restricted supply, especially in an environment of increasing demand. The dairy industry was among the first to benefit from such windfalls in terms of high-value marketing quotas established by the government. Such windfalls were the result of management policies applied by various provincial governments and designed largely to preserve the family-based production of milk.[8]

Subsequently, policies based on supply restrictions also led to the emergence of rents in the fisheries through means such as lucrative licences, permits, and quotas that affected lobster, scallop, crab, and other species. Thus, for example, in the lobster fishery, a licensing system was established along with limitations on the number of traps, size of lobster that could be caught, duration and timing of the fishing season, and the like. These were parts of a new approach by the Canadian government that aimed to organize and manage the fisheries on a sustainable basis.[9]

The reemergence of rents, primarily as a result of supply management policies, stressed the question of distribution, as opposed to factors like production and marketing. In the past, such economic rents were distributed among the various participants according to their relative economic power. Thus, for example, in the 1920s the rents in the fisheries were appropriated by groups that had monopoly power, such as the fish buyers, processors, and merchants, at the expense of the individual fishermen. However, as had begun to occur in the 1930s, these fishermen could increase their economic power and thus change the situation and raise their incomes by forming cooperatives and building their own processing plants. In the process, they were able to appropriate the available rents while also creating opportunities for additional ones. Similar possibilities also existed in the agricultural sector. Indeed, such a process constituted the main driving force that propelled the success of the Antigonish Movement in the early years.

By the 1970s the allocation of rents was transferred out of the primarily economic arena and into the realm of politics. The government and its various departments, at both the federal and the provincial levels, determined the allocation of rents to producers, processors, and communities. This allocation was carried out through mechanisms such as licensing, marketing quotas, total allowable catches, fish quotas, and control of the length and timing of the fishing season. The emergence of rents and their allocation through these mechanisms caused a fundamental change in the behaviour of those involved in the affected sectors. In the main, it shifted the primary concern away from matters such as production, marketing, efficiency, and cost considerations and toward influencing political decisions.

Within this new environment, strategies to maintain and expand economic activity and power along lines consistent with the original vision of the Antigonish Movement were no longer seen as effective in various sectors. Nonetheless, political decisions and actions, such as exerting pressure on politicians through demonstrations, writing letters to political representatives, participating in community meetings, and blocking roads, became more important vehicles to increase the incomes of individual producers and their communities. In the process, there was a significant decline in the importance of cooperatives to the individual members – a decline that was further accentuated by the fact that cooperatives were weak, often isolated, and indeed dismissed in some quarters as being both a cause and an effect of regional underdevelopment.[10] Ironically, the various supply management and other measures could also have been used to strengthen the cooperative organizations, as was indeed the case in the dairy sector.

The decline in the perceived relevance of cooperatives was accompanied by the emergence and expansion of new organizations that were better suited to the exertion of political as well as economic pressure. Thus the latter part of the 1970s saw the emergence of the Maritime Fishermen's Union, whereas the United Maritime Fishermen cooperative became weaker, going into receivership in 1988 and eventually collapsing altogether.[11]

The role of cooperatives and of the movement as a whole in the fisheries was also weakened by the extension of Unemployment Insurance (UI) benefits to the fishermen.[12] Although it was welcomed by those in the fisheries, the program took on a life of its own and hampered cooperatives' efforts to evolve and become more efficient and sustainable. In effect, the extension of UI combined with the management strategies of the federal Department of Fisheries and Oceans to politicize the whole fisheries sector to an extent that proved to be highly detrimental not only for the cooperative approach but also for the fisheries as a whole.[13]

The new socio-economic environment, predicated on a culture of individualism and mobility and heavily reliant on the emergence of the welfare state, the regulatory function of the government, and the political process, made the appeal to the traditional values of the Antigonish Movement less attractive and perhaps even irrelevant to the majority of the region's population. Moreover, given the state of the movement, the changes in attitude were not without justification. The Extension Department and the Antigonish Movement had moved away from the original vision and promise of establishing a dynamic economic system and had also failed to adapt to the changing circumstances, as the trend toward innovations such as greater technological sophistication and larger-scale production not only continued unabated but also became much more pronounced.

In the economic sphere, the continued decline of the region, particularly in industrial Cape Breton, and the persistent regional imbalance prompted the Canadian government to become more fully involved in the attempt to find solutions. Although this process had begun earlier, especially during the 1960s, it reached its peak in the 1970s as the Department of Regional Economic Expansion (DREE) went into full swing. The new strategy entailed government ownership as well as subsidization of key industries and sectors, such as coal, steel, and shipbuilding. The establishment of the Cape Breton Development Corporation (DEVCO) and the Sydney Steel Corporation (SYSCO), both in 1967, was a part of this trend. Thus the solution to regional problems was entrusted fully to the political realm – a drastic reversal of the original inception of the Antigonish Movement, where the political solution was identified as the "lazy" one. DREE was terminated in 1982 and succeeded by the Atlantic Canada Opportunities Agency (ACOA) in 1987, which was to act as the main conduit for development in the region.[14]

The lack of success of many of the government programs and the degree to which they undermined other local initiatives, including cooperatives, constituted a double loss for the region.[15] Yet the Extension Department, which had gone a long way toward transforming itself into a purely adult education institution, could offer relatively little direct support for economic action. Thus it was in a weak position to influence government policy or, more important, to use the new initiatives to bolster the Antigonish Movement and its institutions. Moreover, its virtual divorce from the cooperatives still in operation gave it little leverage over them, and the fact that the cooperative sector itself was disjointed and fragmented added to the problem.

THE EXTENSION DEPARTMENT'S ADJUSTMENT TO CHANGES IN THE SOCIO-ECONOMIC ENVIRONMENT

During the 1960s, the Extension Department had substantially altered both the vision and the strategy of the Antigonish Movement.

In effect, the Antigonish Movement, as envisaged by Rev. Moses Coady and the other early pioneers, had been terminated. The most critical components of the new approach were the adoption of a new community development strategy and the assignment of the leadership role in the economic sphere to the government as opposed to the people themselves. The Extension Department viewed the new approach as more appropriate for the times. By 1970, however, there was a sobering realization that the new approach had yielded few tangible benefits.

The Search for a New Vision

In 1969 Rev. George Topshee, an experienced, dedicated, and respected member of the Extension Department who held the position of associate director under Rev. Dr Joseph N. MacNeil, was appointed director, and he held the position until 1982.[16] Rev. Topshee's appointment signalled a determined effort to search for a way out of the dire predicament that had engulfed both the Extension Department and the Antigonish Movement at the end of the 1960s. Rev. Topshee was not only experienced but also dedicated to the preservation and revitalization of the Antigonish Movement or at least some version of it.

Rev. Topshee took over as the director at a time when the Extension Department had been fundamentally transformed and when what remained of the Antigonish Movement was fragmented and in disarray. Revitalizing the movement and the Extension Department itself was a major task, especially given the prevailing socio-economic environment and fundamental confusion concerning what the Antigonish Movement was all about. His first reaction was an attempt to force such a revitalization through a fundamentally top-down process involving the organization of a development conference, the Eastern Development Conference, modelled after the Rural and Industrial Conferences (RAICS) of earlier times. To prepare for the conference, ten development councils were established.[17] These councils were also to serve as the nucleus for the revival of the study clubs. After six months of study, these councils organized a conference, held in June 1971, to which hundreds of delegates were invited. Although the conference generated initial enthusiasm, it ended in frustration and disappointment, as the delegates could not agree on any common action. Since there was no follow-up to the conference, the development councils became inactive and soon ceased to exist.

Such efforts to revive the movement failed for a number of reasons. First, the success of the early RAICs depended on the economic activities of numerous cooperatives and credit unions and on the educational activities of hundreds of study clubs. The link between education and economic activity was a key source of the inspiration and enthusiasm generated by the RAICs among the participants. In the 1970s there were no study clubs, and very few new economic activities were initiated under the auspices of the Antigonish Movement. The conference, while attempting to put the proverbial cart before the horse, could not possibly generate enthusiasm since there was little to be enthusiastic about. Second, the format of the conference – speeches and panel presentations by invited experts – was not conducive to the promotion of participation and long-term commitment by the people at large. The Eastern Development Conference was thus a far cry from the early RAICs, and rather than enthusiasm and inspiration, it created a great deal of frustration and feelings of hopelessness and helplessness. As a consequence, no attempts were made to revive similar conferences until 1978 when the fiftieth anniversary of the Extension Department and the Antigonish Movement was held.

The failure of the initial Eastern Development Conference forced the Extension Department to change its approach to one that was fundamentally "bottom-up." The new approach involved attempting to go back to what was perceived as the initial vision of the movement. In fact, the 1972–73 annual report of the Extension Department started out by trying to recapture what was perceived as the original philosophy of the Antigonish Movement, asserting that although "circumstances have changed since the early days, members of the movement still believe that the original principles and ideals are valid and applicable."[18] However, the vision that it alluded to was the one implied by the "Six Principles" rather than by the "Big Picture" and the establishment of an economic system. Moreover, it did not translate into programs that would have reversed the decline of the movement or prompted its reemergence, despite the rhetoric and a concerted effort to initiate programs and projects in areas where the Extension Department had been very active in the past, such as the fisheries, the cooperative and credit union sectors, housing, labour education, and community development. As well, the divergence between the objectives and the nature of these various programs gave the appearance of a loss of focus and overall sense of direction, as was confirmed by a 1979 consultant's report.[19] Not surprisingly, the report concluded that the Extension Department's lack of focus was due to the absence of a clearly defined and comprehensive strategy. Nevertheless, some real efforts were made to at least stay engaged with the movement and to renew some of the historically significant relationships.

Much of the work undertaken by the Extension Department during the early and mid-1970s involved the delivery of programs mainly on behalf of government and other entities. This was especially the case for the various housing programs from about 1975 onward, with the Extension Department's own program having been terminated during the 1969–70 period. Although generally beneficial, these programs were in keeping with the reliance on the government to resolve the major problems facing the various communities, albeit in a way that allowed some inputs from the local population in terms of planning and implementation.

In part, the seeming lack of a strategy and of focus was linked to a belief that activities in the various areas that were parts of the past involvement of the Extension Department would mobilize linkages and mutual-reinforcement mechanisms, leading to a de facto restoration of some of the earlier strategies and, in the process, achieving the dual target of both revitalizing the movement and reestablishing the leadership role of the Extension Department within it. Thus several long-lasting programs were initiated in areas such as labour education – with the establishment of the Atlantic Region Labour Education Centre (ARLEC) in 1972 – cooperative and social housing, and community development. However, there were no integrative links between these various programs, and they remained isolated initiatives for as long as they were in existence. They served different clienteles, regions, and communities and were generally funded by agencies with their own specific mandates and objectives. In effect, the Extension Department continued to act as an intermediary for government and other agencies rather than serving the needs of the movement. Thus, although seemingly successful, these programs were not able to revitalize the Antigonish Movement or to reestablish the role of the Extension Department within it. Indeed, the fragmentation of what was left of the movement continued unabated, further splintering it into isolated and often marginal components. The situation persisted for the remainder of Rev. Topshee's tenure as director.

Nevertheless, there was a real concern that the Extension Department was not doing enough, especially as economic difficulties among various components of the original constituencies of the Antigonish Movement worsened. In 1978 it organized a RAIC-type conference on the occasion of its fiftieth anniversary. This conference brought to the fore a number of issues, particularly the need to reestablish contact with the cooperatives and other institutions of the movement. Out of this awareness emerged an attempt to reestablish a program of cooperative education.

The Extension Department recognized that it had been a mistake to leave cooperative institutions to carry out their own educational programs once they were seemingly economically viable. Its 1978 annual report notes, "In the 1950s and 1960s, the umbilical cord to Extension was severed for consumer coops, credit unions and fishermen's coop[s]. Peripheral involvements between Extension and these coop institutions remained but the main responsibility for educational programs fell on the various segments of the cooperative movement. In recent years there has been concern expressed by staff and rank and file members that the lack of member participation in the affairs of coops was leading to control by technicians. The social change, economic reform and educational elements of coops was perceived to be endangered."[20] Thus there was a refocus of the new vision to consider the economic institutions that had been created by the movement but that, particularly over the previous decade, had been cast adrift. Cooperative and credit union education, which had been largely discontinued in the 1960s, became a matter of urgency for the Extension Department in the late 1970s and early 1980s, giving rise to a number of programs and pilot projects. The new focus, however, came at the end of Rev. Topshee's tenure and was a case of too little, too late. Moreover, beyond the delivery of programs that were funded by government or other entities, the Extension Department was limited in its ability to deal with the outstanding socio-economic problems.[21] Already pulled in various directions, it opted to stress advocacy and predominantly political solutions rather than action in the economic sphere. The issue was complicated by the fact that "some coops saw Extension as having a historical responsibility while some in the hierarchy of the organizations saw an Extension Department intervention as interference in their affairs."[22] Indeed, there was a substantial amount of distrust between the Extension Department and the cooperative sector.[23] The implication, of course, is that the cooperative sector itself, or segments of it, had failed to accept that it was a part of a system in which the Extension Department needed to play a critical and broad-based role.

Generally, even while revitalization of the Antigonish Movement was being pursued, it was accepted that the movement could no longer deal with the economic problems of the region.[24] Given the state of the Antigonish Movement, the new socio-economic environment, especially the increased role of government in the economy, and the lack of resources available to the Extension Department, the situation could perhaps not have been otherwise. Nevertheless, the reemergence of cooperative education and the recognition of its importance were significant. It was in keeping with the original vision of the movement and, more important, constituted an acknowledgment that things had somehow gone wrong.

The Emergence of a New Vision in the 1980s

In 1982 Dr Teresa MacNeil, a long-time associate of the Extension Department and one of its bright and highly educated fieldworkers during the 1960s, replaced Rev. Topshee as director. MacNeil, who remained director until her resignation in 1992, held graduate degrees in the area of adult education and headed the university's Adult Education Department when it was established in 1970. Her formal training in adult education had enormous impact in shaping her vision of the Extension Department and the Antigonish Movement as a whole, transforming both into adult education programs. In the process, MacNeil completed the change that had been taking place since the 1960s and that had been only mildly challenged by Rev. Topshee during the 1970s. She moulded the Extension Department to reflect accepted adult education methodology, turning it into "the university's agent for adult education in the community."[25] The process was facilitated by the fact that the continuing education program of the university was transferred to the Extension Department when MacNeil became director, leading to a fundamental bifurcation of the department's programs.[26]

In 1983 a new education strategy designed to bridge the gap between the vision and the programs of the movement was approved by the Senate of the university. This new strategy, referred to as the establishment of "appropriate program goals for the Extension Department," was predicated on four steps:

> 1. to identify on a continuous basis, learning needs of the adult population of Northeastern Nova Scotia as they relate to the economic, social, political and cultural development of the area; 2. to organize groups to meet the shared learning needs of all individuals, with attention to individual differences, to the individual's capacity to know him/herself and with emphasis on the method of problem solving through group action; 3. to arrange for the resources of the university and of other knowledge sources, to be utilized by the respective learning groups as means to achieve required knowledge and skill; 4. to measure the success of the Department's program in terms of improvement in the knowledge and skill of individual participants and in terms of group effectiveness as agents of social change.[27]

Although on the surface the new vision did not seem to be that much different from those articulated in earlier decades, as adult education had always been an integral part of the Extension Department, in reality it constituted a series of radical breaks with the past. The most obvious of these breaks is represented by the fact that education itself, rather than socio-economic development and transformation, became the objective of the Extension Department. In contrast, its traditional focus had been more narrowly on the economic and social development of the various surrounding communities through the promotion of group action and the establishment of cooperative ventures as tools for establishing a new economic system. The new vision, with its emphasis on "educational needs," formally broadened the horizon of the Extension Department to include, for example, political, cultural, and later also environmental issues. The significance, validity, and priority of various issues were to be determined by the "learners" themselves. In addition, the organizations that the Extension Department was to assist could now include any "learning group" that possessed "shared needs," regardless of what these entailed. As well, group action was no longer directed toward ownership and control of economic institutions but toward any action bolstering undefined "agents of social change." Finally, the effectiveness of the Extension Department was no longer to be measured by the number of cooperatives, credit unions, and the like that it helped to organize and/or to thrive but by "improvements in the knowledge of individuals" and "group effectiveness as agents of social change." There was no recognition of either the Antigonish Movement as an attempt to establish an independent economic system or the role that the Extension Department needed to play in such a system.

In addition to its radical departure from the original vision of the movement, which completely delinked education from economic action, the fundamental problem with the new strategy was that it was too broad and all-encompassing. As such, it was of little concrete significance from an operational perspective. Although it was consistent with a learner-driven adult education program, it provided no guidance for the Extension Department in informing its choice and ranking of activities as well as its overall strategy. It was not possible to exclude any programs as falling outside of its scope or as being less desirable or even undesirable. Any program could be justified in terms of the learning needs of the region's adult population. Thus the new strategy simply propagated and in a real sense legitimized the Extension Department's lack of a focus other than adult education generally.

In terms of adult education criteria, the Extension Department's programs of the 1980s, which dealt with a wide range of issues that included economic, social, political, and cultural factors, were highly successful. These programs attracted an ever-increasing number of participants and continually expanded to other regions and most of the provinces in Canada. Its diploma program in adult education, Training for Trainers, acquired a national reputation and spawned numerous such programs. The expansion of the Extension Department's educational program was accompanied by an ever-increasing budget and personnel. However, while the continuing and adult education components of this program were expanding in scope, size, and the resources devoted to them, the remaining programs – now labelled "general extension," which included the economic and community-based programs – were stagnating. The increased gap between the continuing and adult education programs, on the one hand, and "general extension," on the other, resulted in the creation of "two cultures" within the Extension Department – one involving fieldwork and the other involving continuing education.

The focus on adult education courses, often for national audiences, caused the Extension Department to distance itself from the Antigonish Movement and from the economic problems that plagued various local communities and eastern Nova Scotia as a whole. The economic base of the region, along with some of the institutions of the Antigonish Movement itself, continued to be undermined. Output and employment in the steel and coal industries of Cape Breton were steadily declining, leaving government-owned corporations such as DEVCO and SYSCO with continuous deficits. The heavy government involvement in the local economy had proved not to be a panacea. However, the problems were much more widespread: for example, local shipyards were on the verge of bankruptcy, fish stocks were being depleted at an alarming rate, and forests were being harvested at faster than sustainable rates. While all of this was taking place, there were no innovative ideas emerging from the Extension Department and the university.

The deteriorating economic base of the region negatively impacted the performance of the cooperative sector, thus undermining some of the institutions linked to the Antigonish Movement that had managed to survive. The persistent difficulties faced by the United Maritime Fishermen during the decade left many fishing cooperatives that were still in operation further isolated, without support, and vulnerable, especially in the face of the competition from large-scale operations and the worsening crisis in the fisheries. The credit unions, particularly the rural ones, were struggling, which resulted in a number of bankruptcies. Even some of the strongest segments of the cooperative sector, such as the consumers' cooperative stores, were negatively affected.[28] The fragmented remnants of the movement were powerless in the face of these forces, and the Extension Department was unable to offer much help.

The educational offerings of the Extension Department were of little relevance to the pressing economic problems of the region and to the plight of the cooperative sector. In part, the problem can be attributed to the adoption of a methodology predicated on the common but erroneous presupposition that education and knowledge automatically lead to action and social change.[29] Adult education is a tool but by itself not a very effective one, at least in terms of fostering economic action and entrepreneurship.[30] The links between education and economic activity are at best indirect, complex, and varied. Moreover, since the solutions to the socio-economic problems of the region were perceived to rest with the public sector, direct economic action was not seen to be as urgent as in earlier times. At the heart of the matter was the fundamental misconception of the nature of the education process in the context of the Antigonish Movement.

Even during the 1980s, however, the notion that there was more to the Antigonsh Movement than simply adult education did not altogether disappear, particularly among some of the Extension Department's fieldworkers and other supporters of the movement. This perception was reflected not only in some of the work that was being done but also in attempts to revitalize the whole movement through the institution of the Topshee Conference in the early 1980s, which continued to be organized on an annual basis until 1998 and which has been held biannually since then. The Extension Department also inherited and continued some of the programs and initiatives instituted during the latter part of Rev. Topshee's tenure as director.

The Topshee Conferences constituted an attempt to revive what was understood to be the original movement following a largely "top-down" approach. They have been largely unsuccessful for basically the reasons identified earlier in the case of the 1971 conference. Topshee Conferences, normally attended by hundreds of often enthusiastic delegates, have involved attempts at analyzing current economic conditions, have contributed some interesting hypothetical options, have led to the passing of resolutions of various sorts, and in some instances have even led to the appointment of committees. However, as they have evolved, they have generally done little in terms of promoting economic action or providing an understanding of the Antigonish Movement as an integrated, self-contained, and dynamic economic system. Little actual work gets done until the next conference. The reason for this general state of inaction stems from the absence of institutional networks and frameworks, the absence of activities, and perhaps most important, the absence of a grassroots movement to carry out the resolutions, recommendations, and so on. Thus, although some of these conferences have been impressive in terms of the expertise brought in and the topics discussed, they have generally been far removed from the very essence of the Antigonish Movement. They have functioned primarily as an exercise in adult education, allowing various fragmented groups to interact, come into contact, and exchange ideas.

The New Vision and the Program Thrust in the 1980s

The radical reorientation of the vision of the Extension Department under Dr Teresa MacNeil resulted in a greatly expanded scope for its activities, ushering in an avalanche of new programs and projects, in addition to the ongoing ones, such as ARLEC, housing, and community development. Most of these new programs and projects were in the area of adult, continuing, and distance education, but there were also new initiatives involving health education, social justice, unemployment, workers' cooperatives, recreation, senior citizens, youth, rural women, and other perceived disadvantaged and marginalized groups. In addition to this impressive array of projects and programs, the Extension Department also initiated several research projects involving worker cooperatives, programs to deal with family violence, health-related initiatives, and so on. Moreover, its "educational reach" was greatly expanded beyond its traditional area of the Maritimes to include the entire country and even some parts of the United States.

CONTINUING AND ADULT EDUCATION It is difficult to draw a clear distinction between continuing and adult education. In theory, continuing education, as its name implies, is the extension of formal education in time and space. Thus academic courses are offered during the evening hours and summer months and in locations outside of the university campus, often in neighbouring towns or via new electronic media worldwide. These courses are usually a part of the formal accreditation process. Adult education, in contrast, is designed to serve the nonacademic educational needs of members of the adult population, many of whom may lack formal academic training. In practice, the distinction between continuing and adult education is blurred and subject to considerable overlapping given that continuing education often offers noncredit courses for adults and that adult education programs at times include certification, diplomas, and other forms of academic recognition.

St Francis Xavier University, along with other postsecondary institutions in Canada, offers both types of educational programs. However, until 1982 these programs were kept outside of the organizational structure of the Extension Department, as its traditional educational activities were fundamentally different from both continuing and adult education. First, they were initially directed toward the solution of concrete economic problems and hence focused primarily on economic education, to a great extent excluding political, social, cultural, and other issues. Second, they were directed toward significant economic groups such as fishermen, farmers, industrial workers, and consumers but not to single individuals or any other noneconomic group. Third, they were directly linked to the organization and building of economic institutions and through them to economic actions such as organizing marketing cooperatives, establishing credit unions, and building lobster-processing plants. Thus the traditional education program of the Extension Department was largely practical, problem-oriented, economic-group-based, and geared toward institution building.

Unfortunately, the founders of the Antigonish Movement – Rev. Coady, Rev. Tompkins, and others – had attached the generic term "adult education" to their unique education programs, the same term employed by many other institutions to describe an entirely different educational approach. This unfortunate semantic error caused no confusion to the movement or the Extension Department during the first two decades of its activities, as it was clear to all what they were about. During this time, the focus was on the practice, not the label. What was referred to as adult education was a combination of study and research aimed at building up the entrepreneurial capacity to foster economic action and the required expertise to administer the institutions that were created. It was fundamentally a tool, albeit an important one, and as such it could be defined by its objective. However, with the passage of time and the passing of generations, the label created a great deal of confusion, uncertainty, and errors among the staff and even among the succeeding directors of the Extension Department. As a result, the perception of the true nature and identity of the Extension Department as an institution was also affected. This confusion was accentuated by the introduction of various innovative programs beginning with the radio programs of the 1940s, the People's School, and the like.[31] Gradually, the knowledge of the unique educational approach was lost, and the Extension Department became transformed into a largely standard adult education institution, virtually indistinguishable from many others except in terms of its history, location, and size. This transformation was formally recognized in 1982 when the administration of the university incorporated all of its continuing and most of its adult education programs as parts of the Extension Department's activities under the direction of MacNeil.

During the first years of this new arrangement, the more formal adult education component of the Extension Department's activities played a relatively minor role, as the existing programs – ARLEC, housing, community development, cooperative education, and others, which were largely carried over from the Rev. Topshee years – continued to be of primary importance. For example, in 1986 continuing and adult education accounted for less than 20 per cent of the Extension Department's budget, whereas more than 80 per cent was allocated to so-called "general extension," which involved "change-oriented problem-centered projects."[32] However, the situation changed dramatically over time, as the continuing and adult education offerings increased rapidly both in absolute and in relative terms.[33] Furthermore, the success of these programs spawned numerous new courses of the same variety, which also expanded rapidly, with the diploma program in adult education, Training for Trainers, becoming its fastest growing component. This expansion of various continuing and adult education programs, combined with the relative stagnation of the "general extension" ones, resulted in the reversal of their relative importance. Thus in 1997 continuing and adult education courses accounted for more than 80 per cent of the Extension Department's total budget. In fact, it exceeded 90 per cent if ARLEC, which was being phased out, is removed from the "general extension" programs.[34] This change, even though accompanied by a 300 per cent expansion of the Extension Department's total budget between 1985 and 1997, implied a substantial reduction, both in absolute and in relative terms, in the amounts allocated to "general extension."[35] In effect, the Extension Department increasingly became an appendage that served the interests of the academic programs of the university.

THE INTERNAL REACTION The shift in vision and thrust of the Extension Department's programs did not go unnoticed and raised concerns, particularly among those still loyal to the Antigonish Movement as well as some of its long-serving fieldworkers.[36] Interestingly, however, there was no recognition of the fact that what was being labelled as "general extension" work itself constituted a fundamental divergence from the original vision of the Antigonish Movement. In 1991 the Extension Department's Advisory Committee expressed concern that an "increasing number of formal learning opportunities indicated decreasing attention to the significance of the Antigonish movement."[37] Despite these warnings, the expansion of continuing and adult education courses proceeded unabated. By 1995 the diploma course in adult education had expanded to eighteen cities in Canada, attracting 1,747 participants.[38] The success of this program prompted the introduction of similar courses, such as the certification and diploma course for managers of the Nova Scotia Civil Services Association, the Nova Scotia Health Organization, the New Brunswick Hospital Association, Canada Post, the Northern Affairs Drug and Alcohol Program, and many other organizations. Under the increasingly overlapping continuing and adult education labels, the Extension Department expanded its programs to include diverse groups and organizations such as the New Brunswick Union of Indians and Dartmouth General Hospital. Moreover, its range of services expanded to include consultation, assistance with the development of strategic plans, provision of chairs, animators, and facilitators for various workshops, seminars, and conferences, assistance with funding applications, and so on.

In 1990 a distance-based degree program for nurses attracted over 150 practising nurses. The health training program, in particular, has enjoyed remarkable expansion and diversification since the late 1980s. In 1987 the Extension Department's health education program expanded to various cities in Ontario, Quebec, New Brunswick, and Nova Scotia.[39] In addition, the Extension Department initiated various programs directly targeting various groups – such as women, seniors, Natives, and youth and adolescents – and even instituted a grade 8 program for gifted children. Women's programs, in particular, received special consideration following a shift in policy in 1986 away from cooperative education and the People's School, both of which were terminated, and toward those programs aimed at people deemed to be economically, socially, and educationally disadvantaged.[40] Its programs for seniors involved such things as the Elder Hostel, a vacation learning program related to Scottish culture and the Antigonish Movement, and a Grandparents in School program.[41] These initiatives were certainly impressive in terms of both sheer coverage and number, but they moved the Extension Department further away from the vision and needs of the Antigonish Movement.

A Final Attempt to Return to Its Roots

In 1993 Tom Webb, a long-time employee of Moncton-based Co-op Atlantic, was appointed as director of the Extension Department. This appointment signalled an attempt to revive the original vision of the movement. With his background in the cooperative sector, the new director understood the role and importance of cooperatives as well as their needs.[42] His vision was reflected in a new mission statement of the Extension Department that postulated a return to the "principles and goals of the Antigonish Movement" and a strong commitment to the cooperative sector. The new director followed a two-pronged approach. On the one hand, he had inherited a successful adult and continuing education program from MacNeil's years and sought not only to maintain it but also to promote its further expansion by means of initiatives with a potential international reach. On the other hand, he also sought to bring about a rebirth of the Antigonish Movement. A key component of the latter was a two-day colloquium on the Antigonish Movement that was held in October 1995. The colloquium, a part of a process to promote the "full and vibrant renewal of the Antigonish Movement," brought together "a diverse group of the traditional support base of the Movement" to "reflect on what the Antigonish Movement was, what worked and did not."[43] Although the colloquium was intellectually stimulating, the outcome fell short of expectations. Like the Eastern Development Conference of 1971, it produced an abundance of ideas but no clear direction or workable plan that could be used to revitalize the Antigonish Movement and the Extension Department in the context of putting in place an alternate economic system.

Although the colloquium was to be a part of a process leading to the revival of the Antigonish Movement, no substantive follow-up took place. In addition to the colloquium, steps were taken in the mid-1990s to establish new programs for the education of cooperative managers, to promote new economic activities through innovative partnerships involving the Extension Department (including some initiatives with respect to natural gas), to renew efforts to establish cooperation between the Extension Department and various departments of the university, to undertake an analysis of the cooperative movement in parts of Europe, including Mondragon, and to send individuals to study cooperative activities elsewhere, among other initiatives.[44] That it was felt necessary to study cooperative activities elsewhere as a prelude to trying to revive them in eastern Nova Scotia speaks volumes about the extent of the decline of the Antigonish Movement in its home base – a reversal of the days when delegations from other parts of the world came to observe the Antigonish Movement in action on its home turf. These various efforts were generally in the right direction and addressed fundamental aspects and needs of the movement. However, they too ultimately came to naught. Given the resources available to the Extension Department and the state of severe decline of the Antigonish Movement, the initiatives undertaken were too broad and ambitious at the intellectual level and woefully inadequate as practical solutions.

Webb also envisaged the university as a critical component of the whole process, in effect allowing the Extension Department to act as a bridge between the university and the Antigonish Movement – between the campus and the community. However, this bridging occurred at the same time that the university's retrenchment from its traditional community involvement was proceeding rapidly.[45]

Not only did the extensive adult education and continuing education programs from MacNeil's years remain a critical component of the work of the Extension Department, but Webb sought to expand them even further. Thus, for example, there was an expansion in the degree program for nurses both across Canada and internationally, and the diploma in adult education was extended to twenty locations in Canada and the United States, attracting over 2,000 participants in 1997 and employing a number of instructors and facilitators.[46] It provided training to organizations such as the Toronto Police Department and the Canadian Police College. It also introduced a wide variety of new programs such as the Ministry Diploma program and the Real Property Appraisal and Assessment program, which attracted over 600 registrants in its first two years of operation. It became involved in projects dealing with family violence, partner homicides, community literacy, and the like while also offering assistance to an eclectic group of organizations that included the AIDS coalition of Cape Breton, the Nova Scotia Food Banks, the Mental Health Association, and Nova Scotia Voluntary Planning.[47]

By 1997 the conversion of the Extension Department into a purely adult and continuing education institution seemed complete, as the share of "general extension" programs had, as we noted earlier, fallen to a paltry 20 per cent of its total budget. The dominance of the adult and continuing education programs and the extensive incursion into the social, cultural, and political spheres conspired, despite efforts to the contrary, to make the return to the roots of the Antigonish Movement impossible. Despite Webb's attempts to be proactive and to introduce educational programs geared to the enhancement of the cooperative sector, the process could not be reversed.

Interestingly, during Webb's tenure there was an attempt to resurrect the Big Picture, and in fact it showed up on the cover of the one of the annual reports.[48] However, as suggested earlier, the cumulative effect of the past divergence from the original vision of the movement, the absence of any real concrete economic analysis, the general lack of enthusiasm by the university for the cooperative approach, the dire shortage of resources, and the fragmentation among existing cooperative institutions proved to be insurmountable. In particular, it was impossible to shake the misconception that the Antigonish Movement was nothing more than an adult education program.

After Webb decided not to seek another term as director, the university's Board of Governors approved a new mandate for the Extension Department. The new mandate removed continuing and adult education from the Extension Department, along with much of its personnel and funding. Moreover, although on the surface strikingly similar to the original mission of 1928, the new mandate was in reality extremely restrictive, with a very narrow focus, and largely ignored the practices of the Antigonish Movement and its tradition. It confined the Extension Department's involvement primarily to the seven counties of eastern Nova Scotia and to areas linked to economic development, and it directed the department's activities toward projects that could attract outside and long-term funding or that involved nonprofit organizations and community-based associations. It was provided with few resources and very little institutional support, thus ensuring that the Antigonish Movement could not be resurrected through the work of the Extension Department. For better or for worse, the Antigonish Movement, and its vision of establishing a dynamic alternate economic system, was officially laid to rest; the great experiment had ended.[49] In effect, the Webb years constituted the last hurrah for the Antigonish Movement.

PROGRAMS OF THE EXTENSION DEPARTMENT

Despite the failure to revive the Antigonish Movement and the increased involvement in continuing and adult education, over the three decades under consideration the Extension Department remained remarkably active in attempting to at least stay engaged with some of its original programs and in trying to devise new strategies. However, these efforts generally lacked focus and staying power.[50] Many of them were motivated either by the availability of funds or by the interest of some staff member, rather than being a part of an overall strategy that could have been used to select and assign priority to various programs and activities in accordance with some basic logic and objective. The absence of such a strategy meant that any program could be justified as being consistent with the goals and objectives of the movement, resulting in the enormous branching-out observed over the period, especially during the 1980s and 1990s. The result was the introduction of some fundamental contradiction into many of the programs. Although the Extension Department was trying to revive the original vision of the movement, the lack of focus and strategy inherent in its programs and activities reduced the likelihood of success. That the vision of the movement itself was being largely misinterpreted added another dimension to the problem.

The programs and initiatives of the Extension Department also underwent substantial changes over the three decades that reflected, at least in part, the disparities in vision and perspective of the different directors. Whereas in the 1970s, particularly during the latter part of the decade, there was an effort to revive those programs that had proven successful in the past, in the 1980s, with continuing and adult education attached to the Extension Department, there was the evolution of a two-pronged approach that involved adult and continuing education, on the one hand, and what came to be known as "general extension" activities, many of which were at least in the spirit of the original movement, on the other. The latter also entailed some concerted efforts to implement new programs designed to exploit new economic opportunities by promoting research that could generally address some of the local concerns.[51]

Research Program

Despite the shortcomings of the 1960s, faith in the value of applied research to the work of the Extension Department experienced a revival in the 1980s. As a result, a number of research activities were undertaken. Although questionable in terms of their practical value, they became an important part of the work of the Extension Department until the end of the millennium. Predominant among these efforts was the research on workers' cooperatives.

RESEARCH ON WORKERS' COOPERATIVES The concern with workers' cooperatives was consistent with the original vision of the Antigonish Movement and the Big Picture. Moreover, the accelerating unemployment and underemployment experienced during the 1980s provided a strong impetus for the Extension Department to engage in activities designed to alleviate the acute and persistent problems through the organization of new cooperatives, which would be run and operated by the workers themselves. There were very few cooperatives of this nature operating in Nova Scotia in the early 1980s, and these tended to be small, marginal, and unstable. They were plagued by a shortage of capital, an inability to access markets, organizational inefficiency, a lack of skills and technological support, and the like. The Extension Department organized a weekend-long workshop on workers' cooperatives in August 1982, which concluded that both existing and new workers' cooperatives required the assistance of a comprehensive system of supporting services to survive and thrive.[52] The design and organization of such supporting services were to be guided by research specifically tailored to the analysis of the problems encountered by the workers' cooperatives. However, such research required financing. In 1986, after three years of persistent efforts, the Extension Department was able to secure a three-year research grant valued at $511,000 under the Innovations program of Canada Job Strategy.[53] Concurrent with its drive to secure financing for its research program, the Extension Department had also begun to create an institutional structure to supplement the research and to put its findings into practice. Its efforts culminated in the organization of the province-wide Community Development Cooperative (CDC) also in 1986, with the financial support of all major cooperative organizations.[54] Thus the Extension Department was able to launch the workers' cooperative project on a far more solid and secure basis than that of the typical funding-oriented projects that made up much of its postwar work. The research project was not only problem-driven but also contained an institutional component designed to put its findings into action. Moreover, it had the cooperation and financial support of the major cooperative organizations. In fact, this approach was somewhat reminiscent of that of the 1930s, when programs were initiated in response to the major problems of the communities and were also supported by the appropriate institutions, which mobilized the necessary resources.

Despite the comprehensive and problem-driven approach, the workers' cooperative program proved to be both short-lived and of limited success. All three of its major components – its research, its institutional apparatus (i.e., the CDC), and its resources – proved to be inadequate. The research component (i.e., the Innovations project) was funded for only three years and was not subject to renewal. It was also based on the presupposition that research would uncover the hidden obstacles hindering the success of workers' cooperatives, provide the information needed to design an appropriate support system for effectively dealing with these obstacles, and enable the cooperatives to succeed and flourish. Despite the intuitive appeal of such a presupposition, the issues turned out to be much more complex than had been envisioned. Obstacles hindering the success of workers' cooperatives in Nova Scotia did in fact exist, including the lack of capital, inadequate access to technology, shortcomings in organizational experience, and unstable markets, all of which required a much more concentrated and systematic effort to overcome. In any event, they were overwhelming and formidable enough that the efforts of the Extension Department could not overcome them.

The actual research output of the Innovations project fell short of its expectations. Some educational material, including slide presentations, was produced. Several issues of a quarterly newsletter were published, and a clearing house of information pertinent to the subject was established. Furthermore, model bylaws of workers' cooperatives were formulated. Although of some practical value, none of these initiatives had much impact in terms of promoting the emergence of workers' cooperatives. At the very least, the research would have had to be linked to mobilizing some sort of group entrepreneurship, something that it was not designed to do.

The second component of the program, the institutional support of the CDC, was also inadequate. The CDC provided only about $60,000 in financial resources and, moreover, depended on the Innovations project for most of its operational expenses and was not financially self-sufficient.[55] At the same time, workers' cooperatives, by their very nature, are more difficult to organize than the service-oriented cooperatives, such as marketing cooperatives, consumers' stores, farm suppliers, and credit unions. They normally require greater amounts of capital, more advanced technology, a more complex organizational structure, larger markets, and the like to compete against national and international profit-driven corporations, as attested to by the experience of successful efforts such as the Mondragon Movement in Spain.

The Innovations project was terminated in 1989, and the CDC, deprived of most of its financial resources, continued to struggle for a few more years. It assisted in the organization of a few small workers' cooperatives, none of which proved to be sustainable. It is perhaps ironic that at the time when the Extension Department had discontinued its meager educational support of the existing cooperatives, it undertook the far more difficult task of organizing workers' cooperatives with, in retrospect, practically no chances of success. It lacked both the resources and the institutional support that could only have been provided by being a part of a larger and thriving economic system.[56]

THE CENTRE FOR RESEARCH ON THE FUTURE OF WORK The establishment in 1986 of the Centre for Research on the Future of Work, funded by an annual grant from the Social Science and Humanities Research Council of Canada, was another major research-oriented undertaking of the Extension Department. This body, consisting of a group of academic researchers motivated to engage in relevant projects, was to serve essentially as a research arm of the Extension Department, to some extent fulfilling its longstanding objective of having its own research capabilities and of connecting its activities with those of the academic side of the university. It was designed to meet the needs of the Extension Department through relevant research that could act as a useful guide for its programs, as well as those of interested academics, who welcomed the opportunity to engage in socially significant research that addressed the pressing problems of the local communities and of the region.[57]

However, any high expectations on the part of both the Extension Department and interested academics were largely extinguished within a decade. During its relatively short existence, the Centre for Research on the Future of Work produced a research output of academic papers that were generally of little practical value to the work of the Extension Department.[58] In the mid-1990s it was renamed the Centre for Regional Studies, which focused on purely academic research and had no pretense of providing research that could be employed by the Extension Department in its programs to foster socio-economic development.

Many factors contributed to this not entirely unexpected outcome. First, as the Extension Department's main thrust was continuing and adult education and as few of its activities were in its traditional field of economic action, the department offered very little obvious scope for relevant research. Second, the capabilities of academic researchers were confined to their narrowly defined disciplines and were of limited value to the analysis of the multidimensional problems facing the region or to the revitalization of a stagnant and splintered movement. Third, even if significant and practical research findings were uncovered, there was no institutional apparatus in place to put these findings into practice. Fourth, the relevant research interests of the academic community were marginal to their main tasks of teaching and to their professional research.

RESEARCH INTO SOCIAL AND HEALTH PROBLEMS The failure of the predominantly economics-oriented research – the Innovations project and the Center on the Future of Work – may have dampened the Extension Department's enthusiasm for research-oriented activities but did not end it. In the 1990s its research-oriented activities shifted into areas revolving around social and health problems. In 1990 the Extension Department undertook to participate in a five-year project on Heart Health Inequalities, which addressed the problem of higher rates of heart disease among the low-income groups.[59] The project was designed "to confront, through group action, the range of barriers which prevent socially and economically disadvantaged people from having adequate access to the conditions that foster heart health."[60] Two years later, its research involvement in cardiovascular disease was expanded with the initiation of a short-lived project in Glace Bay designed to reduce the incidence of disease in that community.[61] The results of this project were never made public. The incursion of the Extension Department into health research was driven by the availability of funding from Health and Welfare Canada and other agencies. Moreover, its role in these undertakings was "to take responsibility for the day-to-day management of the project" rather than to carry out the actual research.[62]

The drift of the Extension Department away from its traditional role and areas of expertise continued under the directorship of Tom Webb, expanding the department into areas where adequate financing was available. Thus in 1995 it completed a study on partner homicide in Nova Scotia.[63] The termination of funding for this project two years later led the Extension Department back into health research, specifically into health-needs assessment.

None of the research activities of the Extension Department after the 1960s, regardless of their merits, produced any appreciable positive impact on the Antigonish Movement, despite the desire to improve the economic conditions in the local communities and the region as a whole. Increasingly, in the 1990s the research efforts, such as those focusing on health and social problems, were of a noneconomic nature. Given its precarious financial base and increasing de facto retrenchment from the more economic-oriented areas, these research activities met the need of the Extension Department to engage in any activities for which the funding was available in order to justify and ensure its continued institutional existence.

Paradoxically, the most innovative and successful program and projects originated in the 1930s and the 1940s without the aid of formal research. They were guided by the experience, intuition, common sense, pragmatism, and trial and error that characterized the building of a new and radically different economic system. As it turned out, the traditional way of doing things had proven to be much more reliable and effective than the formal research activities undertaken by the Extension Department since the 1960s. The times were different, however, and so were the types of institutions that needed to be put in place. Most tellingly, the university, with its ever-expanding research capabilities, played a marginal role in the process.

Additional New Program Initiatives

The attempt to revive the Antigonish Movement in the 1990s gave rise to a flurry of additional initiatives, attempts, explorations, and proposals. Some of these never materialized, whereas others were introduced but discontinued shortly after. Most of these initiatives were predominantly economic, being designed to enable the Extension Department to increase its presence, profile, and relevance. Their significance rests not on their impact, which was minimal, but on their illustrations of the increasing difficulties of developing economic programs for the region with very limited resources and from outside of a well-established movement or system.

VENTURE AND IDEAS FAIRS The Venture and Ideas Fairs were an attempt to introduce locally an innovative and successful program from North Dakota following an Extension Department–sponsored visit to that state by two St Francis Xavier faculty members.[64] These fairs consisted of one day of displays of various actual or potential ventures, which presumably could stimulate economically viable projects that would be beneficial to the local communities. It was hoped that such displays, demonstrations, and information would encourage various local groups to get involved in devising projects of their own. The Extension Department was prepared to work with such groups and assist them with the development of their projects into viable and economically feasible ventures. It was expected that the success of a few such new projects would, through their demonstration effect, induce other groups to also get involved in the process. The success of these fairs would have allowed the Extension Department to regain some of its economic leadership in the local communities while contributing directly to the revitalization of the Antigonish Movement.

The initiative was to play a role akin to that of the mass meetings and study clubs of the original strategy of the 1930s. The Venture and Ideas Fairs would replace the original community meetings, and the interested groups would assume the role of study clubs. Unlike the original strategy, however, the new projects were no longer tied solely to the cooperative structure but could assume any form of ownership as long as they were financially viable.

Several Venture and Ideas Fairs were organized during the late 1990s, attracting many participants, including numerous local and outside entrepreneurs displaying a wide range of actual or potential projects. Most of these were small, requiring very little capital and using simple organizational structures and technologies. Most of them assumed the form of individual business ownership and appeared to offer very little room for group action or for expansion.

Some of them were untried and appeared to carry a high degree of risk. Furthermore, although there were many individuals interested in some of these projects, no identifiable interested groups or viable projects emerged from any of these fairs, and they were soon discontinued. In retrospect, the initiative suffered from two misconceptions: (1) that there were a number of feasible projects that were unexplored and could easily be identified; and (2) that interested groups would emerge following the demonstration. Generally, the identification of feasible projects involves entrepreneurship, and the fairs were not, unlike the study clubs of old, designed to develop it. In addition, and more important, the Venture and Ideas Fairs were essentially passive and did not challenge people to find their own solutions to pressing problems. The various ventures and ideas were not intrinsically linked to the people's own immediate circumstances and, moreover, were predicated on a reversal of the selection and study sequence for projects. In the original strategy, projects emerged out of study rather than the other way around. Moreover, the fairs were not able to showcase the cooperative approach and its myriad advantages as a means to mobilize interest in it. As well, the initiative involved people coming to the university rather than the university going to the people at a time when a wide gap had already emerged between the campus and the community.

THE "NEW" PEOPLE'S SCHOOL ON THE ECONOMY Although not one of its own initiatives, the Extension Department also helped to sponsor the initial revival of a five-part workshop series on the economy.[65] The workshops were delivered during the fall of 1997 in Antigonish and then in the spring of 1998 in Sydney. Abridged versions were also delivered in Canso and in Annapolis Royal. The workshops, involving substantial opportunity for group discussions, were designed to provide the participants with basic economic knowledge that could be used to understand the economic conditions of their community and the region. This approach was based largely on the premise that the lack of relevant economic knowledge and the prevailing misconceptions and confusion were major stumbling blocks to meaningful economic action as well as participation in various social and political processes. The final workshop in each series introduced the Antigonish Movement as an alternate approach to solving the problems faced by different communities. In this respect, the workshops were somewhat similar to the original community meetings of the 1930s and seemed to generate a great deal of initial enthusiasm among the relatively large number of participants.[66] However, there was no sustained follow-up on the initial program.[67]

MARKETING OUR COOPERATIVE ADVANTAGE The Marketing Our Co-operative Advantage initiative consisted of annual conferences to which senior managers of major cooperative organizations from both Canada and the United States were invited. A driving force behind these conferences was the belief that the globalization process created significant opportunities for cooperative organizations. However, to take advantage of these opportunities, cooperatives would need to come together and pool their resources into a common national and international marketing program. In essence, the cooperatives would need to learn to market their unique advantage in the global market place. These greater marketing opportunities would become an engine of growth for the participating cooperative enterprises, including those from eastern Nova Scotia.

Three such annual conferences were organized. The second, held in Boston and co-sponsored by the Extension Department, attracted over seventy "CEOs, presidents and senior marketing executives from Canada and the USA."[68] However, no common marketing campaign ever materialized, and by the latter part of the 1990s, the Extension Department had withdrawn its support for this project. Nevertheless, the initiative highlighted the new options that were now becoming available to the cooperative sector, including the possibility to network at the international or global level.

SUMMARY OF CHARACTERISTICS OF THE NEW INITIATIVES The various new initiatives shared a number of common characteristics. They constituted efforts to reengage with the vision of the Antigonish Movement while trying to adapt it to the new socio-economic realities. As well, each addressed a specific issue that was believed to be a major stumbling block preventing economic development in the region, such as unexplored economic projects, lack of economic information, and lack of marketing of cooperative advantage. However, such an approach was too narrow and limited to be of much practical value. Generally, the various efforts constituted limited attempts to go back to the beginnings of the Antigonish Movement, ignoring what was already in place. More important, they were devoid of the grand vision that had propelled its original programs. The region's socio-economic problems were numerous, mutually reinforcing, and deeply ingrained, requiring efforts much more comprehensive and sustained than those actually undertaken by the Extension Department. Most important, any attempt to revive the Antigonish Movement or to foster a return to its roots required recognition that it constituted an effort to build an alternate dynamic and efficient economic system based on cooperative principles and fully able to function in the newly emerging global economy.

THE TRADITIONAL PROGRAMS OF THE EXTENSION DEPARTMENT

Despite the changes in vision and the misconceptions regarding what it really was, the revival of the Antigonish Movement remained remarkably imbedded in the rhetoric as well as some of the programs of the Extension Department until the end of the millennium. The failure to develop an adequate internal source of funding, and the increased reliance on external funds, had a major impact on the direction that the Extension Department was able to follow. That cooperative institutions were unwilling, and many also unable, to transfer funds to the Extension Department for its programs was symptomatic of their lack of appreciation of the importance of being a part of a system anchored by such an institution. Nevertheless, the Extension Department tried, albeit neither consistently nor adequately, to at least stay engaged in many of the traditional areas linked to the Antigonish Movement of earlier times.

The Fisheries

Although its partnership with the federal Department of Fisheries had been effectively dissolved, the Extension Department never ceased, throughout the 1970s, to articulate the need to reintroduce a fisheries education program. However, in the absence of other sources of funds, the fisheries program could not be revived without a sizable government grant, and there was no possibility of securing such a grant. The federal Department of Fisheries had established its own network of fieldworkers, or Department of Fisheries officers. The reentry of the Extension Department into the fisheries would have implied competition not only for funds but also for the loyalty of fishermen and would certainly have entailed the duplication of services. Thus, despite seeing the need to play a more active role, the Extension Department was severely constrained by a lack of resources.[69] The degree to which the department had retrenched from involvement in the fisheries, at the very time that the fisheries were in crisis, is reflected by its response in the late 1980s to the proposed shutdown of a fish plant in Canso, which involved helping to organize two public forums, producing an assortment of newspaper articles, and offering assistance to municipal leaders.[70]

Nevertheless, the 1970s involved some efforts to at least stay engaged with the sector. The Extension Department employed a fieldworker to respond to requests for information and generally to deal with immediate problems faced by the fishermen, particularly through getting the fishermen in touch with appropriate groups, agencies, and government departments.[71] It also participated in projects for which funding was available from outside sources, such as in the case of the DEVCO-funded Bras d'Or Lake project, involving the cultivation of oysters.[72] In the mid-1970s, it also attempted, unsuccessfully, to transform the Booth Fisheries plant in Petit de Grat, which had been involved in a strike in 1970, into a cooperative. The workers rejected the cooperative approach, opting instead for public-sector involvement.[73] On a more positive note, the Extension Department influenced the decision of a number of cooperatives to market their fish through the United Maritime Fishermen (UMF) cooperative and contributed to the revitalization of the Blue Ribbon Fisheries cooperative in Little Dover in the early 1980s. It also remained actively involved in carrying out studies and pushing for the amalgamation of existing cooperatives.

In 1978, near the end of Rev. Topshee's years, following its decision to establish closer links with the cooperative sector, to revitalize the cooperative education program, and to become more involved in dealing with the plight of the fisheries, the Extension Department attempted a number of initiatives and pilot projects.[74] These undertakings included the establishment of an outreach program, efforts to establish an ARLEC-type residential school for Cape Breton fishermen, resulting in two pilot projects in 1981, and the implementation of many short study sessions.[75] These programs, generally funded by DEVCO and a number of school boards, fell far short of what was required, but there were no resources to expand them. During the 1982–83 period, there was even a resolution put forth by the UMF to revive the former government-sponsored fisheries program, but these and other initiatives came to naught.[76] There were "no public funding sources to support comprehensive educational programming relating to the inshore fishery."[77]

These efforts were discontinued in the mid-1980s, during the early years of MacNeil's directorship, as the Extension Department again withdrew from cooperative education, causing its involvement in the fisheries to become even more marginal and thus limited to undertakings such as providing help with a marketing analysis for herring roe, providing organizational support to local groups, and assisting with some research activities. Near the end of the decade, after securing adequate funds, primarily from the Atlantic Canada Opportunities Agency, the Extension Department's program became linked mainly to the Coastal Communities program and consisted largely of workshops and conferences as well as short courses and some research activities exploring the possible survival strategies of these communities given the new realities in the fisheries.

The involvement with the Coastal Communities program continued during Tom Webb's tenure as director. However, Webb envisioned a much broader involvement of the Extension Department in the fisheries, as outlined in a document entitled "Opportunity Development Program," which included a wish list of changes and initiatives that could be applied to the sector. These items included using available fish stocks more efficiently, which would have involved both higher standards of quality and greater value added, branching out into aquaculture, finding new markets for underutilized species, and fostering greater cooperation among fisheries cooperatives to take advantage of opportunities and to better penetrate and develop new markets.[78] These ideas, however, did not translate into actual programs. There was no longer a movement or an Extension Department with adequate resources to put such ideas into practice. The programs of the Webb years also had the misfortune of coinciding with the total collapse of the fisheries due to the depletion of fish stocks.

The Housing Program

Throughout the 1970s, the Extension Department remained heavily involved in cooperative housing, working mostly with various government agencies. However, its role underwent a change as the Nova Scotia Housing Commission increased its own staff and activity in the area of cooperative housing. Putting a positive spin on things, the Extension Department announced that it had "been able to phase down its cooperative housing operations in favor of increased involvement in specialized housing projects."[79] These specialized housing projects included subsidized cooperative housing and public housing. From the mid-1970s onward, the Extension Department became heavily involved in the delivery of a number of programs, generally funded by the government through the Central Mortgage and Housing Corporation (CMHC). These programs included the Neighbourhood Improvement Program (NIP); the federal Residential Rehabilitation Assistance Program (RRAP), which itself was linked to NIP; the Rural and Native Housing Program; the Rural Residential Rehabilitation Assistance Program; and the Electrical Safety Program, funded by Canada Works through the Department of Manpower and Immigration and initiated in 1977. In addition, the Extension Department was involved with the Seton Foundation, which was a nonprofit housing foundation; the Co-op Self Help Housing pilot project; and numerous other initiatives.[80] These programs, which were heavily concentrated in the New Glasgow–Pictou and industrial Cape Breton areas, involved a relatively large number of fieldworkers and seem to have been effective, yielding substantial benefits in terms of new and improved housing.

The Extension Department's involvement in the housing program continued throughout the 1980s.[81] However, it was dependent on government funds, and as these began to dry up the Extension Department's involvement diminished as well. In March 1990 the Extension Department's involvement with the delivery of the CMHC housing program was terminated, resulting in a much reduced role in the sector.

Interestingly, the Extension Department's involvement in the government and CMHC cooperative housing programs in many ways harkened back to the original vision of the Antigonish Movement. In the main, this involvement included study, often in relatively small groups, for the purpose of establishing a housing cooperative or bringing about a substantial improvement in the community, as in the case of programs such as NIP. In effect, the programs demonstrated that with adequate resources and the appropriate involvement of fieldworkers, much could still be accomplished.

The Forestry Program

With the Nova Scotia Woodlot Owners' Association (NSWOA) in place and with the establishment of a pulpwood marketing board well on its way, as was noted in the previous chapter, by the early 1970s the Extension Department's forestry program had been largely terminated.[82] Nevertheless, it remained marginally active in the sector over much of the 1970s and early 1980s, during which time both the NSWOA and some of its programs faced difficulties and continued to struggle.

A deepening crisis in the forestry sector, however, sparked the renewed involvement of the Extension Department. The release in 1984 of a royal commission report on the Nova Scotia forestry sector prompted the Extension Department to put together an educational program for the sector, implemented in 1985 with meager and uncertain funding.[83] At the same time, it also increased its involvement with the forestry sector through its workers' cooperatives initiative. Nevertheless, the Extension Department's involvement in the sector remained largely marginal, and the trend continued during the 1990s despite the recognition that it needed to play a more active role.[84]

Community Development Program

The Extension Department maintained its involvement in the community-development program, which it had enthusiastically embraced during the 1960s, but to a more limited extent given its dependence on the availability of government funding. Starting in the mid-1970s and continuing until about 1982, it became involved with the Community Employment Strategy Association (CESA) in Guysborough County and with its subsidiary Mulgrave Guysborough Canso Development Incentives Limited (MGCDIL). The Extension Department's involvement was deemed quite productive since it yielded a number of cooperative organizations, such as a bakery in Canso, a woodcraft shop in Sunnyville, and a boat builders' cooperative in Little Dover, as well as the revitalization of the Blue Ribbon Fisheries cooperative, also in Little Dover.[85] These and other initiatives were touted as having a substantial impact on the area, particularly in terms of employment creation, although the evidence suggests much more modest accomplishments.[86] These projects were funded by the government with relatively little resource input by the Extension Department, aside from a limited number of fieldworkers. Moreover, the majority of the projects were judged to be of a social or at best socio-economic nature rather than to be economic or economic-development projects, even though the focus was on employment creation with strong community input.

Other initiatives linked to community development also took place in other parts of eastern Nova Scotia, particularly in the counties of Inverness and Pictou.[87] However, after 1982, aside from the already discussed Innovations project of 1986, which had a community development component, there was very little concrete involvement in the community development program, aside from helping to establish Local Employment Assistance and Development corporations, and a lack of funding plagued efforts to establish a Co-operative Development Institute.[88] As had been the case in the 1960s, there was seemingly little recognition that the traditional strategy of the Antigonish Movement entailed community development on a broader scale so that economic activities could be integrated not only within communities but also between them.

Other Programs

Of the various other programs in place, the Atlantic Region Labour Education Centre, a residential school for labour leaders, was the most prominent.[89] Established in 1972, ARLEC, which continued until 1997, was seen as particularly important by Rev. Topshee, given his background in labour education. Moreover, this attachment also prevailed during the MacNeil and Webb years. It was a program funded and determined by the labour movement, with the Extension Department entrusted with its delivery. Nevertheless, it maintained the link between the Extension Department and labour that dated back to the earlier years of the Antigonish Movement. To the extent that it was successful, ARLEC was intended to help the labour movement to thrive and become stronger so as to better the conditions of workers largely within the existing socio-economic system rather than through the establishment of an alternate system where the people themselves, whether as workers, consumers, or owners of resources, had ownership and control of economic activity.

Starting in the late 1970s, the Extension Department became involved in a social justice program.[90] Over time, its involvement in social issues increased even further, although the availability of funds remained an important determinant of what could actually be pursued. Although valuable in their own right, these programs had, as we suggested earlier, little relevance to the main thrust of the Antigonish Movement.

The mid-1970s also saw the emergence of the Welfare Rights program, which aimed at organizing welfare recipients in order to improve their bargaining position, increase their welfare payments, and improve their self-image and confidence. This short-lived program sought to create a more effective political pressure group rather than to foster self-reliant economic activity among a marginalized entity.[91]

THE COOPERATIVE EDUCATION PROGRAM

Cooperative education, although formally discontinued during the 1960s, was never completely abandoned or fully resurrected.[92] Rev. Topshee attempted to revive it in the latter part of the 1970s through the establishment of residential schools, the first of which took place in Antigonish during November 1980, outreach programs, and other initiatives aimed at cooperatives and credit unions – particularly at the members of cooperative boards and committees.[93] These efforts were partly in response to the fiftieth anniversary conference of 1978, where those who attended had asked that the Extension Department "establish schools in co-operation with the Atlantic Co-operative Council 'to provide members of credit unions and co-operatives with an educational program concerning the goals, policies and objectives of these institutions and training in appropriate leadership skills.'"[94]

These efforts were complemented by a number of additional activities, including attempts to establish study programs in parts of Cape Breton, participation in various training sessions, the organization of a cooperative directors' training program, and the introduction of instructional material in schools. However, these initiatives were largely limited in scope, were dependent on the availability of external funding, and did not address such fundamental issues as cooperative management, investment, expansion, and linkages.

The cooperative education program established by Rev. Topshee was continued in the early years of MacNeil's directorship but under the presumption that, by acting jointly, the cooperative organizations would be able "to gather the necessary resources to attend to their education and development requirements," leaving the Extension Department to assume "a supportive role in relation to these organizations and ... not initiate programs without their expressed request to do so."[95] Eventually, by the mid-1980s, even such a supportive role was discontinued, with the Extension Department once again no longer formally including cooperative education as a part of its program and once again officially severing the umbilical cord that tied it to the cooperative sector.[96] To a large extent, the decision was made necessary by the lack of resources available to the Extension Department.

This official termination of what was a very limited involvement in cooperative education did not have much of a direct impact. However, it was symbolic of the widening gap between the Extension Department and what was left of the Antigonish Movement and its vision. The justification that cooperatives could draw upon their own resources to meet their educational needs introduced two basic misconceptions. The first was that, in fact, the cooperative organizations themselves had adequate resources. Although some did, others did not, and these included umbrella organizations such as the UMF.[97] The second was that the cooperatives themselves could effectively carry out the education that was required. As we argued earlier, the individual organization, given its narrow scope and concerns, was unsuited to carrying out the educational function required of it as a part of a movement.

The termination of the education program did not entirely eliminate the Extension Department's involvement with the cooperative sector but made it subject to requests and available funding. Moreover, especially from the late 1970s onward, it had been actively supporting the establishment of Community Co-operative Councils, and these umbrella-type organizations were expected to facilitate cooperation among local cooperatives and, in the process, foster educational and other supports.[98] The proliferation of such councils helped to ease the Extension Department's official exit from cooperative education.[99]

The state of affairs vis-à-vis cooperative education continued during the 1990s, although there was increased recognition that the Extension Department and perhaps the university itself needed to become more involved in the whole process. A particularly critical and longstanding shortcoming of cooperative education revolved around the lack of formal training for cooperative managers. Management problems had in fact plagued many cooperative organizations from the outset, but these problems became more serious as economic activities became more complex and as competition from large-scale and highly efficient profit-driven enterprises increased. The adoption of standard private-sector management techniques introduced the danger of alienating the membership of cooperatives, precipitating the Rochdale cul-de-sac effect. Efforts in the late 1970s to introduce cooperative education at the bachelor's or master's level and requests in the 1980s for courses in cooperative economics came to naught. However, when Tom Webb took over as director, the matter took on greater urgency, leading to exploratory work first on a proposal for a master's-level program and later on an undergraduate-level diploma program in cooperative management. These initiatives stopped when Webb left the post of director.

THE ECONOMIC INSTITUTIONS OF THE MOVEMENT

Cooperatives and credit unions constituted the key economic institutional components of the economic system that the Antigonish Movement sought to put in place. Some of these institutions still managed to survive and thrive, largely on their own, in the difficult and challenging environment of the period.

The Cooperative Sector

By the 1970s the Extension Department and the cooperative institutions had gone their separate ways. The attempt to reestablish the link during the latter part of the 1970s through the revival of cooperative education was reversed during the mid-1980s. Despite efforts in the 1990s to reverse the trend, the separation continued unabated.

Table 7.1
Leading indicators of the cooperatives' performance in Nova Scotia, selected years, 1970–98

Year	*Cooperatives*	*Sales*	*Equity*	*Profit*
1970	117	79	11	0.6
1975	119	179	17.2	3.7
1980	124	302	29.0	4.4
1985	162	435	50.6	2.4
1990	228	512	62.6	3.8
1995	241	609	70.6	2.2
1998	217	646	71.5	1.4

Note: Figures are in millions of dollars and based on reporting cooperatives.

Source: Nova Scotia Department of Economic Development, Co-operatives Branch, *Co-operatives Annual Report 2000* (2000).

The cooperative sector itself, in what might at first seem paradoxical, continued to grow in number of organizations as well as in membership and business volume for the province of Nova Scotia as a whole. After remaining quite stable over the 1970s, the number of cooperatives almost doubled between 1980 and 1992. Moreover, as table 7.1 indicates, both sales and members' equity increased dramatically. The only unfavourable development that could be detected from the overall statistics of the cooperative sector was its consistently low profitability, which averaged below 1 per cent of total sales throughout the period and also followed a downward trend.[100] These data were strongly influenced by what was taking place in the housing sector. The availability of government funds allowed numerous housing cooperatives to be established and to flourish, even as the Extension Department's own highly successful Self-Help Housing program came to a close in the mid-1970s.[101] However, there were also other factors at work.

During this period, a relatively large number of new cooperatives were organized by younger and more educated individuals that involved activities such as theatre, filmmaking, crafts, and bookstores. These were generally established separately from the Antigonish Movement and driven by fundamentally different forces. They were established mostly by people who were looking for new independent options and opportunities and who were largely making a lifestyle choice within the existing system and under conditions of relative overall prosperity. These cooperatives were fundamentally different from the old and primarily economics-driven cooperatives organized among the farmers and fishermen and were never envisaged as parts of an integrated system.[102]

In reality, despite the seemingly increasing number of entities, the cooperative sector was being driven by a relatively small number of organizations that had managed to survive and grow. Predominant among these were the larger agricultural marketing cooperatives, particularly those linked to the dairy industry. A small number of large cooperatives accounted for over 60 per cent of the sales and equity and for an even greater percentage of the profits or surplus of the entire sector. Most of the other traditional cooperatives, such as fisheries cooperatives, consumers' stores, and workers' cooperatives, were either barely able to cover their costs or in some cases losing a great deal of money. The share of the sector's profit or surplus earned by the agricultural marketing cooperatives, which were dominated by the dairy cooperatives, increased from 42 per cent in 1984 to 91 per cent a decade later and to a remarkable 139 per cent in 1999, as shown in table 7.2. A dramatically different situation was faced by the consumers' cooperatives, whose profits had been driven down to nearly zero by 1994, to be followed by very large losses in 1999. Facing increased competition from national and international chains, such as Sobeys and Loblaws, and from a number of smaller discount stores as well, these important components of the cooperative sector were increasingly being driven to the brink of bankruptcy and, in the process, were weakening Co-op Atlantic (formerly Maritime Co-operative Services), the most important cooperative organization in Atlantic Canada.[103] The fisheries cooperatives, which were the engine of the sector's growth during the 1930s and the 1940s, were reduced to insignificance by the 1980s and 1990s. Their contribution to total cooperatives sales hovered around 5 per cent, and their overall cumulative profitability was even lower over the period, with the relative improvement in 1999 dictated largely by the poor performance of the consumers' cooperative sector. The demise of many fishing cooperatives was accelerated by the financial difficulties and eventual bankruptcy of the UMF.

The situation of the cooperative sector at the end of the millennium was quite precarious. The failure of the cooperative sector to

Table 7.2
Relative significance of various types of cooperatives in Nova Scotia, selected years, 1984–99

	Agricultural marketing			*Fishing*			*Consumers' store*		
Year	*Sales*	*Profit*	*Equity*	*Sales*	*Profit*	*Equity*	*Sales*	*Profit*	*Equity*
1984	70	42	65	4	-6	4.9	26	57	26
1989	65	56	55	5.5	-5	7	28	45	36
1994	61	91	62	5	6	5	31	1.8	31
1999	64	139	67	6	46	6	28	-88	23

Note: Figures are percentages and based on reporting cooperatives.

Source: Nova Scotia Department of Agriculture and Marketing, *Annual Report of Co-operative Associations in Nova Scotia* (selected 1985); Nova Scotia Department of Small Business Development, *Co-operatives Nova Scotia 1990* (1990); Nova Scotia Economic Renewal Agency, Co-operatives Branch, *Co-operatives Nova Scotia 1995* (1995); Nova Scotia Department of Economic Development, Co-operatives Branch, *Co-operatives Annual Report 2000* (2000).

become a part of an integrated economic system as had been envisaged by the Antigonish Movement must be considered a critical component of this unfolding story.

The thriving dairy cooperatives faced an unusually favourable set of circumstances, which included high prices for milk products and the protection of sales levels by provincial policies on the supply management of farms and by the establishment of marketing quotas. Moreover, consolidation and amalgamation among dairy cooperatives reduced their number to a few relatively large ones, allowing them to benefit from economies of scale, longer production runs, and regional specialization. Increased capital requirements, due to the greater size of operations, were met by levies imposed on the cooperative members in proportion to their sales. Such an arrangement ensured that as sales rose, so too did the available stock of capital, enabling the cooperatives to access adequate financing and thereby avoid the danger of becoming undercapitalized.

The dairy cooperatives demonstrated that it is possible for some cooperatives to become large, efficient, and adequately financed. Cooperatives do not have to be small, inefficient, and starved of capital. The difficulty does not lie with the cooperative organizational structure but with its management, marketing strategies, and operational set-up. However, the importance of the fact that the dairy cooperatives were protected by government policy and had a relatively limited membership, given the relatively large size of dairy farming operations, cannot be discounted. There is a very strong vested interest in maintaining and promoting the cooperative approach among producers, whose wellbeing depends upon it. Nevertheless, if they had remained small and marginal operations, they would likely not have been as successful even if they had managed to survive.

The dairy cooperatives, however, were the exception rather than the norm. Other cooperatives, faced with deteriorating market conditions, low business volume, high production costs, and shortages of capital, generally collapsed or struggled to survive. For example, in 1984 the average workers' cooperative in Nova Scotia had sales of $51,000, profits or surplus of $6,000, and members' equity of about $40,000.[104] In 1995 over 97 per cent of cooperatives were placed in the small-business category, with only eight being classified as medium-size businesses.[105] Small, hardly profitable, and underfinanced cooperatives had very little chance to grow and survive, especially on their own. Even the larger ones, such as those referred to as medium-size business entities, were in jeopardy since each was operating on its own, not as a part of a system.

Perhaps the most obvious indicator of the problem facing the cooperative sector as a whole was its almost negligible contribution to the provincial economy. Its share of Nova Scotia's gross domestic product in 1995 was 4 per cent, and its share of provincial employment was even lower, amounting to 1 per cent of the labour force.[106] Furthermore, wages and salaries paid by cooperative enterprises were only 75 per cent of the provincial average, which supports the position of those who link the existence of cooperatives with underdevelopment.[107] Although cooperatives still benefited thousands of their members, they could hardly be characterized as "robust," a fact used to justify the termination of the cooperative education program, or as effective agents of change and socio-economic transformation.

The Credit Unions

The credit unions of Nova Scotia experienced what seems to have been steady growth during the 1970-2000 period. Their assets and deposits underwent rapid expansion, increasing eleven- and thirty-seven-fold respectively, between 1972 and 1997, as shown in table 7.3.

Table 7.3
The expansion of the credit unions of Nova Scotia, selected years, 1972–97

Year	*Membership*	*Deposits*	*Assets*
1972	112,000	20	70
1973	120,000	31	90
1985	156,138	n.a.	308
1986	n.a.	342	338
1989	166,000	440	472
1992	166,000	554	591
1994	171,000	616	662
1997	162,000	753	817

Note: Figures are in millions of dollars.

Source: Credit Union Central of Nova Scotia, *Annual Reports* (selected years, 1972–97).

Such impressive growth was due largely to greater contributions by existing members rather than to the expansion of membership, which increased by only 45 per cent over the same period and remained virtually constant from 1989 onward. Furthermore, with the notable exception of the Bergengren Credit Union of Antigonish, most of the growth was due primarily to the expansion of urban and occupational credit unions, with the community-based rural credit unions lagging behind. Over the 1975-85 period, the Halifax County credit unions alone accounted for about 40 per cent of the credit union assets in the province.[108] This proportion has likely risen even more in subsequent years.

Faced with rising costs, increased investment in computational equipment, rising wages, declining populations, and lagging deposits and assets, many of the small credit unions had no other option but to consolidate and amalgamate, leading to the establishment of numerous branches.[109] Thus there was a consolidation process whereby smaller rural credit unions were incorporated into nearby larger organizations, continuing their operations as branches. Such a development was in itself not undesirable and, indeed, was consistent with the need to increase efficiency. However, over time many of the smaller communities were abandoned altogether, and many credit unions began to function like banks, alienating some of the membership; they had fallen into the Rochdale cul-de-sac trap.

RESOURCES OF THE EXTENSION DEPARTMENT

Lack of resources to mount its programs remained a critical challenge to the Extension Department throughout the period. Without an adequate and secure financial base, the Extension Department could survive only by carrying out projects and programs for which the necessary funding could be found. However, these programs were shaped by the objectives of the funding agencies rather than by those of the Extension Department, the Antigonish Movement, and the various communities of eastern Nova Scotia and elsewhere. That much of the funding came from government sources further skewed the Extension Department's programs toward politically motivated objectives and perceived solutions.

Financial Resources

The constraints and dangers that the dependence on program-specific funding, especially from government sources, posed for the Extension Department were well understood. Thus in the early 1970s, in calling for the establishment of a million-dollar fund, the Extension Department noted that "With increasing funding from government our independence diminishes. This is much more serious for our type of programs, which arouse public controversy."[110] Along the same lines, in the 1980s it lamented that "financial support for all university extension programs tends to favour those adults who already have an advantage."[111] The dependence on outside funding gave groups and special interests, which controlled the funding, leverage over the programs of the Extension Department in favour of their own specific interests and objectives. In this vein, it was possible to mount ARLEC and carry out the program over three decades because the funding was available. The same was true in the cooperative housing sector during the 1970s and 1980s. In contrast, there were inadequate sources of funds for cooperative education, so the various programs were discontinued. The university and the cooperative institutions were unwilling or unable to increase their commitment to the Extension Department in order to carry out its traditional programs.

From the early 1980s onward, the adult and continuing education component of the Extension Department steadily expanded, whereas

Table 7.4
Summary of the overall budget of the Extension Department, 1982–97

Year	*Endowments and funds*[a]	*Services-related funds*[b]	*ARLEC*	*University*
1982–83	14.2	65.0	34.9	11.5
1983–84	17.6	71.3	35.4	11.1
1984–85	18.1	71.9	35.1	10.0
1985–86	18.4	72.1	34.9	10.0
1986–87	25.7	62.0	29.7	12.3
1987–88	20.0	68.0	31.0	12.0
1988–89	17.9	74.5	24.6	7.6
1989–90	14.7	77.4	31.8	8.0
1990–91	15.3	73.2	17.5	11.5
1991–92	11.9	81.9	27.7	6.2
1992–93	11.6	84.6	19.3	3.8
1993–94	11.5	88.5	17.9	—
1994–95	9.7	90.3	20.5	—
1995–96	8.8	85.4	17.7	5.8
1996–97	8.5	88.7	20.7	2.8

[a] Includes the Greening Fund, the Antigonish Movement Endowment Fund, the Cape Breton Endowment, the Murphy Endowment, the Catholic Episcopal Corporation, and the Sisters of St Martha. A number of these sources were not contributors for the whole period under consideration.
[b] Includes ARLEC, all funds that in later years were identified with training and development, as well as other grants and donations.

Note: Figures are percentages of the Extension Department's total general funds.

Source: Extension Department, St Francis Xavier University, *Annual Reports* (1982–97).

the relative importance of the "general extension" program declined. Moreover, the actual amount earmarked for economic-related activity became increasingly smaller over time, as we suggested earlier. The extent to which the general extension programs became dependent on program-specific funding is made clear in table 7.4. The funds linked to the provision of specific services and programs clearly dwarfed the other main sources, and their importance generally increased over time, reaching a highpoint of 90 per cent of all general extension funds in 1994–95. Endowments and funds generally declined in relative importance and even in absolute terms during the 1990s. ARLEC remained a strong contributor, although it too became less important in relative terms as the Extension Department expanded its various training and educational programs. The contribution by the university, which was limited to begin with, became virtually negligible, especially in relative terms, during the 1990s.

Despite the overall increase in the funds available to the Extension Department, its ability to carry out a function that would provide more substantive support for the formation of new cooperative entities and, perhaps more important, would strengthen those already in place was severely constrained. Given the new socio-economic environment, its altered vision, and the need to gain access to resources in order to remain in operation, the Extension Department followed a strategy that overall seems to have been quite successful, although it continued the process of undermining the Antigonish Movement that had started during the 1960s and in many respects even earlier. That the funding structure became even more skewed in favour of the services-related funding during the Webb years seems somewhat surprising. However, Webb believed not only that the Extension Department could, in fact, carry out all of the programs that it already had in place but also that these could be expanded and improved while also facilitating the revival of the more traditional programs aimed at enhancing the cooperative sector. There was a perception that the Extension Department could take advantage of synergies that arose from the active pursuit of both streams of activity. Webb also envisaged the university as playing a much more vital role in the whole process, whereas, if anything, the university was, as we have already noted, divesting itself of its linkages, at least in terms of the movement.

Human Resources

The hallmark of the Extension Department was that it had traditionally been able to do much with severely limited human as well as financial resources. This was also largely the case during the period under consideration. In addition to its dedicated and capable fieldworkers, the Extension Department could still count upon the contribution of volunteers, although to a much lesser extent than in the 1930s and the 1940s, when volunteers played a critical role in the mobilization of resources and the establishment of economic institutions. After 1982, it also acquired staffing for the continuing education program.

With much of the Extension Department's work linked to funded activities, involving mainly adult education and training programs as well as cooperative housing, only a small number of fieldworkers still remained engaged in various more traditional activities. Moreover, much of this involvement comprised providing information, assisting in organizing meetings, establishing contact with various government and other organizations, and the like. The lack of adequate resources not tied specifically to the provision of specific services, as well as the shifts in vision, severely constrained the traditional functions of field-workers. Although they were still able to help in the initiation of a number of co-operative enterprises, these were small in scale and generally not very successful, especially over the longer term. Along with the fieldworkers, the Extension Department also maintained a number of offices in the region. Over time, these were reduced until only those in Antigonish, Sydney, and New Glasgow remained by the time that Tom Webb left office.

CONCLUSION

The 1970s found the Extension Department and the Antigonish Movement in a state of disarray. Many of the department's traditional programs had been terminated, and the link between it and the cooperative sector had been broken. A succession of directors, all exceptional individuals, took up the challenge of revitalizing the Antigonish Movement. In the process, there was a widening of the involvement of the Extension Department, especially in the social, cultural, and educational spheres, shifting attention ever further away from the Antigonish Movement. Rather than the dynamic centre of a movement predicated on the establishment of an independent economic system, it became essentially a Jack of all trades, providing services and programs, usually for hire, to a wide and varied clientele. Although "People's School" broadcasts continued well into the 1980s and although there was still, from time to time, some reference to kitchen meetings and even study clubs, these methods were no longer relevant to the new approaches.

Given the circumstances, the various attempts to revitalize the movement and to revive old programs were doomed to failure, regardless of whether they involved "top-down" or "bottom-up" approaches. The success of most of these programs in earlier periods had been due largely to the integrated strategy adopted by the Extension Department. Thus they were parts of a greater whole and did not stand entirely on their own. Moreover, the socio-economic environment had changed drastically over time, and the various programs of the past needed to be adapted to fit the new circumstances while remaining true to their vision.

Ultimately, by the start of the new millennium, the institution that originated with the promise of helping the people of the region to become the "Masters of Their Own Destiny" had been reduced to the rank of a minor organization of subregional scope involved in a few projects of an exploratory nature. The institution, which had dared to envision and organize its own economic system – owned and controlled by the people themselves and based on the principles of self-help and economic cooperation – was reduced, after its last hurrah during the Webb years, to one that could only offer limited assistance to some of the region's marginalized and disadvantaged groups and communities. Its presence in the region was hardly visible. Even in its own university, it had lost its rank, prestige, and usefulness. At the same time, the Antigonish Movement had been relegated to the realm of history.

8

Conclusions and Prospects

INTRODUCTION

The Antigonish Movement emerged out of the desperation, poverty, exploitation, rural decline, and out-migration that plagued eastern Nova Scotia in the 1920s. Still, such desperate conditions were by themselves not sufficient to give rise to a unique and dynamic socio-economic movement predicated on the establishment of a unique alternate economic system. There were other regions and countries experiencing similar or, in some cases, even more deplorable conditions, yet they did not generate a similar movement aimed at socio-economic improvement. Although the desperate conditions facing the population of eastern Nova Scotia showed the failure of the existing system to meet the people's basic needs and aspirations, other factors needed to be present in order to establish sufficient conditions for the emergence of the movement. These factors included a political, social, moral, and spiritual environment that conditioned the people's responses to the appeals by the leadership of the movement.

At the political level, the liberties enjoyed by the population of the region, such as the freedom of assembly, were combined with a long-standing tradition of undertaking voluntary economic activities. At the same time, strong social and cultural bonds, cohesiveness, and solidarity prevailed within the communities and the region as a whole. These bonds were forged by economic hardship and insecurity, necessitating mutual self-help and assistance for survival, and were strengthened by the memories of past persecution and discrimination experienced by all three of the region's major ethnic groups – the Scots,

Acadians, and Irish. The moral and spiritual guidance of the Roman Catholic Church, with its emphasis on being one's "brother's keeper" and its emergent social-action imperative, inspired by the encyclicals *Rerum Novarum* and *Quadragesimo Anno*, fortified these bonds. Although the moral and spiritual fabric of the communities was being battered and undermined by the corrosive forces of poverty, exploitation, and sheer struggle for survival, it proved remarkably resilient and served as the base for the emergence of the movement. The critical component in establishing the sufficient conditions was, however, the emergence of an inspiring, community-oriented leadership that was trusted by the people and that was able to articulate a vision and plan of action that made sense to them.

The movement was, in effect, a concrete expression of the notion of a "Middle Way" between unbridled capitalism and state socialism, as embodied in the British doctrine of Distributism, which was also a product of Catholic social teaching and strongly influenced by *Rerum Novarum* and *Quadragesimo Anno*. Indeed, Race Mathews suggests that the Antigonish Movement, with its focus on people being "Masters of Their Own Destiny" and stress on practical economic action, was the de facto embodiment of what Distributism looked like if put into practice.[1] The Antigonish Movement embodied the key elements of Distributism expressed in an appealing way, including equality, broad-based control over economic activity, mutualism, and subsidiarity. Thus it was at the forefront of the search for an alternate solution to existing problems that had worldwide implications and that remains as valid in the present circumstances as in the past.

LEADERSHIP OF THE MOVEMENT

The leadership of the Antigonish Movement came from the most unlikely quarters: a small group of Roman Catholic priest-professors at the small and isolated diocesan university of St Francis Xavier, supported by many parish priests and other religious persons, including Roman Catholic sisters. The emergence of this group as the leaders of a dynamic movement was slow and not without some degree of controversy, largely due to the fact that the primary preoccupation of its members was far removed from the objective of engineering socio-economic transformation.[2] Collectively, they had to overcome many obstacles and barriers as they struggled to find solutions to various vexing and seemingly intractable problems. Their first major obstacle was to go beyond the moral and spiritual guidance of the faithful and to address their most pressing economic needs. The prevailing attitude among the clergy of the region, imbedded in the Bible and enshrined in centuries-old tradition, was based on the belief that there existed a strong negative relationship between economic and material fulfilment, on the one hand, and spiritual welfare, on the other. In fact, there was still a prevailing belief, perhaps best captured in the notion of "blessed are the poor," that poverty was conducive to salvation, whereas wealth presented a grave danger to it. This traditional outlook was not accepted by a group of progressive priest-professors and parish priests who believed that poverty, in fact, endangered the spiritual welfare of the faithful, as their struggle for survival often forced them to abandon higher moral and spiritual standards.

Although these leaders felt obligated to defend themselves against their more conservative colleagues, they had a very powerful ally in the social teachings of the Catholic Church, particularly in the encyclicals *Rerum Novarum* and *Quadragesimo Anno*. Largely educated outside of the region, especially in Rome, Rev. Moses Coady and his colleagues had a broad worldview and were aware of the socio-economic experiments conducted in various European countries, such as Ireland, Denmark, France, and England, and were determined to put their beliefs into practice. They would also have been aware of some of the elements of British Distributism, particularly as defined by co-religionists such as Cardinal Henry Edward Manning and Gilbert Keith Chesterton.[3] Their wide exposure to ideas from abroad, intimate knowledge and understanding of the people and their circumstances, remarkable pioneering spirit, willingness to put their ideas into action, and forceful personalities presented a formidable combination.

Their first ventures in the area of socio-economic action date back to the 1910s, when Rev. Dr Hugh MacPherson conducted pioneering work in organizing cooperatives in the agricultural sector and when Rev. Jimmy Tompkins became involved in the so-called Progressive Movement in Antigonish County. These initiatives were promising and sowed the seeds for the future, especially in terms of providing a clearer sense of the needs of the area and the logistics inherent in formulating appropriate action to address them.

A particularly formidable obstacle that faced the early leaders who were also priest-professors was the large gap separating St Francis Xavier University and its culture of formal education, in which they were professionally immersed, from the lives of the ordinary people of the diocese, who were struggling for survival. This obstacle was partially bridged by the indomitable Rev. Tompkins, who, in his 1921 pamphlet *Knowledge for the People*, denounced the formal education approach as elitist and advocated the direct education of farmers, fishermen, and industrial workers as a primary vehicle for their economic betterment. The pamphlet was followed by a series of initiatives and experiments, such as the People's Schools, which, even if not entirely successful, served to connect with the people and also to cement the evolution of the vision of the emerging movement. In particular, they strengthened the belief in the value of education and knowledge as a means of alleviating the economic suffering of the population. These various initiatives contributed to the mounting pressure from various quarters to establish the Extension Department in 1928 with a mandate to assist in the economic improvement of the people of eastern Nova Scotia.

The early leaders also had the advantage of being members of a group that people generally trusted. In addition to the priest-professors, there were others, including dedicated and down-to-earth parish priests, who were very concerned about the plight of their parishioners and whom the people knew and trusted. Despite their position within the university, both Rev. Coady and Rev. Tompkins were men of the people; they shared the same background, understood the challenges and difficulties that the people faced, and spoke in a language that all could understand. The Roman Catholic Church itself carried sway among a large segment of the people of the region at this time as an entity that could be trusted. Rev. Coady and Rev. Tompkins also pursued an ecumenical approach, inviting different religious groups to work together to deal with common problems and achieve common goals. In essence, a key component in Rev. Coady's notion of scientific thinking involved leaving behind the prejudices and narrow perspectives that constrained human actions and possibilities. There was a concern with the plight of all people, not just Catholics, which remained a constant throughout the evolution of both the Extension Department and the Antigonish Movement as a whole.[4]

INITIAL PROBLEMS OF THE MOVEMENT

The establishment of the Extension Department was a significant step toward the emergence of the Antigonish Movement, but a great deal of additional work remained to be done. The resources at its disposal were miniscule compared to the needs of the population, creating the problem of how to spread them over the region without losing effectiveness. Furthermore, the people in the region, apart from their dire economic circumstances, were dispirited, suspicious, frightened, and disoriented. How was it possible to lift their spirits, to inspire them and mobilize them to initiate risky and uncertain economic ventures that had never been tried in the region before? The problem was further aggravated by the fact that the resources available to individual families fell far short of those required to take advantage of existing or emerging economic opportunities. Also, there was the need to maintain momentum once a few projects had been initiated.

These and many other problems were solved, one by one, by experimentation, trial and error, ingenuity, audacity, and daring. The meager resources of the Extension Department were magnified by the ingenious approach whereby the people themselves took an active part in their own education and in initiating economic activities. The Extension Department provided support and guidance. The people were shaken from their lethargy by the knowledge that they, and their forefathers, were responsible for their misfortunes and economic hardship due to the people's "Great Default" in allowing others to control and own the economic institutions in their communities. They were inspired by the possibility that they could reverse the situation by creating and taking control of their own economic institutions, thereby becoming the "Masters of Their Own Destiny." In addition, the movement could count on the efforts of a wide array of volunteers. Thus, from its inception, the Antigonish Movement followed a fundamentally bottom-up approach. However, the strategy was not simply the outcome of the meagreness of the resources available but was also fundamental to the whole philosophy and vision behind the movement, based on people doing things for themselves so that they could "own" their livelihood and exert some control over their economic "destiny." This approach was a manifestation of both mutualism and subsidiarity in action.

The inadequacy and meagreness of the resources of individual families were solved through the novel approach of pulling their resources together through the formation of groups – study clubs and associated study clubs – and collectively establishing various economic ventures. Such a process involved not only the pooling of resources and sharing of risks but also the mobilization of group entrepreneurship. Education and study served not only to mobilize group entrepreneurship but also to promote and foster the build-up of individual skills and knowledge – that is, human capital. The problem of maintaining momentum was to be overcome by forging a highly integrated system of institutions and programs in which each part contributed to the good of the whole. This integrated system came to be embodied in the "Big Picture."

The Antigonish Movement and the Extension Department quickly adopted a clear operational vision and strategy bent on the creation of an alternate economic system. The critical components of this system were cooperation, self-reliance, and control by the people themselves.

INITIAL SUCCESSES OF THE MOVEMENT

Despite their ingenious approaches and devices, the beginnings of both the Antigonish Movement and the Extension Department were difficult, being fraught with disappointments, uncertainty, and frequent failures. Yet the Extension Department, under the charismatic and inspiring leadership of Rev. Coady, persevered, introducing the necessary adjustments, modifications, and innovations and adopting a highly eclectic approach. By 1936 a critical mass of participants and resources had been reached, and the dynamic mass movement was well on its way. Its activities spread to numerous local communities to which people were flocking in order to study and to organize new economic projects. Newly formed local cooperatives and credit unions became integrated into secondary societies. New areas of activities were discovered and exploited, and the membership of the study clubs and local economic organizations exploded. The daring vision of creating an independent economic system was gradually being implemented in the various communities, capturing the imagination and forging the collective will of the masses.

The extraordinary early success of the Antigonish Movement rested on a number of factors. First, the movement established a vital and direct link between education and economic action. This link was continuously supported, nourished, and fortified by the numerous mass meetings, study clubs, leadership training courses, Rural and Industrial Conferences, and the like. Second, the movement's organization of educational and economic activities proved to be extremely cost-effective since the people themselves were required to do the work. The participation of the people in education and self-help economic activities evoked strong motivation and unbending resolve. The movement belonged to them, as they educated themselves and organized new economic ventures though their sacrifices, hard work, ingenuity, and cooperation. They became conscious of the fact that they were shaping their own economic future and wellbeing. Third, the self-learning that took place in the small groups of friends and neighbours was very effective not only in facilitating the acquisition of new knowledge but also in building the trust, loyalty, commitment, and willingness to take risks that were necessary for the initiation and operation of economic projects. Fourth, the first wave of projects turned out to be extraordinarily profitable, within the context of the region, as rents and quasi rents were captured by the cooperative organizations and transferred to the individual members. That they did experience some gain and could now see that they had more options and possibilities was of paramount importance. Fifth, the movement became a coherent, self-generating, dynamic process in which various elements – educational, social, economic, moral, and so on – were tightly integrated into a network of programs, activities, and institutions, creating and maintaining its own momentum. Sixth, the momentum was guided by an inspiring yet practical vision expressed in the program of action known as the Big Picture.

INTERNATIONAL RECOGNITION

By the end of the 1930s the Antigonish Movement's remarkable achievements had attracted national and international attention. These achievements appeared even more dramatic against the backdrop of widespread unemployment, poverty, and despair of the Great Depression. The recognition, however, proved to be a mixed blessing. In the short run, it added strength and resources to the movement, enabling it to expand to other maritime provinces. The steady stream of national and international visitors increased the confidence and moral resolve of the participants, convincing them that they were building a unique and lasting system that would benefit not only themselves but also their brothers and sisters elsewhere. In the long run, however, the international recognition brought grave dangers and difficulties whose destructive power was never recognized, even when it contributed to undermining the vitality and effectiveness of the movement in the decades to come. In particular, it created the impression that the task that the movement had set out to accomplish had largely been completed – when, in fact, the work had just begun. Some of the groundwork was in place, but most of the economic system was still being built and still very much a work in progress.

WARTIME CHALLENGE

The Second World War resulted in the first formidable challenge to the young movement, testing its resilience and adaptability. Thousands of young men, many of them among the most active members of study clubs and local economic institutions set up by the movement, enlisted and went to serve overseas. Those who remained behind, and the female labour force, were preoccupied with maximizing their contributions to the war effort. Furthermore, the enormous financial burden of the war had greatly reduced the funds available to the Extension Department. The movement had to adapt to the new reality if it was to survive. The educational programs of the Extension Department were revised and scaled down. The cooperatives and the credit unions adapted to the wartime restrictions and established strong roots in their communities, with women taking up new and expanded roles. The movement not only survived but had seemingly managed to solidify some of its gains from the previous decade and was poised to take advantage of the expected postwar expansion.

POSTWAR GROWTH

The conditions prevailing in the postwar period, characterized by reconstruction and economic growth, were initially highly conducive to the further expansion of the Antigonish Movement, allowing it to regain much of its earlier dynamism and vitality. The Extension Department launched a new and ambitious experiment in mass education using radio and later television. There was an expansion in cooperative housing, which attracted volunteers and numerous self-help housing groups and resulted in the construction of hundreds of affordable cooperatively built houses for low- and middle-income families. The economic pillars of the movement – the fisheries, agricultural, and consumers' cooperatives and the credit unions – experienced continued expansion and growth in terms of membership, sales, and assets. In the late 1950s, the movement launched its large-scale project in agricultural processing and services, Eastern Co-operative Services, which was designed to fill an important gap in its integrated system by establishing a direct relationship between agricultural marketing cooperatives and consumers' cooperatives.

In the national and international spheres, the movement spread to the many Canadian provinces outside of the Maritimes, to various parts of the United States, to the Caribbean, to Latin America, and to other continents. To service the increasing international involvement, an international arm of the movement, the Coady International Institute, was established in 1959.

The outward signs of dynamism and expansion, however, masked the reality that as early as the 1950s the movement was beginning to unravel. Rather than being parts of an integrated system, the various components underwent a nearly continuous process of drifting apart. Moreover, whether as a result of the so-called Rochdale cul-de-sac or other and more fundamental factors, attachment to the cooperatives began to weaken. The cooperatives themselves began to lag behind the more traditional profit-oriented enterprises. Whereas in the 1930s the entities established by the Antigonish Movement were in many ways more efficient than the family-based enterprises, this was no longer the case in the postwar years. Thus the movement found itself in the contradictory position of seeming to thrive and to be dynamic while being undermined both from within and from without.

LIMITATIONS OF THE LEADERSHIP AND THE DECLINE OF THE MOVEMENT

Despite the impressive array of accomplishments, the postwar years witnessed the emergence of fissures and widening cracks in the seemingly solid system that was being built by the movement. Vital links among its different components began to weaken and, in some cases, were severed. To a large extent, these emerging problems were not recognized by the leaders of the movement or by the authorities of St Francis Xavier University. In some instances, the opposite seems to have been occurring. The leaders of the movement, particularly Rev. Coady, who were intimately knowledgeable of what had been accomplished, came to believe that they had discovered an important and stable scientific formula of universal applicability that might assist in improving the living standards of the masses and perhaps even in alleviating global poverty. The early manifestation of this conviction was perhaps Rev. Coady's acceptance of the misleading interpretation of the movement incorporated by Harry Johnson in his articulation of the "Six Principles," even though in practice Rev. Coady still adhered to the seemingly more modest, even if grounded in reality, socio-economic action plan of the Big Picture. In addition to their abstract nature, the Six Principles ignored the importance of ownership and control of economic activity, which were the central components of the Antigonish Movement and integral to the notion of the Middle Way. Although they did not constitute a refutation of the movement, the Six Principles failed to capture what was truly unique about it and did not offer anything resembling a blueprint for action.

Being visionaries, social reformers, and men of action, Rev. Coady and his associates understood, even if not fully, the complexity of the system that was being put in place. Rev. Coady, in particular, was keenly aware of the crucial relationship between education and economic action, and he addressed the issue continuously, even when he was no longer director of the Extension Department in the 1950s. He also understood the forces that could undermine this relationship, such as the free rider problem and the lack of commitment to cooperation and to the vision of the movement. However, the need for the various economic activities to be integrated into a self-generating system was not recognized or appreciated fully. In any event, the state of precariousness in which the movement progressively found itself during the 1950s went largely unnoticed. Once Rev. Coady and the other leaders of the movement had left the scene, the nature of the crucial relationship between the program of adult education that had been devised and the economic activities that emanated from it was effectively lost, especially from the 1960s onward. As the Extension Department moved toward becoming a formal adult education institution, study and education largely ceased to be seen as tools for the mobilization of group entrepreneurship, decision making, and economic action.

Although the Big Picture pointed to an understanding that the economic system that was being put in place had to be integrated, the various components of the movement had in fact begun to move in separate directions nearly from the outset. The whole notion of an integrated economic system was further weakened by the abandonment of the Big Picture and the adoption of the Six Principles. In the 1930s the commitment of the people was fostered by the successes of the movement, as they were asked not only to make sacrifices but also to lay the groundwork for their own economic, social, and political betterment. What it provided was of fundamental importance to the people and their way of life. In the postwar years, as the options available to people increased and the movement was unable to adjust and evolve, its impact began to weaken, which gave rise to a weakening of commitment as well. The often weak and marginal cooperatives had little to offer to their members and certainly did not reflect an inspiring vision. The Rochdale cul-de-sac, whereby struggling and even successful cooperative enterprises abandoned cooperative principles and became indistinguishable from more traditional ones, also played a role.

The link between education and economic action was also not a permanent force of universal applicability, contrary to what the leaders of the movement had erroneously assumed. It was strongly dependent on the type of education and study strategy that had been adopted in the early years, which had involved especially the mobilization of group entrepreneurship. This vital link had already begun to unravel at the end of the 1930s when mass meetings were largely discontinued, and it was left up to the economic institutions of the movement to organize the study clubs. In the latter part of the 1940s this unravelling was heightened by additional changes in education strategy, particularly with the introduction of the radio programs. Programs of mass education such as "Life in These Maritimes" and the "People's School" failed to inspire or initiate any meaningful economic action. These were replaced by television in later decades and remained in place for some time largely as providers of public information. Although these programs were informative, they could do very little to initiate new economic ventures or to strengthen existing cooperative enterprises, especially since, over time, these needed to be bigger, employ more complex technologies, and the like. The new mass media programs could also not provide the in-depth economic analysis that was required to make sense of what had actually been accomplished and why and to point to what to do next, including what needed to be done to strengthen the existing economic institutions and the links between them.

The lack of effective management was a problem that had plagued cooperative entities from the outset. Although the problem was not serious at first, particularly given the small scale of the earlier cooperatives, it increased in seriousness over time, especially from the 1950s onward, as larger and more efficient cooperatives, as well as a more highly integrated cooperative sector, were required to remain competitive with the expanding profit-driven private sector. The leaders of the movement, despite being seemingly aware of the problem, were unable to adequately address it. In addition, neither its leaders nor the movement itself had been able to develop the skills and expertise required to design and implement larger-scale projects, as became evident with ambitious but ill-fated Eastern Co-operative Services (ECS) during the latter part of the 1950s and the early 1960s. Indeed, the failure of ECS highlighted the weaknesses that had emerged in the movement, which included inadequate management skills, fragmentation within the cooperative sector, the lack of appreciation for the importance of such a project, and the failure to branch out beyond the traditional resource-based sectors.

Ironically, the establishment of the Coady International Institute, despite fulfilling Rev. Coady's dream of providing the Antigonish Movement with an international or global outreach, also inadvertently weakened it. The institute diverted resources and attention from the growing problems at home, giving the misleading impression that the movement was dynamic and expanding when, in fact, it was disintegrating and fragmenting into separate components.

The Antigonish Movement was also severely harmed by fundamental confusion about its nature and what it involved. Such confusion also extended to the role and function of the Extension Department. From the outset, the department was referred to as primarily an adult education institution, with the Antigonish Movement being labelled an adult education program. However, these terms were misleading as to the true nature of both. The Extension Department was in fact the dynamic centre of a program of socioeconomic development. The Antigonish Movement itself constituted an ambitious attempt to establish an independent economic system with the clout to effect fundamental socio-economic changes that would allow people to become "Masters of Their Own Destiny." This confusion existed from the very beginning but become significant after the early leaders and participants had largely left the scene, especially from the 1950s onward.

In part, the confusion arose from the absence of an in-depth analysis that would have provided a clear, rigorous, and definitive blueprint of the movement both in terms of its past achievements and in terms of its future direction. Rev. Coady's failed attempt in the 1950s to provide a definitive statement of its vision proved to have important implications for the future evolution of the movement. He was a visionary and a man of action but not a theoretician and, in any event, was too close to his creation to be able to provide the required analysis.

Despite the limitations arising from the lack of adequate analysis and the increasing misconception about their very nature, both the Antigonish Movement and the Extension Department still possessed a great deal of vitality and energy during much of the 1950s, which saw the emergence of new programs, institutions, and instruments. Thus, for example, the kitchen meetings, although not an effective replacement for the study clubs in terms of the generation of new cooperative activity, were able to revitalize and strengthen existing enterprises and to some extent maintain the link between education and economic activity in many rural communities. Other initiatives, such as the Model Fisherman program in the fisheries, created an economic hybrid of individual and cooperative activities. There was also a lot of activity in the cooperative housing sector. Perhaps the most obvious sign of apparent vitality was the creation of ECS. Nevertheless, the movement was beginning to unravel even while some of its leaders were travelling to other continents to expound its universal relevance.

The difficulties and problems that emerged during the 1950s were magnified and compounded in the following decade by a new and inexperienced leadership with little direct knowledge of the early movement. Thus there was greater confusion about the nature of the Antigonish Movement and the role of the Extension Department. Moreover, whereas the early leaders of the movement had been able to develop a great deal of intuitive knowledge forged by practice and experience, the new leadership, emerging from different backgrounds and into a socio-economic environment that was much different from that of earlier decades, was much less capable of doing so. It adopted strategies and policies that proved disastrous for both the movement and the Extension Department. By the end of the 1960s the original movement had virtually ceased to exist. It had lost its fiery vision, and its two major components, the Extension Department and the cooperative economic institutions, had severed their already weak links. The Extension Department, the dynamic driving force of the movement in the previous decades, was in disarray and becoming increasingly marginalized within the university. Its major programs, such as those in the fisheries, cooperative housing, credit unions, and cooperative education, were terminated, and it lost development partners, including the federal Department of Fisheries, the provincial Department of Agriculture, and the Nova Scotia Housing Commission.

Over the 1960s, the original vision of the Antigonish Movement, predicated on the people themselves being able to solve their own problems by creating their own economic institutions and their own alternate economic system, thereby becoming effective "Masters of Their Own Destiny," was repudiated and replaced by a vision that in effect sought to improve the wellbeing of the people within the existing system by following the leadership of the government. In the process, economic activity, rather than the means for the attainment of loftier goals of moral and spiritual enrichment, became increasingly perceived as an end in itself.

The new vision looked to the power of the social sciences to devise appropriate solutions largely independent of the history and evolution of the Antigonish Movement. The Extension Department largely abandoned its function as a key component of socio-economic development as it deferred to the government and to traditional private, for-profit enterprise and, its rhetoric aside, no longer looked to the Middle Way in its approach to the region's problems and difficulties. Despite still doing some very useful work and still being able to attract many remarkable people to carry out its programs, the Extension Department after the 1960s could no longer be regarded, even remotely, as the anchor of an alternate economic system based on the widespread ownership and control of economic resources and activities by the people themselves that would allow them to become "Masters of Their Own Destiny." The movement, as it was effectively envisaged and put into action by its founders, no longer existed.

Whereas in earlier periods the reference to the movement as an adult education program was not of much importance, this mislabelling began to play a more important role as adult education became more formalized as an academic discipline. In the 1960s and increasingly in the 1970s and beyond, references to the Antigonish Movement as an adult education program distorted its true nature and obscured the factors that had made it successful in the first place. This distortion became increasingly prominent as the practice of the movement and the notion of the Big Picture effectively disappeared from view, particularly with the full acceptance of the Six Principles in their stead. As there was less to directly observe, the labelling and description became more important, with serious negative consequences for the Antigonish Movement.

The new programs of the Extension Department, which involved a host of undertakings such as participation in studies conducted by the Agricultural and Rural Development Agency (ARDA), community development initiatives, working with Aboriginal communities through its "Indian" program, providing education in the African Canadian communities, and organizing woodlot owners in the forestry sector, were generally of limited impact and short-lived. The new development partners, which included ARDA and the federal Departments of Municipal Affairs and Indian Affairs, could provide only short-term, often nonrenewable contracts, and they also set the agenda for the work that was being done. At the same time, the cooperative sector, largely left to its own devices, faced daunting prospects in its struggle for survival in the face of the vicious cycle of undercapitalization, high costs and declining profitability, membership withdrawals, loss of sales, and increased marginalization. As they struggled to survive, cooperatives also increasingly adopted strategies that widened the gap between management and the membership – giving rise to the so-called Rochdale cul-de-sac by creating a dichotomy between the interests of the institutions and those of the membership.

The last three decades of the century witnessed the inevitable further fragmentation and decline of what remained of the movement, culminating in its de facto official termination at the end of the millennium. During this long period, the Extension Department, under three different directors, all of whom were in some way associated with the movement, veered in different directions and introduced various programs and initiatives in an attempt to remain relevant and regain its vitality. A fundamental factor that worked to undermine such efforts was the loss of the initial vision of the movement. In the process, it became increasingly drawn into the formalized academic discipline of adult education.

During the 1970s, attempts were made to revitalize both the Extension Department and the Antigonish Movement by returning to the past. Various initiatives were implemented and others proposed. However, even when in the right direction, these efforts fell far short of their mark. The 1980s saw the Extension Department attempting to forge a new role, independent of its past, as a purely adult education institution that offered a wide range of educational programs to an increasingly Canada-wide constituency. Although the movement continued in the general direction established during the 1980s, the 1990s witnessed another attempt to return to some of its original roots. However, what was done was essentially too little and too late. There was too little of the original vision and institutional set-up to latch on to.

Although the many major new programs, such as the Atlantic Region Labour Education Centre, social housing, and Training for Trainers, were useful and beneficial to many individuals, groups, and organizations, they failed to restore purpose, meaning, and dynamism to this once famous institution, which remained unable to reclaim its past role as the vital centre of the Antigonish Movement. Arguably, the Extension Department had become the prisoner of its past, a past that it could neither return to nor escape from. It found itself in an unenviable situation. Shorn of its inspiring vision, separated from its institutional offspring (the cooperative sector), denied adequate resources by the university and other sources, lacking influential development partners, and bereft of clear knowledge of the causes of its past success that could also serve as a guide for the future, it had no option but to increasingly provide services for hire and to pursue initiatives for which funds were available.

The Board of Governors of St Francis Xavier University restored the original 1928 mandate to the Extension Department in the symbolic year of 2000. Yet the board also limited the department's coverage to eastern Nova Scotia and, most revealing, provided it with very limited, short-term funding, a new director unfamiliar with the movement, and a pared-down skeleton staff. Regardless of the motivation behind it, the result has been the de facto official termination of the Extension Department's participation in the great experiment that was the Antigonish Movement.

The cooperative sector, for its part, is continuing its fragmentary and precarious existence. Some selected groupings, such as fisheries cooperatives and most of the agricultural suppliers, have largely disappeared, along with their secondary societies. Other groupings, such as the consumers' cooperatives, are facing the onslaught of national and international chains, such as Sobey's and Loblaws. Only the credit unions and milk-processing cooperatives were able to establish and maintain their presence. The latter has also benefited from government regulation and protection. The extent to which these can survive on their own is brought further into question by the formidable changes that are occurring as a result of globalization.

PROSPECTS FOR THE MOVEMENT

The Antigonish Movement had sought to establish an alternate economic system that effectively addressed many of the concerns that are as relevant in today's globalized world as they were in the 1920s. The issues raised by *Rerum Novarum* and *Quadragesimo Anno* have been reiterated by more recent encyclicals of John Paul II and are as compelling in the present context as they were in the past. The inequities of the present economic system are no less serious than they were in the past, and the same applies to the risks and uncertainties facing the masses. In much of the Western world, although the building-up of the social-welfare safety net has cushioned the costs associated with economic changes and fluctuations, these costs have not been eliminated, and the owners of capital have never been as dominant, owing to their freedom to scour the globe in search of higher returns. The patterns of globalization and the demise of state socialism have if anything made the search for a Middle Way along the lines of the Antigonish Movement more relevant than ever before. Moreover, new technological innovations have made it easier than ever before for alternate economic institutions, such as cooperatives, to thrive and to link up globally.

Nevertheless, in the present socio-economic, intellectual, and political environment, any attempt to revive the Antigonish Movement is likely to face even more serious challenges than in the past. The environment has changed dramatically since the golden years of the movement from one that was highly favourable to one that is in many ways decidedly hostile. Yet, despite this development, its revival is not impossible.

Natural resources, which constituted the economic base of the movement and which were in abundance in early decades, have become much less so, and some, like the fish stocks, have been severely depleted. The newly discovered natural resources, such as offshore gas, require such an enormous volume of capital and sophisticated technology that only large multinational corporations, working in consortiums, can afford the risk. There seem to be very few obviously idle or underutilized resources that the movement could use. As well, the primary sectors are much less important to the economy as a whole, and their growth potential is generally very limited. This suggests that a revival of the movement cannot be based solely on natural resources but must also look to other sectors – including manufacturing and services.

The technology prevailing in the 1930s was relatively easy to access for small-scale projects, as it was simple, primitive, and labour-intensive and required few specialized skills to operate. In contrast, today's technology tends to be highly capital-intensive and much more sophisticated, to be embodied in specialized and complex machinery, and often to require highly skilled employees. To the extent that such technology is highly indivisible, it has increased the threshold size of enterprises to well beyond the limits of community-based groups and in some instances also well beyond the limits of the region as a whole. Nonetheless, there is a possibility for some of the newer technologies to be highly divisible and scale-neutral, which could have the opposite effect, increasing rather than decreasing the accessibility of economic activity. Furthermore, some of the new technology has made it possible to establish networks so that, working as integrated units, even small cooperative entities can thrive. The new technology, by enabling networking among cooperatives, confers advantages that the initial cooperative enterprises of the Antigonish Movement did not have. That there may be less scope for "sweat capital" or "sweat equity" does not constitute a problem.

Another important development is the large number of highly trained individuals emerging from the various higher-education institutions, including St Francis Xavier University, which could sustain economic activities based on human capital as opposed to natural resources. Indeed, an extreme irony is that if the movement had adapted to changing circumstances and survived, it would now be faced with a number of technological and human-capital conditions that could have enhanced its ability to thrive.

The market structure has also changed. Whereas small, inefficient, and fragmented local institutions were once predominant, the present market is characterized by large national and international, highly efficient, and specialized enterprises driven by ever-increasing advertising and sale-promotion expenditures in the constant struggle for market shares, the proliferation of logos and brand-name associations, battles for consumers' loyalty, protection granted by patents, and the like. Most markets are seemingly difficult, if not impossible, to penetrate. Nonetheless, the possibility also exists to enhance the value and appeal of cooperative logos and brands. Moreover, fuelled by the new information technology, the new economy has, at least in theory, rendered economic activity increasingly footloose and has also allowed smaller, more dynamic, and more agile entities to thrive, particularly as parts of networks, and there is no reason why these networks cannot be based on principles similar to those of the Antigonish Movement – that is, self-reliance, cooperation, and ownership and control of economic institutions by the people themselves.

Equally fundamental changes have occurred in the labour markets. Despite its many institutions of higher learning, eastern Nova Scotia, and to some extent the whole of Atlantic Canada, faces substantial deficits in skilled and educated labour due to out-migration and the brain drain, which have been motivated by the expansion of opportunities elsewhere and the rapid increase in mobility. In an increasingly globalized economy, the position of labour is being undermined, creating not only increased uncertainty and stress but also social breakdowns engendered by forced migrations and dislocations. In many ways, these issues are similar to those addressed by the initial pioneers of the Antigonish Movement, which included out-migration and the relative powerlessness of workers and the masses in general. Indeed, much of the opposition to the notion of globalization rests on the imbalance that exists between owners of capital, on the one hand, and workers and the masses in general, on the other.

The rural sector, which the Antigonish Movement set out to revive and to protect and where it achieved some of its most important early successes, has experienced a marked decline, at least in relative terms, as a consequence both of the changes in structure of production that have characterized all Western countries and of a decades-long hemorrhaging of human and material resources. In the 1930s the rural sector, although poor, exploited, and depressed, had at least the potential for development, as it included a large portion of the population. Today, this sector has become much less important economically, socially, and politically. With few exceptions, the current situation in rural eastern Nova Scotia is one of economic decline due to an aging and scattered population that often lacks the critical mass, initiative, and energy to mount any significant revival of the movement through the initiation of viable economic projects. For there to be a revival, the more urban areas, as well as the younger and more educated generations, must also be, once again, more fully integrated into the process. However, these people would also need to be inspired by a grand vision that extolled, as was the case in the 1930s, the broad range of benefits emanating from the movement rather than simply calling for sacrifices to be made. Such a vision must address issues that really matter, not relatively minor areas of concern. As Race Mathews points out, having access to cooperative stores where one can purchase things that may be available elsewhere at close to the same price may in itself not be important enough in people's lives to prompt strong commitment[5] – as had been very clear to Rev. Coady and the other leaders of the Antigonish Movement.

There has also been a loss of commonality of interests and concerns as the population has become increasingly fragmented into conflicting and competing occupations, trades, unions, associations, professions, and specialized interests, each protecting and jealously guarding its licences, permits, quotas, occupational privileges and entitlements, monopolies, and the like. The problem is further compounded by increased social stratification. In the 1930s there tended to be limited social stratification among a large segment of the population. Whether industrial workers, fishermen, or farmers, the people were bound together by poverty and limited options. The "common man" of the 1930s, who was the foundation of the movement, was to a great extent a self-employed and entrepreneurial individual. There is still evidence that the entrepreneurial spirit has remained strong in the maritime region of Canada as a whole.[6]

Arguably, the biggest obstacle to the reemergence of the Antigonish Movement, or of something along similar lines, is the need to mobilize adequate leadership. The traditional local leaders, such as parish priests and school teachers, have largely disappeared, especially from the smaller communities, along with the bulk of the educated youth. We have also witnessed the complete disappearance of the priest-professors from St Francis Xavier University. These traditional leaders have often been replaced by distant experts, bureaucrats, and specialists of every description who have been ill suited to fostering fundamental changes and economic action. The university itself has long distanced itself from the community, partly due to a lack of interest in, commitment to, and understanding of its historical role in the community. In this context, the virtual disappearance of the Extension Department looms particularly large.

Political conditions have also been altered dramatically. In the 1920s and 1930s the federal government followed a policy that could be characterized as largely laissez-faire or economic noninterference, although exceptions were made in cases involving the national interest or groups suffering unusual hardship, such as the inshore fishermen of the Maritimes. Indeed, the federal government's response to the plight of the maritime fishermen, in addition to the recommendations of the MacLean Commission, was to introduce the fisheries grant, which allowed the Extension Department to carry out some of its work in this sector from the late 1930s onward. However, that this grant was awarded by the House of Commons, not by the federal Department of Fisheries per se, underlies its exceptional nature. The provincial governments followed a less strict laissez-faire policy, occasionally assisting politically important groups – such as farmers, who benefited from the network of agricultural representatives, a provincially owned abattoir, and other measures.

One of the benefits of the laissez-faire policy was that it gave the people unimpeded freedom and incentive to become active in solving their own economic problems. If the people wanted to improve their economic conditions, they had to do it themselves. The situation changed in the postwar period, particularly from the 1960s, when the traditional noninterference policy was replaced by Keynesian-inspired government interventions in various aspects of the economy. These many initiatives have included the creation of an elaborate social-welfare safety net, an enormous expansion of the social infrastructure, equalization payments to the poorer provinces, and regional development programs. In recent years, forces that advocate retrenchment in these areas have gained strength, especially as the forces of globalization have become more pervasive. Such retrenchment in itself puts greater pressure on communities to find alternatives if they are to survive. Nonetheless, although the greater involvement of the government in the economy may reduce the urgency to act, this involvement does not undermine the rationale behind the Antigonish Movement or the relevance of its vision and the notion of the Middle Way, which would assure people greater ownership and control of economic institutions.

TRENDS, TENDENCIES, AND POSSIBILITIES

Despite the fundamental changes that have occurred and their impacts on the population in the region, the future is not all bleak for a revival of the Antigonish Movement or some variant of it. To be sure, some of the early strategies would no longer work, and other more appropriate ones would have to be devised. What is important to keep in mind, however, is that the movement was based on the creation of a dynamic and effective economic system with substantial clout to bring about a fundamental transformation of the then existing socio-economic environment and values. The movement perceived the establishment of such a system not as an end in itself but as a tool for achieving moral, spiritual, social, and cultural enlightenment. The outcome was not only the attainment of the "full and abundant life" but also the achievement of full democratic participation in the economy, the political system, and society at large. Attaining these lofty goals required ownership and control of economic activity and resources, which would provide empowerment for the common people and make them "Masters of Their Own Destiny."

In terms of the socio-economic environment of eastern Nova Scotia, many of the current pressing problems are not much different from those that gave rise to the emergence of the Antigonish Movement in the first place, even though some of the underlying causes may be different.[7] Problems in the fisheries and the industrial centres, especially with the demise of the coal and steel sectors, out-migration, and rural decline, are still dominant, as the region is becoming increasingly affected by the forces of globalization. Many communities are fighting to remain viable in the face of unemployment, economic decline, and the exodus of the young and more educated.

Community-based activities, although generally disjointed and marginal, are still much in evidence in the region. Of particular note are some of the initiatives in Cape Breton, such as New Dawn.[8] Some of the institutions established by the Antigonish Movement are still in place and offer an important glimpse of what was and can be accomplished. Nevertheless, the overarching vision of establishing a vital alternate economic system is no longer in evidence and constitutes the key missing component.

One particular development that must be considered favourable and that could, under the right conditions, prompt the revival of the movement is the information revolution. Although it has not yet run its course, it has already had a great impact in reducing geographical distance and "democratizing space." This democratization process can play an important role in reducing the advantage that larger cities and urban areas have traditionally enjoyed over the countryside and more rural areas, especially in attracting resources and people due to, among other things, their access to superior information and knowledge and their agglomeration economies. This historical advantage is presently being eroded by the information revolution, which provides rural and urban communities equal access to information and knowledge. The emerging democratization of information and communication, combined with improvements in transportation and the mounting environmental, social, and other problems of the cities, might improve the attractiveness of the rural communities and provide the impetus to put in place the economic activities that would effectively reverse the population and brain drain flows. In terms of economic activity, the perceived disadvantages of more rural eastern Nova Scotia would be reduced. In many ways, this set of conditions is conducive to more rural-based economic activity, somewhat similar to the situation in the 1930s. Arguably, under proper conditions, especially if linked to a vision similar to that of the Antigonish Movement, there would be not only an increase in the number of available economic opportunities but also the generation of new hope, new vitality, and especially, new leadership.

Perhaps of even greater importance is that the new technology offers the potential to overcome the barrier to communication, which in the past kept the various economic institutions of the Antigonish Movement separate from one another. The possibility for networking, the creation of linkages, and the exploitation of agglomeration economies as well as knowledge and expertise, something that even large corporations are beginning to do at the global and local levels, would be a boon to cooperative enterprises, allowing even small ones to survive. In effect, the new technology provides the means whereby the integrated economic system envisaged by the Antigonish Movement could actually be realized by overcoming many of the movement's earlier constraints. It needs to be understood that cooperative enterprises, although more complex, do not constitute an inferior way of organizing production of goods and services; under proper conditions, they possess many advantages over conventional profit-driven entities.

Another important development that could foster the reemergence of the Antigonish Movement, both in eastern Nova Scotia and elsewhere, is the gradual unravelling of the successful postwar economic system, which was based on a symbiosis between the public and private sectors. This system has worked eminently well, reducing the incentives to create an alternative by putting in place a social-welfare safety net that addresses the negative impacts of economic growth and expansion. This system has succeeded in satisfying the material needs of the majority of the population like never before but arguably at the expense of greater loss of control and increased powerlessness on the part of the population at large, leading to increased stress and uncertainty and undermining both collective creativity and a sense of community. In effect, the system has propagated something akin to Rev. Coady's notion of the "Great Default of the People." At the same time, inequities are becoming more pronounced and increasingly difficult to deal with through transfers and other redistributive programs, especially as these become more difficult to maintain. Arguably, this has set the stage for a weakening of the collective desire for continued sheer economic growth, with some of the main assumptions about the working of the system as a whole coming increasingly into question. In many ways, increased powerlessness, combined with the natural desire for greater meaning and purpose in life, constitutes an important precondition for the search for alternate economic systems. To some extent, at both the local and global levels, this search is manifested in outcomes such as environmentalism, human rights activism, and various aspects of antiglobalization, as well as in the protests that arise from these concerns.[9]

During the postwar years, government involvement in the economy through social programs, income-redistribution strategies, and regional equalization, development, and stabilization policies has been instrumental in keeping economic instability in check. Government-sponsored and -funded development initiatives and programs have also attempted to foster growth at the regional level. Indeed, as we noted above, the belief that economic development was a task more effectively undertaken by the government and the conventional free market was an important contributor to the decline of the Antigonish Movement. Despite the government intervention, inequalities between individuals, communities, and regions have persisted and proliferated. All have not shared equitably in postwar growth, and this inequality is becoming more pronounced as a consequence of the new economy, which has weakened the position of labour and added a great deal of risk, insecurity, stress, and uncertainty, particularly as a consequence of the mobility of capital and the rapid changes that are taking place in both the structure and organization of production. To these trends we can add the decline in the ability of governments to strengthen the social safety net and to meet the demands of the population. At the same time, economic decision making and control are becoming increasingly concentrated in a small number of large corporate entities, often far removed from where the people are, heightening the "Great Default." Moreover, the gap that exists between those who have the skills and other attributes to take advantage of the new global opportunities and those who do not is widening, creating an environment that is not benefiting a large segment of the population and hence is not working for them.[10]

To a great extent, the end of the twentieth century and the beginning of the twenty-first century have replicated, albeit in a vastly different socio-economic environment, the same basic initial conditions that prevailed in the 1920s in eastern Nova Scotia, namely industrial decline, the devastation of rural communities, and problems in the fisheries. In the current context, these conditions have arisen from the demise of coal and steel in the industrial heartland of Cape Breton, the abandonment of rural communities, and the collapse of the fisheries. As was the case in the 1920s, the prevailing system does not seem to be working for a large portion of the population. The time is perhaps ripe for the consideration of an alternate economic system along the lines of the original version of the Antigonish Movement.

THE ENDURING LEGACY OF THE ANTIGONISH MOVEMENT

Regardless of whether the Antigonish Movement is revived in the future – in its original form or in some novel form, in part or in its entirety – the movement's legacy is important and must be preserved. It must be preserved not only because of its fundamental impact on the region but also to motivate, inspire, and guide future grassroots movements. However, to preserve this legacy, we must first fully understand what the movement was all about and why it failed, and it is providing this understanding that has motivated the writing of this book.

The legacy of the Antigonish Movement, and indeed that of Rev. Moses Coady, Rev. Jimmy Tompkins, A.B. MacDonald, and the many other pioneers of the movement, is embedded not only in its achievement of putting in place a dynamic and integrated alternate economic system but also in its grand vision and holistic approach to life and the human condition. The movement was able to inspire dispirited, poverty-stricken, unschooled farmers, fishermen, and industrial workers to become empowered by engaging in and creating a network of economic institutions that they owned and controlled. In the process, it established a strong and vital link between education – which involved study and inquiry into alternate possibilities – and economic activity. The movement proved that the combination of studying and working in groups is a very effective vehicle for acquiring knowledge and mobilizing for economic action. It also demonstrated that a grassroots movement that was based on self-reliance, education, and economic cooperation and that was accessible to the poorest, most exploited, and most ignorant segments of the population could succeed and thrive through hard work, mutual respect, and adherence to a vision. Indeed, coming together, studying in groups, and acting jointly to implement economic activities constitute a very effective template for socio-economic development. So too does the broad-based notion of scientific thinking based on the use of knowledge in all of its attributes and on the abandonment of petty prejudices in order to improve the human condition not marginally but substantively by enabling people to become "Masters of Their Own Destiny."

Notes

CHAPTER ONE

1 On these economic movements, see, for example, Prinz, "German Rural Cooperatives"; MacLeod, *From Mondragon to America*; Whyte and Whyte, *Making Mondragon*; Wiener and Oakeshott, *Worker-Owners*; Thomas and Logan, *Mondragon*; and Boyle, *Poor Man's Prayer*. Economic movements have also emerged in the less developed countries. The latter include the much celebrated Grameen Bank in Bangladesh; see Yunus and Jolis, *Banker to the Poor*.

2 Ash, *Social Movements in America*, 1.

3 Indeed, in recent years there seems to have been a virtual explosion of social movements of various sorts and various spheres of influence. These range from lifestyle ones to esoteric religious cults. In part, their proliferation has been bolstered by the communication revolution and mass media, which have allowed many of these to achieve recognition while also providing them with a forum for pressing their demand for social change. In part, they are also a product of an increasingly fragmented society and of an existing social order that cannot accommodate the perceived needs and aspirations brought about by such fragmentation.

4 Religious movements can be traced back to very early times. For example, the emergence of Christianity, the Reformation, and the establishment of various denominations have had great influence on the development of Western countries. Moreover, this effect has been primarily apolitical, although there have been undeniable political outcomes. Similarly, intellectual movements such as those of the Renaissance and the Enlightenment also did not rely on political action. To some extent, the same holds true in the case of the Temperance Movement of the 1930s.

5 Symbolic actions such as marches, hunger strikes, and the blockage of highways normally result in immediate media attention, which magnifies their significance and emotional appeal. By comparison, establishing manufacturing plants, marketing activities, and the like is much more laborious and of longer duration, requiring substantial commitments of time and resources as well as careful assessment and cost-benefit analysis. Moreover, they have very little emotional appeal and are seldom the recipients of media attention and promotional assistance.

6 Most economic activities require a wide range of inputs as well as the existence and/or setting-up of infrastructure and all sorts of ancillary facilities. For example, resources and/or commodities usually need to be transported, which requires both good communication and good transportation. These requirements act as a critical constraint on economic activity and, moreover, are more likely to be met if the activity is concentrated within a region rather than within a national or international sphere. This is not to say that elements of a movement or a movement as a whole cannot be adopted in other parts of a country or by other countries.

7 Aside from Mondragon, the last wave of economic movements in Western countries occurred during the time of the Great Depression. Since then, in Canada and in other Western countries, there have been sporadic, widely dispersed, short-lived, and unsuccessful attempts falling far short of what we can term grassroots movements.

8 However, the general prosperity has not been equitably shared but has bypassed large groups of people and in some instances entire regions.

9 These objectives include greater economic security and are influenced by the notion that work and participation in the economy have their own intrinsic value, as reflected, for example, in Thorstein Veblen's "instinct for workmanship" and in what Paul Honigsheim refers to as "the work ethic." See Veblen, *Theory of the Leisure Class*, 29; and Honigsheim, *On Max Weber*, 114.

10 We should note that this is not necessarily the case in different manifestations of the cooperative sector as a whole. For example, Uma Lele laments "the top down nature of the movement and the consequent tendency of governments to form organizations without much regard to factors that are likely to influence a group's motivation to co-operate." See Lele, "Co-operatives and the Poor," 66.

11 See De Soto, *Mystery of Capital.*

12 For more details on the theory of economic rent and on rent-seeking behaviour, see, for example, Blaug, *Economic Theory in Retrospect*; and Krueger, "Political Economy."

13 The theoretical issues are straightforward and can be gleaned from most intermediate and advanced microeconomics textbooks.

14 Cooperation between groups is normally required to set up wholesale marketing or purchasing organizations, financial intermediation, and the like.

15 To ensure that such cooperation is maximized so that social welfare is enhanced, a vast array of institutional factors must normally be put in place. Thus to foster cooperation between buyers and sellers interacting in a market at arms length, there must be an apparatus offering some guarantee that contracts will be honoured, disputes settled, and adequate information made available.

16 According to the Economic Council of Canada, *From the Bottom Up*, 4, the supply-side initiatives would comprise the following:
- utilizing idle human and physical resources;
- expanding the community's resource base; and
- increasing the productivity of local resources.

17 In reality, there are various dimensions to economies of scale that need to be addressed. Economies may be internal to a firm or production unit, to a whole industry or sector, or to the economy of a region or country as a whole. In the first instance, the economies would arise simply as a result of the increased size or capacity of the individual firm or production unit. In simple economic terms, these economies reflect expansion of the size of the production unit along the negatively sloped segment of the long-run average cost curve until this expansion reaches the point where the average, or per unit, cost is at its lowest. In the other two instances, as a consequence of the expansion of economic activity around the individual firm or production unit, the whole cost structure of this activity shifts downward. Thus the cost reductions are shared by the entire industry or sector or by the economy as a whole.

18 See Olson, *Logic of Collective Action.*

19 Ibid., 62.

20 Ibid., esp. 64.

21 Closely linked to the free rider problem is the notion of the prisoner's dilemma. The prisoner's dilemma effect arises when there is uncertainty about how others will behave, leading to a suboptimal outcome as each individual tries to insure against the worst possible outcome. Like the free rider problem, the prisoner's dilemma effect normally works toward the dissolution of the group or collective. Just as it is not rational for individuals to pay for something that they may have access to anyway, so too is it not rational to incur sacrifices without any assurance that others, who also

share in the benefits, are doing likewise. The free rider and prisoner's dilemma problems have long been recognized, even if often only implicitly in the economic development literature, particularly within the context of efforts to generate capital through the mobilization of excess or idle labour, as discussed in the seminal work by Ragnar Nurkse, *Problems of Capital Formation*.

22 Essentially, the choice open to them is either to cooperate or to accept things as they are, which may entail continuous stagnation and impoverishment.

23 Here, we refer to the notion of perfect competition and the perfectly competitive market, which can be envisaged as involving a great deal of cooperation between suppliers and demanders carried out through the price mechanism.

24 See Smith, *Inquiry into the Nature*, 437–49. For additional discussion of the link between economics and moral philosophy, see, for example, Hausman and McPherson, *Economic Analysis*.

25 See, for example, Bruyn, *Civil Economy*; Powelson, *Moral Economy*; and Randall and Charlesworth, eds, *Moral Economy and Popular Protest*.

26 Our notion of wealth here is linked not to greed and accumulation for its own sake but to the notion of having access to all that is required to lead a "full and abundant life."

27 This is the sixth of the "Six Principles" of the Antigonish Movement, first articulated in Johnson, *Antigonish Movement*, 9.

28 This often occurred during periods of national economic decline, which hit some regions, usually those less advanced to begin with, particularly hard.

29 In the Spanish case, it was the military devastation created by the vicious civil war that precipitated the emergence of the movement.

30 The problem is also very much in evidence in less developed countries, particularly in the context of the very rapid rural-urban migration usually to a small number of large cities, where much modern formal economic activity and investment, both public and private, takes place.

31 Arguably, some transfer would take place but only up to some social and/or political minimum.

32 The latter is interesting in view of the extensive uses of collectivization employed under communism. However, since everything is established and enforced from the top, these do not constitute grassroots approaches.

33 The role of the political apparatus is of particular importance to present-day less developed countries, where dictatorships, of various sorts, are still common. Dictatorial systems seldom permit independent economic movements

to arise and flourish. What exists at the grassroots level in these countries, therefore, is generally under full government control and essentially a government policy tool. Independent economic activity of any consequence is normally perceived as a threat to the power of the regime. Although, in principle, countries with some degree of democracy should be more receptive to grassroots activities, this is often not the case due to the instability and fragility of such democratic governments. Again, these governments tend to view grassroots movements either as potential threats, which are to be discouraged, or as potentially useful tools for gaining popular support, which are to be controlled. In either case, the political and social barriers that exist to both the emergence and working of grassroots movements in less developed countries are great. Moreover, they are far from being the only problem.

34 Related to this sort of nonformal education is what John Simmons refers to as education for self-reliance. According to Simmons, this type of education "teaches groups of people how to study together and become aware of the political and economic determinants of their poverty. They learn how to organize themselves to improve their own circumstances, and in the process they learn to build roads, manage water distribution, reduce neighbourhood crime and grow more food. Individual groups select members to be trained as paramedics and teachers. Through co-operative saving, they reduce their dependence on the moneylenders." See Simmons, "Education and Development," 264.

35 Such infrastructure serves not only to facilitate economic activity but also to counter or weaken monopolistic tendencies on the part of economic agents.

36 See, for example, Tompkins, *Knowledge for the People*; Coady, *Masters of Their Own Destiny*; and Freire, *Pedagogy of the Oppressed*.

CHAPTER TWO

1 The movement also spread to other parts of the Maritimes as well as Newfoundland.

2 See Cameron, *For the People*; MacInnes, *Clerics, Fishermen*; Campbell and MacLean, *Beyond the Atlantic Roar*; Campbell, *Compassion on the Multitude*; and Coutinho, *Community Development*. There were also black and Aboriginal communities, in addition to English and other groups mainly of European backgrounds.

3 For more information about these remarkable men, see especially Arnold, *Father Jimmy*; Boyle, *Father Tompkins*; Lotz and Welton, *Father Jimmy*; Lotz,

Humble Giant; MacLellan, *Coady Remembered*; Laidlaw, ed., *Man from Margaree*; and Welton, *Little Mosie*.

4 See, for example, Cameron, *For the People*; and Campbell, *Compassion on the Multitude*. As P.J. MacKenzie Campbell suggests, in the case of the Scots – the Highland settlers – the possibility that they could own land, something denied them in Scotland, was an important consideration.

5 See Cameron, *For the People*.

6 The Acadians also settled along the western shores of Nova Scotia as well as in Prince Edward Island and New Brunswick.

7 For a comprehensive survey of St Francis Xavier University from its inception in 1853 until 1970, see Cameron, *For the People*.

8 The favourable demand conditions were also affected by the Crimean War (1854–56) and by the Civil War in the United States (1961–64).

9 See Conrad and Hiller, *Atlantic Canada*, 101–4.

10 See Norrie and Owram, *History of the Canadian Economy*, 377, 379.

11 See ibid. 379.

12 Conrad and Hiller, *Atlantic Canada*, 104.

13 The importance of linking the Maritimes to potential North American market areas had been realized for some time, particularly in the context of fostering greater North-South trade under Reciprocity. On this issue, see, for example, Conrad and Hiller, *Atlantic Canada*, 115. The main obstacle was finance. For more details, see also Norrie and Owram, *History of the Canadian Economy*, 299–300.

14 On this situation, see, for example, Conrad and Hiller, *Atlantic Canada*, 122–3.

15 Ibid., 124.

16 In contrast, Conrad and Hiller, *Atlantic Canada*, 127, suggest that opponents of Confederation "tended to look east and south – to the North Atlantic, Britain, the oceanic trades and the promising American market – whereas supporters of Confederation looked west, seeing the future in economic integration with the central provinces and expansion to the Pacific."

17 On this decline, see, for example, Acheson, "National Policy"; and Conrad and Hiller, *Atlantic Canada*, 129, who note that "shipbuilding gradually declined into insignificance" as iron and steam increased in prominence.

18 Conrad and Hiller, *Atlantic Canada*, 129.

19 Although the notion that freight rates were established to promote the interests of the region still has wide currency, it has not gone unchallenged; see, for example, Cruikshank, "Intercolonial Railway." Acheson, "National

Policy," also notes the problem of the relatively high freight rates and the general failure to get the government to lower them.

20 Forbes, *Challenging the Regional Stereotype*, 118. See also Conrad and Hiller, *Atlantic Canada*, 131.

21 Forbes, *Challenging the Regional Stereotype*, 118.

22 Conrad and Hiller, *Atlantic Canada*, 131.

23 See Heron, *Working in Steel*, 16; and Conrad and Hiller, *Atlantic Canada*, 131–2.

24 The bulk of the central Canadian market was being supplied by the United States. See Conrad and Hiller, *Atlantic Canada*, 131.

25 Ibid., 132. For a more detailed discussion of this issue, see Inwood, "Maritime Industrialization"; and Alexander, "Economic Growth."

26 See Acheson, "National Policy," 103–5.

27 See Savoie, *Visiting Grandchildren*, esp. 31–3.

28 See Conrad and Hiller, *Atlantic Canada*, 131. Here, Margaret Conrad and James Hiller suggest that "Maritimers were well-placed to meet the demand for fish, both fresh and frozen, from the United States and central Canada, primarily because of improvements in railway connections and refrigeration technology."

29 See Norrie and Owram, *History of the Canadian Economy*, 379.

30 See Conrad and Hiller, *Atlantic Canada*, 150.

31 See ibid.

32 Ibid.

33 For more details, see Frank, "Cape Breton Coal Industry."

34 On this situation, see, for example, Inwood, "Maritime Industrialization."

35 Ken Cruikshank, "Intercolonial Railway," 192, questions the role of freight rates and the overall importance of the intercolonial railway. Nevertheless, he also argues that the freight rate structure of the intercolonial railway did allow Maritime shippers "to penetrate the larger markets of Central Canada" and that, as a result of the higher rates in the postwar period, "they faced increased barriers" to accessing these markets.

36 See Forbes, *Challenging the Regional Stereotype*, esp. 123; Savoie, *Visiting Grandchildren*, 35; and Conrad and Hiller, *Atlantic Canada*, 165.

37 As pointed out by Acheson, "National Policy," 108, the Nova Scotia Steel and Coal Corporation "represented the most fully integrated industrial complex in the country" at the end of the nineteenth century.

38 For more detail on the role of immigrants in the Canadian steel industry, see Heron, *Working in Steel*.

39 For example, Sowder, *Present Status*, 22–3, notes that in the period 1891–1931 the population of eastern Nova Scotia declined by 26,607 – from 131,886 in 1891 to 105,279 in 1931. In the same vein, Coady and associates, *Antigonish Way*, 1, state that "in one fifty-year period Eastern Canada has lost four hundred and fifty thousand of its people to other parts of America." On this issue, see also Cameron, *For the People*, among others.

40 Thornton, "Problem of Out-Migration," provides a good summary of the effects of out-migration. Conrad and Hiller, *Atlantic Canada*, 135, note that "Out-migration was both an effect and a cause of the region's shaky economic performance."

41 See, for example, MacInnes, *Clerics, Fishermen*; Sacouman, *Social Origins* and "Underdevelopment,"; Mifflen, *Antigonish Movement*; Coady, *Masters of Their Own Destiny*; Coady and associates, *Antigonish Way*; and Sowder, *Present Status*.

42 For a similar approach, see Dodaro and Pluta, *Antigonish Movement as a Model*; and Dodaro, Pluta, and Amoako-Tuffour, *Relevance of the Human Factor.*

43 See, among others, Lotz and Welton, *Father Jimmy*; and Delaney, *By Their Own Hands*.

44 McKay and Morton, "Maritimes," 53.

45 As pointed out in McCann, "Mercantile-Industrial Transition," 32, "Glace Bay, New Waterford, Stellarton, Westville, and Springhill were essentially the products of externally controlled corporations."

46 The charge has sometimes been levelled that local financiers and entrepreneurs ignored local opportunities in order to take advantage of opportunities elsewhere, partly underestimating the potential of the region. See, among others, McCann, "Mercantile-Industrial Transition"; Frank, "Cape Breton Coal Industry"; Forbes, *Maritime Rights Movement*; and Inwood, "Maritime Industrialization".

47 See, for example, McKay and Morton, "Maritimes," 73–5; and Conrad and Hiller, *Atlantic Canada*.

48 Campbell, *Compassion on the Multitude*, 6, notes that "As conditions changed, quantity, or even quality, in farm animals and other productive phases of farming, didn't provide adequately for increasing necessities ... the matter of purchasing farm- machinery, clothing and other factory-produced articles became increasingly important, and income couldn't match the demand." In the agricultural sector, the drover system prevailed, whereby the farmers had little bargaining power or control over prices; see ibid., 7.

49 Campbell, ibid., 6, refers to a host of poor practices that led to the depletion of the soil. There were also problems getting farm produce to potential markets, especially for those who were some distance away. Here, Campbell further notes that there was "no established or practical avenue through which farm products could be marketed profitably." In addition, he alludes to issues concerning the notions of ownership and control that may have had a negative effect on the ability and/or willingness of people to take fuller advantage of their resources.

50 "Monopsony" refers to the case where there is a single buyer, whereas "monopoly" refers to the case where there is a single seller or supplier. Monopsony is associated with low prices for what is being sold – in this case, farm produce. Monopoly is associated with high prices for what is being bought.

51 See, among others, Campbell, *Compassion on the Multitude*, 11–12.

52 See, for example, MacPherson, "Patterns"; and MacPherson, *Each for All.*

53 See, for example, Croteau, *Cradled in the Waves*.

54 Arguably, the political system did not work very well for the rest of Canada either, especially with the onset of the Great Depression.

55 However, there were some tensions, particularly along religious, cultural, and linguistic lines.

56 On the state of the roads and the precariousness of winter travel, see, among others, Delaney, *By Their Own Hands*; and MacDonald, *Memoirs*.

57 See Cameron, *"And Martha Served."*

58 The same also held true of clergymen from other denominations such as J.D. Nelson MacDonald, who was a United Church minister. See MacDonald, *Memoirs.*

59 Thus Lotz and Whelton, "Knowledge for the People," Cameron, *For the People*, and others note that Rev. Tompkins was influenced by Bishop O'Dwyer of Ireland, as well as being familiar with the Danish Folk School concept, the Swedish Discussion Circles, and many other approaches.

60 See Forbes, *Challenging the Regional Stereotype*, 16–20.

61 On the spread of unionization, see, for example, McKay and Morton, "Maritimes," 50.

62 See ibid., 54–5.

63 See ibid., 68–71.

64 See, among others, Alexander, *Antigonish Movement*, 67; and Cameron, *For the People*, 151. Rev. Coady and Rev. Dr Hugh MacPherson were also prominent leaders in the Forward Movement.

65 See, among others, Alexander, *Antigonish Movement*, 67; and Cameron, *For the People*, 167–9.

66 MacPherson, a priest-professor at St Francis Xavier University, was appointed as an agricultural fieldworker in 1915 and did much to promote the cooperative approach. For details on Rev. MacPherson's contribution, see, among others, Alexander, *Antigonish Movement*; Cameron, *For the People*; Coutinho, *Community Development*; and Campbell, *Compassion on the Multitude*. MacPherson remained a force in promoting the rural sector, especially through the adoption of more efficient production methods and practices; see, for example, MacPherson, *Kitchen Chats on Farming*.

67 See, for example, Forbes, *Maritime Rights Movement*; Cameron, *For the People*.

68 See, for example, Forbes, *Challenging the Regional Stereotype*, 126–7; and Savoie, *Visiting Grandchildren*, 36.

69 See Savoie, *Visiting Grandchildren*, 36–9.

70 See, among others, Forbes, *Maritime Rights Movement*.

71 See Alexander, *Antigonish Movement*, 33.

72 See, Alexander, *Antigonish Movement*, 72–3; and Cameron, *For the People*, 166. Coady, *My Story*, 13, paid tribute to this organization and its leader, Rev. Michael Gillis, as "the real author of the Extension Department."

73 The importance of existing local conditions is clearly articulated by Coady, *My Story*, 16, particularly in his advice to those from elsewhere who were interested in the movement to "go home and find your lobster."

74 Indeed, the process never really stopped even during the 1930s.

75 This notion was popularized especially through pamphlets and broadcasts. See, for example, Coady and associates, *Antigonish Way*; Coady and associates, *Antigonish Way: A Series of Broadcasts*; and Anselm, *Antigonish Idea*. Moreover, over time, it was used to imply different things.

76 It was based on the Danish People's Schools. See Cameron, *For the People*, 171.

77 For details concerning the first People's School, see Alexander, *Antigonish Movement*, 68–9; and Cameron, *For the People*, 169–72.

78 This development reflected the view that had often been expressed by Rev. Tompkins, both before and after the publication of his *Knowledge for the People*. It helped that this view was shared by many others as well.

79 See, for example, Alexander, *Antigonish Movement*, 71. These conferences played an important role in the establishment of the Antigonish Movement and also in its early success in the 1930s.

80 An example of this clarity of purpose is the experience of Rev. Tompkins in Canso, as described by Lotz and Welton, *Father Jimmy*.

81 For details about Rev. Tompkins's work in Canso, see ibid., among others. On Coady's work in Margaree, see, for example, Coady, *Masters of Their Own Destiny*, 10; and Coady, *My Story*, 10.

82 The Rochale Principles can be stated as follows: (1) democratic control (one member, one vote), (2) open membership, (3) quality goods at current market prices, (4) division of profits on a patronage basis, (5) limited rate of interest, (6) strict religious and political neutrality, and (7) education of members and non-members; see O'Hearn Cameron, "Birthday of the People's Business." Boyle, *Democracy's Second Chance*, 152–74, provides slightly different wording: (1) one man, one vote, (2) fixed rate of interest on capital, (3) goods shall be sold for cash, (4) goods shall be sold at the market price, (5) patronage dividends, (6) political and religious neutrality, and (7) funds are to be set aside and used for education.

83 See, for example, Boyle, *Poor Man's Prayer*.

84 As Ida Delaney points out in *25c a Week*, her pamphlet on the Coady Credit Union, the study club that organized this union studied subjects such as credit union legislation, the Credit Union Movement in Germany, the United States, and Quebec, and the Rochdale Principles.

85 It may also be argued that the period should in fact be specified as that between 1921 and 1930 since the Extension Department did not actually come into effect with its programs until 1930, even though it was established in 1928.

86 Tompkins had been advocating this view for some time in various writings, as is made clear in Lotz and Welton, *Father Jimmy*, among others. However, it was the first formal articulation of this view in the form of a pamphlet.

87 For some interesting details concerning the first People's School, see, for example, ibid.

88 Rev. Tompkins was transferred as a consequence of his championing of university amalgamation, not because of his social activism. On this issue, see Cameron, *For the People*; and Lotz and Welton, *Father Jimmy*.

89 Coady, *Masters of Their Own Destiny*, 8.

90 As is pointed out in Lotz and Welton, "Knowledge for the People," and elsewhere, Tompkins and others read and studied these encyclicals and were heavily influenced by them. This was the case especially with *Rerum Novarum*, as it was published prior to both Tompkins's and Coady's studies in Rome. Their studies in Rome also provided Tompkins and Coady with access to the many ideas in circulation at the time.

91 See Coady, *My Story*, 10.

92 For a restatement of this notion, see Coady, *Masters of Their Own Destiny*, 17–29.

93 However, the contributions by Tompkins, Coady, MacPherson, and others to this process can be traced back to the previous decade – in the case of Tompkins, at least to as early as 1912. See, for example, Alexander, *Antigonish Movement*; Lotz and Welton, *Father Jimmy*; and Cameron, *For the People*.

94 Delaney, *By Their Own Hands*, 99.

95 Johnson, *Antigonish Movement*, 6–9.

96 See Coady, *Social Significance*.

97 Delaney, *By Their Own Hands*, 103–4.

98 As Delaney, ibid., 21, points out, Coady believed that "adult education had to result in the rise of institutions."

99 See, among many others, Cameron, *For the People*; Lotz and Welton, *Father Jimmy*; and Alexander, *Antigonish Movement*.

100 The initial staff when the Extension Department became operational consisted of Rev. Coady and A.B. MacDonald, who was hired as associate director.

101 The MacLean Commission had been instigated by Rev. Tompkins in Canso to bring the plight of the fishermen to the attention of the government. For details, see Lotz and Welton, *Father Jimmy*, among others.

102 According to Alexander, *Antigonish Movement*, 83, "the United Maritime Fishermen paved the way for a future partnership." For some early history of this cooperative, see Donovan, *Sharing the Catch*.

103 On the contribution made by A.B. MacDonald, see, among others, Alexander, *Antigonish Movement*; and Delaney, *By Their Own Hands*.

104 Lotz and Welton, *Father Jimmy*. Similar sentiments were expressed by other leaders of the movement, especially Rev. Coady.

105 On this point, see, among others, Lotz and Welton, "Knowledge for the People"; and Lotz and Welton, *Father Jimmy*. Coady had also applied the concept in Margaree in the 1920s, as we pointed out above.

106 Indeed, as early as 1930, the Extension Department put out a pamphlet on the study clubs. This pamphlet, which was periodically reissued and revised, provided basic guidelines on the operations of the study clubs. It covered areas such as the purpose of the clubs, membership, officers, time and place of meetings, what to study, how to study, general regulations, and suggestions for study club leaders.

107 See, among others, MacPherson, "Patterns"; MacPherson, "Appropriate Forms"; and MacSween, *History of Nova Scotia*.

108 See MacPherson, "Patterns."

109 For additional discussion of pertinent issues, see MacPherson, "Patterns," "Appropriate Forms," *Each for All*, and *Co-operative Movement*.

110 For example, Delaney, *25c a Week*, points out that acceptance of the benefits that could accrue from the formation of a credit union was facilitated by the fact that the British Columbia Co-operative Society already operated a large general store in Glace Bay.

111 See, for example, Flannery, *Economic Evaluation*, 14; and Moody and Fite, *Credit Union Movement*, 1–25. The American Credit Union Movement was also influenced by the Raiffeisen–Schultze Credit Cooperative Movement of Germany, among others.

112 The credit union in Antigonish is in fact called Bergengren, in honour of Roy Bergengren, the American credit union pioneer.

113 However, the social dimensions were also close to the surface. On this situation, see, for example, Anselm, *Antigonish Idea*; and St Francis Xavier University Extension Department, *Social Significance*.

114 That is, the Antigonish Movement was revolutionary as opposed to evolutionary, as suggested, for example, by Lotz, "Antigonish Movement"; and Lotz, "Historical and Social Setting."

115 For the often cited story of Little Dover, see, for example, Coady, *Masters of Their Own Destiny*, 49.

116 In any event, the outside resources to which the masses would have had access were very limited. The assumption here is that substantial resources did in fact exist, which is consistent with the much more recent argument by De Soto, *Mystery of Capital*.

117 For example, lawyers, doctors, consultants, and a wide array of experts are able to earn a comfortable living by selling services based on the knowledge that they possess.

118 Coady, *Masters of Their Own Destiny*, 17. This quotation is also cited in Arnold, *Father Jimmy*, inside cover.

119 The notion of group entrepreneurship is not new in itself. However, it is generally associated with large-scale conglomerates rather than with the small and essentially grassroots types envisaged as parts of the Antigonish Movement. According to Leff, "Entrepreneurship and Development," 52, "the 'Group' is a large scale firm that invests and produces in several product lines that involve vertical integration or other economic and technological complementarities." The issue is captured forcefully in Coady, *Masters of Their Own Destiny*, 25: "If it is lawful for seven men to form a joint stock company and obtain a charter for commercial purposes, there is no reason that is should not be right for seven hundred, seven thousand, or even seven million to do the same!"

120 See, among others, Hagen, *Economics of Development*.

121 As Delaney, *By Their Own Hands*, 44–5, points out, "The most important function of the Associated Study Clubs was to prepare the way for organizing credit unions and other co-operatives. When the decision was made to start a credit union the Associated Study Clubs meeting became the forum where all questions were answered and all details were planned. It was the Associated Study Clubs meeting that appointed a provisional board of directors, charged with the duty of obtaining a charter, drawing up by-laws and planning the first annual meeting of the new credit union."

122 See, for example, ibid., 43–4.

123 For some formal economic analysis of cooperatives, see, for example, Bonin and Putterman, *Economics of Co-operation*; Bonin, Jones, and Putterman, "Theoretical and Empirical Studies"; and Helm and Ushirika, *Economics of Co-operative Enterprise*. For a discussion within the development context, see, for example, Thordarson *Banking on the Grass Roots*.

124 This is similar to the process suggested within the context of developing countries by, for example, Nurkse, *Problems of Capital Formation*.

125 See, for example, Coady, *Masters of Their Own Destiny.*

126 Delaney, *25c a Week*, for example, describes elements of all three methods.

127 On these informal forces, see, for example, Mancur Olson's seminal *The Logic of Collective Action*.

128 In some cases, there was a doubling of the incomes earned by the movement's members over the period of one year.

129 The issue of whether to allow purchases on credit was a contentious one that plagued some of the organizations well into the 1960s.

130 See MacDonald, "Credit Union and Cash Trading."

131 See Mckay and Morton, "Maritimes," 57.

132 George Keen, quoted in Neal, *Brotherhood Economics*, 66.

133 Without Rev. Coady, Rev. Tompkins, A.B. MacDonald, and the other early leaders, the movement would not have taken off as it did.

134 These visitors included, for example, correspondents of prestigious newspapers such as the *New York Times* and the *Times of London* and many other well-known individuals. See Cameron, *For the People*.

135 The negative effects of downplaying the role and importance of education were recognized even as early as the late 1930s, as can be gauged from Delaney, *25c a Week*.

136 On this approach within the context of Prince Edward Island, see, for example, Croteau, *Cradled in the Waves*.

137 Nevertheless, we need to recognize the importance of other factors that played a role. In particular, there was the presence of legislation that covered

housing within a certain price range, and then there was the donation of land by Rev. Tompkins, who had been transferred to Reserve Mines in 1935 and soon set about stirring things up. No doubt, therefore, there was an important providential component at work, including the contribution by Mary Arnold, a noted American cooperative pioneer who was instrumental in the emergence of Tompkinsville. See, among others, Coady, *Masters of Their Own Destiny*, 77–80; Arnold, *Story of Tompkinsville*; Ward, *Nova Scotia*, 96–110; Boyle, *Father Tompkins*; and Lotz and Welton, *Father Jimmy*, 137–50.

138 See, for example, Fowler, *Lord Helps Those*.

139 These included primarily the standard backward, forward, and final demand linkages, which set up the sorts of growth impulses suggested, for example, by Hirschman, *Strategy of Economic Development*.

140 New ventures also produced this effect simply by creating new and generally obvious economic opportunities.

141 Tompkins's handling of the reports of stealing among his parishioners in Little Dover illustrates this concern most eloquently. See, for example, Lotz and Welton *Father Jimmy*, esp. 69–70.

142 This approach is evident in Coady, *Masters of Their Own Destiny*, as well as in the writings of the other early leaders of the movement.

143 Ibid., 163.

144 See Carroll, *Influence of H.H. Stevens*, 11.

145 The party emerged spontaneously shortly after Stevens left the Conservative Party, and although it had a fifteen-point program (the Reconstruction Manifesto), it lacked not only resources and organization but also a clear vision or platform that would appeal to all of its target groups. Moreover, even Stevens often referred to it as a movement rather than a party. See Carroll, *Influence of H.H. Stevens*.

146 Ibid., 116. Fishermen were also included in the category of forgotten men.

147 This evidence emerged from the price spread probe undertaken over the 1934–35 period, first as a select commission (i.e., the House of Commons Select Committee on Price Spreads and Mass Buying) and then as a royal commission (i.e., the Royal Commission on Price Spreads and Mass Buying), both of which were instigated by Stevens while he was still with the Conservative Party. See Carroll, *Influence of H.H. Stevens*.

148 The main recommendations of the Royal Commission on Price Spreads and Mass Buying are listed in ibid., esp. 104–13. The shelving of these recommendations precipitated Stevens's resignation from the Conservative Party.

149 See ibid., 192–4.

150 In fact, nationwide only Stevens managed to win a seat, getting reelected in the British Columbia riding that he had held as a member of the Conservative Party.

151 Although Stevens paid tribute to Coady and his work during his campaigning in eastern Nova Scotia and although there is no doubt that participants in the early work of the Atigonish Movement were sympathetic to the Reconstruction Party (in fact, one of the early fieldworkers of the Extension Department, the United Church minister J.D. Nelson Macdonald, was nominated as a Reconstruction Party candidate), there was no allegiance between the two. Coady had made it clear, especially in his submission to the Royal Commission on Price Spreads and Mass Buying, that the plight of the fishermen and other primary producers could be alleviated only through cooperation, not through government action. See Carroll, *Influence of H.H. Stevens*.

CHAPTER THREE

1 See, for example, Fowler, *Lord Helps Those*; and Ward, *Nova Scotia*.

2 See Coady, *Masters of Their Own Destiny*, 105–9.

3 See ibid., esp. 30–41. Ida Delaney writes, "the mass meeting was the place to explode the intellectual dynamite that would break up apathy and prejudice, shock the people out of their complacency and fire them with enthusiasm to rebuild society"; see Delaney, *By Their Own Hands*, 23. This approach reflects what John Tougas Croteau refers to as the "rawhide lash" one, intended to shake people out of their complacency. Croteau also argues that such a method can be effective only if employed by someone of "great personal prestige" or someone "who was well known to the group." Arguably, the early leaders of the Antigonish Movement who addressed the mass meetings, particularly Rev. Coady, can be said to have possessed both attributes. Croteau also suggests that in the case of outsiders, the more gentle "shot in the arm" approach would be more effective; see Croteau, *Cradled in the Waves*, 22.

4 See Coady, *Masters of Their Own Destiny*, 31. Rev. Coady's notion of scientific thinking was a broad one. It referred not only to the acceptance of scientific ideas and new technologies but also to thinking based on logic and reason rather than on superstition, biases, and accepted practices. Thus it was also used to fight against bigotry, intolerance, and parochialism. He further used the term as a defence against the accusation, particularly by other members of the clergy, that the movement was pursuing crass materialism.

5 See ibid., 42.

6 In 1937 the responsibility was assumed by associated study club executives. In 1938 the organization and reorganization of study clubs was passed on to officers of cooperative organizations. See St Francis Xavier University Archives (SFXUA), RG 30.3/25/975–976.

7 Delaney, *By Their Own Hands*, 35, points out, "Prospective leaders were told that their role was simply to be the link between the study club and the Extension Department, to receive and distribute literature and to report on the progress of the club. In practice, the leader was expected to take charge of the meeting and to lead in the discussion."

8 See Coady, *Masters of Their Own Destiny*, 43–4.

9 Ibid., 44.

10 Ibid., 43.

11 See ibid., 49. Rev. Tompkins provided a $300 loan and arranged for another loan of $700 at low interest; see Lotz and Welton, *Father Jimmy*, 98; and Fowler, *Lord Helps Those*, 43–4. To indicate the success of the venture, Bertram Fowler notes that "At the end of the season ... they found that they had enough money to pay off the $1,000 borrowed and return an extra two cents a pound to the individual fishermen"; see Fowler, *Lord Helps Those*, 44.

12 Coady, *Masters of Their Own Destiny*, 51. Interestingly, this project was also instigated by the parish priest Rev. James Boyle, who was also a former professor at the university.

13 Ibid.

14 See ibid., 52.

15 This figure represented a collective increase of an estimated $7,000 for the thirty-five fishermen involved compared to what "they would have received if they had to rely upon an independent packer for the canning and sale of their lobsters." See SFXUA, RG 30.3/25/910a.

16 See Delaney, *25c a Week*, 10–11, 14.

17 See ibid., 18.

18 Ibid., 18–19. In 1938 economic disaster hit the community, with miners unable to get even one shift per week for extended periods of time. Yet their cooperative bank not only survived but also continued to thrive.

19 See MacDonald, *Memoirs*, 64–5.

20 Ibid., 65.

21 Ibid.

22 See Coady, *My Story*, 20.

23 See Coady, *Masters of Their Own Destiny*, 47.

24 See ibid., 48–9.

25 See, among others, ibid.; and Campbell, *Compassion on the Multitude*.
26 See Neal, *Brotherhood Economics*, 141–2.
27 See ibid., 149.
28 See SFXUA, RG 30.3/25/968.
29 See MacInnes, *Clerics, Fishermen*, 237.
30 Coady, *Masters of Their Own Destiny*, 10, refers to the "willingness of the more intelligent members of the group to place their abilities at the disposal of the slower members."
31 Cameron, *For the People*, 224, reports a range between 39 and 145 over the 1932–40 period.
32 See, among others, ibid., esp. 224.
33 This funding was introduced with the passing of the Regional Libraries Act in 1937 by the provincial government. See, for example, Lotz and Welton, *Father Jimmy*, 132.
34 See Mathews, *Jobs of Our Own*, 6. As Race Mathews points out here, the doctrine dictates "that a higher body should not assume on behalf of a lower body functions that the lower body is able to perform for itself."
35 See Dutcher, "'Big Business,'" 65–8.
36 See ibid., esp. 75–98.
37 See ibid., 85. Interestingly, McEwen, *Faith, Hope*, 31, identifies 1944 as the date of the official name change.
38 Walsh, *We Fought*.
39 See SFXUA, RG 30.3/25/1009, RG 30.3/25/1014.
40 On the MacLean Commission, see chapter 2, note 100.
41 Nevertheless, there was a great deal of overlap involving not only guidelines provided by the Extension Department but also some common study issues such as the Rochdale Principles on cooperation.
42 Quoted in Walsh, *We Fought*, 83; and in Lotz and Welton, *Father Jimmy*, 87.
43 The fisheries unions that were in place were both weak and ineffective.
44 This work included instigating the agitation that led to the MacLean Commission. See, among others, Lotz and Welton, *Father Jimmy*; and Fowler, *Lord Helps Those*.
45 On this disposition of the fisheries sector within the context of Prince Edward Island, but with application to the whole sector, see Croteau, *Cradled in the Waves*.
46 Coady, *Masters of Their Own Destiny*, 87.
47 See Coady, *My Story*, 16. See also Coady, *Masters of Their Own Destiny*, 105.
48 See SFXUA, RG 30.3/25/985. Coady, *Masters of Their Own Destiny*, 46–53, pro-

vides a description of how the various cooperatives were established and the role played in each case by the various parish priests.

49 Coady, *Masters of Their Own Destiny*, 102.

50 Cooperative lobster-canning plants were also established in New Brunswick and Prince Edward Island. Coady, ibid., 102, suggests that by 1938 eastern Nova Scotia and north-eastern New Brunswick had a combined total of thirty-five cooperative lobster-canning plants.

51 Ibid., 103.

52 See, for example, ibid., 99–101.

53 See SFXUA, RG 30.3/25/899.

54 Nevertheless, not all problems in the fisheries were resolved. See, for example, MacSween, "Problems of the Fishing Industry."

55 See Walsh, *We Fought*, 28, as well as Campbell, *Compassion on the Multitude*, 9, among others.

56 For a discussion of some of the benefits, see Coady, *Masters of Their Own Destiny*, 92.

57 See Walsh, *We Fought*, 38; and McEwen, *Faith, Hope*, 2.

58 Coady, *Masters of Their Own Destiny*, 90.

59 On this point, see ibid., 92–4.

60 Ibid., 93.

61 Ibid.

62 See ibid., 98.

63 SFXUA, RG 30.3/25/910a.

64 Ibid.

65 A similar pattern also characterized their expansion in both New Brunswick and Prince Edward Island, which had seventy-nine and thirty-seven credit unions respectively near the end of the decade. See SFXUA, RG 30.3/25/1016.

66 The same issue was addressed later by Hirschman, *Strategy of Economic Development*, and much later still by De Soto, *Mystery of Capital*, who refers to vast amounts of capital lying essentially dormant that can be mobilized, in his view, through the establishment of an appropriate legal framework for property rights.

67 See Coady, *Masters of Their Own Destiny*, 84–8.

68 See ibid., esp. 69–74.

69 This view is consistent with the much later work on the pattern of development that was undertaken by Kuznets, *Modern Economic Growth*, and later by Chenery and Syrquin, *Patterns of Development*, among others.

70 Coady, *Masters of Their Own Destiny*, 75.

71 The first cooperative store in Canada was in fact established in 1861 in Stellarton; see Lotz and Welton, "Knowledge for the People." The British Canadian Co-operative Society established its first outlet based on the Rochdale Principles in Sydney Mines in 1906; see Campbell, *Compassion on the Multitude*, 33.

72 Coady, *Masters of Their Own Destiny*, 76.

73 The issue of cash trading was one that was never fully resolved and continued to be a source of tension for some time.

74 This was an initiative of the cooperative store in the rural community of St Andrews, just outside Antigonish. It was instituted in 1937 and seems to have had some success. See SFXUA, RG 30.3/25/975; and Coady, *Masters of Their Own Destiny*, 77.

75 Especially important here was the provision, under the instigation of Rev. Tompkins, that of the $500 required to build cooperative housing, $400 could be in the form of "sweat capital." For more details, see, for example, Lotz and Welton, *Father Jimmy*, 138–9.

76 Coady, *Masters of Their Own Destiny*, 44.

CHAPTER FOUR

1 Whereas the First World War was based on trench warfare fought by huge armies of foot soldiers, the Second World War involved highly mobile and mechanized approaches to land, sea, and air combat. The military equipment employed was of unprecedented complexity, sophistication, and size, involving panzer divisions of mobile tanks, squadrons of bombers and fighter planes, fleets of battleships, air carriers, and the like. Financing such a war also required a radical departure from the past, with important consequences for the economy both during and after the war years. Canada's war effort had to be financed entirely by Canadians through a combination of taxation, domestic borrowing on the bond market, and as Graig McIvor attests, "the development of an unprecedented variety of direct government controls"; see McIvor, *Canadian Monetary*, 165. For a comprehensive overview of the financial and other economic aspects of financing the war, see ibid., 165–201.

2 See, for example, Cameron, *For the People*, 246. Arguably, the state of events may have prevented the Extension Department from being co-opted by the federal Department of Fisheries at a very early stage.

3 This success can be gleaned from numerous accounts, including Delaney, *By Their Own Hands*.

4 For example, Cameron, *For the People*, 260, cites Alexander Laidlaw's estimate that "the business of Nova Scotia's consumer cooperatives rose from about $2.5 million in 1939 to over $4.5 million in 1944." This is consistent with the experience of consumers' cooperatives in the country as a whole. On this subject, see, for example, MacPherson, *Building and Protecting*.

5 St Francis Xavier University Archives (SFXUA), RG 30.3/25/1019, emphasis added.

6 SFXUA, *Scrapbooks*, 1943. Rev. Coady was joined by W.G. Good, representing the Co-operative Union of Canada, and by H.L. Fowler, representing the view from Saskatchewan, in presenting briefs before the Canadian federal government; see MacPherson, *Building and Protecting*, 117–18.

7 For a discussion of the effort mounted by the cooperative sector, see MacPherson, *Building and Protecting*. The Extension Department also participated in the process by preparing a brief highlighting the fundamental nature and importance of cooperation within the framework of the Antigonish Movement; see Coady, *Social Significance*.

8 For example, Delaney, *By Their Own Hands*, 39, notes, "It is a striking fact that many of the charter members, directors and officers of the credit unions, were in their early twenties."

9 Urquhart and Buckley, eds, *Historical Statistics*, F-88, R-17.

10 See, for example, McIvor, *Canadian Monetary*. To the extent that these savings were directed at the war effort, they would not have been available to local cooperative activities. Nevertheless, they contributed to the rush of economic activity that accompanied the war effort.

11 In economic terms, the costs – including opportunity costs – of engaging in study were increased, whereas its relative benefits were decreased.

12 Indeed, in searching for a middle way, the leaders of the Antigonish Movement were particularly aware of the dangers that these totalitarian systems posed, even in the context of the chaotic 1930s when all sorts of well-intentioned people were duped by one side or the other. The encyclicals *Rerum Novarum* and *Quadragesimo Anno* provided a very important sense of direction.

13 The war, in particular, had laid bare the shortcomings of both systems, although in the case of communism, the full evidence of its massive failings came later.

14 The Nova Scotia Co-operative Union was incorporated under the Co-operative Associations Act of 1949. It was preceded by the formation of a cooper-

ative educational council with two members each from the Extension Department (Rev. Coady and A.B. MacDonald), the Nova Scotia Credit Union League, the United Maritime Fishermen, Cape Breton Co-operative Services, the United Mineworkers of America, and later the Steelworkers' Union. Its objective was "to link together all co-operatives in a co-ordinated program of education and to promote the co-operative movement throughout the province"; see MacSween, *History of Nova Scotia*, 59.

15 The generally scant evidence that is available from the early 1940s suggests that for the cooperative sector, direct financing of education took precedence. Thus, for example, in 1941 the Credit Union League spent $4,202.82 on education and expansion while giving $1,000 to the Educational Council. In 1942 it spent $5,000 on its own educational programs and gave $1,200 to the Educational Council. See SFXUA, RG 30.3/25/1019, RG 30.3/25/1029.

16 Delaney, *By Their Own Hands*, 59–60.

17 Ibid., 59.

18 However, the Extension Department documents of the period express the belief that, despite their declining number, there were still enough study clubs to ensure a healthy and active continuation of the Extension Department's program. However, as the war dragged on, the study clubs were decreasingly emphasized, even in the rhetoric of the movement, with greater attention paid to the short courses as well as to the increased number and "quality" of Regional and Vocational Conferences.

19 Delaney, *By Their Own Hands*, attributes the suspension of the course largely to the economic circumstances brought about by the war, as do the documents available for the period.

20 This change was motivated primarily as a cost-saving function due the financial difficulties faced by St Francis Xavier University; see Cameron, *For the People*, 246. On the emergence of the *Maritime Co-operator*, see also Delaney, *By Their Own Hands*, 49–52.

21 See Delaney, *By Their Own Hands*, 59–60.

22 See Cameron, *For the People*, 248.

23 Delaney, *By Their Own Hands*, 63. Delaney, ibid., 60–5, presents some interesting details about the short courses and the extent that they proliferated throughout the maritime provinces. In some cases, short courses were offered at night. Generally, these night courses were better attended than those offered during the day; for example, for the courses offered during the fall and winter of 1943–44, whereas the average day course attendance was

about 45 people, the average night course attendance ranged from 50 to 200 people. Essentially, this difference was the result of some participants not being able to take time off work during the day to attend the courses, whereas at night they were free. See SFXUA, RG 30.3/25/944.

24 Delaney, *By Their Own Hands*, 62.

25 Ibid., 64.

26 The diagram itself came under the heading of "The Program for Social Change" and exists in various forms. It owes a lot to the artistry of Sister Mary Anselm (Irene Doyle). See ibid., 130.

27 Ibid.

28 This course covered (1) cooperative bookkeeping (the main thrust of the course), (2) cooperative principles and practices, (3) banking, (4) business English, and (5) the manager-member relationship. See SFXUA, RG 30.3/25/944.

29 See SFXUA, RG 30.3/25/1023.

30 The number of books, both in the Antigonish and Sydney branches, increased somewhat over the period, and these works seem to have been read extensively. See SFXUA, RG 30.3/25/943.

31 These broadcasts were delivered by Rev. J.A. MacDonald, a former professor of economics at St Francis Xavier University. They were terminated after ten weeks when Rev. MacDonald became ill. See SFXUA, *Scrapbooks*, 1943.

32 See Cameron, *For the People*, 248. The "University of the Air" broadcasts offered broad coverage aimed at a wide range of constituencies.

33 Thus, as Dutcher, "'Big Business,'" 240, notes, "female co-operators were largely relegated to the role of foot soldiers." On this matter, see also Neal, *Brotherhood Economics*; and Delaney, *By Their Own Hands*.

34 Dutcher, "'Big Business,'" 91.

35 Some of these concerns are noted in Delaney, *By Their Own Hands*, 117–28.

36 See, for example, ibid., esp. 122–7.

37 Dutcher, "'Big Business,'" 91. Dutcher, ibid., 124–5, also notes that some of the women themselves extolled the importance of homemaking over holding a position in a cooperative.

38 See Delaney, *By Their Own Hands*, 115. As Delaney, ibid., puts it, "The war had brought many changes to the homemaker's life. The bread winners were now employed and there was, for the first time in many years, assurance of a pay envelope at the end of the week. It was a transition period during which women began to move into employment outside the home in industry and service jobs."

39 In 1945 the federal government issued the policy white paper *Employment and Income*, which "implicitly embraced Keynesian philosophy." See Strick, *Canadian Public Finance*, 211.

40 For example, government expenditures as a percentage of gross domestic product (GDP) were 21.4 per cent in 1939 and 20.5 per cent in 1944. They increased to 24.3 per cent in 1947 and then dropped again to 21.3 per cent in 1950. These figures are a far cry from the, say, nearly 48 per cent achieved in 1995. We also note that government expenditures were between 15 and 17 per cent of GDP during the 1920s. They were higher over much of the 1930s (e.g., 27.4 per cent in 1933) due to the Great Depression; see, for example, Strick, *Public Sector*, 65. However, initiatives such as the introduction of unemployment insurance as early as 1941 and the family allowance program of 1945 signalled important beginnings; see Strick, *Canadian Public Finance*, 41–2. Also important were some of the changes that followed the Rowell-Sirois Commission of 1937; see ibid., 152–4.

41 Returning soldiers brought back with them a broader view of the world as a result of their experiences overseas.

42 A.B. MacDonald was hired as fieldman for the Co-operative Union of Canada (CUC) in late 1943 to help in the restructuring of the organization. He was then appointed to the permanent position of national organizer and in 1945 became general secretary of the restructured CUC, a post that he occupied until his death in 1952. For more discussion on his contribution to the CUC, see MacPherson, *Building and Protecting*, 119–48. A.B. MacDonald's brother, Rev. Dr Daniel J. MacDonald, professor of economics and the president of St Francis Xavier University from 1936 to 1944, also passed away in 1948. He had been a strong supporter of the Antigonish Movement and had even made scholarly presentations on aspects of it. For more details, see Cameron, *For the People*, esp. 241–2.

43 A.S. MacIntyre also died in 1952.

44 Rev. Tompkins's health had been in decline for some time before his official retirement; see Lotz and Welton, *Father Jimmy*; and Boyle, *Father Tompkins*. He died in 1953.

45 Rev. Tompkins viewed libraries in terms of promoting broad "education and intellectual development ... to prepare now to fight with the weapons of IDEAS"; see Neal, *Brotherhood Economics*, 173–4.

46 Ibid., 173.

47 Ibid.

48 Among these new members were Rev. Michael J. MacKinnon, who was later to replace Rev. Coady as director of the Extension Department, and Rev.

Francis J. Smyth, who was later to become the first director of the Coady International Institute, serving from 1959 to 1970.

49 SFXUA, RG 30.3/25/1035.

50 To these members, we can add people such as Kay Thompson, Zita Cameron, Ellen Arsenault, and others who were remarkably active in the operations of the program.

51 Indeed, 1,400 study clubs were reported organized in Ohio at the time and over 100 in British Columbia.

52 See various writings and speeches by Rev. Coady compiled in Laidlaw, ed., *Man from Margaree*.

53 The notion of the "Middle Way" was part of the Antigonish Movement from the outset. For an early articulation, see, for example, Boyle, *Middle Way*.

54 Arguably, this has continued to be the case in the bureaucratic approach to regional economic development since then.

55 SFXUA, Coady, "My Unwritten Book," 6.

56 The groups, at various times, sought to improve their lot by throwing their support behind the United Farmers, the Independent Labour Party, the Co-operative Commonwealth Federation, and the Reform Party, among others.

57 For additional insight into this sort of collaboration, see, for example, Walsh, *We Fought*.

58 See Henderson, *Angus L. MacDonald*, esp. 13–17.

59 For further insight into Angus L. MacDonald's views concerning the economy and his accomplishments as premier, see ibid.

60 Interestingly, the shift to radio programs during the war years was also motivated by financial considerations, namely the need to shift to a lower-cost method of carrying out the Extension Department's education program. See Cameron, *For the People*, 247.

61 See, for example, ibid.

62 The "Life in These Maritimes" broadcasts were a part of the "University of the Air" program. In 1948 "This Is Your Library," a series on books and reading hosted by Sister Marie Michael, was added to the program. The "University of the Air" program also included broadcasts on health, poetry, home economics, and science. See SFXUA, *Scrapbooks*, 1946.

63 See, for example, SFXUA, *Scrapbooks*, 1947–48; and Laidlaw, *Campus and the Community*, 118. The Education for Urban Adults program was predicated on weekly industrial classes. It employed Kenneth E. Boulding's book *The Economics of Peace* (1945) as a sort of textbook. Richard Pattee gives a glowing account of such classes conducted by Rev. J.A. MacDonald, where work-

ers grappled with assorted economic concepts. Pattee was one of many who wrote glowing reports about the work of the Antigonish Movement; see Pattee, "Good Life." Others included Neil MacNeil, "All Roads."

64 Tapes of the various programs could be sent to different radio stations, further enhancing their coverage with very little additional cost.

65 See SFXUA, RG 303/11/2049-2050, RG 30.3/11/2059, RG 30.3/11/2060.

66 Often, the "People's School" broadcasts contained little that addressed the people's own economic conditions.

67 See Cameron, *For the People*, 248–51. Students from various parts of the world were beginning to flock to St Francis Xavier University in order to observe the work of the Extension Department. In addition to Cameron, ibid., see, for example, Laidlaw, *Campus and the Community*; and SFXUA, RG 30.3/25/1035. Eventually, the Coady International Institute was established to cater to their needs.

68 It was at such a conference held in 1949 that a motion was made to once again introduce the Rural and Industrial Conferences – which occurred in 1950. See SFXUA, RG 30.3/28/363.

69 A.S. MacIntyre, "Report to the Annual Meeting of NS Co-operative Union" (1947), in SFXUA, *Scrapbooks*, 1947.

70 SFXUA, Coady, "My Unwritten Book," notes, 3.

71 No Extension Department reports could be found for the 1944–48 period. However, the *President's Report* for 1948–49 makes no mention of study clubs whatsoever. As well, the Extension Department's *Annual Report* for 1949–50 mentions them only in passing when referring to something else, namely the decision to allow adult education teachers-in-training to get a better insight into community problems through weekly visits to study clubs in several rural areas in Antigonish County. The 1949–50 report, however, praises the cooperative club that provided administrative assistance to the Extension Department and that also established "The Volunteer Workers of Extension" on the campus of St Francis Xavier University. See SFXUA, RG 30.3/25/1034.

72 Kitchen meetings held in January 1947 in St Andrews succeeded in turning around the ailing local credit union, giving rise to a sharp increase in both membership and assets. See SFXUA, *Scrapbooks*, 1947.

73 For example, estimates mostly for the 1938 period suggest that there were in place some 227 credit unions, 47 consumers' stores, 26 lobster factories, 18 other cooperatives and community enterprises, and about 12 smelt-marketing organizations. See SFXUA, RG 30.3/25/1016.

74 On these changes in the cooperative sector, see, for example, MacSween, *History of Nova Scotia*. Roderick MacSween, Canada's first inspector of cooperatives, attributes this slowing down during the latter part of the 1940s to the "inflation, high employment and prosperity" that characterized the postwar period; see ibid., 42.

75 See SFXUA, RG 30.3/25/942. In 1950 total assets were $9 million.

76 SFXUA, RG 30.3/25/942.

77 Ibid.

78 Nova Scotia Department of Agriculture and Marketing, *Annual Report of Co-operative Associations in Nova Scotia* (1950).

79 For more discussion on this issue, see, for example, Dutcher, "'Big Business.'"

80 The Nova Scotia Credit Union League was formally established in 1935 with A.E. MacIntyre as president and A.B. MacDonald as managing director. (Roy Bergengren was named honorary president.) The headquarters of the league was established in the office of the Extension Department of St Francis Xavier University. The Credit Union League Act was passed in 1938. See MacSween, *History of Nova Scotia*, 50–2. MacSween also provides a concise desription of the rationale behind the league's formation and its functions.

81 The Sydney branch of the Canadian Livestock Co-operative for the Martimes eventually evolved into Cape Breton Co-operative Services in 1942. For more details concerning the three cooperative wholesalers, see Dutcher, "'Big Business'"; MacSween, *History of Nova Scotia*; and McEwen, *Faith, Hope*.

82 As McEwen, *Faith, Hope*, 52, notes, "These newly incorporated stores did not operate long before they felt the need for a Co-operative controlled source of supply if they were to avoid becoming simply a distributive service for existing wholesales. Hence, under the study club work, demand or enquiry began to come in to St. F. X. Extension asking re the possibility of organizing a wholesale." Both McEwen and MacSween also describe in some detail the process that was followed and its myriad complications as well as the role of the leaders of the Antigonish Movement, especially A.B. MacDonald and A.S. MacIntyre, in setting the whole process going; see McEwen, *Faith, Hope*, 52–65; and MacSween, *History of Nova Scotia*, 43–8. MacSween, ibid., 48, also notes that a third institution was set up in 1946, Cumberland Co-operative Services, but this organization was much narrower in scope. Additional details can be found in Dutcher, "'Big Business.'"

83 For a discussion of the seriousness and longstanding nature of the problem, see Dutcher, "'Big Business.'"

84 See ibid. As Dutcher, ibid., 165, points out, in the case of Eastern Co-operative Services, there were plans for an abattoir, a creamery, a woolen mill, a co-operative fishery hatchery, and central cold-storage facilities, among other ventures.

85 See SFXUA, *Scrapbooks*, 1948–49. There were a number of earlier initiatives in the area of cooperative healthcare. For example, in 1944 there was an arrangement that, for a small fee, cooperators could qualify for thirty-five days of hospitalization and allied services at no extra cost.

86 See SFXUA, *Scrapbooks*, 1947–48.

CHAPTER FIVE

1 In the 1930s, due to the relatively small threshold size of productive units, resources were by and large more readily available, and the existing technology was relatively simple and accessible to the relatively small number of people who made up the study clubs and associated study clubs. Thus it was possible for small groups to set up and operate viable economic projects once the study process had been completed. The threshold size refers to the level of output required for the firm or enterprise to break even.

2 For example, Alexander Laidlaw left the Extension Department to assist cooperatives in Ceylon (now Sri Lanka) under the Colombo Plan. See, for example, MacPherson, *Building and Protecting*, 160.

3 Also relevant in this context was that the declining positions of both agriculture and the fisheries, especially in terms of the overall economy, would limit the expansion possibilities of the movement unless there was a breakthrough into industrial and processing activities as envisaged in the Big Picture.

4 Indeed, as quoted in Cameron, *For the People*, 333, Rev. Coady believed that eastern Nova Scotia could be seen as "a great social laboratory for the undeveloped parts of the world." Efforts were made in the late 1940s and early 1950s to establish an international arm of the Antigonish Movement, but these were not successful; see, for example, ibid., 289.

5 The transportation difficulties that plagued the Maritimes throughout the 1930s and 1940s are well documented in, among others, MacDonald, *Memoirs*; Delaney, *By Their Own Hands*; and Croteau, *Cradled in the Waves*. Angus L. MacDonald, the premier of Nova Scotia during much of the 1930s, parts of the 1940s, and the early 1950s, was a strong proponent of improving the transportation network, carrying out numerous road-paving and road-improvement projects; see, for example, Henderson, *Angus L. MacDonald*.

6 During the war years, the demand for information about the war situation had created a large increase in radio and film communication. After the war, these communication vehicles were put to other uses, such as advertising, sale promotion, and entertainment, in addition to the provision of information.
7 Although advertising and marketing were also carried out in newspapers, magazines, and other print media, radio and particularly television proved much more effective. Radio listeners and television viewers could be bombarded with strategically placed and often repeated messages, affecting not only consumption choices but also fundamental values and aspirations. The print media, in contrast, gave people more control over messages and information since people could choose not to read something or could skip something, which was much more difficult to accomplish with radio and television programming.
8 These values included thrift, self-reliance, and cooperation.
9 See, for example, Haley, *Tested by Fire*, 219, in the case of the expansion of grocery stores such as Dominion utilizing "marketing and merchandizing methods perfected in the prime markets of Ontario and Quebec."
10 In effect, the threshold size of enterprises was now greater.
11 St Francis Xavier University Archives (SFXUA), RG 30.3/25/1044.
12 At the same time, Canada was beginning to experience substantial postwar immigration of people from war-torn Europe, who settled mostly in the larger cities of central and western Canada.
13 See Urquhart and Buckley, eds, *Historical Statistics*, M1–22. Although some of this decline was the result of consolidation into larger and presumably more efficient holdings, the numbers are nevertheless staggering. Indeed, the Nova Scotia Voluntary Planning Board, *Report on Progress* (1965), 36, reported that "the farm population declined by 26% between 1951 and 1961." On this situation, see also, among others, Dutcher, "'Big Business.'"
14 In the six counties of eastern Nova Scotia, between 1931 and 1951 some 4,918 farms were abandoned. See SFXUA, RG 30.3/25/85.
15 See SFXUA, RG 30.3/25/84; and Sowder, *Present Status*, 61.
16 Labour productivity in the agricultural sector more than doubled over the 1946-60 period, with the productivity index increasing from twenty-seven in 1946 to fifty-seven in 1960. Such a change was, in relative terms, greater than the productivity increase of 72 per cent in the industrial sector over the same period. See Urquhart and Buckley, eds, *Historical Statistics*, F268–76.
17 During the 1930s, and earlier, education, as well as other social activities, was generally the responsibility of individual families and private voluntary

and other institutions, such as the church and religious orders. The government kept its involvement to a minimum and confined it to primary education. For example, private, mostly denominational universities received only limited and ad hoc help.

18 See Cameron, *For the People*, esp. 319–27. The desire to increase the academic standing of the university, especially in terms of promoting research and expanding the natural sciences, can be traced back to the 1940s.

19 During the 1950s, despite severe resource constraints, the Extension Department was encouraged to expand in order to offset the rural-sector decline. See, for example, ibid., 289.

20 Moreover, it was still the subject of lavish praise. See, for example, MacDonald, "How STFX Saved the Maritimes."

21 For more details, see, for example, Cameron, *For the People*, 292.

22 As Cameron, ibid., 291, notes, Coady's "resignation was a hefty blow for extension. Much of the magic that it had exercised resided in his personality. It is surely rare to find so many leadership qualities – energy, oratory, imagination, vision, commitment, service, optimism, and courage – combined in one person."

23 However, Rev. MacKinnon lacked the ability to effectively network with other institutions, particularly the provincial Department of Agriculture, which contributed to his dismissal as director of the Extension Department in 1958. For more details, see Cameron, ibid., 343–5.

24 Referring to Rev. MacKinnon, Joseph Hernon noted that "He found himself with the workaday tasks of trouble-shooting and consolidation; of safeguarding the growing independent co-operative enterprise from smugness, carelessness and lack of modern merchandising knowledge." Quoted in Laidlaw, *Campus and the Community*, 158.

25 See Cameron, *For the People*, 345–8.

26 Many of Rev. Coady's speeches, articles, and letters are reproduced in Laidlaw, ed., *Man from Margaree*.

27 SFXUA, Coady, ad lib, 2 March 1959, in notes for *My Unwritten Book*, 2.

28 SFXUA, Coady, "In Search of Possibilities," in notes for *My Unwritten Book*, 1.

29 SFXUA, Coady, *My Unwritten Book*, 1.

30 Ibid., 4.

31 Although Rev. Coady's faith in the power of science and technology was far too optimistic, it was an extension of his belief in the power of scientific thinking, including rational thinking, to help one escape from the constraints of prejudices and traditional ways of doing things. More important,

it reflects that Rev. Coady understood that the changes taking place could in fact foster cooperation and overcome many of the fundamental traditional constraints to cooperation among cooperators.

32 SFXUA, Coady, "Notes: Co-operation in Industrial Society," 1–2. Rev. Coady was fully aware that there were conflicts among cooperators and that not all who benefitted from the institutions that were promoted by the Antigonish Movement were fully committed to its vision. These issues are perhaps most clearly identified in Delaney, *By Their Own Hands*.

33 This sequence is consistent with that envisioned in the original specifications for the Big Picture. As Delaney, ibid., 98, 102, puts it, "The eager co-operators wanted to put in the picture more powerful credit union organizations and the most desired economic institution, the co-operative factory." "Co-operative members were continually reminded that their loyalty would help to put co-operative factories in the big picture."

34 SFXUA, Coady, "Random Notes for the Book," 1.

35 See, for example, Delaney, *By Their Own Hands*, esp. 96–7.

36 Even though he was not willing to jump on the urbanization bandwagon, Rev. Coady was not inimical to the urban sector but envisioned the possibility of a fundamentally different society in which the rural and smaller urban areas played vital and leading roles. That the fundamental changes permeating the social fabric, even within eastern Nova Scotia, pointed to an increasing urban and industrial society did not invalidate his vision.

37 See Tompkins, *Knowledge for the People*.

38 See, for example, Coady, *Masters of Their Own Destiny*, 22–3.

39 See Dutcher, "'Big Business,'" 240–1; and Delaney, *By Their Own Hands*, esp. 127–8.

40 The Rural and Industrial Conference was perhaps the easiest components of the original program to revive since similar but smaller-scale conferences had proliferated in the 1940s. In fact, it was at a similarly named Rural and Industrial Conference held in 1949 that a resolution for the Extension Department to reinstate the old conference was passed. See SFXUA, RG 30.3/28/364.

41 See SFXUA, RG 30.3/25/1062.

42 SFXUA, *Scrapbooks*, 1953. The content of these courses was influenced by the workshops for cooperative managers and bookkeepers that had emerged during the 1940s.

43 The overseas students were normally also enrolled in the university's Social and Co-operative Leadership program.

44 See SFXUA, RG 30.3/25/1067.

45 For example, courses on social action for Seminarians (i.e., students of the Seminarian Vacation School) were started in 1949, with the first running from 24 August to 2 September of that year. Also, there were numerous courses offered to consumers' organizations and aimed at directors of cooperatives, store managers, and the like. These courses tended to be very practical and focused on matters such as management principles. Other courses were aimed at the fisheries and forestry sectors as well as at specific groups, such as Aboriginals.

46 Sowder, *Present Status*, 35.

47 See SFXUA, *Scrapbooks*, esp. 1953, 1954, and 1956.

48 See, for example, Sowder, *Present Status*, 36; and SFXUA, *Scrapbooks*, 1954.

49 On a trial basis in 1957, these courses were offered at four centres in Nova Scotia in addition to St Francis Xavier University: Brookfield, Lawrencetown, Bridgewater, and Tatamagouche; see Sowder, *Present Status*, 40. These centres were selected to enable local leaders, largely active members of cooperatives and credit unions and those serving as directors or chairpersons of various cooperative committees, to attend the courses without travelling great distances.

50 See, SFXUA, RG 30.3/25/1063.

51 See, SFXUA, RG 30.3/25/1065. In addition, 553 conferences, conventions, short courses, and rallies were either organized or attended by Extension Department staff, along with 7,031 personal interviews.

52 See, SFXUA, RG 30.3/25/1071.

53 Coady, *Masters of Their Own Destiny*, 8.

54 Twenty-one individuals who had actively contributed to various areas of the Antigonish Movement were conferred honorary degrees. See SFXUA, RG 30.3/25/1066.

55 A paper presented at the conference by Alex E. MacIsaac noted that credit unions "organized while men were on relief, have done so well in the field of savings that today they are operating as full-time modern banks; some of them with money lying idle while the development of the Co-operative Movement and related social services are sometimes hampered from lack of funds. The co-operative stores that were organized at that time have grown in volume, progressed in services and are today among the best equipped in that field. Yet, these Credit Unions and stores are looked upon too often, and by too many as ends in themselves. The potential power of these organizations is being short-circuited by lack of vision and an integrated program"; see SFXUA, RG 30.3/28/389–390. MacIsaac also criticized labour

unions for not entering into "wider fields of ownership" and for strengthening the status quo and power of corporations; see SFXUA, RG 30.3/28/390–392. In the case of primary producers, he argued that "the terrific savings made in marketing were not pooled and invested in the ownership of processing plants, cold storage plants and other facilities connected with the complete job of marketing"; see SFXUA, RG 30.3/28/392. He also noted that farmers "clumsily engaged in a short-sighted program of sabotaging their co-operative organizations; sucking away the little drops of rebates and dividends which, if left in a co-operative pool, would have gradually and automatically given them ownership of these and many other plants"; see SFXUA, RG, 30.3/28/393.

56 The programs also lacked a well-defined audience, unlike the traditional approach, which was aimed at members and potential members of the movement mobilized through mass meetings and then organized into study clubs. The new "shotgun approach" was much more of a hit and miss affair intended to appeal even to segments that were hostile to the movement.

57 This approach also constituted adopting a tool because it was available and then allowing it to dictate the nature and direction of the new education strategy.

58 These broadcasts included the series "This Is Your Library," introduced by Sister Marie Michael in 1949, and various instalments of the "University of the Air" program.

59 More specifically, the program sought to "encourage serious discussion and study of the urgent social problems of our time, so that we may have a large body of well-informed leaders among citizens in general but in the ranks of organized labor in particular"; see "Summary of Extension Activities," in "President's Annual Report, 1950–51," 2, SFXUA, RG 30.3/25/1039. The appointment of Rev. MacKinnon, a priest from Sydney Mines who was on good terms with labour unions, could only further strengthen this preoccupation.

60 Thus, for example, 16,000 study bulletins of radio broadcasts and 9,000 lecture bulletins of weekly classes were distributed in 1950. See SFXUA, RG 30.3/25/1039.

61 Ibid.

62 Ibid.

63 SFXUA, RG 30.3/25/1069.

64 Ibid.

65 In 1957–58 the total number of registrants in the weekly classes was 400. In 1959–60 classes (with Rev. Andy Hogan as instructor) were held only in

Sydney, Sydney Mines, and Glace Bay, and junior People's School classes were held in Sydney, Sydney Mines, New Waterford, and Antigonish; see SFXUA, RG 30.3/25/1140. In contrasts, during 1950–51 such classes were held in seven industrial centres in Cape Breton, three in Pictou County, and one in Inverness; see SFXUA, RG 30.3/25/1039.

66 SFXUA, RG 30.3/25/1069.

67 See SFXUA, various documents pertaining to the "Life in These Maritimes" broadcasts. The Extension Department itself described the program as dealing with rural problems, practical agricultural issues, and best methods of production and marketing; see SFXUA, RG 30.3/11/2005.

68 Out of these groups, fifty-three were in Antigonish, Inverness, and Richmond Counties. See SFXUA, RG 30.3/11/2067.

69 In 1949 the National Film Board completed its film on the Antigonish Movement, *The Rising Tide*, which also captured these rural roots.

70 See SFXUA, RG 30.3/25/19. In 1956–57, the new program consisted of a series of eighteen half-hour radio broadcasts.

71 Although actual figures are hard to come by, in 1951–52 some 50,000 individual bulletins were distributed, dropping to about 42,000 in 1953–54. See SFXUA, RG 30.3/25/1061, RG 30.3/25/1068–69.

72 SFXUA, RG 30.3/25/1069.

73 See SFXUA, various documents pertaining to the radio programs.

74 See Sowder, *Present Status*, 42–4.

75 Delaney, *By Their Own Hands*, 65; MacDonald, *Memoirs*, 44–5.

76 MacDonald, *Memoirs*, 25.

77 See "1951–52 Report of the Extension Department's Activities among the Fishermen of Eastern Canada," SFXUA, RG 30.3/25/1043.

78 Essentially, the Model Fisherman program was intended to provide a powerful demonstration of Rev. Coady's notion of the translation of "scientific thinking" into practice.

79 See, for example, SFXUA, RG 30.3/25/1097. The Fishermen's Loan Board was established in 1935 to administer federal funds that were allocated to the maritime fisheries of Nova Scotia; see Walsh, *We Fought*, 72–4.

80 See, for example, SFXUA, RG 30.3/25/1093, on the decision to dispense with study clubs altogether in favour of monthly meetings in the case of the Point Sapin–Baie Ste Anne area of New Brunswick in the mid-1950s.

81 These cooperatives were seen largely as the main success stories in the eastern Nova Scotia fisheries sector. See SFXUA, RG 30.3/25/1097–1105.

82 See SFXUA, RG 30.3/25/1088.

83 By 1959 there were 4,393 credit unions with a total membership of 2,369,833. See Chiasson, *Co-operation*, 50.

84 For example, in 1951 seven credit union charters were cancelled and three new charters were granted. There was also the emerging problem of uncollectible loans for some of the credit unions, attributed to "laxity on the part of credit union officers and their neglect in regard to enforcing an adequate collective system"; see Nova Scotia Credit Union League, *Annual Report* (1952), 24.

85 In 1954 the membership and asset amounts of credit unions for the whole of Nova Scotia were 51,952 and $7,927,069.37. In each of the seven counties in eastern Nova Scotia, the figures for 1954 were as follows:

County	*Membership*	*Assets ($)*
Antigonish	3,858	487,235.93
Cape Breton	21,352	3,798,112.48
Guysborough	847	116,872.49
Inverness	3,120	411,056.15
Pictou	1,627	178,290.48
Richmond	2,447	235,928.24
Victoria	724	67,278.93

Halifax County was also a big contributor, making up about 21 per cent of both membership and total assets. See Nova Scotia Credit Union League, *Annual Report* (1954).

86 In 1949 the membership in Nova Scotia cooperatives was 24,267. See chapter 4, table 4.3.

87 CBCS reported total sales of $1,000,000.00 in 1946, $1,400,051.60 in 1949, $1,656,169.92 in 1952, and $1,553,612.15 in 1956. ECS reported total sales of $282,126.00 in 1945, $762,228.00 in 1948, $934,446.36 in 1953, and $1,333,904.39 in 1956. See Dutcher, "'Big Business,'" 161, 167, 244, 247.

88 Sowder, *Present Status*, 62.

89 See Dutcher, "'Big Business,'" 149–84. As pointed out by Stephen Dutcher, additional factors included the growth of big business (particularly Dominion and Sobey's), the small population base of the area, the egalitarian cooperative structures, and the decline in commitment to cooperation as reflected in the loss of interest in cooperative education. Other factors included the decision by the government to allow the production of margarine (which undermined the local cooperative creameries), the increasingly

urban population, and the proliferation of co-op brands from outside the area.

90 See ibid., 247–50.

91 This merger would reduce the institutional fragmentation that emanated from the conflict between consumers and producers; see, for example, Delaney, *By Their Own Hands*, 96–7, 100. On the amalgamation process, see Dutcher, "'Big Business,'" esp. 250–71.

92 See Cameron, *For the People*, 345.

93 Rev. Coady went further, maintaining that "Our credit unions, co-operative stores, co-operative fish plants and other farming and fisheries co-operatives, all were built for the day when the whole movement would be topped off by a comprehensive, central organization, such as Eastern Co-operative Services, to give our fishermen, farmers, townspeople and industrial workers the necessary facilities for conducting their economic affairs." See SFXUA, RG 30.3/25/11.

94 What was envisioned in terms of rural development is perhaps best captured in Chisholm, *Program for Rural Development*.

95 Interestingly, Dutcher, "'Big Business,'" 269, identifies McEwen, along with R.J. MacSween, the director of marketing for Nova Scotia's Department of Agriculture, as supporters of the merger. However, this support seems to have been based on the view that amalgamation was better than the way things were, particularly in the case of CBCS.

96 See Haley, *Tested by Fire*, 216.

97 See, for example, SFXUA, RG 30.3/25/87.

98 See, for example, Sowder, *Present Status*, 69–72.

99 See Cameron, *For the People*, 345.

100 For more details, see, among others, McEwen, *Faith, Hope*; and Walsh, *We Fought*.

101 Haley, *Tested by Fire*, 216. A more complete picture can be obtained from the organizational chart of ECS, reproduced in Sowder, *Present Status*, 63-4. The plan also included, among other things, the provision of burial services and automobile service stations.

102 See Dutcher, "'Big Business,'" 281–93.

103 In some quarters, as Cameron, *For the People*, 345, reports, this souring was attributed to Rev. MacKinnon's "bulldozing fighting spirit" rather than simply to disagreement about ECS. For example, Roderick MacSween, the director of marketing services in the Nova Scotia Department of Agriculture, was very supportive of the proposed ECS; see SFXUA, RG 30.3/25/87. As well, the Department of Agriculture was represented in the committee that recom-

mended the amalgamation of the two wholesalers into ECS. See SFXUA, RG 30.3/25/88; and Sowder, *Present Status*, 60.

104 See Cameron, *For the People*, 345.

105 Sowder, *Present Status*, 56. Sowder also notes here that "there were sixty-nine cooperative housing groups in Nova Scotia already living in their own homes," with an additional fifteen groups at various stages of preparation. By the 1960s twenty-five such groups were purported to be in operation; see SFXUA, RG 30.3/25/1140.

106 Sowder, *Present Status*, 83.

107 Managers of cooperatives, in particular, did not appreciate the need for continuous adult education.

108 See SFXUA, RG 30.3/25/1064, RG 30.3/25/1148.

109 Again, the dependence on an outside source of funding, linked in this case to a particular sector, created a fundamental imbalance in the focus of the movement that could only compromise both the Extension Department and the whole Antigonish Movement.

110 See SFXUA, RG 30.3/25/1066.

111 See Coady, *Masters of Their Own Destiny*, 164.

112 Dodaro, Pluta, and Amoako-Tuffour, "Relevance of the Human Factor," argue that the approach of the Antigonish Movement is of relevance to the development process, even within the context of the "Six Principles."

113 For additional details about the establishment of the Coady International Institute, see, for example, Cameron, *For the People*, esp. 332–6.

CHAPTER SIX

1 Another of the early pioneers and a stalwart of the movement, Rev. Dr Hugh MacPherson passed away in 1962.

2 The devolution of education to the various economic institutions had already made substantial headway during the 1950s and even earlier. The matter was complicated by the fact that the various cooperatives did not see themselves as parts of a system whereby their own narrower institutional interests were fundamentally linked to those of the movement as a whole.

3 Those who watched the television programs, however, had to spend time to do so and, in the process, incurred an opportunity cost. As well, they were bombarded by ads whose sole purpose was to change their tastes and preferences in favour of the goods and services of interest to the advertisers. Such educational programs often carried with them a mix of different and often inconsistent messages.

4 The introduction of the welfare state or social safety net could, if appropriately managed, have effectively complemented the Antigonish Movement. However, it could not replace the movement since it was not a program of fundamental socio-economic transformation. In the main, it constituted an effort to ensure against the negative consequences of the existing order. To a large extent, the failure of the emerging social-welfare safety net to complement the movement and its tendency, in fact, to weaken the movement were due to the Antigonish Movement itself being in disarray.

5 Details can be gleaned from various textbooks on economic development, such as Todaro, *Economic Development*, and Meier, ed., *Leading Issues*, as well as from some of the literature on regional economic development, such as Savoie and Higgins, eds, *Regional Development Theories*.

6 For more details, see, among others, Bradfield, *Regional Economics*; and Savoie, *Visiting Grandchildren*. These were in addition to the institutions put in place in the 1950s, such as the Maritime Provinces Board of Trade (1951), the Atlantic Provinces Economic Council (1954), and the Atlantic Provinces Research Board (1958).

7 Although these forces had already been at work in earlier periods, particularly during the 1950s, they became even stronger during the 1960s and later. See, among others, Cameron, *For the People*.

8 Thus the Catholic Church's influence was greatest in eastern Nova Scotia, the eastern parts of both New Brunswick and Prince Edward Island, and the predominantly Catholic areas of Newfoundland. However, many ministers and members of other denominations were also actively involved in the work of the Antigonish Movement, meaning that it was not simply a Catholic movement.

9 The Sisters of St Martha and the Sisters of Charity were very active in filling the void by providing these services. On the contribution of the Sisters of St Martha, see Cameron, *"And Martha Served."*

10 The improved economic conditions brought greater material welfare and higher standards of living within the grasp of more people, particularly those who were young, educated, and highly motivated within the existing general economic framework.

11 Or at least, as we argued earlier, the new social reality favoured the notion that economic wellbeing and moral and spiritual factors could be treated as separate issues. Faith in science at the expense of religious beliefs has long been a part of the Western intellectual tradition. In the past, however, this was confined to a narrow intellectual and cultural elite. The vast majority of the population remained grounded in the principles of the Christian

faith as propagated and delineated by different denominations. In the years following the Second World War, however, there emerged the widespread belief that science and technology held the solutions to all social problems, with the tendency among many being to relegate religion to the status of private beliefs and preferences.

12 Brennan, "Commentary on the Decree," 64, notes that "the clerical and religious states are not to be thought of as higher or better than the life of the laity."

13 In some areas, the mines had shut down in the early 1950s, as in the case of Inverness. See Campbell, *Banking on Coal*, 86.

14 See, for example, Williams and Theriault, "Crisis and Response," 106.

15 On this competition, see ibid. Ironically, government policies that were meant to promote local development by fostering economic activity through various incentives also played a role in some of the emerging difficulties, especially by favouring the expansion of the offshore fleet and larger-scale, and presumably more efficient, profit-driven processing activities.

16 *Extension Newsletter*, 9 May 1962, St Francis Xavier University Archives (SFXUA), RG 30.3/25/201.

17 That such was the case is suggested by the emergence of the Maritime Fishermen's Union in the 1970s and its efforts to represent fishermen in bargaining with their own cooperative organizations. See, for example, Williams and Theriault, "Crisis and Response."

18 Rev. Gillis's term as director had been laden with controversy and conflict, as is made clear in his summary of his 1,107 days at the Extension Department. This term was characterized by numerous attempts to remove him as director and to reduce his influence, with the highpoint being the change of the administrative structure in 1960 to four co-directors – with Rev. Gillis being in charge of rural development, agriculture, fisheries, and forestry – and one coordinator, a position assumed by the then president of St Francis Xavier University. Without making any judgments on the personalities involved in the turmoil, we note that Rev. Gillis did have a sense that all was not well with the Antigonish Movement, especially with ECS. Although he formally resigned as director, it is clear that by 1961 he was in an untenable position at the Extension Department. See Rev. Gillis's summary of his time at the Extension Department in SFXUA, *My Side of the Story*; and Cameron, *For the People*, 347–8.

19 Rev. MacNeil, in fact, had taken economic courses in 1944 with Harry Johnson, the economist who had penned the Six Principles; see SFXUA, RG 30.3/25/3095. Johnson, a leading monetarist and free enterpriser at the Uni-

versity of Chicago, spent a day, 15 September 1962, advising the Extension Department on its proposed research for Cape Breton in response to an invitation by Rev. MacNeil; see SFXUA, RG 30.3/25/2110.

20 This strategy included the reappointment of Dr Remi Chiasson, a former inspector of schools in Cape Breton with a particular interest in adult education, who had initially been hired by Rev. Gillis, and also the appointment to the Sydney office of Rev. George Topshee. See Cameron, *For the People*, 348.

21 The consultants, appointed at various times, were Rev. Michael Gillis (one of the prime movers behind the initial establishment of the Extension Department), W.H. McEwen, J. MacKinnon, R.J. MacSween, F. Waldo Walsh, and J.H. MacKichan. All of them had long been involved in the cooperative field and/or had some sort of association with the Antigonish Movement.

22 Cameron, *For the People*, 348, points out that, "by 1969, out of twenty-five extension staff members, about twenty did not know personally the founding fathers of the Antigonish Movement – Dr. Coady, Father Tompkins, and A. B. MacDonald."

23 SFXUA, RG 30.3/25/1275.

24 Extension Department, *Annual Report* (May 1963–June 1964), 4.

25 Arguably, the notion of a quick fix was also prevalent in the application of various theories to the economies of Third World countries. The failure of the so-called "development decade" of the 1960s can be taken as evidence that quick fixes cannot deal with deep and entrenched problems – regardless of how sophisticated they may be or seem to be.

26 Thus it was argued that "Only government departments and agencies have the resources and sufficient competent personnel required to prepare a comprehensive plan of development, and the financial resources to ensure its implementation. Local citizens and their organizations should participate intelligently in the development of these plans and especially, in putting them into effect." See Extension Department, *Annual Report* (1965–66), 6.

27 The community development approach had also been adopted by government agencies such as the Agricultural and Rural Development Agency as their "quasi-official method"; see SFXUA, RG 30.3/25/1235. Given that the Extension Department increasingly viewed itself as a junior partner of public-sector agencies, such a coincidence of approaches is not surprising.

28 The concern raised in the 1950s, and even in the early 1960s in view of the difficulties faced by ECS, that the various cooperative entities were not work-

ing together, as they should have, largely disappeared over the decade. Nonetheless, it was evident that some of the cooperative organizations were weak and stagnant.

29 Extension Department, *Annual Report* (May 1963–June 1964), 4.

30 More of them would require a university-level education, possibly also supplemented by appropriate training at the graduate level.

31 These pilot projects normally served a variety of purposes, including allowing fieldworkers to gain experience in conducting the required research and in testing for its appropriateness. They also served the purpose of developing a standard methodology that could be applied elsewhere, fostering community support and participation in the novel approach, mobilizing community leadership, and the like.

32 For example, in 1964 a follow-up meeting after a survey of the fishing industry in L'Ardoise reported a disappointing attendance of "eleven out of sixty-three fishermen." See SFXUA, RG 30.3/25/292.

33 See SFXUA, RG 30.3/25/1200.

34 See A.A. MacDonald, *Report* (1964–65), SFXUA, RG 30-3/25/1308. In the same report, MacDonald goes on to say that "The social Science Department and the Extension Department are in the process of working out a modus operandi for carrying out this research."

35 See SFXUA, RG 30.3/25/1411.

36 SFXUA, RG 30.3/25/1418.

37 See SFXUA, RG 30.3/25/1411.

38 SFXUA, RG 30.3/25/1317.

39 Extension Department, *Annual Report* (1965–66), 12.

40 Extension Department, *Annual Report* (1963–64), 3.

41 SFXUA, RG 30.3/25/1154.

42 Extension Department, *Annual Report* (May 1961–June 1962), 14.

43 Extension Department, *Annual Report* (May 1967–June 1968), 5.

44 SFXUA, RG 30.3/25/1435.

45 The pattern was so well established that in a letter to Rev. MacNeil, dated 13 February 1963, Rev. Topshee referred, somewhat in jest, to "each member of the staff taking his or her turn going away to study." See SFXUA, RG 30.3/25/3603.

46 "Memorandum on StFX Extension," 13 October 1964, 3, SFXUA, RG 30.3/25/1285.

47 New cooperatives could, however, still emerge on their own or, possibly, through the sponsorship of those already in operation. In effect, the Exten-

sion Department fell short in providing for the needs of the existing cooperative enterprises while also not providing any set mechanism for the establishment of new ones.

48 "Memorandum on StFX Extension," 13 October 1964, 5, SFXUA, RG 30-3/25/1287. See also, Extension Department, *Annual Report* (May 1963–June 1964), 5.

49 Rural and Industrial Conferences were organized in both 1960 and 1962.

50 See SFXUA, *Scrapbooks*, 1964. The books were moved to the Angus L. MacDonald Library, and Sister Marie Michael, the librarian, was transferred to the Coady International Institute.

51 The various *Annual Reports* of the Extension Department during the 1960s identified a wide array of topics, including consideration of the problems facing various sectors, such as steel and coal, the economic prospects of particular regions, and issues pertaining to unemployment and education, as well as the consideration of items such as the price of drugs, issues surrounding medicare, and local government.

52 In 1966 the broadcast time was also changed from Sunday afternoon to Monday evening, which was perceived to be a better, albeit more expensive, viewing time.

53 For example, in 1963 classes were held in Petit de Grat, New Glasgow, Sydney, Bras D'Or, and Inverness. Efforts to organize such classes in Antigonish ended in failure, and one that had been started in Port Hawkesbury was discontinued due to a lack of interest. See SFXUA, RG 30.3/25/239–240.

54 Extension Department, *Annual Report* (May 1961–June 1962), 8.

55 Ibid., 11–12.

56 "Memorandum on StFX Extension," 13 October 1964, 3, SFXUA, RG 30.3/25/1285.

57 This outside influence was largely a consequence of the Extension Department's increasing involvement in carrying out education and other work on behalf of other institutions and government agencies.

58 This was especially the case as the emphasis shifted to doing surveys and the like in conjunction with government agencies. Arguably, even in earlier times, the work of the Extension Department among the fishermen was highly conditioned by government funding and, as a consequence, government objectives.

59 Starting in 1962, this television program involved broadcasts during the fall and winter months that covered a wide range of issues of interest to the fisheries.

60 This was particularly the case with respect to places like Cheticamp, Grand Etang, Alder Point, Port Bickerton, and a few others in eastern Nova Scotia. See, for example, SFXUA, RG 30.3/25/1189, RG 30.3/25/1240.

61 See SFXUA, RG 30.3/25/194. The fisheries in New Brunswick generally continued to face difficulties, especially in the case of lobster despite the establishment of a central lobster cannery at Richibucto. See, for example, SFXUA, RG 30.3/25/1241.

62 The greater reliance on Community Development Councils, of course, signalled the acceptance of the approach championed by newly emerging government agencies.

63 Extension Department, *Annual Report* (1965–66), 13.

64 Ibid., 14.

65 In some instances, the fishermen had come to believe that their interests were no longer truly represented by the cooperatives, although such membership still provided advantages that others did not have. On this situation, see, for example, Williams and Theriault, "Crisis and Response."

66 Williams and Theriault, ibid., note the resilience of cooperatives in more remote areas and attribute both their emergence and their survival to underdevelopment and, in turn, suggest that they kept underdevelopment alive in the region, instead of being the agents of change and progress that they were envisaged as being within the context of the Antigonish Movement.

67 See, for example, Roy, "Impact of Social Insurance."

68 Extension Department, *Annual Report* (1966–67), 12.

69 Extension Department, *Annual Report* (1967–68), 10.

70 See, for example, Extension Department, *Annual Report* (1969–70), 10.

71 Extension Department, *Annual Report* (1968–69), 6.

72 Extension Department, *Annual Report* (1969–70), 10.

73 However, in addition to being a top-down approach, this also involved a bias toward the offshore and large-scale production and processing units, as pointed out in Williams and Theriault, "Crisis and Response," among others.

74 See, SFXUA, RG 30.3/25/2826.

75 See, for example, Rev. J.A. Campbell, "Report to the Extension Department, 1964-65," SFXUA, RG 30.3/25/1300. There was also generally weak coordination with the Nova Scotia Credit Union League.

76 See SFXUA, 30.3/25/1301.

77 In the mid-1960s, kitchen meetings in conjunction with local credit unions were established in communities such as Petit de Grat, Lower River Inhabi-

tants, L'Ardoise, Main-a-Dieu, and Florence. See SFXUA, RG 30.3/25/1220, as well as RG 30.3/25/252 and RG 30.3/25/1302.

78 See Nova Scotia Credit Union League, *Annual Reports* (1960, 1965, 1970).

79 The critical role played by having a financial institution as part of the system is perhaps best illustrated by the case of Mondragon. See, among others, MacLeod, *From Mondragon*; and Whyte and Whyte, *Making Mondragon*.

80 See, for example, SFXUA, RG 30.3/25/2850.

81 See Extension Department, *Annual Report* (May 1961–June 1962), 10; and Extension Department, *Annual Report* (1966–67), 9.

82 See Extension Department, *Annual Report* (May 1968–June 1969), 8; and Extension Department, *Annual Report* (June 1969–June 1970), 7.

83 See, for example, Extension Department, *Annual Report* (May 1968–June 1969), 8–9.

84 Rev. Gillis was concerned that the whole enterprise was predicated on an unsustainable base, as the region of eastern Nova Scotia could not expand its production of various agricultural crops to sustain it. Soil and climatic conditions combined with inefficient farming methods to compromise the whole undertaking. He was also concerned about its management.

85 SFXUA, *Report to the Board of Governors* (17 May 1960), RG 30.3/25/1139.

86 SFXUA, *Report to the Board of Governors* (15 May 1961), RG 30.3/25/1162.

87 Thus Rev. Gillis goes on to say, "The board of directors is aware of the problems and steps are being taken to solve them. I am confident that, with some changes, the organization will weather the storm." See SFXUA, *Report to the Board of Governors* (15 May 1961), RG 30.3/25/1162.

88 SFXUA, *Report* (18 October 1961), RG 30.3/25/1153.

89 Extension Department, *Annual Report* (May 1961–June 1962), 10.

90 See McEwen, *Faith, Hope.* Haley, *Tested by Fire*, 233, paints an even gloomier picture, stating that "From 1960 onwards, it was effectively bankrupt, sustained on an unsatisfactory basis from year to year by negotiating deals with its creditors, with the Nova Scotia Credit Union League, with any organization that could forestall the inevitable."

91 See, for example, Dutcher, "'Big Business,'" 286–7.

92 As suggested by Dutcher, ibid., esp. 296, some believed that whereas the dairy industry was viable, others such as poultry were not.

93 The reorganization also included the appointment of Maritime Co-operative Services's McEwen as supervisor of ECS. See ibid., 310.

94 For details on ECS's operations from 1961 to 1964, see ibid., 311–44.

95 Quoted in Cameron, *For the People*, 348.

96 See ibid. Cameron further notes here that "agricultural representatives considered ECS an example of clerical domination – imposing a program on the people without their approval."

97 The Extension Department's previous involvement with forestry was through its agricultural-sector programs.

98 Extension Department, *Annual Report* (1966–67), 7.

99 Extension Department, *Annual Report* (May 1968–June 1969), 5.

100 Extension Department, *Annual Report* (June 1969–June 1970), 12.

101 The challenges facing the woodlot owners and the new organization were nevertheless daunting. Even with some degree of unity and bargaining power, the sector was still plagued by problems of efficiency, scale of operation, and management. See Extension Department, *Annual Report* (May 1968–June 1969), 5.

102 The Extension Department was fully aware that there was much more to the problems facing the Aboriginal communities than simply inadequate leadership. It recognized, for example, the effects of the lack of jobs and training, poor housing, inadequate access to services, discrimination, and existing traditions. See Extension Department, *Annual Report* (May 1967–June 1968), 9.

103 Nonetheless, the Extension Department claimed that it fostered improvement in leadership as well as social development and the like among the Aboriginal population. See, for example, Extension Department, *Annual Report* (May 1968–June 1969), 10.

104 What the Extension Department did, for good or bad, reflected the position of the federal department more than anything else.

105 In addition to some of the ones cited in the chapter, there were also the Local Government project of 1967–68 and the PEI Development Plan project of 1969–70.

CHAPTER SEVEN

1 Dr John T. Sears, the academic vice president of the university, occupied the position of acting director over the 1992–93 period.

2 Starting with the early 1980s, an increasing amount of Extension Department activity and funding was linked to academic programs involving continuing education and adult education.

3 See Extension Department, *Annual Report* (June 1970–June 1971), 13, which quoted Alexander J. Laidlaw: "the curse of the Maritime divisiveness fell upon the fishermen's cooperatives and they were never able to unite in such a way as to secure the benefits of large-scale enterprise."

4 Starting with the 1930s and continuing into the 1960s, there was a commonality of interests as well as a fundamental complementarity between the Extension Department and the federal Department of Fisheries. Both were concerned with improvements in the fisheries – although their objectives were not necessarily coincident. Moreover, the Department of Fisheries had no fieldworkers of its own to reach the fishermen. The Extension Department, in contrast, had the fieldworkers but lacked the funds. Thus the arrangement whereby the Extension Department received a grant directly from the government – or the House of Commons – to use for hiring fieldworkers and promoting economic activities and development in the fisheries was beneficial for both. Through this arrangement, the Extension Department could spread the Antigonish Movement among the fishermen, and the Department of Fisheries gained indirect access to the sector.

5 This process has, of course, been further heightened by the spread of computers and the Internet.

6 Generally, their standards of living either declined or remained low, and some would also have been afflicted by insecurity and a sense of inferiority as a result of their lack of independence. Some became drawn into welfare dependency due to the lack of other options.

7 See, for example, Williams and Theriault, "Crisis and Response."

8 Traditionally, this has been associated with the effects of low elasticities respecting both price and income as well as with the impact of technological change.

9 On this issue, see, for example, Williams and Theriault, "Crisis and Response." For details on the rationale and shortcomings of the strategy, see, among others, Grafton and Lane, "Canadian Fisheries Policy"; Gordon and Munro, eds, *Fisheries and Uncertainty*; Arai, "Policy and Practice"; Parsons, *Management of Marine Fisheries*; Matthews, *Controlling Common Property*; Davis and Thiessen, "Public Policy"; and Lamson and Hanson, eds, *Atlantic Fisheries*.

10 For a clear and concise exposition on this issue, see, for example, Williams and Theriault, "Crisis and Response."

11 See, for example, A.A. MacDonald, "Antigonish Movement."

12 For some of the standard arguments, see, among others, Grafton and Lane, "Canadian Fisheries Policy."

13 There is much debate on this issue. See, for example, ibid.

14 The ACOA was established in 1987 by the ACOA Act.

15 See, for example, Williams and Theriault, "Crisis and Response."

16 In addition to being the director of the Extension Department, Rev. Topshee also served as the director of the Coady International Institute from 1973 to 1979. Rev. Topshee died in January 1984, a little more than a year after leaving his post as director of the department.

17 See Extension Department, *Annual Report* (June 1970–June 1971).

18 Extension Department, *Annual Report* (June 1972–June 1973), 5. On this view, see also Extension Department, *Antigonish Movement*, 33–44.

19 The report was commissioned by the Sisters of St Martha in 1978 on the occasion of the fiftieth anniversary of the establishment of the Extension Department. See Dods, *Organizational Review*.

20 Extension Department, *Annual Report* (1978), 28.

21 Extension Department, ibid., states the position that "staff, as individual members and with the support of the Department, would become involved with local coops and credit unions in order to foster member participation and education. In addition, Extension would make known to coop institutions its willingness to conduct educational programs for members and to support the Director Training Program of the Coop College of Canada."

22 Ibid.

23 Indeed, in conjunction with the university's fundraising campaign of the late 1970s, where the Extension Department was asked to help by approaching the cooperative institutions, serious concern was raised about the reluctance of maritime Canada cooperatives to support the department. Moreover, there is reference to the "mistrust of [the] Atlantic Co-op sector towards STFX" and also reference to the need to convince key people in the cooperative sector about the Extension Department's "place in Co-op education"; see SFXUA, RG 30.3/25/3631–32. The erosion of the department's standing in cooperative education is also highlighted by St Francis Xavier University's exclusion as a site for the Co-operative College of Canada's bachelor's and master's program in co-op studies at the time when the university was interested in establishing such programs; see SFXUA, RG 30.3/25/3628, RG 30.3/25/3631.

24 The first annual report produced under the directorship of Rev. Topshee stated that the Extension Department's "secondary mission would appear to be that of raising [the] economic and social standards of the community through such projects as low-cost housing and training for community development, [and] various group action programs. These latter would

include work among the Indian and black communities of Eastern Nova Scotia, the organization of woodlot workers, seminars for leaders of cooperatives, and participation in a variety of other programs sponsored by Extension or other agencies"; see Extension Department, *Annual Report* (June 1969–June 1970), 3.

25 Extension Department, *Annual Report* (1984), 9.

26 During the Topshee years, the continuing education program was under a separate academic department of the university. Now, all components of continuing education, except the master's program in adult education, were transferred to the Extension Department.

27 Extension Department, *Annual Report* (1982–83), 3. These were also reproduced in Extension Department, *Annual Report* (1984), 11–12.

28 In fact, so many of the rural cooperative stores, along with other cooperatives as well, applied for receivership that one of the areas longest-serving cooperators, Leonard Oja, who had been assisting in the establishment of cooperatives since 1948, found, after his retirement in the 1970s, a new career as a liquidator of cooperatives.

29 Arguably, information that is disjointed and is not subjected to appropriate or relevant analysis may, rather than foster action, be paralyzing. Action within the context of the Antigonish Movement depended on the existence of an appropriate analytical framework and vision in addition to adequate and appropriate information. Even these elements, however, were not enough: there also needed to be in place a strong commitment to the vision and an institutional framework able to foster economic action. Aside from the educational component, these elements were generally lacking.

30 We do not question adult education's intrinsic value. However, to be effective, it must have a sense of purpose and be a part of a broader vision.

31 As already noted in chapter 4, the issue also became a bone of contention between Coady and Tompkins in the 1940s. Whereas the former maintained that the Extension Department was relevant strictly in terms of its link to economic action, the latter increasingly moved the department in the direction of education for its own sake.

32 Extension Department, *Annual Report* (1986), 18.

33 This increase was in step with the trends affecting the university and its programs as a whole.

34 Extension Department, *Annual Report* (1996–97), 11.

35 Ibid.

36 By the end of the 1980s and the beginning of the 1990s, the level of dissatisfaction within the Extension Department led to the formation of the Exten-

sion Program Staff Association and to further polarization within the department. As a consequence, an external review of the Extension Department was undertaken in 1991, and one year later the director of the Extension Department resigned from her position.

37 Extension Department, *Annual Report* (1991–92), 1.

38 Extension Department, *Annual Report* (1995), 8.

39 See Extension Department, *Annual Report* (1987), 12.

40 See Extension Department, *Annual Report* (1986), 7–8. Specifically, the Extension Department produced educational material on women in business and trained women as personal-care and transitional-house workers. In addition, it assisted in organizing the Second Stage Housing project in Pictou for abused women leaving shelters.

41 Extension Department, *Annual Report* (1987), 16; Extension Department, *Annual Report* (1988), 13; Extension Department, *Annual Report* (1989), 8–9.

42 In contrast, Rev. Topshee's background was in labour education, and MacNeil's background was in adult education. Webb's interest in cooperatives and the cooperative approach is well documented in some of his writings. See, for example, Webb, *Worker's Co-operatives*.

43 Extension Department, *University and Community*, 1–2. For the contribution of the present authors to the colloquium, see Dodaro and Pluta, *Antigonish Movement*. The colloquium also elicited the participation of Sister Mary Anselm (Irene Doyle), one of the pioneers of the Antigonish Movement, as well as Hon. Allan J. MacEachen, who had been heavily involved in the Extension Department's education programs, especially in the late 1940s and 1950s, and Dr A.A. MacDonald, a former director of the Coady International Institute, who had been heavily involved with the Extension Department as a fieldworker, especially in the 1960s.

44 These other initiatives included a trip by one of the authors, Dr Leonard Pluta, and Dr Monica Diochon to North Dakota to study undertakings such as the establishment of a cooperative pasta-making facility and a bison-raising cooperative and its central processing facility; see Diochon and Pluta, *North Dakota*. Also, there was a trip to the prairie provinces to assess the possibility of establishing a cooperative organization in natural gas.

45 This retrenchment can perhaps best be seen in the fact that the St Francis Xavier Enterprise Development Centre (XEDC) was established in 1997, in partnership with the ACOA, to provide help primarily to the small-business sector – in order to help new businesses to get started and others to grow – although it lays claim to a broader mandate. Since it generally offered little

support to the cooperative sector, the XEDC was set up as an entity separate from the Extension Department. Such an initiative, if linked to the Extension Department, could have provided a boost both to the revitalization of some of the "general extension" programs and to the Extension Department's bridging function. More recently, the XEDC partnership has also been extended to Human Resources Canada and DEVCO. Equally important from the perspective of gauging the new direction of the university was the establishment of the Gerald Schwartz School of Business, first announced in 1999. Named after the founder and chief executive officer of the Onex Corporation, the school, in effect, established a strong working relationship between the university and large-scale private enterprise.

46 Extension Department, *Annual Report* (1996–97), 5.

47 See Extension Department, *Annual Report* (1996–97), 8.

48 See Extension Department, *Annual Report* (1996–97).

49 Even the movement's importance as a publicity tool has declined enormously, with attention shifting almost completely to its offspring, the Coady International Institute.

50 Numerous programs and projects were introduced and quickly terminated, Extension Department offices were opened and closed in different communities, and so on.

51 Research, including increasing research capability, was an important component of the Extension Department's strategy in the 1960s, and although it was not overly dominant in the 1970s, it remained an important area of concern, especially starting in the mid-1980s when applied research initiatives became more predominant.

52 See Extension Department, *Annual Report* (1982–83), 6.

53 See Extension Department, *Annual Report* (1986), 11.

54 See ibid.

55 Arguably, these would have been substantial sums in earlier periods, particularly the 1930s, especially when supplemented by "sweat labour" and other resources.

56 In describing the function of the Innovations program, the Extension Department's annual report for 1988 notes, "the project is creating support services for worker co-operatives. It does this by gathering data about the need for support among existing co-operatives, by developing educational materials which will enable worker-owned enterprises to be effective businesses, and by establishing vehicles for communication among workers co-operatives"; see Extension Department, *Annual Report* (1988), 16.

57 See Extension Department, *Annual Report* (1986), 14.

58 These academic papers included a three-part evaluation of the Extension Department undertaken by the present two authors.

59 The project was conducted in partnership with the Nova Scotia Health Program, the Nova Scotia Heart and Stroke Foundation, and Health and Welfare Canada.

60 Extension Department, *Annual Report* (1990), 12.

61 Extension Department, *Annual Report* (1991–92), 5.

62 Ibid., 6.

63 Extension Department, *Annual Report* (1995), 6.

64 See Diochon and Pluta, *North Dakota*.

65 The initiative was the result of interest on the part of a number of people in understanding the economy and its various dimensions, including moral. The materials used in the workshops were prepared and delivered by Santo Dodaro (a co-author of this study).

66 There were between sixty and seventy participants at each session in both Antigonish and Sydney, with many travelling some distance to attend. For example, there were people from Sydney, Inverness, and other locations at the Antigonish workshops.

67 The only follow-up entailed three additional workshops in the spring of 1998 in Antigonish, which were conducted, in addition to Santo Dodaro, by Dr A.A. MacDonald and by Dr Greg MacLeod, from University College of Cape Breton (now Cape Breton University), who has a longstanding involvement in programs inspired by the Antigonish Movement.

68 Extension Department, *Annual Report* (1996–97), 8.

69 In itself, the fact that the fisheries program had been dependent on government financing for so long had precluded the need to develop alternate sources of funds or to follow a different fisheries program altogether. In any event, being overly reliant on government sources of funding created a dependency on those funds. This has been recognized as a major pitfall of many attempts to find solutions to local problems. See, for example, Blakely and Bradshaw, *Planning Local.*

70 Apologetically, the Extension Department noted, "These earnest, modest gestures seemed to be all that was possible for the University to contribute at the time when there was tremendous political activity involving all levels of government, several labour unions, at least one fishery corporation, and a strong public outcry." See Extension Department, *Annual Report* (1990), 14.

71 Thus, in response to a call for help by the fishermen of Inverness, in addition to providing some resources in the formation of a fishermen's association, the Extension Department "established liaison with the appropriate

agencies which could provide the assistance they required." See Extension Department, *Annual Report* (1972–73), 13.

72 The Extension Department provided organizational and educational help for about 500 people who were involved in the project. The work involved numerous meetings, rallies, seminars, committee meetings, and the like. See Extension Department, *Annual Report* (June 1971–June 1972), 12.

73 In effect, they opted to have the government purchase the plant and and to have a PEI-based American company operate it. See Extension Department, *Annual Report* (June 1974–June 1975).

74 Indeed, Extension Department, *Annual Report* (1978), 21, called for a renewed approach in which the role of the department would be the following:

   1 To promote co-operation development among fishermen as the ultimate level of control in the fishing industry and to assist individuals and groups interested in acting co-operatively.
   2 To promote organization of fishermen (Co-operative, Union or Association) as a critical need in the Maritime fishery.
   3 To encourage and take whatever action possible to have the existing organizational forces in the fisheries (Unions, Co-ops and Associations) provide the fishermen with a united voice in negotiations with governments and companies.
   4 To provide information and study opportunities to fishermen (a) on fishermen's organizations and (b) on the industry and the fishermen's place in it.
   5 To carry out general community development activities in fishing communities in the eastern counties of N.S.

75 These included study sessions held in March and April 1983 to study the recommendations of the Kirby Commission, supported by funds obtained from the federal Department of Fisheries and Oceans.

76 See Extension Department, *Annual Report* (1982–83), 9, where the resolution is reproduced as follows: "that ... United Maritime Fishermen Co-op attempt to persuade the Federal Government to provide financial assistance to the St. F.X. Extension Department so as to permit the latter to reinstate the service of fieldworkers as we had in the early years of our co-operatives when Dr. Coady and his associates brought education to the fisherman on the wharf or at his familiar meeting place."

77 Extension Department, *Annual Report* (1985), 15.

78 Extension Department, *Opportunity Development Program* (1996), 4–6.

79 Extension Department, *Annual Report* (1969–70), 7.

80 See Extension Department, *Annual Report* (1978).

81 For example, in 1981 the Extension Department administered $3 million under the RRAP alone. The RRAP seems to have peaked around 1983–84, when in excess of 300 houses were being rehabilitated, with the total falling to forty-five two years later.

82 See Extension Department, *Annual Reports* (1969–70, 1970–71).

83 In part, the new impetus was instigated by the president of the university, Rev. Gregory MacKinnon, who had co-authored a Forestry Commission report. In response, staff members of the Extension Department set up meetings with various interest groups, including woodlot owners and mill workers, to study the problems. See Extension Department, *Annual Report* (1986).

84 Extension Department, *Opportunity Development Program*, 7, notes, "With new technologies, innovative thinking, and a linked enterprise approach, there are significant opportunities for growth in forestry products," with particular emphasis on value added and more imaginative use of the resource with a clear view of taking advantage of opportunities arising in the global market.

85 See Extension Department, *Annual Report* (1981–82). Half of the cooperative organizations operating in the area are attributed to the Extension Department's involvement in this program.

86 According to ibid., 1, since its inception, CESA-MGCDIL had "established 98 projects, provided 83 permanent jobs and 718 temporary jobs." There is also a claim that, in fact, more than 1,300 jobs were created.

87 In the case of Inverness, four economic projects were put in place, none of which seems to have lasted very long.

88 Extension Department, *Annual Report* (1984), 25, notes that "five initiatives to secure funding for the proposed institute were unsuccessful."

89 ARLEC's main contribution was the training that it provided for numerous labour leaders.

90 This program was designed to promote Christian social action and adopted the study club technique with some success, although not to foster economic activity.

91 The concern with marginalized groups had also served as the basis for the Extension Department's programs in the Aboriginal and black communities, especially in the 1960s, and for the Rural Women program of the 1980s. Indeed, Extension Department, *Annual Report* (1987), 9, stated that "the principal focus of the Department is on the improvement of the status of the disadvantaged."

92 The Extension Department had remained somewhat active in cooperative education by responding to specific requests from the cooperative sector as well as by hosting institutes, such as the Association of Co-operative Education Institute, by participating in symposia and seminars of various sorts, and by encouraging cooperative activities. These included attempts to establish workers' cooperatives, especially among skilled trades people (as in the case of attempts to foster skilled-trades and builders' cooperatives in order to promote tradesmen-owned and controlled operations). Such cooperatives seem to have been established in Pictou and Guysbrough Counties – in the case of the latter, the Whitehead Carpentry Shop. See Extension Department, *Annual Report* (1978).

93 For example, during the 1980–81 period, outreach programs were carried out in Antigonish, Richmond County, and Cheticamp; see Extension Department, *Annual Report* (1980–81). The school held in Antigonish lasted three and a half days and aimed at increasing participants' understanding of the problems, benefits, and philosophy of economic cooperation.

94 Extension Department, *Annual Report* (1980–81), 29.

95 Extension Department, *Annual Report* (1982–83), 5.

96 Extension Department, *Annual Report* (1986), 17, offered the following justification: "within the cooperative organizations there are abundant resources for achieving their respective educational goals."

97 Thus, for example, Extension Department, *Annual Report* (1982–83), 9, noted that "neither the United Maritime Fishermen nor this Department is in a position to finance increased educational activity."

98 The Community Co-operative Councils were made up of representatives from the various cooperative enterprises in a given area and were expected to "coordinate social and educational and other co-operative activities" for the area. See Extension Department, *Annual Report* (1981–82), 9.

99 In addition, the Extension Department also participated in a number of other projects and programs, such as the Co-op Future Directions project. These initiatives, however, did not amount to much in concrete terms.

100 The available data exhibit a great deal of variability. For example, in the case of 1994, total sales were around $590 million and profits were around $7.8 million, which translates into a profit rate of about 1.3 per cent, in contrast to the 1995 profit rate of about 0.4 per cent and that of 1998 of about 0.2 per cent. These figures are based on the data reported in Nova Scotia Department of Economic Development, Co-operatives Branch, *Co-operatives Annual Report 2000* (2000).

101 The Self-Help Builders Co-op program ended in 1976. Over the 1936–76 period, it had prompted the building of more than 7,000 homes. See Extension Department, *Annual Report* (1981–82).

102 These cooperatives were also driven by idealism but in the pursuit of objectives that would have clashed with the idealism and vision that imbued the early pioneers of the Antigonish Movement.

103 The weakening of Co-op Atlantic, in turn, also weakened the affiliated consumers' cooperatives in the same way that the weakening of the UMF negatively impacted the fisheries cooperatives.

104 Nova Scotia Department of Agriculture and Marketing, *Annual Reports of Co-operative Associations in Nova Scotia* (1985), 14. These figures are based on nine reporting worker cooperatives (out of a total of fifteen).

105 Nova Scotia Economic Renewal Agency, Co-operatives Branch, *Co-operatives Nova Scotia 1995*, 17.

106 Ibid.

107 Ibid.

108 The figure is based on data presented in Nova Scotia Department of Consumer Affairs, *Nova Scotia Credit Unions* (1975, 1985).

109 Thus Credit Union Central of Nova Scotia, *Annual Report* (1997), 7, noted that in the province as a whole there were "63 credit unions with a total of 92 branch locations."

110 Extension Department, *Annual Report* (June 1971–June 1972), 15.

111 Extension Department, *Annual Report* (1984), 10. Here, it was further noted about the Extension Department that "If it does succeed in assisting groups to alter their circumstances, it faces yet another barrier of a disapproving sector of the population whose power was eroded by the successful work of a formerly disadvantaged group."

CHAPTER EIGHT

1 Mathews, *Jobs of Our Own*.

2 Although priests, church leaders, and Catholic thinkers have a long tradition of being concerned with the inequity and unfairness of the evolving capitalist system – as attested to, for example, by the work of Cardinal Henry Edward Manning in England – the transformation of this concern into concrete action, at least to the extent envisioned by the Antigonish Movement, was relatively rare.

3 See, for example, Mathews, *Jobs of Our Own*.

4 This concern is evident in numerous statements by Rev. Coady, Rev. Tompkins, and others, as well as, for example, in the work done for the Antigonish Movement by Rev. J.D. Nelson Macdonald, who was a minister of the United Church of Canada.

5 Mathews, *Jobs of Our Own*, 176.

6 See, for example, Organization for Economic Cooperation and Development, *Implementation of an Entrepreneurship*.

7 See also Dodaro and Pluta, *Antigonish Movement*.

8 New Dawn was instigated by Rev. Greg MacLeod, a Roman Catholic priest-professor at the University of Cape Breton College (now Cape Breton University). See, for example, Hanratty, *New Dawn*; and MacSween, "New Dawn Limited."

9 Of particular relevance in this context has been the emphasis on freedom as a requirement for development and for the improvement of human welfare. See, for example, Sen, *Development as Freedom*.

10 These issues are debated extensively in the vast literature on globalization. For a good introduction, see, among others, Rodrik, *Has Globalization Gone Too Far?*

Bibliography

Acheson, T.W. "The National Policy and the Industrialization of the Maritimes, 1880–1910." 1972. Reprinted in P.A. Buckner, Gail G. Campbell, and David Frank, eds, *The Acadiensis Reader*, vol. 2, *Atlantic Canada after Confederation*, 3rd ed., 90–115. Fredericton, NB: Acadiensis, 1999.

Alexander, Anne. *The Antigonish Movement: Moses Coady and Adult Education Today.* Toronto: Thompson Educational, 1997.

Alexander, David. "Economic Growth in the Atlantic Region, 1980 to 1940." *Acadiensis* 8, no. 1 (Autumn 1978): 47–76.

Anselm, Sister Mary (Irene Doyle). *The Antigonish Idea and Social Welfare.* Antigonish, NS: St Francis Xavier University, 1955.

Arai, A. Bruce. "Policy and Practice in the Atlantic Fisheries: Problems and Regulatory Enforcement." *Canadian Public Policy* 20, no. 4 (December 1994): 353–64.

Arnold, Mary Ellicott. *Father Jimmy of Nova Scotia.* Chicago: Cooperative League of the U.S.A., n.d.

– *The Story of Tompkinsville.* New York: Cooperative League of the U.S.A., 1940.

Ash, Roberta. *Social Movements in America.* Chicago: Markham, 1972.

Blakely, Edward J., and Ted K. Bradshaw. *Planning Local Economic Development: Theory and Practice.* 3rd ed. Thousand Oaks, CA: Sage, 2002.

Blaug, Mark. *Economic Theory in Retrospect.* 4th ed. Cambridge, UK, and New York: Cambridge University Press, 1985.

Bonin, John, and Louis Putterman. *Economics of Co-operation and the Labour-Managed Economy.* Chur, Switzerland: Harwood Academic, 1987.

Bonin, John, Derek C. Jones, and Louis Putterman. "Theoretical and Empirical Studies of Producer Co-operatives: Will Ever the Twain Meet?" *Journal of Economic Literature* 31, no. 3 (September 1993): 1290–320.

Boyle, George. *Democracy's Second Chance: Land, Work and Co-operation.* New York: Sheed and Ward, 1941.

– *Father Tompkins of Nova Scotia.* New York: P.J. Kenedy, 1953.

– *The Poor Man's Prayer.* Baltimore, MD: Helicon, 1962.

Boyle, James. *A Middle Way.* Antigonish, NS: Extension Department, St Francis Xavier University, 1937.

Bradfield, Michael. *Regional Economics: Analysis and Policies in Canada.* Toronto: McGraw-Hill Ryerson, 1988.

Brennan, Margaret. "Commentary on the Decree on the Appropriate Renewal of Religious Life." In George P. Schner, ed., *The Church Renewed: The Documents of Vatican II Revisited*, 63–73. Lanham, MD: University Press of America, 1986.

Bruyn, Severyn T. *The Civil Economy: Transforming the Market in the Twenty-First Century.* Ann Arbor: University of Michigan Press, 2000.

Cameron, James D. *"And Martha Served": History of the Sisters of St. Martha, Antigonish, Nova Scotia.* Halifax: Nimbus, 2000.

– *For the People: A History of St Francis Xavier University.* Montreal and Kingston: McGill-Queen's University Press, 1996.

Campbell, Donald F., and Raymond A. MacLean. *Beyond the Atlantic Roar: A Study of Nova Scotia Scots.* Toronto: McClelland and Stewart, 1974.

Campbell, Douglas F. *Banking on Coal: Perspectives on a Cape Breton Community within an International Context.* Sydney, NS: University College of Cape Breton Press, 1997.

Campbell, P.J. MacKenzie. *Compassion on the Multitude.* Sydney, NS: N.p., 1966.

Carroll, Carman V. "The Influence of H.H. Stevens and the Reconstruction Party in Nova Scotia, 1934–35." MA thesis, University of New Brunswick, 1972.

Chenery, Hollis B., and Moises Syrquin. *Patterns of Development, 1950–70.* London: Oxford University Press for the World Bank, 1975.

Chiasson, Remi J. *Co-operation: The Key to Better Communities.* Antigonish, NS: Extension Department, St Francis Xavier University, 1961.

Chisholm, John. *A Program for Rural Development for Eastern Nova Scotia.* Antigonish, NS: Extension Department, St Francis Xavier University, 1955.

Coady, Moses M. *Masters of Their Own Destiny.* New York: Harper and Brothers, 1939.

– *My Story: Text of an Interview for CBC-TV, July 8, 1957.* Antigonish, NS: Extension Department, St Francis Xavier University, 1957.

– *The Social Significance of the Co-operative Movement.* Antigonish, NS: Extension Department, St Francis Xavier University, 1945.

– and associates. *The Antigonish Way.* Antigonish, NS: Extension Department, St Francis Xavier University, 1943.
– and associates. *The Antigonish Way: A Series of Broadcasts over CBC.* Antigonish, NS: Extension Department, St Francis Xavier University, 1948.
Conrad, Margaret R., and James K. Hiller. *Atlantic Canada: A Concise History.* Don Mills, ON, and New York: Oxford University Press, 2006.
Coutinho, Boavida. *Community Development through Adult Education and Cooperatives: The Story of the Antigonish Movement.* Rome, Borgo Santo Spirito: Institute of Pastoral Sociology, 1966.
Credit Union Central of Nova Scotia. *Annual Reports.* 1972–97.
Croteau, John Tougas. *Cradled in the Waves: The Story of a People's Co-operative Achievement in Economic Betterment in PEI.* Toronto: Ryerson Press, 1951.
Cruikshank, Ken. "The Intercolonial Railway, Freight Rates and the Maritime Economy." 1992. Reprinted in Kris Inwood, ed., *Farm, Factory and Fortune: New Studies in the History of the Maritime Provinces*, 171–96. Fredericton, NB: Acadiensis, 1993.
Davis, Anthony, and Victor Thiessen. "Public Policy and Social Control in the Atlantic Fisheries." *Canadian Public Policy* 14, no. 1 (March 1988): 66–77.
De Soto, Hernando. *The Mystery of Capital: Why Capitalism Triumphs in the West and Fails Everywhere Else.* New York: Basic Books, 2000.
Delaney, Ida Gallant. *By Their Own Hands: A Fieldworker's Account of the Antigonish Movement.* Hantsport, NS: Lancelot, 1985.
– *25c a Week: The Coady Credit Union's First 10 Years, 1933–1943.* Antigonish, NS: Extension Department, St Francis Xavier University, n.d.
Diochon, Monica, and Leonard Pluta. *The North Dakota Success Story.* Report prepared for the Extension Department, St Francis Xavier University, Antigonish, Nova Scotia, 3 January 1996.
Dodaro, Santo, and Leonard Pluta. *The Antigonish Movement: Past Successes, Current Circumstances, Future Options.* Truro, NS: Nova Scotia Economic Renewal Agency, Cooperative Branch, 1995.
– and Leonard Pluta. "The Antigonish Movement as a Model of Regional Economic Development." In Masudul Alam Choudhury, ed., *Political Economy of Development in Atlantic Canada*, 48–70. Sydney, NS: University College of Cape Breton Press, 1988.
– Leonard Pluta, and Joe Amoako-Tuffour. "The Relevance of the Human Factor and a Grassroots Approach to Economic Development: A Case Study of the Antigonish Movement of Canada." In Senyo B-S.K. Adjibolosoo, ed., *International Perspectives on the Human Factor in Economic Development*, 55–76. Westport, CT, and London: Praeger, 1998.

Dods, R.A. *Organizational Review for St. Francis Xavier University.* Antigonish, NS: St Francis Xavier University, 1979.

Donovan, Alvin. "Sharing the Catch: The Origin and Development of the United Maritime Fishermen to 1938." MA thesis, University of New Brunswick, 1989.

Dutcher, Stephen. "'Big Business for the People': Co-operative Wholesaling in the Maritime Provinces, 1934–1965." PhD diss., University of New Brunswick, 2001.

Economic Council of Canada. *From the Bottom Up.* Ottawa: Economic Council of Canada, 1990.

Extension Department, St Francis Xavier University. *Annual Reports of the Extension Department.* Antigonish, NS: Extension Department, St Francis Xavier University, 1961–97.

– *The Antigonish Movement: Yesterday and Today.* Antigonish, NS: Extension Department, St Francis Xavier University, 1976.

– *Opportunity Development Program.* Antigonish, NS: Extension Department, St Francis Xavier University, 1996.

– *President's Report.* Antigonish, NS: Extension Department, St Francis Xavier University, 1948–49.

– *The Social Significance of the Cooperative Movement.* Antigonish, NS: Extension Department, St Francis Xavier University, 1945.

– *Study Clubs.* Antigonish, NS: Extension Department, St Francis Xavier University, 1930.

– *University and Community: The Antigonish Movement: Beyond 2001.* Antigonish, NS: Extension Department, St Francis Xavier University, 1995.

Flannery, Mark J. *An Economic Evaluation of Credit Unions in the United States.* Boston: Federal Reserve Bank of Boston, 1974.

Forbes, Ernest R. *Challenging the Regional Stereotype: Essays on the 20th Century Maritimes.* Fredericton, NB: Acadiensis, 1989.

– *The Maritime Rights Movement, 1919–1927: A Study in Canadian Regionalism.* Montreal and Kingston: McGill-Queen's University Press, 1979.

Fowler, Bertram Baynes. *The Lord Helps Those ...: How the People of Nova Scotia Are Solving Their Problems through Co-operation.* New York: Vanguard, 1938.

Frank, David. "The Cape Breton Coal Industry and the Rise and Fall of the British Empire Steel Corporation." *Acadiensis* 7, no. 1 (Autumn 1977): 3–34.

Freire, Paulo. *The Pedagogy of the Oppressed.* Rev. ed. New York: Continuum, 2000.

Gordon, Daniel Vernon, and Gordon Ross Munro, eds. *Fisheries and Uncertainty: A Precautionary Approach to Resource Management.* Calgary, AB: University of Calgary Press, 1996.

Grafton, R. Quentin, and Daniel E. Lane. "Canadian Fisheries Policy." *Canadian Public Policy* 24, no. 2 (June 1998): 133–47.

Hagen, Everett E. *The Economics of Development.* 4th ed. Homewood, IL: Irwin, 1986.

Haley, Stefan. *Tested by Fire: The Life and Work of W.H. McEwen.* Saskatoon, SK: Co-operative College of Canada, 1980.

Hanratty, John. *The New Dawn: An Experiment in Economically Based Community Development*. Ottawa: Health and Welfare Canada, 1981.

Hausman, Daniel M., and Michael S. McPherson. *Economic Analysis and Moral Philosophy.* Cambridge, UK, and New York: Cambridge University Press, 1996.

Helm, Franz C., and Chuo Cha Ushirika. *The Economics of Co-operative Enterprise.* London: University of London Press, 1968.

Henderson, T. Stephen. *Angus L. MacDonald: A Provincial Liberal.* Toronto: University of Toronto Press, 2007.

Heron, Craig. *Working in Steel: The Early Years in Canada, 1883-1935.* Toronto: McClelland and Stewart, 1988.

Hirschman, Albert O. *The Strategy of Economic Development.* New Haven: Yale University Press, 1958.

Honigsheim, Paul. *On Max Weber.* New York: Free Press, 1968.

Inwood, Kris. "Maritime Industrialization from 1870 to 1910: A Review of the Evidence and Its Interpretation." 1991. Reprinted in P.A. Buckner, Gail G. Campbell, and David Frank, eds, *The Acadiensis Reader*, vol. 2, *Atlantic Canada after Confederation*, 3rd ed., 116–39. Fredericton, NB: Acadiensis, 1999. Also reprinted in Kris Inwood, ed., *Farm, Factory and Fortune: New Studies in the History of the Maritime Provinces*, 149–70. Fredereicton, NB: Acadiensis, 1993.

Johnson, Harry G. *The Antigonish Movement: A Lecture to the Students of Acadia University.* Antigonish, NS: Extension Department, St Francis Xavier University, 1944.

Krueger, Anne O. "The Political Economy of the Rent-Seeking Society." *American Economic Review* 64, no. 3 (June 1974): 291–303.

Kuznets, Simon. *Modern Economic Growth: Rate, Structure and Spread.* New Haven, CT: Yale University Press, 1966.

Laidlaw, Alexander F. *The Campus and the Community: The Global Impact of the Antigonish Movement.* Montreal: Harvest House, 1961.

– ed. *The Man from Margaree: Writings and Speeches of M.M. Coady.* Toronto: McClelland and Stewart, 1971.

Lamson, Cynthia, and A.J. Hanson, eds. *Atlantic Fisheries and Coastal Communities: Fisheries Decision Making Case Studies.* Halifax, NS: Dalhousie Ocean Studies Program, 1984.

Leff, Nathaniel. "Entrepreneurship and Development: The Problem Revisited." *Journal of Economic Literature* 17 (March 1979): 46–74.

Lele, Uma. "Co-operatives and the Poor: A Comparative Perspective." *World Development* 9, no. 1 (January 1981): 55–72.

Lotz, Jim. "The Antigonish Movement: A Critical Analysis." *Studies in Adult Education* 5, no. 2 (1973): 97–112.

– "The Historical and Social Setting of the Antigonish Movement." *Nova Scotia Historical Quarterly* 5, no. 2 (1975): 99–116.

– *The Humble Giant: Moses Coady, Canada's Rural Revolutionary.* Ottawa: Novalis, 2005.

– and Michael R. Welton. *Father Jimmy: Life and Times of Jimmy Tompkins.* Wreck Cove, NS: Breton Books, 1997.

– and Michael R. Welton. "Knowledge for the People: The Origins and Development of the Antigonish Movement." In Michael R. Welton, ed., *Knowledge for the People: The Struggle for Adult Learning in English Speaking Canada, 1928–1973*, 97–111. Toronto: OISE Press, 1987.

MacDonald, A.A. "The Antigonish Movement after the 1950s: Restructuring and the Response to New Constituencies." Paper presented at the conference "University and the Community: The Anatigonish Movement beyond 2001," Antigonish, Nova Scotia, 4–5 October 1995.

MacDonald, Colin. "Credit Union and Cash Trading." Address to Associated Club Rally, Antigonish, Nova Scotia, 26 April 1938.

MacDonald, Daniel J. "The Philosophy of the Antigonish Movement." Paper read before the Canadian Academy of St Thomas Aquinas, 1938.

MacDonald, David. "How STFX Saved the Maritimes." *Maclean's Magazine*, 1 June 1953, 24–5, 69.

MacDonald, J.D. Nelson. *Memoirs of an Unorthodox Clergyman.* Truro, NS: Cooperative Resources, 1986.

MacInnes, Daniel William. "Clerics, Fishermen, Farmers and Workers: The Antigonish Movement and Identity in Eastern Nova Scotia, 1928–1939." PhD diss., McMaster University, 1978.

MacIsaac, Alex A. "The Future." Speech delivered at the Rural and Industrial Conference, July 1953.

MacLellan, Malcolm. *Coady Remembered.* Antigonish, NS: St Francis Xavier University Press, 1985.

MacLeod, Greg. *From Mondragon to America: Experiments in Community Economic Development.* Sydney, NS: University College of Cape Breton Press, 1998.

MacNeil, Neil. "All Roads Lead to Antigonish." *The Sign*, January 1948, 33–5.

MacPherson, Hugh. *Kitchen Chats on Farming.* Antigonish, NS: Extension Department, St Francis Xavier University, 1937.

MacPherson, Ian. "Appropriate Forms of Enterprise: The Prairie and Maritime Co-operative Movements, 1900–1955." *Acadiensis* 8, no. 1 (Autumn 1978): 77-96.

– *Building and Protecting the Co-operative Movement: A Brief History of the Co-operative Union of Canada.* Ottawa: Co-operative Union of Canada, 1984.

– *The Co-operative Movement in the Prairies, 1900–1955.* Ottawa: Canadian Historical Association, 1979.

– *Each for All: A History of the Co-operative Movement in English Canada, 1900–1945.* Toronto: Macmillan of Canada, 1979.

– "Patterns in the Maritime Co-operative Movement, 1900–1945." *Acadiensis* 5, no. 1 (Autumn 1975): 67–83.

MacSween, Rankin. "New Dawn Limited: A Community Economic Development Experiment." In Gertrude Anne MacIntyre, ed., *Perspectives on Communities: A Community Economic Development Roundtable*, 79–89. Sydney, NS: University College of Cape Breton Press, 1998.

MacSween, Roderick J. *A History of Nova Scotia Co-operatives.* Truro, NS: Nova Scotia Department of Agriculture and Marketing, 1985.

– "Problems of the Fishing Industry." Speech delivered at the Rural and Industrial Conference, August 1939.

Mathews, Race. *Jobs of Our Own: Building a Stake-Holder Society: Alternatives to the Market and the State.* Sydney, Australia: Pluto, 1999.

Matthews, David Ralph. *Controlling Common Property: Regulating Canada's East Coast Fishery.* Toronto: University of Toronto Press, 1993.

McCann, L.D. "The Mercantile-Industrial Transition in the Metal Towns of Pictou County, 1857–1931." *Acadiensis* 10, no. 2 (Spring 1981): 29–64.

McEwen, W.H. *Faith, Hope and Co-operation: A Maritime Province's Story.* Moncton, NB: Maritime Co-operative Services, 1969.

McIvor, R. Craig. *Canadian Monetary, Banking and Fiscal Development.* Toronto: Macmillan of Canada, 1958.

McKay, Ian, and Suzanne Morton. "The Maritimes: Expanding the Circle of Resistance." In Craig Heron, ed., *The Workers' Revolt in Canada, 1917–1925*, 43–86. Toronto: University of Toronto Press, 1998.

Meier, Gerald M., ed. *Leading Issues in Economic Development.* 4th ed. New York: Oxford University Press, 1984.

Mifflen, Francis J. "The Antigonish Movement: A Revitalization Movement in Eastern Nova Scotia." PhD diss., Boston College, 1974.

Moody, J. Carroll, and Gilbert C. Fite. *The Credit Union Movement: Origins and Development, 1850–1970*. Lincoln: University of Nebraska Press, 1971.

Neal, Rusty. *Brotherhood Economics: Women and Co-operatives in Nova Scotia.* Sydney, NS: University College of Cape Breton Press, 1998.

Norrie, Kenneth H., and Douglas Owram. *A History of the Canadian Economy.* Toronto: Harcourt Brace Jovanovich, 1991.

Nova Scotia Credit Union League. *Annual Reports.* 1940–60.

Nova Scotia Department of Agriculture and Marketing. *Annual Reports of Co-operative Associations in Nova Scotia.* 1938–85.

Nova Scotia Department of Consumer Affairs. *Nova Scotia Credit Unions: Financial and Statistical Reports on Operations*. 1975, 1985.

Nova Scotia Department of Economic Development, Co-operatives Branch. *Co-operatives Annual Report 2000*. 2000.

Nova Scotia Department of Small Business Development. *Co-operatives Nova Scotia 1990*. 1990.

Nova Scotia Economic Renewal Agency, Co-operatives Branch. *Co-operatives Nova Scotia 1995*. 1995.

Nova Scotia Voluntary Planning Board. *Report on Progress: Overall Plan Nova Scotia to 1968*. 1965.

Nurkse, Ragnar. *Problems of Capital Formation in Underdeveloped Countries.* Oxford: Blackwell, 1958.

O'Hearn Cameron, Zita. "Birthday of the People's Business." *Railway Employee Monthly*, August 1944, 218–19, 222.

Olson, Mancur. *The Logic of Collective Action: Public Goods and the Theory of Groups.* Cambridge, MA: Harvard University Press, 1971.

Organization for Economic Cooperation and Development (OECD). *The Implementation of an Entrepreneurship Development Strategy in Canada: The Case of the Atlantic Region.* Paris: OECD, 1996.

Parsons, L.S. *Management of Marine Fisheries in Canada.* Ottawa: National Research Council of Canada and Department of Fisheries and Oceans, 1993.

Pattee, Richard. "The Good Life in Antigonish." *Columbia*, May 1947, 3, 17.

Pope Leo XIII. "Rerum Novarum: The Condition of Labour." 1891. Reprinted in Gerald C. Treacy, ed., *Five Great Encyclicals: With Discussion Club Outlines*, 1–36. New York: Paulist Press, 1939.

Pope Pius XI. "Quadragesimo Anno: Restructuring the Social Order." 1931. Reprinted in Gerald C. Treacy, ed., *Five Great Encyclicals: With Discussion Club Outlines*, 125–76. New York: Paulist Press, 1939.

Powelson, John P. *The Moral Economy.* Ann Arbor: University of Michigan Press, 1998.

Prinz, Michael. "German Rural Cooperatives, Friedrich-Wilhelm Raiffeisen and the Organization of the Trust, 1850–1914." Paper delivered at the Thirteenth International Education Association of Australia (IEAA) Conference, Buenos Aires, July 2002.

Randall, Adrian, and Andrew Charlesworth, eds. *Moral Economy and Popular Protest: Crowds, Conflict and Authority*. New York: St Martin's Press, 2000.

Rodrik, Dani. *Has Globalization Gone Too Far?* Washington, DC: Institute of International Economics, 1997.

Roy, Noel. "The Impact of Social Insurance on the Length of the Fishing Season." Paper delivered at the Eighth Biennial Conference of the International Institute of Fisheries Economics and Trade, Marrakech, Morocco, July 1996.

Sacouman, R. James. "Social Origins of Antiogonish Movement Cooperative Associations in Eastern Nova Scotia." PhD diss., University of Toronto, 1976.

– "Underdevelopment and the Structural Origins of the Antigonish Movement Co-operatives in Eastern Nova Scotia." *Acadiensis* 7, no. 1 (Autumn 1977): 66–85.

Savoie, Donald J. *Visiting Grandchildren: Economic Development in the Maritimes.* Toronto: University of Toronto Press, 2006.

– and Benjamin Higgins, eds. *Regional Development Theories and Their Applications.* New Brunswick, NJ: Transaction Books, 1995.

Sen, Amartya K. *Development as Freedom.* New York: Anchor Books, 2000.

Simmons, John. "Education and Development Reconsidered." 1979. Reprinted in Michael P. Todaro, ed., *The Struggle for Economic Development*, 262–76. New York: Longman, 1983.

Smith, Adam. *An Inquiry into the Nature and Causes of the Wealth of Nations.* Bungay, Suffolk, UK: Pelican, 1970.

Sowder, Ellie Mae. "The Present Status of the Antigonish Movement in Nova Scotia." PhD diss., George Peabody College for Teachers, 1967.

St Francis Xavier University. *Academic Calendars*. 1940–60.

Strick, John C. *Canadian Public Finance.* 4th ed. Toronto: Holt, Rinehart and Winston, 1992.

– *The Public Sector in Canada: Programs, Finance and Policy.* Toronto: Thompson Educational, 1999.

Thomas, Henk, and Chris Logan. *Mondragon: An Economic Analysis.* London and Boston: Allen and Unwin, 1982.

Thordarson, Bruce. *Banking on the Grass Roots: Co-operatives in Global Development.* Ottawa: North-South Institute, 1990.

Thornton, Patricia A. "The Problem of Out-Migration from Atlantic Canada, 1871–1921: A New Look." *Acadiensis* 15, no. 1 (Autumn 1985): 3–34.

Todaro, Michael P. *Economic Development in the Third World.* 5th ed. New York: Longman, 1994.

Tompkins, Rev. James John. *Knowledge for the People: A Call to St. Francis Xavier College.* Antigonish, NS: St Francis Xavier University, 1921.

Urquhart, Malcolm Charles, and Kenneth Arthur Haig Buckley, eds. *Historical Statistics of Canada.* Toronto: Macmillan of Canada, 1965.

Veblen, Thorstein. *The Theory of the Leisure Class.* Boston, MA: Houghton Mifflin, 1973.

Walsh, F. Waldo. *We Fought for the Little Man: My Sixty Years in Agriculture.* Moncton, NB: Co-op Atlantic, 1978.

Ward, Leo Richard. *Nova Scotia, the Land of Co-operation.* New York: Sheed and Ward, 1942.

Webb, J.T. *Worker's Co-operatives: A People Centered Approach to Regional Development.* Moncton, NB: Institut Canadien de Recherche sur le Développement Régional, 1987.

Welton, Michael R. *Little Mosie from Margaree: A Biography of Moses Michael Coady.* Toronto: Thompson Educational, 2001.

Whyte, William Foote, and Kathleen King Whyte. *Making Mondragon: The Growth and Dynamics of the Worker Cooperative Complex.* 2nd ed. Ithaca, NY: Cornell University Press, 1991.

Wiener, Hans, and Robert Oakeshott. *Worker-Owners: Mondragon Revisited.* London: Anglo-German Foundation, 1987.

Williams, Rick, and Gilles Theriault. "Crisis and Response: Underdevelopment in the Fisheries and the Evolution of the Maritime Fishermen's Union." In Bryant Fairley, Colin Leys, and James Sacouman, eds, *Restructuring and Resistance from Atlantic Canada*, 105–29. Toronto: Garamond, 1990.

Yunus, Muhammed, and Alan Jolis. *Banker to the Poor: Micro-lending and the Battle against Poverty.* New York: Public Affairs, 2003.

Index